PARALLELISM AND IMPLEMENTATION OF LOGIC AND CONSTRAINT LOGIC PROGRAMMING

PARALLELISM AND IMPLEMENTATION OF LOGIC AND CONSTRAINT LOGIC PROGRAMMING

Editors:

Inês de Castro Dutra

Manuel Carro

Vítor Santos Costa

Gopal Gupta

Enrico Pontelli

Fernando Silva

Nova Science Publishers, Inc.
Commack, New York

Editorial Production: Susan Boriotti
Office Manager: Annette Hellinger
Graphics: Frank Grucci and John T'Lustachowski
Information Editor: Tatiana Shohov
Book Production: Donna Dennis, Patrick Davin, Christine Mathosian
and Tammy Sauter
Circulation: Maryanne Schmidt
Marketing/Sales: Cathy DeGregory

Library of Congress Cataloging-in-Publication Data

Parallelism and Implementation of Logic and Constraint Logic Programming / [edited by]
Inês de Castro Dutra ... [et al.].
p. cm.
Selected papers presented at workshops in 1996 and 1997.
ISBN 1-56072-673-3
1. Parallel processing (electronic computers) 2. Logic Programming.
3. Constraint Logic Programming (Computer Science) I. Castro Dutrs, Inês de.
QA76.58.P3789 1999 99-23165
004'.35—dc21 CIP

6080 Jericho Turnpike, Suite 207
Commack, New York 11725
Tele. 516-499-3103 Fax 516-499-3146
e-mail: Novascience@earthlink.net
e-mail: Novascil@aol.com
Web Site: http://www.nexusworld.com/nova

Printed in the United States of America

Contents

Introduction

One of the main areas of research in logic programming is the design and implementation of sequential and parallel (constraint) logic programming systems. This research goes broadly from the design and specification of novel implementation technology to its actual evaluation in real life situations. A series of workshops on *Implementations of Logic Programming Systems*, previously held in Budapest (1993), Ithaca (1994), Portland (1995), Bonn (1996), and Port Jefferson (1997), as well as the Compulog Net Area Meetings on Parallelism and Implementation Technologies, previously held in Madrid (1993 and 1994) and Utrecht (1995) provided a forum for ongoing research on the design and implementation of sequential and parallel logic programming systems.

This book is a collection of selected papers presented at the Fourth Compulog-Net Work- shop on Parallelism and Implementation Technologies for (Constraint) Logic Languages, held in Bonn on September 6 th , 1996, in conjunction with JICSLP'96, and at the Fifth Workshop on Parallelism and Implementation Technology for (Constraint) Logic Programming Languages, held in Port Jefferson on October 16th and 17th, 1997, in conjunction with ILPS'97. Both workshops were sponsored by the ESPRIT BR Project #7230 COMPULOG NET (*Network of Excellence in Computational Logic*) and ALP (Association for Logic Programming).

The 1997 workshop was organised under the ACM SIGPLAN in cooperation programme. Papers from both academia and industry were invited. Preference was given to the analysis and description of implemented systems (or currently under implementation) and their associated techniques, problems found in their development or design, and steps taken towards the solution of these problems.

Topics included, but were not limited to:

- standard and non--standard sequential implementation schemes (e.g., generalization/modification of WAM, translation to C, etc.);
- implementation of parallel logic programming systems;
- balance between compile--time effort and run--time machinery;
- techniques for the implementation of different declarative programming paradigms based on, or extending, logic programming

(e.g., constraint logic programming, concurrent constraint languages, equational--logic languages);
- performance evaluation of sequential and parallel logic programming systems, both through benchmarking and using real world applications;
- other implementation--related issues, such as memory management, register allocation, use of global optimisations, etc.

We were very fortunate to have so many interesting research papers, ranging over widely different subjects and giving a broad coverage of current research in sequential and parallel implementation of logic programming systems. Papers on sequential logic programming systems, focus on varied topics: constraint evaluation, support for extensions to logic programming, and abstract machines for performance evaluation. Papers on parallel logic programming systems also focus on diverse topics ranging from distributed implementations, garbage collection, to optimisations for exploiting and-or parallelism.

The editors would like to thank all authors that chose to submit their work to this book, and also for their cooperation in making this document possible. We would also like to thank the JICSLP'96 and ILPS'97 organisers for their support in the organisation of the workshops.

Vítor Santos Costa and Fernando Silva would like to thank the PRAXIS PROLOPPE and JNICT MELODIA projects for their support. Gopal Gupta and Enrico Pontelli would like to thank the NSF. Inês Dutra .would like to thank the APPELO project (CNPq/Protem).

The editors,

Ines de Castro Dutra
COPPE/Systems Engineering and Computer Science Department
Universidade Federal do Rio de Janeiro
Centro de Tecnologia, Bloco H-319
Cx. Postal 68511
Rio de Janeiro, RJ, Brazil, CEP: 21945-970
Email: `ines@cos.ufrj.br`

Manuel Carro
Facultad de Inform'atica
Universidad Polit'ecnica de Madrid
Boadilla del Monte
E-28660 Madrid Spain
Email: `mcarro@fi.upm.es`

Vítor Santos Costa
Fernando Silva
LIACC and DCC/FCUP,
Universidade do Porto Rua do Campo Alegre,
823 4150 Porto, Portugal
Email: `fvsc,fdsg@ncc.up.pt`

Gopal Gupta
Enrico Pontelli
Department of Computer Science
New Mexico State University
Box 30001/CS
Las Cruces, NM 88003 USA
Email: `fepontell,guptag@cs.nmsu.edu`

List of Referees

María José García de la Banda, Monash University, Australia
Francisco Bueno, UPM, Spain
Daniel Cabeza, UPM, Spain
Vanusa Menditi Calegario, COPPE/UFRJ, Brazil
Manuel Eduardo Correia, UPorto, Portugal
Vítor Santos Costa, UPorto, Portugal
Inês de Castro Dutra, COPPE/UFRJ, Brazil
Gopal Gupta, NMSU, USA
Manuel Hermenegildo, UPM, Spain
Luis Barros Lopes, UPorto, Portugal
Pedro López, UPM, Spain
Enrico Pontelli, NMSU, USA
Germán Puebla, UPM, Spain
Kish Shen, IC-Parc, UK
Fernando Silva, UPorto, Portugal

VisAll: A new Tool to Visualise Parallel Execution of Logic Programs

Nuno Fonseca and Vítor Santos Costa
{nf,vsc}@oat.ncc.up.pt

LIACC, Universidade do Porto

Inês de Castro Dutra
ines@cos.ufrj.br

COPPE/UFRJ

Abstract. Logic programming allows the exploitation of parallelism in a transparent manner. Several systems were developed to exploit this implicit parallelism. The development of these systems involves hard problems such as parallel debugging and dynamic distribution of varied sized work among processors. This paper describes **VisAll**, a new tool to visualise the parallel execution of logic programs, whose main objective is to help users to develop parallel logic programming systems. VisAll can visualise several kinds of parallelism including or-parallelism, independent and dependent and-parallelism, and combined systems. The system is modular and reasonably flexible in order to visualise a great spectrum of parallel logic programming systems. VisAll allows users or system developers to modify or add new trace formats, define the visualisation of new forms of parallelism, and define the icons associated to each trace event.

Keywords: logic programming, parallelism, visualisation tool, trace files.

1 Introduction

One of the most important advantages of logic programming is that it allows the transparent exploitation of parallelism. Several forms of paralellism can be exploited in logic programming systems. The major forms are or-parallelism, independent and-parallelism and dependent and-parallelism. Independent and-parallelism was exploited in systems such as &-Prolog [12] and &-Ace [11, 9], or-parallelism in systems such as Aurora [14] and Muse [1], and dependent and-parallelism in systems such as KLIC [23], Parlog [3] and DASWAM [21]. More recently, parallel logic programming systems have been developed to exploit a combination of these forms of parallelism. These include Andorra-I [19], ACE [10], SBA [2], Penny [17], ParAKL [18] and the EAM [25].

Experience from these systems has shown that the development of *efficient* parallel logic programming systems is not an easy task. System implementors need to tackle hard problems such as parallel debugging and dynamic distribution of varied sized work among processors. Some applications use a sequential programming style and have a very low degree of parallelism, be it and-parallelism or or-parallelism. Moreoveor, this parallelism can be rather fine-grained. Better performance for these applications often depends on smart scheduling decisions.

Logic programs that present reasonable amounts of paralellism can have good, even excellent, performance on parallel systems. However, in practice, there are several issues that may result in bad performance of the parallel system even when the application has sufficient parallel tasks to supply the available processors. In most parallel logic programming systems these problems are directly related to workload distribution strategies since task switching is not a constant time operation. In order to achieve good performance and scalability, parallel systems need to be optimised to the target parallel machine used.

Added to the difficulties posed above, parallel systems developers face the problem of debugging a complex system on a parallel environment where the response time is non-deterministic due to the interference of operating system operations.

To deal with these problems parallel system designers and users need tools that can allow a high-level view of a parallel execution. Visualisation tools are particularly important towards this goal, as good visualisation tools can both allow a general overview of an execution and focusing on the important execution details of the execution of the logic program. This work gives a major contribution in this direction with the design and implementation of a flexible visualisation tool for parallel logic programming systems, the **VisAll** system.

VisAll is a *flexible* and *universal* tool designed to support the visualation of all kinds of parallelism in logic programming. The main goals of VisAll are (i) to allow developers to identify points of the parallel implementation that need to be optimised for the target parallel architecture used; and (ii) to help in parallel debugging. Initially, the system was designed to help the development of SBA [2], a parallel logic programming system that exploits both or-parallelism and independent and-parallelism. Currently, VisAll is capable of visualising synthetic tracefiles for the target SBA system and also other tracefiles taken from parallel systems such as Muse, Aurora and &-Prolog. The system is flexible because users can specify graphical objects and trace events to be visualised. It is universal in that VisAll is capable of visualising all major forms of parallelism that are exploited in parallel logic programming systems.

Our systems follows other visualisation tools have been developed to parallel logic programming systems, such as WAMtrace [5], VisAndOr [7], Must [22], and VACE [24]. Each of these systems supports a different parallel logic programming system. VisAll is the first attempt at unifying the visualisation paradigms exhibited by the other visualisation tools whilst adding the extra features important to system optimisation and debugging.

The paper is organised as follows. Some basic notions on visualisation of parallel execution of logic programs are given in Section 2 Description of VisAll and its implementation is done in section 3 We compare VisAll with two other well-known visualisation tools in section 4 And finally, the conclusions and future work are given in section 5

2 VisAll In Operation

In this section we present some terminology used throughout this paper and demonstrate some VisAll applications. We borrow terminology from VisAndOr [15] whenever possible.

VisAll is a trace-based event-driven visualisation tool. An *event* describes a relevant point in the execution, together with the information needed to distinguish it from other event in the same execution. VisAll reads and interprets a set of these events from a *trace* file and transforms them into a graphical visualisation.

Typically an event contains its type, a timestamp, a process agent, references to related events and additional information. The *timestamp* corresponds to the time that the event occurred. The *process agent* corresponds to the process that generated the given event. A *trace* is thus a collection of events that corresponds to a particular execution of a program.

VisAll transforms the trace-file in a dependency graph, where nodes correspond to events and arcs to dependencies (or relations) between two events. For example, a colour line between two nodes represents a process at work. In VisAll each process will receive a different colour. Moreover, black lines indicate that no worker has taken this work. Each event is represented by an icon. The vertical axis represents either the time-line or event order, that increases from the top to the bottom of the image. In this paper we use event order for the VisAll pictures.

The main objective of VisAll is to help the user to understand his/her parallel system execution. In order to do so VisAll gives to the user three views of the parallel execution: (1) a static view of the whole execution tree and processor allocation; (2) a dynamic view of the execution for a more detailed study of an application's behaviour; and (3) a view of process utilisation along time. Note that the dynamic view of the execution is obtained from the static execution tree.

One important characteristic of VisAll is that it is built in such a way that it can visualise traces of different parallel systems. This includes visualising traces for well known logic programming systems, and also visualising synthetic trace files that can be used to predict the performance of parallel systems not yet implemented. To do so, VisAll is distributed with several filters that can translate from the formats used in other tools to the more general internal VisAll format.

In the following sections we show how VisAll is applied to some well known parallel logic programming systems.

2.1 Visualising Or-parallel Execution

Or-parallelism arises in applications when one executable goal matches more than one clause in the database. Or-parallel execution can be described through or-trees. VisAll can display, but is not limited to, parallel execution of the Muse [1] and Aurora [14] or-parallel systems.

Implementors of or-parallel systems must deal with problems such as side-effects, that sequentialise execution, and work distribution. Moreover, and depending on the system, or-trees for the same problem from different systems may look quite different.

Figure 1 shows how VisAll visualises the parallel execution of the queens problem, as run in Muse with four processors for a 8x8 board size. The small picture to the bottom left shows the whole picture of the parallel execution, and gives the structure of the search tree. The main picture shows the zoomed part of the execution tree. The triangles represent events associated to branches. An upwards pointing triangle (▲) indicates that a branch has been completed successfully, while a downwards pointing triangle (▼) represents the start of a branch. The downwards pointed stripped triangle represents branch suspension while an upwards pointing triangle after a suspension indicates resumption of the suspended branch.

One of the utilities of our tool can be immediately identified with this picture. By observing figure 1, one can see that for this execution too many suspensions were made in very short intervals right after starting goals. This may indicate that Muse is being too eager to suspend branches and seek for better (less speculative) work in the tree.

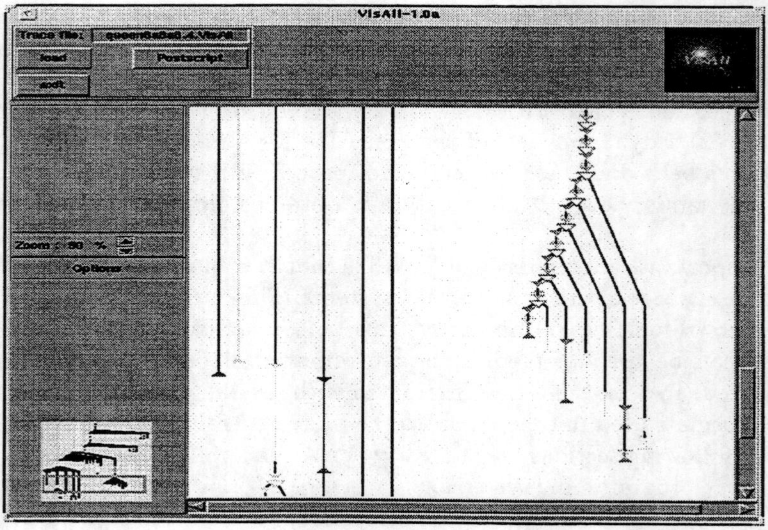

Fig. 1. Or-parallelism: Visualisation of the eight queens problem in Muse by VisAll

VisAndOr shows the same kind of tree, but its precision does not allow one to spot the "too many suspensions" problem. Figure 2 shows the same trace file as visualised by VisAndOr. We do not compare VisAll with ViMust in this work, since the dynamic part of VisAll is not yet implemented.

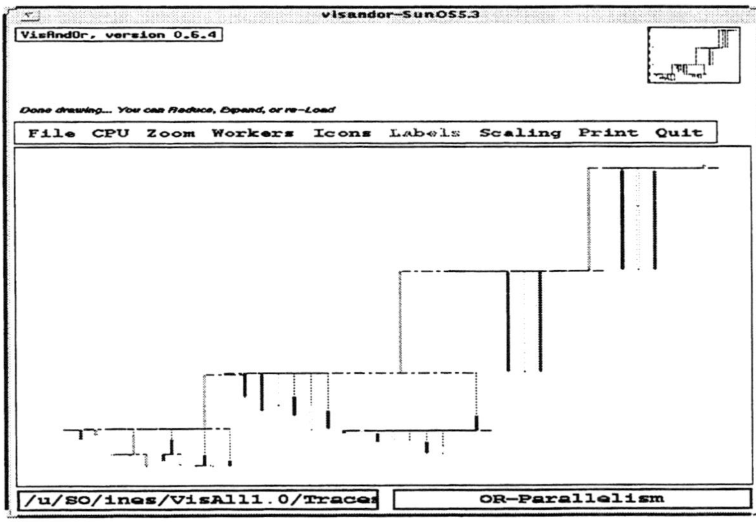

Fig. 2. Or-parallelism: Visualisation of the eight queens problem in Muse by VisAndOr

Aurora [14], as Muse, exploits or-parallelism in logic programming applications. Aurora and Muse have major differences in their design. They use different data structures to manage conditional bindings and use different or-scheduling techniques. Using different data structures to manage or-parallel bindings does not necessarily make the execution trees look different, but different scheduling strategies definitely will make the trees look different. Figure 3 shows the parallel execution of the eight queens problem[1] with four processors, in Aurora.

VisAll clearly shows how the execution trees of Muse and Aurora are quite different. While Aurora concentrates workers on the left hand side of the search tree, Muse spreads workers evenly across branches, suspending work in a given branch from time to time in order to seek for better sources of work.

2.2 Visualising And-parallelism

And-parallelism arises in applications where several sub-goals can execute in parallel and has been exploited in systems such as &-Prolog [13]. In these systems

[1] Returns all solutions

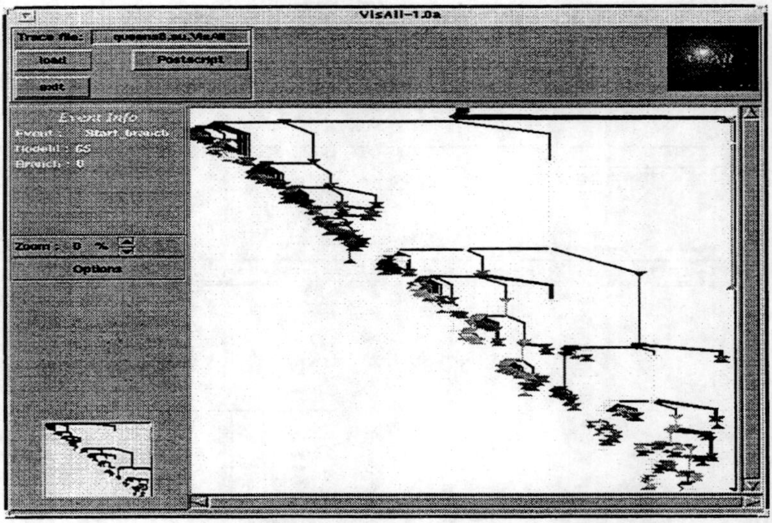

Fig. 3. Or-parallelism: Visualisation of the eight queens problem in Aurora by VisAll

goals that do not share variables are allowed to execute in parallel. Independent and-parallelism arises in divide and conquer problems, for example.

VisAll can visualise parallel execution of systems that exploit dependent and independent and-parallelism. Figure 4 shows an &-Prolog execution. The trace-files generated by &-Prolog have the same format as the ones for VisAndOr and can be converted to the VisAll format. We present the visualisation of a parallel execution of the quicksort program run in &-Prolog with four workers. Notice that the work always *forks* from a conjunction, is run in parallel by the individual workers, and at the *joins* to provide a partial solution. Although the structure of the execution is quite regular, tasks at the same level have quite different execution times, showing the need for good load-balancing.

The figure also shows for the first time the VisAll's *activity map* for each processor. At any time if a worker is idle its bar is painted black, otherwise it is painted in the worker's color. One can move from the activity map to the main visualisation and back, allowing for easy investigation of the points at which workers became idle for longer, and vice-versa. In the example, the map indicates some load imbalance, especially at the beginning and end of the execution.

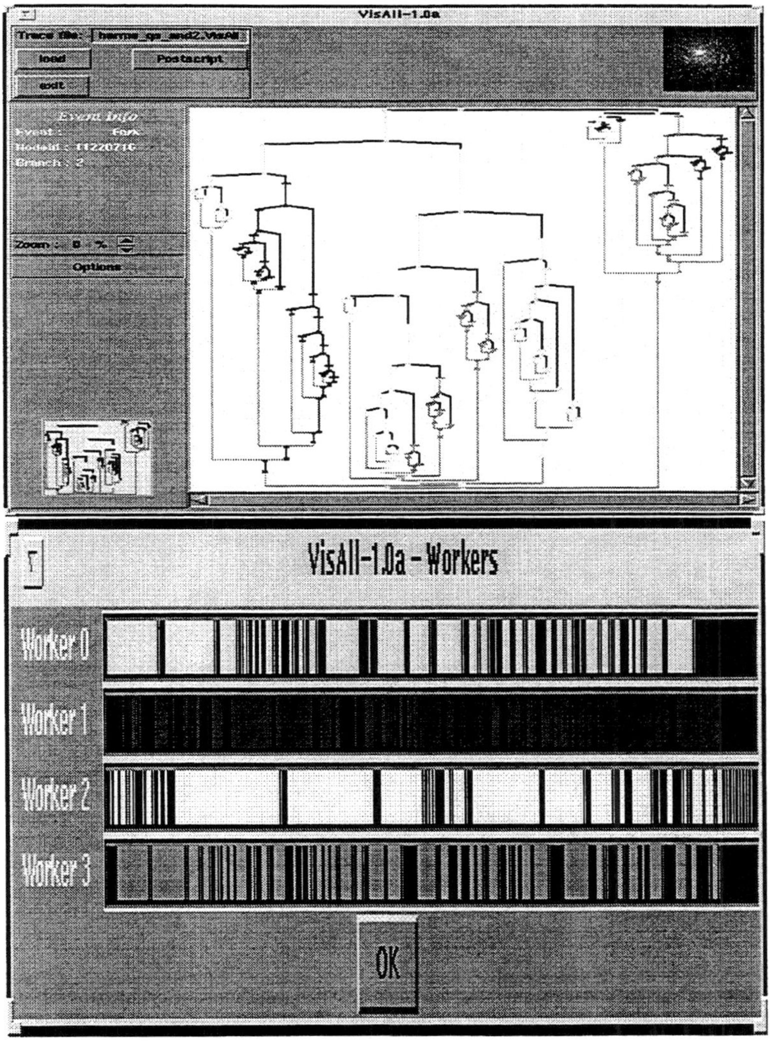

Fig. 4. &-Prolog according to VisAll

2.3 Visualising both And-parallelism and Or-parallelism

Andorra-I [27, 20, 26, 6] is a system that exploits *or-parallelism* and *determinate and-parallelism*. By determinate and-parallelism we mean that the system only allows parallel execution of goals when they match at most one clause in the database. This makes the parallel execution tree looks like an or-tree with some "bushes" that indicate the parallel execution of determinate and-goals in a branch.

Figure 5 shows the last phase of the parallel execution of a flight allocation program run in Andorra-I. The program first sets constraints on the flights by using the Pandora method and then evaluates the system of constraints by first propagating the constraints and then trying the available alternatives to the unsolved constraints. Execution has two sources of parallelism: and- and or-. And parallelism is dominant in a first phase, where initial constraints are set and some resolved deterministically. In a second phase the system searches through a space of possible solutions and both and- and or-parallelism are available. The picture only shows this second phase.

Note that and-parallelism is depicted by parallel coloured lines that join in a same main branch of the execution tree. Both figures seem to indicate lack of sufficient work to sustain eight workers. The search tree is pretty small, and workers are quite often idle or jumping to find work in other branches. The activity map confirms this insight, with long periods of idleness for most processors.

A different approach for combining different kinds of parallelism in logic programs is to support both or-parallelism and independent and-parallelism. The combination of these two forms of parallelism in a recomputation based approach offers the promise to obtain good performance and low overheads in relation to sequential Prolog systems. The SBA model was designed to exploit combined parallelism by introducing a novel approach to the problem of variable binding representation, the sparse binding array. In this representation, each position in the shared stacks is shadowed by a position in a binding stack, so that the complex problems of memory management for independent and-parallel systems need only to be resolved for the shared area.

The SBA system [2] is being developed at LIACC. VisAll is being developed in the context of the same project and therefore should be able to visualise parallel execution of the model subsumed by the SBA system. Ultimately, the main objective of this project is to build a parallel logic programming system that integrates all sorts of parallelism, dependent, independent and-parallelism, and or-parallelism. Currently, VisAll is capable of visualising **synthetic** trace-files for the SBA system, since this system is not fully implemented yet.

Figure 6 shows the visualisation of a synthetic trace-file to the SBA model, as visualised by VisAll. The file was generated by Dutra's recomputation *Or* plus *Independent &*-parallelism simulator.

The execution of `?-a.` is shown in figure 6, and the corresponding Prolog program is shown in the next lines.

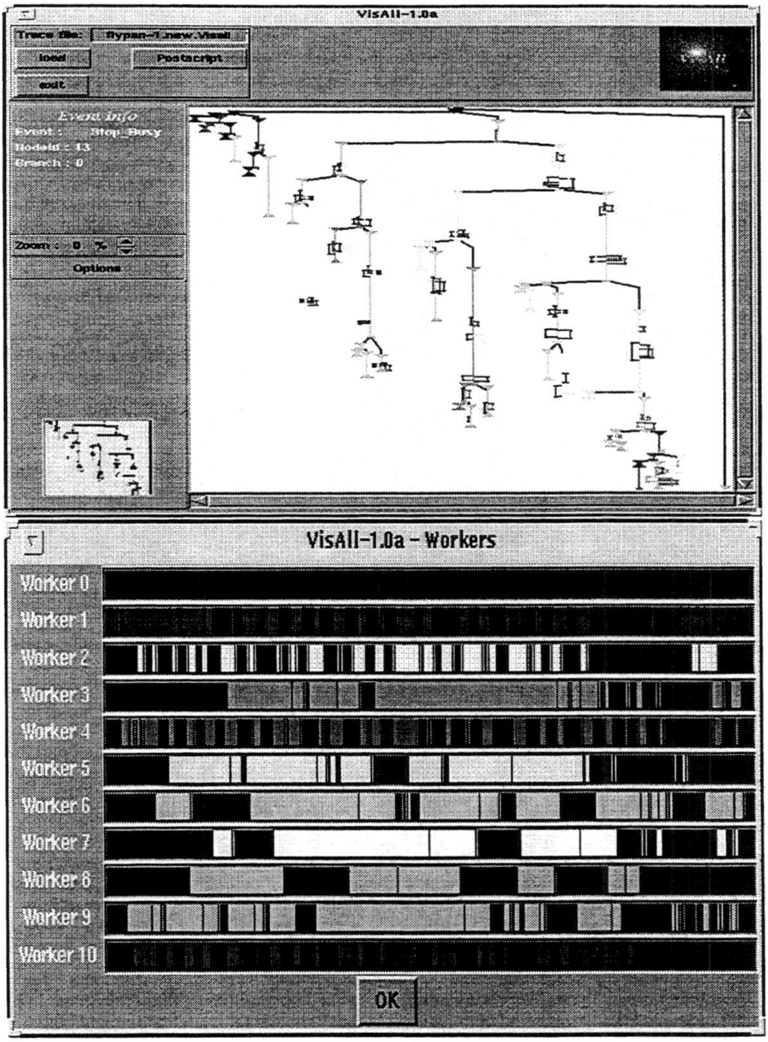

Fig. 5. VisAll Visualisation of an Andorra-I Benchmark

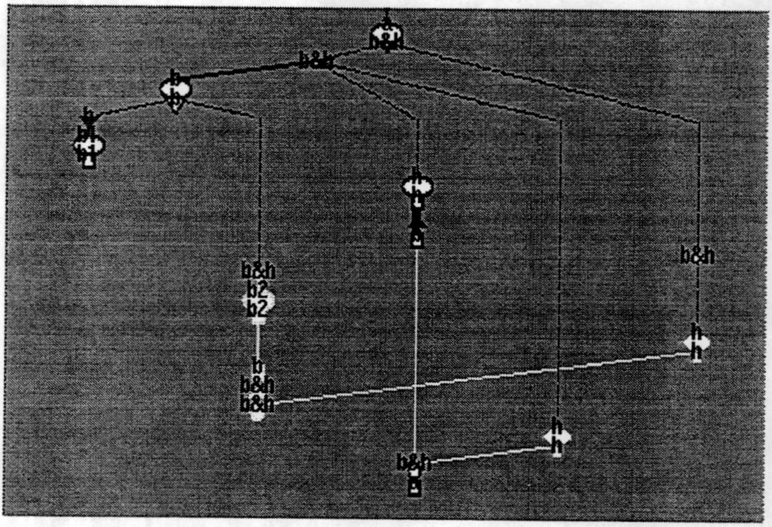

Fig. 6. VisAll representation of independent-and and or-parallelism

```
a :- b & h.
b :- b1 ; b2.
b1. b2. h.
```

The simulator generates VisAll traces, so information on the name of goals is also available. The goal a unfolds in `b & h`. A C-node is created for this goal just at the top of the figure. The C-node has two alternatives. The first is obtained by taking `b1` and running `h` in parallel. The second by taking `b2` and running `h` in parallel with it.

Notice that differently from VisAndOr and VACE, VisAll represents join nodes. These joins connect and-goals that can be executed in parallel inside a CGE (Conditional Graph Expression) [4]. They are particularly useful when the and-parallel computation is not the last goal in a clause.

3 VisAll Implementation

One of the objectives of VisAll was to allow developers of parallel logic programming systems to debug and optimize their implementations. To do so, the system should be extremely flexible. Moreover, we wanted for VisAll to be an universal system, that could be useful in the new systems being developed. Note that implementors are still required to capture in their programs the events understood by VisAndor in order to generate trace events whenever appropriate.

VisAll's contribution is that it allows implementors to add new forms of visualisation or to modify existing forms. In order to do so, VisAll was designed as three components: (1) an *event configurer*, (2) a *visualisation program* and (3) *translators*:

- The *event configurer* is a program based in TCL/TK that allows users to configure symbols associated to events. For example, the user may wish to represent a *cut* by [!] or he may wish to use another icon.
- The *translators* have the job of converting a given trace file and to create a VisAll trace format file containing a dependency graph representing the trace.
- The *visualisation program* displays the VisAll files created by the translators.

The algorithms used by VisAll do not pose any limit to the size of the trace files. Trace file size is only restricted by the computer's virtual memory size.

Figure 7 shows a scheme of the system, including the system's components and their relationship.

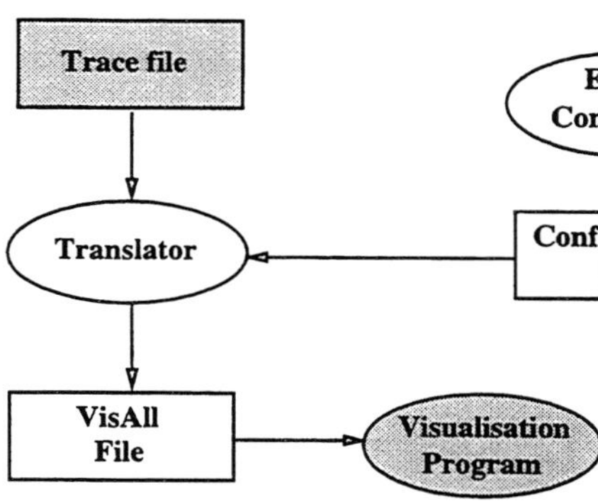

Fig. 7. The VisAll Tool

3.1 The Trace Files

The trace files are the basis for the visualisation process. The use of trace files makes unnecessary the direct access to the parallel system during visualisation, thus reducing overheads. It also allows to visualise the parallel execution in an environment different from the system where the trace was generated. Note that the use of trace files is not new to VisAll.

In order to create trace-files, the developer of the parallel system must instrument the parallel system to generate events. These events must be written on a disk trace-file. Each trace file line must refer to only one event at a time, and has to be ordered chronologically (by the timestamp value). VisAll accepts several events on the same timestamp.

Event	Description
Start Time	Start the execution of a program
End Time	End the execution of a program
Create C-Node	C-Node was created
Create CGE	New alternative to C-Node (CGE)
Start Goal	Parallel goal started execution
Finish Goal	Parallel goal completed
Join	Parallel conjunction completed
Make Public	Or-node available to other teams
Start Branch	Branch in or-node taken
Succ Branch	Branch finished successfully
Suspend Branch	Team left non-completed branch
Resume Branch	Team returns to completed branch

Table 1. Main VisAll Events

Currently, VisAll accepts two trace formats. One is VisAndOr's original format. The internal VisAll format generalises the VisAndOr format in that it includes (1) new fields to visualise icons related to new forms of parallelism; and (2) a string field used to store source program information. The main events for VisAll closely follow the Visandor's events and are described in table 3.1 The *Start* and *End Times* events indicate the beginning and the end of the execution. The *Create C-Node* events corresponds to a a set of and-parallel goals which can have both and and or-parallelism according to the Composition tree model [8]. The *Create CGE* event corresponds to starting a traditional and-parallel conjunction for independent and-parallelism. *Start* and *Finish Goal* correspond to and parallel goals. Lastly, *Join* corresponds to the end of parallel conjunction execution. The next events correspond to or-parallelism. *Make Public* corresponds to making a goal available for parallel execution, and *Start Branch* to some processor taking a branch from that node. A branch may succeed or may be suspended and then later resumed, as shown in the next events.

3.2 The Translators

The task of a translator is to take a trace in a format specific to that translator and to create a VisAll file. The file includes a list of events, in a format similar to the Trace-files described in the previous section, and an associated dependency graph. The graph is also represented as ASCII text, as a sequence of lines of the form *Command: Fields*, where the number of fields depends on the commands. The main commands are *addInfo* and *addNode*, that together describe a node, and *addEdge*, that describes an edge of the graph. Note that the translator could be included in the visualiser. Implementing it separately avoids the overheads of always building and setting the coordinates of the graph whenever we visualise a trace.

Translators are currently written in C. Each translator includes a common set of routines and two separate modules: (1) the *trace module* that defines the trace format, and (2) the *graph module*, that defines the dependencies of each event (defines a graph). To define a new trace format it is only necessary to write a new trace module that understands the new trace format and converts to the internal representation. The graph module that defines the graph is essentially implemented as a series of rules, one for each kind of event, that introduce the edges to the graph. In this way one can generate different graphs supporting different visualisation paradigms by rewriting just this module.

The common code provides control and is responsible for the general look of the visualisation graph. The translator inputs the trace file line by line. For each line, or in other words, each event, the translator calls the trace module function for the event. This function will in its turn call the `addNode` glue function, which calls the graph module for the visualisation dependent rules defined for the event. After all events are loaded, the X and Y coordinates of the nodes (events) and edges of the graph must be calculated. The Y values can be obtained either from the timestamp field or from the event order, and the X values are obtained from an algorithm designed to balance the graph width. If necessary, the algorithm adjusts the Y coordinates in order to prevent that icons are overlapped. By default, each unit of time corresponds to one pixel on the screen, which makes the visualisation accurate in terms of time.

Each edge has associated a type and a color. The types are either dotted or full line. The color indicates the worker that generated that event. The dotted lines are used to show relations between events, while full lines show working agents.

3.3 The Visualisation Program

The visualisation program is implemented on top of the Tcl/TK script language and toolkits. It currently displays the dependency graph contained in a VisAll file, shows some information associated to each event, a legend with information about each icon, and individual execution time for each processors.

The whole graph is reduced and showed in the small picture on the left. The small picture also has a small box indicating the part that is being visualised in the larger image. The image on the right shows the graph at different sizes controlled via a zoom button. When the graph does not fit in the window, scrollbars are used to navigate through the graph. On the left hand side top corner of the graph, VisAll shows information about each event (node). It is sufficient to click on any node to obtain the information that corresponds to that event.

VisAll also allows the user to associate the processor execution time with the branch of the tree where the worker is positioned. It is sufficient to click on the worker bar in order to obtain the position where the worker is in the tree.

4 Related Work

To the best of our knowledge, VisAndOr [16] was the first system that attempted to visualise more than one parallel logic system execution. It was originally designed for &-Prolog, and then extended to support Aurora, Muse, and Andorra-I. VisAll differs from VisAndOr in three characteristics: (1) it allows for visualisation of more parallel systems; (2) it represents information for individual execution of each process; (3) it implements a more sophisticated scheme of zoom, where the user can examine information attached to each node of the execution tree.

Figure 8 shows two visualisations of the same program. The left one is the one shown by VisAll. The right one shows the same program visualised by VisAndOr. Note the extra info provided by VisAll for this program.

Another well-known tool for visualisation is VACE. VACE was designed to visualise parallel execution of the ACE system. VACE uses an approach different from VisAll to visualise parallel logic programming systems. VACE builds a graph that is then designed by using the DaVinci system.

VisAll is different from VACE in two main aspects: (1) VisAll visualises more parallel logic programming systems, and (2) VisAll visualises parallel execution according to event time and by according to execution flow and shape of the tree. Figure 9 gives a flavour of VACE and VisAll displays.

5 Conclusions and Future Work

This work presented **VisAll**, a flexible and universal tool to visualise the parallel execution of logic programs.

VisAll is capable of visualising several kinds of parallelism, and-parallelism and or-parallelism, and displaying individual processor execution times. It can visualise traces of different parallel logic programming systems allowing the user to zoom in and out at parts of the execution tree to see dynamic execution and to obtain information about the logic program source. It integrates two paradigms of visualisation allowing the user to see execution through an execution tree or through individual process execution. VisAll capable of visualising more sources of parallelism than other visualisers.

VisAll is a tool still under construction. Our next steps are (1) to add new forms of parallelism, namely non-determinate dependent and-parallelism, (2) to implement an animated simulation of the execution, and (3) to extend the tool to give more detailed information about the system, such as why a processor (or worker) suspended, why it positioned somewhere in the tree, and where in the source program is is executing code. We are particularly interested in finding what kinds of information are of interest to parallel logic programming system designers.

Needless to say, we are continuing experimentation of VisAll with the recent parallel systems in order to demonstrate its utility.

Acknowledgments

This work has been supported by the PRAXIS Proloppe project, PRAXIS/3/-3.1/TIT/24/94. Vítor Santos Costa would like to acknowledge support from the JNICT Melodia project. Inês Dutra would like to acknowledge support from the PROTEM Appelo project. Nuno Fonseca would like to acknowledge support from the Subprograma Ciência e Tecnologia do 2º Quadro Comunitário de Apoio.

References

1. Khayri A. M. Ali and Roland Karlsson. The Muse or-parallel Prolog Model and its Performance. In *Proceedings of the 1990 North American Conference on Logic Programming*, pages 757–776. MIT Press, October 1990.
2. Manuel Eduardo Correia, V tor Santos Costa, and Fernando Silva. The SBA: Exploiting Orthogonality in AND–OR Parallel Systems. In *ILPS'97, Port Jefferson, NY, USA*,, 1997.
3. J. A. Crammond. The Abstract Machine and Implementation of Parallel Parlog. Technical report, Dept. of Computing, Imperial College, London, June 1990.
4. Doug DeGroot. Restricted And-Parallelism. In Hideo Aiso, editor, *Proceedings of the 1984 International Conference on Fifth Generation Computer Systems*, pages 471–478. Institute for New Generation Computing, Tokyo, 1984.
5. Terrence Disz and Ewing Lusk. A Graphical Tool for Observing the Behavior of Parallel Logic Programs. In *Proceedings of the 1987 International Logic Programming Symposium*, pages 46–53, 1987.
6. I. C. Dutra. *Distributing And- and Or-Work in the Andorra-I Parallel Logic Programming System.* PhD thesis, University of Bristol, Department of Computer Science, February 1995.
7. Luis Gómez, Manuel Carro, and Manuel Hermenegildo. Some Paradigms for Visualising Parallel Execution of Logic Programs. In *Proceedings of the Tenth International Conference on Logic Programming*, pages 184–202, 1993.
8. Gopal Gupta, M. Hermenegildo, and V. Santos Costa. And-Or Parallel Prolog: A Recomputation based Approach. *New Generation Computing*, 11(3,4):770–782, 1993.

9. Gopal Gupta and M. V. Hermenegildo. ACE: And/Or-parallel Copying-based Execution of Logic Programs. In *LNCS 569, ICLP'91 Pre-Conference Workshop on Parallel Execution of Logic Programs*, pages 146–158. Springer-Verlag, June 1991.
10. Gopal Gupta, M. V. Hermenegildo, E. Pontelli, and V. Santos Costa. ACE: And/Or-parallel Copying-based Execution of Logic Programs. In *Proceedings of the Eleventh International Conference on Logic Programming*, Italy, June 1994.
11. Gopal Gupta, Enrico Pontelli, and Manuel Hermenegildo. &ACE: A High Performance Parallel Prolog System. In *Proceedings of the First International Symposium on Parallel Symbolic Computation, PASCO'94*, 1994.
12. M. V. Hermenegildo and K. Greene. &-Prolog and its Performance: Exploiting Independent And-Parallelism. In *Proceedings of the Seventh International Conference on Logic Programming*, pages 253–268. MIT Press, June 1990.
13. Manuel Hermenegildo. An Abstract Machine for Restricted And-Parallel Execution of Logic Programs. In Ehud Shapiro, editor, *Proceedings of the Third International Conference on Logic Programming*, pages 25–39. Springer-Verlag, 1986.
14. Ewing Lusk, David H. D. Warren, Seif Haridi, et al. The Aurora Or-parallel Prolog System. *New Generation Computing*, 7(2,3):243–271, 1990.
15. M.Hermenegildo M. Carro, L. Gómez. Implementation of an event driven scheme for visualizing parallel execution of logic programs. In *JICSLP'92 Workshop on the Parallel Execution of Logic Programs*, 1992.
16. M.Hermenegildo M. Carro, L. Gómez. Some paradigms for visualizing parallel execution of logic programs. In *Proceedings of the Tenth International Conference on Logic Programming*, pages 184–200. MIT Press, June 1993.
17. Johan Montelius. *Penny, A Parallel Implementation of AKL*. PhD thesis, Swedish Institute for Computer Science, SICS, Sweden, May 1997.
18. Remco Moolenaar and Bart Demoen. Hybrid tree search in the Andorra Model. In Pascal Van Hentenryck, editor, *Proceedings of the Eleventh International Conference on Logic Programming*, pages 110–123. MIT Press, June 1994.
19. V. Santos Costa, D. H. D. Warren, and R. Yang. Andorra-I: A Parallel Prolog System that Transparently Exploits both And- and Or-Parallelism. In *Third ACM SIGPLAN Symposium on Principles & Practice of Parallel Programming*, pages 83–93. ACM press, April 1991. SIGPLAN Notices vol 26(7), July 1991.
20. Vítor Santos Costa, David H. D. Warren, and Rong Yang. The Andorra-I Preprocessor: Supporting full Prolog on the Basic Andorra model. In *Proceedings of the Eighth International Conference on Logic Programming*, pages 443–456. MIT Press, 1991.
21. Kish Shen. Memory Management and Goal Scheduling for Parallel Execution Revisited. Internal Report, Bristol University, 1993.
22. J. Sunberg and C. Svensson. Muse trace: A graphic tracer for or-parallel prolog. Technical report, SICS, 1990.

23. T. Chikayama, T. and Fujise, and H. Yashiro. A Portable and Reasonably Efficient Implementation of KL1. In *Proceedings of the Eleventh International Conference on Logic Programming*, June 1993.
24. Richard S. Vaupel. Vace - a visualization system for ace. Internal Report, New Mexico State University, 1995.
25. David H. D. Warren. The Extended Andorra Model with Implicit Control. Presented at ICLP'90 Workshop on Parallel Logic Programming, Eilat, Israel, June 1990.
26. Rong Yang, Tony Beaumont, Inês Dutra, Vítor Santos Costa, and David H. D. Warren. Performance of the Compiler-Based Andorra-I System. In *Proceedings of the Tenth International Conference on Logic Programming*, pages 150–166. MIT Press, June 1993.
27. Rong Yang, Vítor Santos Costa, and David H. D. Warren. The Andorra-I Engine: A parallel implementation of the Basic Andorra model. In *Proceedings of the Eighth International Conference on Logic Programming*, pages 825–839. MIT Press, 1991.

This article was processed using the LaTeX macro package with LLNCS style

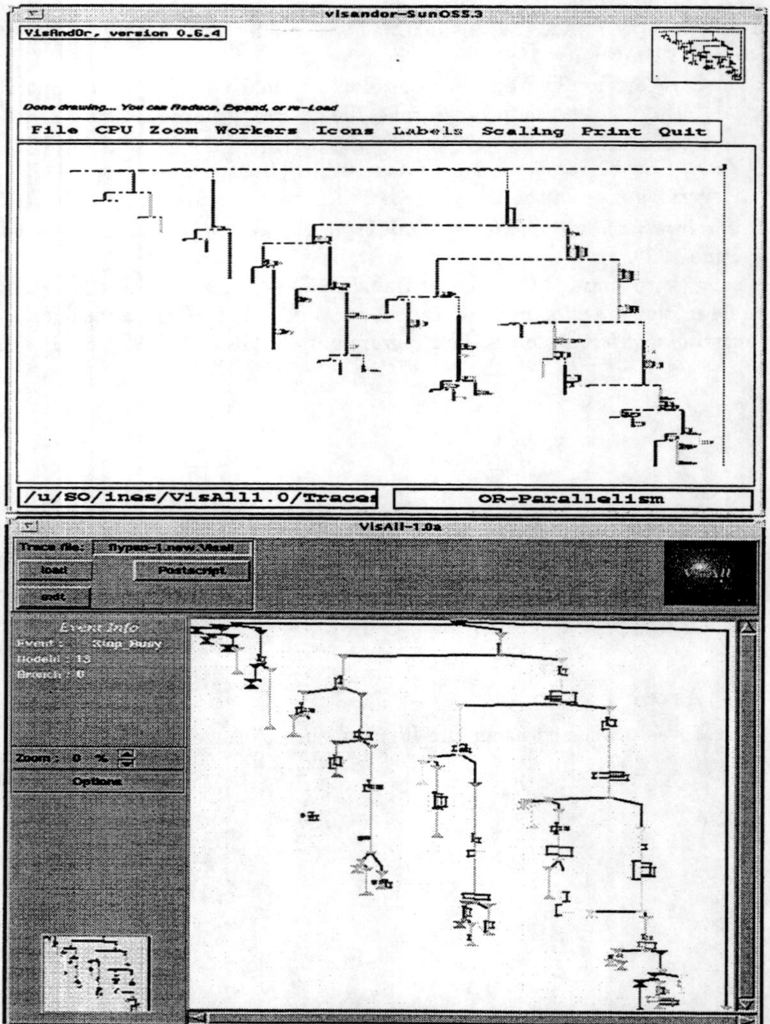

Fig. 8. Flight allocation application executed in Andorra-I according to VisAndOr and VisAll, respectively

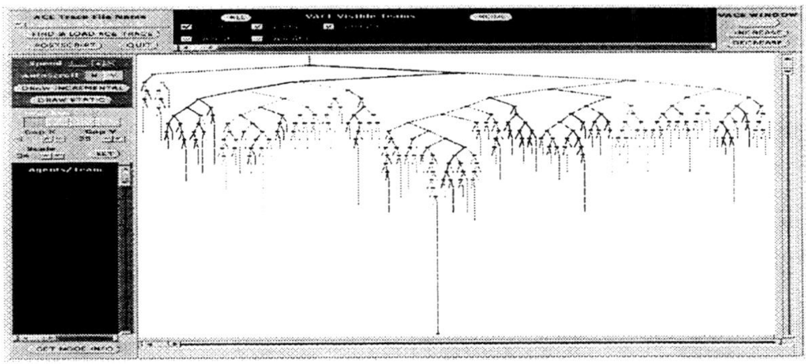

Fig. 9. VACE visualisation

A Concurrent Implementation of Curry in Java

Michael Hanus and Ramin Sadre

RWTH Aachen, Informatik II, D-52056 Aachen, Germany
{hanus,ramin}@i2.informatik.rwth-aachen.de

Abstract. Curry is a multi-paradigm declarative language aiming to amalgamate functional, logic, and concurrent programming paradigms. Curry combines in a seamless way features from functional programming and (concurrent) logic programming. Curry's operational semantics is based on the combination of lazy reduction of expressions together with a possibly non-deterministic binding of free variables occurring in expressions. Moreover, (equational) constraints can be executed concurrently which provides for passive constraints and concurrent computation threads that are synchronized on logical variables. This paper sketches a first prototype implementation of Curry in Java. The main emphasis of this implementation is the exploitation of Java threads to implement the concurrent and non-deterministic features of Curry.

Keywords: Functional logic programming, lazy evaluation, concurrency, implementation

1 Introduction

Curry [11, 12] is a multi-paradigm declarative language aiming to integrate functional, logic, and concurrent programming paradigms. Curry combines in a seamless way features from functional programming (nested expressions, lazy evaluation, higher-order functions), logic programming (logical variables, partial data structures, built-in search), and concurrent programming (concurrent evaluation of expressions with synchronization on logical variables). Moreover, Curry provides additional features in comparison to the pure languages (compared to functional programming: search, computing with partial information; compared to logic programming: more efficient evaluation due to the deterministic and demand-driven evaluation of functions). Moreover, it also amalgamates the most important operational principles developed in the area of integrated functional logic languages: "residuation" and "narrowing" (see [9] for a survey on functional logic programming).

Curry's operational semantics is based on a single computation model, described in [11], which combines lazy reduction of expressions with a possibly non-deterministic binding of free variables occurring in expressions. Thus, purely functional programming, purely logic programming, and concurrent (logic) programming are obtained as particular restrictions of this model. Moreover, due to the use of an integrated functional logic language, one can choose the best of the two worlds in application programs. For instance, input/output (implemented in logic languages by side effects) can be handled with the monadic I/O concept

[20] in a declarative way. Similarly, many other impure features of Prolog (e.g., arithmetic, cut) can be avoided by the use of functions.

Beyond this computation model, Curry provides higher-order functions, a parametrically polymorphic type system, modules, monadic I/O, a connection to external functions, and primitives to encapsulate non-deterministic computations (committed choice, encapsulated search). To provide the full power of logic programming, (equational) constraints can be used in conditions of function definitions. Such basic constraints can be combined to more complex constraint structures by a concurrent conjunction operator which evaluates them concurrently. The concurrent conjunction of constraints is useful to reduce the search space with passive constraints or to model concurrent objects as functions synchronizing on a stream of messages.

Since Curry is an amalgamation of functional and logic programming languages, it can also serve as a common basis to unify research efforts and to boost declarative programming in general. Actually, Curry has been successfully applied to teach functional and logic programming techniques in a single course without switching between different programming languages [10].

In order to provide a portable implementation of Curry, we have developed an interpreter for Curry in Java. Each function defined in a Curry program is translated into a Java class containing instructions of an abstract machine for Curry programs.[1] These instructions implement the pattern matching and control flow of a Curry program. They are executed by a small interpreter implemented in Java.

In this implementation we exploit the concurrent features of Java in two ways. *Don't know* non-deterministic computations (corresponding to search in logic programming) are implemented by starting independent computation threads (this corresponds to OR-parallel implementations of logic languages). The *concurrent conjunction* of constraints is implemented by starting two threads evaluating these constraints. Such a thread suspends if it requires the value of a currently unbound variable (consumer of the variable), or if it tries to bind a variable to different values (non-deterministic binding to compute potential solutions) while its corresponding twin thread is already active. The latter case avoids the duplication of processes for don't know non-deterministic computations which is also known as *stability* from AKL [15]. This scheme implements coroutining features of current Prolog systems [18] as well as features of concurrent constraint languages [22].

In the next section, we review the basic computation model of Curry. Its concurrent implementation in Java is described in Section 3. Section 4 discusses some extensions of the basic computation model, and Section 5 contains our conclusions.

---

[1] A straightforward direct translation of defined functions into Java functions is not possible in a simple way due to the potential non-deterministic evaluation of Curry expressions which we want to implement concurrently (by Java threads) rather than sequentially as in Prolog. Thus, standard techniques to translate (sequential) logic programs into procedures of imperative languages (e.g., [19]) cannot be applied here.

2 The Computation Model of Curry

This section provides an informal introduction to the computation model of Curry. A formal definition can be found in [11, 12].

The basic computational domain of Curry is, similarly to functional or logic languages, a set of *data terms* constructed from constants and data constructors. These are introduced through data type declarations like[2]

```
data bool    = true | false
data nat     = z    | s(nat)
data list(A) = []   | [A|list(A)]
```

`true` and `false` are the Boolean constants, `z` and `s` are the zero value and the successor function to construct natural numbers,[3] and polymorphic lists (`A` is a type variable ranging over all types) are defined as in Prolog.

A *data term* is a well-formed expression containing variables, constants and data constructors, e.g., `s(s(z))`, `[true|Z]` etc. *Functions* (or *predicates* in logic programming, but throughout this paper we consider predicates as Boolean functions for the sake of simplicity) operate on data terms. Their meaning is specified by *equations* (or *rules*) of the form $l = r$ where l has the form $f(t_1, \ldots, t_n)$ with f being a function, $t_1, \ldots, t_n$ data terms and each variable occurs only once (expressions of this form are also called *patterns*), and r is a well-formed *expression* which may also contain function calls. A *conditional equation* has the form l | $\{c\} = r$, where the condition c is a constraint consisting of a conjunction of equations. A conditional equation can be applied if its condition is satisfiable. A *head normal form* is a variable, a constant, or an expression of the form $c(e_1, \ldots, e_n)$ where c is a data constructor. A *Curry program* is a set of data type declarations and equations.

Example 1. Assume that the above data type declarations are given. Then the following rules define the addition and the predicate "less than or equal to" for natural numbers:

```
add(z   ,Y) = Y                   leq(z   ,X   ) = true
add(s(X),Y) = s(add(X,Y))         leq(s(X),z   ) = false
                                  leq(s(X),s(Y)) = leq(X,Y)
```

The following rules define the concatenation of lists and the last element of a list:

```
concat([]    ,Ys) = Ys
concat([X|Xs],Ys) = [X|concat(Xs,Ys)]
last(Xs) | {concat(Ys,[X])=Xs} = X
```

[2] In the following we use a Prolog-like syntax which is slightly different from the actual Curry syntax.

[3] Curry has also built-in integer values and arithmetic functions (see Section 3.3). We use here the explicit definition of naturals only to provide some simple and self-contained examples.

If the equation `concat(Ys,[X])=Xs` is solvable, then `X` is the last element of the list `Xs`. □

From a functional point of view, we are interested in computing *values* of expressions, where a value does not contain function symbols (i.e., it is a data term) and should be equivalent (w.r.t. the program rules) to the initial expression. The value can be computed by applying rules from left to right. For instance, we compute the value of `add(s(z),s(z))` by applying the rules for addition to this expression:

`add(s(z),s(z))` → `s(add(z,s(z)))` → `s(s(z))`

The difficulty in computing such values is to find a *normalizing* strategy which selects a reducible function call ("*redex*") such that a value is always computed (provided that it exists). Since it is well known that innermost reduction is not normalizing, Curry is based on a lazy (outermost) strategy. This also allows the computation with infinite data structures and provides more modularity by separating control aspects [13].

A subtle point in the definition of a lazy evaluation strategy in combination with pattern matching is the selection of the "right" outermost redex. For instance, consider the rules of Example 1 together with the rule `f = f`. Then the expression `leq(add(z,z),f)` has two outermost redexes, namely `add(z,z)` and `f`. If we select the first one, we compute the value `true` after one further outermost reduction step. However, if we select the redex `f`, we run into an infinite reduction sequence instead of computing the value. Thus, it is important to know which outermost redex is selected. Since most lazy functional languages follow a left-to-right pattern-matching strategy and choose the leftmost outermost redex, Curry follows the same approach.[4] Thus, in order to evaluate the expression `leq(add(z,z),f)`, the first subterm `add(z,z)` must be evaluated to head normal form (in this case: `z`) since its value is required by all rules defining `leq` (we also call such an argument *demanded*). If the first subterm evaluates to an expression of the form `s(·)`, then the second subterm needs to be evaluated.

Sometimes there is no single argument in the rules' left-hand sides demanded by all rules. In particular, functions defined by rules with overlapping left-hand sides, like the "parallel-or"

```
 true ∨ X     = true
    X ∨ true  = true
false ∨ false = false
```

have this property. For the expression $e_1 \vee e_2$, it is not clear which subterm must be evaluated first. Since our computation model must already include some kind of non-determinism in order to cover logic programming languages, we *non-deterministically evaluate* the first or the second argument, i.e., rules with

[4] Since the exact evaluation strategy of Curry is specified using definitional trees [1, 11], Curry also supports more powerful evaluation strategies than current functional languages.

overlapping left-hand sides cause don't know non-deterministic computations similarly to logic programming.

Up to now, we have only considered functional computations where ground expressions are reduced to values. In logic languages, the initial expression (often an expression of Boolean type, called a *goal*) may contain free variables. A logic programming system should find values for these variables such that the goal is reducible to `true`. Fortunately, it requires only a slight extension of the reduction strategy to cover non-ground expressions and variable instantiation: if the value of a free variable is demanded by the left-hand sides of program rules in order to proceed the computation, the variable is non-deterministically bound to the different demanded values. For instance, if the function `f` is defined by the rules

```
f(a) = c
f(b) = d
```

(where `a`, `b`, `c`, `d` are constants), then the expression `f(X)` with the free variable `X` is evaluated to `c` or `d` by binding `X` to `a` or `b`, respectively. In order to reflect not only the computed *value* (like in functional programming) but also the different variable bindings (*answers*, like in logic programming), the *computational domain* of Curry is a disjunction of answer/expression pairs. For instance, in the previous example the evaluation of `f(X)` is reflected by the following (non-deterministic) computation step:

```
f(X)  →  {X=a}c | {X=b}d
```

(Here `|` denotes a disjunction, `{X=a}` denotes a substitution (binding), and `{X=a}c` represents a answer/expression pair.) A single *computation step* performs a reduction in exactly one unsolved expression of a disjunction. This reduction may yield a single new expression (*deterministic step*) or a disjunction of new expressions together with corresponding bindings (*non-deterministic step*). For inductively sequential programs [1] (these are, roughly speaking, function definitions without overlapping left-hand sides), this strategy, called *needed narrowing* [2], computes the shortest possible successful derivations (if common subterms are shared) and a minimal set of solutions, and it is fully deterministic if free variables do not occur.[5]

Note that Curry is not based on a backtracking strategy. Backtracking is one possible (but unfair) implementation of disjunctions. However, the concrete evaluation order is not important for the computed results, since Curry has no side effects. Because there is no need to ensure a sequential backtracking semantics as in Prolog (e.g., unlike in the ACE parallel Prolog system [21]), we will implement disjunctive computations by independent threads. However, this implementation issue is less important than in Prolog since most parts of larger computations are purely deterministic due to the use of functions in Curry.

---

[5] These properties also shows some of the advantages of integrating functions into logic programs, since similar properties for purely logic programs are not known.

Functional logic languages are often used to solve equations between expressions containing defined functions. For instance, consider the function `add` defined in Example 1 and the equation `add(X,z)=s(z)`. This equation can be solved by evaluating the left-hand side `add(X,z)` to the answer expression `{X=s(z)}s(z)` (here we omit the other alternatives in the disjunction). Since the resulting equation is trivial, the equation is valid w.r.t. the computed answer `{X=s(z)}`. In general, an *equation* or *equational constraint* e_1=e_2 is satisfied if both sides e_1 and e_2 are reducible to a same data term. As a consequence, if both sides are undefined (non-terminating), then the equality does not hold.[6] Operationally, an equational constraint e_1=e_2 is solved by evaluating e_1 and e_2 to unifiable data terms where the lazy evaluation of the expressions is interleaved with the binding of variables to constructor terms [16]. Thus, an equational constraint e_1=e_2 without occurrences of defined functions has the same meaning (unification) as in Prolog. The basic kernel of Curry only provides equations e_1=e_2 between expressions as constraints. Since it is conceptually fairly easy to add other constraint structures, future extensions of Curry will provide richer constraint systems to support constraint logic programming applications. Note that constraints are solved when they appear at the top level or in conditions of program rules (cf. Section 4) in order to apply this rule.

The use of functions together with lazy evaluation and demanded instantiation of free variables can reduce the number of non-deterministic choices compared to pure logic programming. On the other hand, it is also known that the guessing of free variables should not be applied to all functions or predicates, since some of them (in particular, those defined on recursive data structures) may not terminate if demanded arguments are unknown. Moreover, many logic languages provide flexible selection rules (coroutining, i.e., concurrent computations based on the synchronization on free variables). To support such features, Curry provides the *suspension of function calls* if a demanded argument is not instantiated. Such functions are called *rigid* in contrast to *flexible* functions which instantiate their arguments if it is necessary to proceed their evaluation. As a default in Curry (which can be easily changed), non-Boolean functions are marked as rigid and predicates are marked as flexible. Thus, pure logic programs behaves as in Prolog, and pure functional programs are executed as in lazy functional languages like Haskell.

If function calls may suspend, we need a mechanism to specify concurrent computations. For this purpose, constraints can be combined with the *concurrent conjunction* operator $\wedge$. If c_1 and c_2 are constraints, $c_1 \wedge c_2$ is a constraint which is evaluated by solving c_1 and c_2 concurrently. In a sequential implementation, $c_1 \wedge c_2$ can be evaluated by an attempt to solve c_1. If the evaluation of c_1 suspends, an evaluation step is applied to c_2. If a variable responsible to the suspension of c_1 was bound during the last step, the left expression will be evaluated in the subsequent step. In this way we obtain a concurrent behavior with an interleaving semantics. In our concurrent implementation, we assign different threads to the

[6] This notion of equality is also known as *strict equality* [7, 17] and is the only reasonable notion of equality in the presence of non-terminating functions.

evaluation of c_1 and c_2. These computation threads synchronize on the bindings of common variables.

This fairly simple model for concurrent computations is able to cover applications of Prolog systems with coroutining [18]. For instance, if `gen` is a predicate or constraint which instantiates its argument with potential solutions (i.e., `gen` is flexible) and `test` checks whether the argument is a correct solution (i.e., `test` is rigid), then a constraint like "`test(X)`$\wedge$`gen(X)`" specifies a "test-and-generate" solution where the test is activated as soon as its argument is sufficiently instantiated.

It is also interesting to note that this model is able to cover recent developments in parallel functional computation models like Eden [4] or Goffin [5]. For instance, a constraint of the form "`X=f(t1)`$\wedge$`Y=g(t2)`$\wedge$`Z=h(X,Y)`" specifies a potentially concurrent computation of the functions `f`, `g` and `h` where the function `h` can proceed its computation only if the arguments have been bound by evaluating the expressions `f(t1)` and `g(t2)` (provided that `h` is rigid in all arguments).

The advantage of Curry's computation model is the clear separation between sequential and concurrent parts. Sequential computations, which could be considered as the basic units of a program, could be expressed as usual functional (logic) programs, and they are composed to concurrent computation units via concurrent conjunctions of constraints. Since constraints could be passed as arguments or results of functions (like any other data object or function), it is possible to specify general operators to create flexible communication architectures similarly to Goffin [5]. Thus, the same abstraction facilities could be used for sequential as well as concurrent programming. On the other hand, the clear separation between sequential and concurrent computations supports the use of efficient and optimal evaluation strategies for the sequential parts, where similar techniques for the concurrent parts are not available. This is in contrast to other, more fine-grained concurrent computation models like AKL [15], CCP [22], or Oz [23].

3 Implementation of Curry Programs

In this section we sketch a Java-based implementation of an abstract machine for executing Curry programs. We describe the implementation of data terms, defined functions, and the computational model of Curry (variable bindings, non-determinism, concurrency).

The main motivation for using Java is to provide a portable implementation of Curry and its concurrency features. Due to the use of Java, it is also evident that this implementation cannot compete with other highly optimized implementations of Prolog. On the other hand, the use of Java provides automatic memory management and support for concurrent programming which largely simplifies the implementation task for Curry.

3.1 Representation of Data Terms and Functions

The run-time system of our implementation is completely written in Java [24]. This has influenced some implementation choices, in particular, the run-time representation of constructors and functions. Java is an object-oriented programming language where the compiler transforms source code not into native machine code but into code (the *bytecode*) for the Java Virtual Machine (JVM), an abstract machine dedicated to execute Java programs. The JVM code is independent of a particular hardware. Therefore, a compiled Java program can run on different hardware architectures provided that a JVM implementation is available on this hardware. The JVM interprets the compiled bytecode and manages a heap where all objects constructed by the program reside. It is not necessary to call a destructor for unused objects, since the memory of unused objects is automatically reclaimed by the garbage collector of the JVM.

In order to simplify the implementation task, we use Java's object system for the representation of dynamically created data terms and expressions. Thus, expressions in Curry are represented as Java objects in a straightforward way. Constructors and functions are instances of the classes `Constructor` and `Function`, respectively. Every instance of this class represent an expression of Curry, where the possible arguments of the expression are references from this instance to other objects representing the arguments. Therefore, these classes have the following structure (`Term` is a superclass of both `Constructor` and `Function`):

```
class Constructor extends Term {
  private ConsDesc cd ;  // infos about name and type
  Term [] args ;         // reference to arguments
  ...
}
abstract class Function extends Term {
  ...
  Term [] args ;         // reference to arguments
  static Command code[] ;
}
```

In the following, we will show the principles of our implementation by discussing the implementation of the simple function `add` of Example 1. For instance, a data term like `s(z)` is represented by two instances of the class `Constructor` where the instance for the constructor `s` refers to the instance representing `z`.

Function calls are represented as instances of a subclass of `Function`. Each function object has a component `code` containing the instruction sequence to be executed if this function call must be evaluated (due to the `static` declaration, the code is represented only once for all instances). Thus, the Curry compiler translates each function definition into a definition of a subclass of `Function`. For instance, the function `add` is translated into the class `Function_add` which contains in the component `code` the corresponding instructions for an abstract Curry machine, which will be described below.

The creation of instances of these classes is performed by the Curry run-time system. As an example, consider that the user enters the expression "`add(s(z),z)`" to be evaluated. Then the run-time system performs the following operations:

1. It searches for the class `Function_add` and loads it into memory (loading of classes during run-time is supported by the JVM).
2. An instance of the class is created that represents the initial expression. This instance refers to representations of the actual arguments `s(z)` and `z` which are also created as instances of the class `Constructor`.
3. The abstract Curry machine is started. Since the entered goal is the function `add`, the machine starts the execution of the code stored in the class `Function_add`.

Now we discuss more details of the code instructions. The operational model of Curry requires that the code of the function `add` should do something like this:

```
if <1st argument is a function>
   <evaluate the function (to head normal form)>
if <1st argument is a constructor c>
   switch on c:
        case 'z':
            <return argument 2 as result>
        case 's':
            T = <first argument of this constructor 's'>
            <return result expression 's(add(T,argument 2))'>
```

Note that the lazy evaluation of expressions requires the creation of new, partially evaluated expressions. Thus, the abstract Curry machine must be able to execute instructions

- to test the type of arguments (function or constructor),
- to construct new expressions (the right-hand sides of rules), and
- to change the execution path (e.g., call functions and return results).

To perform these tasks, the machine has the following registers and data areas:

- Argument registers that holds the actual arguments of a function call.
- Some auxiliary registers for pattern matching, i.e., to get access to the arguments of constructor terms (see "T" in the pseudo code above).
- A result register containing the result of a function call.
- A program counter pointing to the next instruction.
- A small stack for the construction of expressions.
- A call stack to store the actual machine state when a function is called.

Single commands are represented by instances of classes that are derived from the abstract class `Command`:

```
abstract class Command {
```

```
    abstract void execute(...) ;
  }
```

Thus, a command is executed by calling its execute-method. A machine program (i.e., a sequence of commands) is implemented as an array of Command-objects (stored in the component code of functions). The complete code of the function add looks like this:

```
public class Function_add extends Function {
 ...
 private static final Command code[]={
 // Argument 1 is in register 0, Argument 2 in register 1
     new CmdSwitchOnType(0,11),         // is reg. 0 function?
                                        //          -> line 11
 // code for case 'isConstructor'
     new CmdSwitchOnCons(0,{2,4}),      // Constructor in reg. 0:
                                        //           z -> line 2
                                        //           s -> line 4
 // code for rule 1, line 2:
     new CmdPushReg(1),
     new CmdReturn(),                   // return register 1
 // code for rule 2, line 4:
     new CmdLoadArgs(0),
     new CmdLoadReg(0,0),               // get argument of s(X)
     new CmdPushReg(0),
     new CmdPushReg(1),
     new CmdPushFunc("add",2),
     new CmdPushCons("s",1),
     new CmdReturn(),                   // return s(add(X,Y))
 // code for case 'isFunction', line 11:
     new CmdCall(0,2),                  // execute function call
                                        // referred by register 0
     new CmdGetResult(0),
     new CmdJump(0)                     // and try again
 };
}
```

This is only a brief description of the abstract machine. The current implementation additionally performs some optimizations (e.g., right-hand sides of rules which do not contain control transfer instructions are directly compiled into Java code in order to avoid the stepwise execution of the command sequence).

In this section we have described only the implementation of the purely functional part of Curry. However, Curry also inherits from logic programming free variables and non-determinism. The implementation of these features are sketched in the following section.

3.2 Free Variables and Disjunctive Computations

Since Curry subsumes purely logic languages, we have to implement free variables and their (non-deterministic) bindings. Free variables may be bound by pattern matching or by unification of an equational constraint. We describe only the binding by pattern matching, since the unification of data terms can be similarly implemented (iterative pattern matching). The main problem to bind a free variable by pattern matching is caused by the fact that a variable may be bound to different constructors leading to alternative solutions. We implement such non-deterministic bindings by starting several abstract Curry machines which evaluate the expressions with the different bindings of the variable.

Example 2. Consider the rules for `add` of Example 1 and the evaluation of the expression `add(Y,z)`. Since `Y` must be bound to `z` *or* `s(X)` (where `X` is a new free variable) to proceed the evaluation, we create *two* machines for the further evaluation: one machine works with the binding {`Y=z`} and the other with {`Y=s(X)`}. □

The run-time system of our implementation uses threads to implement different abstract machines. Each machine needs a data structure that stores the bindings initiated by the machine (see [8] for an overview of different implementation methods). Our current implementation is based on *binding arrays*: every variable has a unique number that is interpreted as an index in an array of expressions. This array (the binding array) contains the expressions the variables are bound to. Thus, variables are represented as instances of the class `Variable` containing the index in the binding array:

```
class Variable {
  int index ;
  ...
}
```

The binding array method guarantees constant variable access but results in a non-constant machine creation time: in fact it is linear in the number of used logical variables. In contrast to logic programming, this is not a problem in a functional logic language: free variables do not occur so often in application programs compared to logic programs, since they are not necessary for passing intermediate values due to the use of nested expressions. Moreover, the larger part of Curry programs are purely functional computations which do not need free variables and non-deterministic bindings at all.

In order to extend the code for the `add` example of the previous section to include the possible binding of free variables, we replace the first command (`SwitchOnType`) by the instruction

```
SwitchOnType(0,11,14)     // register 0: function -> line 11
                          //             variable -> line 14
```

Thus, the command SwitchOnType(n,$l1$,$l2$) inspects the contents of argument register n and jumps to line $l1$, if it is a function call, and to line $l2$, if it is a free variable. Otherwise, it proceeds with the next instruction.

Furthermore, we append the following code sequence (case 'isVariable') at the end of the previous code for add (here we show the generated code instead of the creation commands "new Cmd..."):

```
// handling of free variable as first argument (this is line 14)
   NewMachine(18),              // start a copy of this machine
                                // at line 18
// choice 1:
   PushCons("z",0),
   SimpleBind(0),               // bind register 0 to 'z'
   Jump(2),
// choice 2 (this is line 18)
   PushVar(),                   // create new variable X
   PushCons("s",1),
   SimpleBind(0),               // bind register 0 to 's(X)'
   Jump(4)
```

If the first argument of a call to add is a free variable, the current computation thread is duplicated. One thread binds the free variable to the constructor z and proceeds with the first rule, while the other thread binds the variable to s(X) (where X is a newly created variable) and proceeds with the second rule.

3.3 Concurrent Execution of Constraints

As introduced in Section 2, Curry also supports the suspension of function evaluations that are not sufficiently instantiated. As known from logic programming with coroutining [18], this feature is quite useful to avoid an unrestricted generation of infinite solution sets and also supports a concurrent programming style like in concurrent constraint/logic programming languages. Moreover, the suspension of function calls is also essential to connect *external functions* in a clean way [3]. For instance, the integer numbers can be considered as an infinite set of constants where the addition on integers is conceptually defined by an infinite set of rules:

```
0+0 = 0
0+1 = 1
...
2+3 = 5
...
```

These rules are not explicitly available in the program but this addition is implemented by some external operation. Therefore, an addition with unknown values, like X+3=Y must be delayed until the arguments are known. Since Curry supports the concurrent execution of constraints by the concurrent conjunction operator $\wedge$, a goal like "X+3=Y $\wedge$ X=2*3" is executed by suspending the first constraint, evaluating the second constraint which binds X to 6, and activating the first constraint which evaluates 6+3 and binds Y to 9.

It is reasonable to implement the concurrent conjunction of constraints by different threads in Java, where the threads evaluate different constraints. The synchronization of these threads is organized through the binding of common variables. This has the consequence that the run-time system must start new evaluation machines not only for OR-parallel computations but also for AND-parallel computations.

To implement this feature, our previous concept of a strong connection between a machine and the expression/goal to be evaluated must be replaced by a new data structure. This structure (the so-called *computation structure*) contains—apart from the binding array that is now shared by all AND-parallel machines—the AND-tree representing the structure of concurrent conjunctions. This tree organizes the AND-parallel evaluation of a goal:

- The leaves represent working machines evaluating a constraint.
- An evaluation of a concurrent conjunction $c_1 \wedge c_2$ replaces the calling leaf (i.e., the machine which attempts to evaluate this constraint) by an AND-node with two sons that represent the constraints c_1 and c_2, respectively.
- If the two sons of an AND-node terminate successfully (i.e., the constraints are solved), this AND-node is replaced by a leaf which continues the evaluation thread containing this conjunction.
- A failure of one leaf results in a failure of the entire computation structure, since the entire constraint is unsolvable.
- The computation structure terminates successfully only if all leaves have terminated successfully.

Since function calls may suspend if free variables are passed as arguments (e.g., X+3), an AND-tree may contain two types of leaves:

1. *Active leaves* represent running machines.
2. *Suspended leaves* represent machines that are waiting on a variable binding in order to proceed their computation. Since this binding can only be done by an active leaf, the lack of any active machine in the tree will cause a failure of the entire computation structure.

Since the binding array for variables is shared by all machines of the computation structure, it is fairly simple to organize the access to a variable in a synchronized way, which is supported in Java by the monitor concept. Only one machine at a time can access and bind the value of a variable shared by the computation structure. A problem occurs if one thread wants to bind a variable to different values (OR-parallelism). The two extreme solutions to this problem are the complete copying of the entire computation structure (which corresponds to full OR-parallelism) or to forbid the non-deterministic binding inside concurrent computations. We prefer a middle course and adopt a solution which is also known as *stability* from AKL [15]:

- Leaves which want to bind a variable deterministically are allowed to do it immediately.
- Non-deterministic binding will cause the leaf to suspend. This leaf can only be reactivated
  - if there is no other active leaf, or
  - if another active leaf has bound the variable.

This can avoid unnecessary duplications of active threads and prefers deterministic parts of the computation, similarly to the Andorra computation model [14]. If all leaves in a computation structure are suspended but there are several leaves waiting to bind a variable non-deterministically, then only one of them (e.g., the leaf corresponding to the leftmost constraint) is reactivated.

A small example helps to see how this works. Our program consists of one predicate (i.e., a function that returns a Boolean value):

```
digit(0) = true
...
digit(9) = true
```

This (flexible) function acts in goals like

```
X+X=Y ∧ X*X=Y ∧ digit(X)=true
```

as a generator for values of X. The bindings produced by this generator are consumed by the (rigid) arithmetic functions + and *:

1. When the goal is started, a computation structure with three leaves for the constraints X+X=Y, X*X=Y and digit(X)=true is created.
2. If the machine evaluating digit(X) attempts to bind X in a non-deterministic way, it suspends as long as there are other active leaves.
3. The evaluations of the functions + and * suspend since all arguments are uninstantiated.
4. Now all consumers are suspended. This permits the machine for digit(X) to create bindings for the variable X.
5. The leaves which represent the consumers receive a message that the variable has been bound. This cause the reactivation of the machines.

Note that the entire computation structure must be copied before reactivating the machines in case of a non-deterministic binding.

3.4 Global Synchronization

The user interface of the run-time system consists of a main thread waiting for user-input. When an expression or goal has been entered, the main thread creates a new computation structure for this expression (containing initially only one leaf) and starts its execution.

A terminating computation structure sends a message to the main thread. This message may include a solution for the goal or simply signals a failed computation. In the former case, the main thread writes the solution on the terminal and re-enters into the message-loop, ready to receive further messages.

Note that—unlike the backtracking mechanism of Prolog—an infinite computation can not inhibit the output of other solutions, since the OR-parallel computation paths are executed as independent threads.

4 Extensions of the Basic Computation Model

Higher-order functions has been shown to be very useful to structure programs and write reusable software [13]. Although the computation model described so far includes only first-order functions, higher-order features can be implemented by providing a (first-order) definition of the application function (as shown by Warren [25] for logic programming). Curry supports the higher-order features of current functional languages (partial function applications, lambda abstractions) by this technique, where the rules for the application function are implicitly defined. In particular, function application is *rigid* in the first argument, i.e., an application is delayed until the function to be applied is known (this avoids the expensive and operationally complex synthesis of functions by higher-order unification).

To recognize partially applied functions, every function call (i.e., instance of a subclass of `Function`) stores the arity of the function *and* the number of arguments currently bound to the function object. If a partial function call (i.e., an object whose number of arguments is less than its arity) is applied to an argument, it simply adds the new argument to the function object and increments the argument counter.[7]

Conditional rules, in particular with *extra variables* (i.e., variables not occurring in the left-hand side) in conditions, are one of the essential features to provide the full power of logic programming. Our implementation can be easily extended to conditional rules following the approach taken in Babel [17]: consider a conditional rule "l | $\{c\} = r$" (the condition c is a constraint) as syntactic sugar for the rule $l = (c \Rightarrow r)$, where the right-hand side is a *guarded expression*. The operational meaning of a guarded expression "$c \Rightarrow r$" is defined by the predefined rule

$$(\{\} \Rightarrow x) \quad = \quad x \ .$$

Thus, a guarded expression is evaluated by an attempt to solve the constraint. If this is successful (i.e., leads to the empty constraint $\{\}$), the guarded expression is replaced by the right-hand side r of the conditional rule.

5 Conclusions and Results

We have presented the structure of a first implementation of the multi-paradigm language Curry in Java. Since Curry contains features from functional, logic,

[7] Note that the machine has to make a copy of the function object because it may be shared with other OR-parallel computation structures.

and concurrent programming, the implementation also reflects them: functional computations are implemented by an elementary stack-based machine, and the concurrent features of Java are exploited to implement the logic (OR-parallelism) and concurrent (AND-parallelism) elements of Curry.

The fact that Curry does not depend on a backtracking semantics like Prolog (since Curry has no side effects) has simplified the structure of the implementation. The user does not need to take any precautions when he want to use parallelism in his program. The explicit notion of a concurrent conjunction results in a transparent AND-OR-parallelism that can be controlled with the high-level concept of constraints. For example, the evaluation of a goal like "**`generate(X)`**$\wedge$**`test(X)`**" does not show any difference—neither in result nor in execution time—to the evaluation of "**`test(X)`**$\wedge$**`generate(X)`**". Concerning this, the implementation is comparable with the Andorra model [14].

Since the run-time system of our implementation is written in Java, its speed is highly dependent on the efficiency of the JVM. First results of our implementation indicate that our implementation is much slower than highly optimized implementations of Prolog. This is not due to the use of threads to implement AND/OR-parallelism, but it is caused by the fact that the JVM performs many run-time checks to ensure a reliable execution of Java programs. For instance, the (completely deterministic) execution of the classical "naive reverse" benchmark (note that it is executed by Curry in a (more costly) lazy manner in contrast to Prolog) is performed with approximately 10000 LIPS ("**L**ogical **I**nferences **P**er **S**econd", where a logical inference is here a reduction step with an equation) on a Pentium 100MHz-system. The use of an intermediate abstract machine in our implementation causes only a limited overhead. A direct translation of the functions occurring in the naive reverse example into Java procedures, which is possible due to absence of non-deterministic choices in this example, yields an efficiency improvement with a factor around 2. We have also tested the behavior of generating threads to implement the non-deterministic search (OR-parallelism). For this purpose, we executed a highly non-deterministic program (a map coloring problem with 47 solutions) with our system. To compute all solutions for this problem, our implementation created 124 threads during an execution time of 2.2 seconds.

Since Java is relatively new and Java compilers (in particular Just-in-Time-compilers) are not comparable to highly developed compilers like GNU-C, we can expect further efficiency improvements in the future. On the other hand, a good efficiency was not the main motivation to use Java. The concurrency features of Java together with its automatic memory management simplified our implementation. Moreover, the use of objects to represent data structures supports an easy connection of Curry and external functions directly implemented in Java.

The use of Java as an implementation language has—in spite of its efficiency—also other advantages: the ability of the JVM to load classes during run time allows the user to hold only those functions in memory that are actually needed (this feature has also been used by other projects like the Prolog-to-Java-compiler JProlog [6]). And last but not least: since the Java-compiler produces bytecode for the JVM, the entire Curry run-time system is portable to other platforms: any computer with an installed JVM (e.g., a WWW-browser) is able to run an application written in Curry without recompilation of the source files.

Future extensions of this implementation will include methods to restrict and control the non-determinism by a committed choice and the encapsulation of search. Furthermore, we will investigate program analysis methods to detect deterministic subcomputations and to transform lazy into eager evaluation. This would provide a method to translate parts of a Curry program directly into Java code which avoids the indirect execution by our abstract Curry machine.

References

1. S. Antoy. Definitional trees. In *Proc. of the 3rd International Conference on Algebraic and Logic Programming*, pages 143–157. Springer LNCS 632, 1992.
2. S. Antoy, R. Echahed, and M. Hanus. A needed narrowing strategy. In *Proc. 21st ACM Symposium on Principles of Programming Languages*, pages 268–279, Portland, 1994.
3. S. Bonnier and J. Maluszynski. Towards a clean amalgamation of logic programs with external procedures. In *Proc. 5th Conference on Logic Programming & 5th Symposium on Logic Programming (Seattle)*, pages 311–326. MIT Press, 1988.
4. S. Breitinger, R. Loogen, and Y. Ortega-Mallen. Concurrency in functional and logic programming. In *Fuji International Workshop on Functional and Logic Programming*. World Scientific Publ., 1995.
5. M.M.T. Chakravarty, Y. Guo, M. Köhler, and H.C.R. Lock. Goffin - higher-order functions meet concurrent constraints. *Science of Computer Programming (to appear)*, 1997.
6. B. Demoen and P. Tarau. JProlog. Available at `http://www.cs.kuleuven.ac.be/~bmd/PrologInJava/`, 1996.
7. E. Giovannetti, G. Levi, C. Moiso, and C. Palamidessi. Kernel LEAF: A logic plus functional language. *Journal of Computer and System Sciences*, 42(2):139–185, 1991.
8. G. Gupta. *Multiprocessor Execution of Logic Programs.* Kluwer Academic Publishers, 1994.
9. M. Hanus. The integration of functions into logic programming: From theory to practice. *Journal of Logic Programming*, 19&20:583–628, 1994.
10. M. Hanus. Teaching functional and logic programming with a single computation model. In *Proc. Ninth International Symposium on Programming Languages, Implementations, Logics, and Programs (PLILP'97)*, pages 335–350. Springer LNCS 1292, 1997.
11. M. Hanus. A unified computation model for functional and logic programming. In *Proc. of the 24th ACM Symposium on Principles of Programming Languages (Paris)*, pages 80–93, 1997.
12. M. Hanus (ed.). Curry: An integrated functional logic language. Available at `http://www-i2.informatik.rwth-aachen.de/~hanus/curry`, 1997.
13. J. Hughes. Why functional programming matters. In D.A. Turner, editor, *Research Topcis in Functional Programming*, pages 17–42. Addison Wesley, 1990.

14. S. Janson and S. Haridi. Kernal Andorra Prolog and its computation model. In *Proc. of the 7th International Conference*, pages 31–46. MIT Press, 1990.
15. S. Janson and S. Haridi. Programming paradigms of the Andorra Kernel Language. In *Proc. 1991 International Logic Programming Symposium*, pages 167–183. MIT Press, 1991.
16. R. Loogen, F. Lopez Fraguas, and M. Rodríguez Artalejo. A demand driven computation strategy for lazy narrowing. In *Proc. of the 5th International Symposium on Programming Language Implementation and Logic Programming*, pages 184–200. Springer LNCS 714, 1993.
17. J.J. Moreno-Navarro and M. Rodríguez-Artalejo. Logic programming with functions and predicates: The language BABEL. *Journal of Logic Programming*, 12:191–223, 1992.
18. L. Naish. *Negation and Control in Prolog.* Springer LNCS 238, 1987.
19. J.F. Nilsson. On the compilation of a domain-based Prolog. In *Proc. IFIP'83*, pages 293–298. Elsevier Science Publishers, 1983.
20. S.L. Peyton Jones and P. Wadler. Imperative functional programming. In *Proc. 20th Symposium on Principles of Programming Languages (POPL'93)*, pages 71–84, 1993.
21. E. Pontelli and G. Gupta. Implementation mechanisms for dependent and-parallelism. In *Proc. of the Fourteenth International Conference on Logic Programming (ICLP'97)*, pages 123–137. MIT Press, 1997.
22. V.A. Saraswat. *Concurrent Constraint Programming.* MIT Press, 1993.
23. G. Smolka. The Oz programming model. In J. van Leeuwen, editor, *Computer Science Today: Recent Trends and Developments*, pages 324–343. Springer LNCS 1000, 1995.
24. Sun Microsystems. Java documentation. Available at `http://java.sun.com/docs/`, 1997.
25. D.H.D. Warren. Higher-order extensions to Prolog: are they needed? In *Machine Intelligence 10*, pages 441–454, 1982.

Unfolding WAM Code

Michel Ferreira and Luis Damas
{michel,luis}@ncc.up.pt

LIACC, Universidade do Porto,
Rua do Campo Alegre, 823, 4150 Porto, Portugal

Abstract. We present a Prolog compiler that can unfold WAM code towards obtaining efficient code for Prolog programs. The unfolder implements the principles of efficiency as stated by Van Roy: reduce instruction granularity, exploit determinism, specialize unification. It can operate without requiring abstract interpretation.

1 Introduction

Since the development of the WAM [7] in 1983 by D.Warren, Prolog compilation has been the subject of a great amount of investigation, deriving new optimizations and solutions [6], aiming at leveling the execution time of Prolog programs and the execution time of programs written in imperative languages such as C or PASCAL. However, and in spite of this effort in the compilation of Prolog and of other logic programming languages, there is still a considerable gap between execution time for these languages and for traditional imperative languages.

The major reason for this gap has not to do with the way compilation is done, because we now know how to compile Prolog efficiently. In fact, Prolog execution is a generalisation of the execution of imperative languages, as the WAM has made clear. Then, why such a difference in the execution time for a program written in C or PASCAL and for a program written in Prolog? That reason has to do with what is compiled in Prolog programs, i.e., what is written in Prolog programs, and not in how that compilation is done.

The major advantage that logic programming languages have over imperative languages is that they allow the programmer to say what he wants without having to say how to get it. In an imperative language, the essence of programming is the description, step by step, of the operations to do in order to obtain what he or she wants. In Prolog we program concepts and definitions, leaving the details of its execution to the compiler. The problem of Prolog programs is that the simplicity of writing such concepts and definitions makes the programmer write more general code than what is needed.

Consider the following example: suppose that we wanted a program that concatenates two lists, for instance [1,2] and [3,4], giving the result [1,2,3,4]. A program in an imperative language to do that would be something like that: "take the first element of the first list and copy it to the first element of the output list; continue copying from the first list to the output list until we reach the end of the first list; make the continuation of the output list be the second list".

In Prolog we simply write the definition of concatenating two lists, and write the intended query:

```
append([],L,L).
append([H|T],L,[H|R]) :- append(T,L,R).

:- append([1,2],[3,4],R).
```

The difference between both programs should be clear. Firstly, because of the simplicity of Prolog, the programmer does not need to concern herself or himself on how the program executes. Secondly, because the Prolog definition is more general than the procedural definition. While the program in the imperative language can only concatenate two known lists, the Prolog program can do a lot more, because it has the definition of concatenating two lists. It can do, for instance:

```
:- append([1,2],L,[1,2,3,4]).
```

asking what is needed to concatenate to [1,2] to obtain [1,2,3,4].

However, the imperative language program will be much more efficient, because it has a much more simpler task to perform. And if what we wanted was a program that only concatenates two given lists, why generate a code that does more than that?

The gap between the execution time of imperative languages and Prolog will disapear when we generate *specialised* code for Prolog programs that executes only what the programmer needs to answer the query, instead of having general code that is only used in a certain way.

The traditional approach to this problem in logic programming is to use abstract interpretation [2] to obtain information about execution of program for standard queries. This information then allows program specialisation. Abstract interpretation can take a high percentage of compilation time, and the complexity of logic programs makes obtaining precise data rather difficult, hence sometimes abstract interpretation may not give the precise results one would need.

The solution we propose is based in the following idea: information implicitly present in each WAM instruction, translated in different cases of instructions like `xxxx_var`, `xxxx_value`, `xxxx_list`, `xxxx_const`, etc, allows not only the simplification of execution instruction itself (the reason why it was implemented in WAM), but also the simplification of the next instructions that encode the predicate. Therefore, as go through predicate code we collect the information present in WAM instructions, propagating it from instruction to instruction, and allow the simplification of the execution of the next instructions.

The only information needed is the WAM code of the clauses of the program. Figure 1 shows the WAM code for the program presented above.

Suppose that we were executing the WAM code of the predicate `$exec_1`. From the `put_list(2)` instruction we know that register `X[2]` has type *list*, from

```
Prolog Code:

append([],L,L).
append([H|T],L,[H|R]) :- append(T,L,R).

:- append([1,2],[3,4],R).


Output types:
append(struct,any,any)
```

```
WAM Code:

append/3: [get_nil(1),
           get_x_value(2,3),
           procceed],
          [get_list(1),
           unify_x_variable(4),
           unify_x_variable(1),
           get_list(3),
           unify_x_value(4),
           unify_x_variable(3),
           execute(append/3)]

$exec_1:   put_list(2),
           unify_integer(2),
           unify_nil,
           put_list(1),
           unify_integer(1),
           unify_x_value(2),
           put_list(3),
           unify_integer(4),
           unify_nil,
           put_list(2),
           unify_integer(3),
           unify_x_value(3),
           put_x_variable(3,3),
           execute(append/3)
```

Fig. 1. WAM code for the append/3

instruction **put_list(1)** we deduce the same for register X[1], and from instruction **put_x_variable(3,3)** we know that register X[3] is a new variable. When we find the **execute(append/3)** instruction, we can use the data we collected to specialise the call to the predicate, creating a predicate that will directly unify with the types of the arguments of the goal being executed, that we know are of type *list*, *list*, *var*, respectively. This idea has some similarities with what is done in the VAM (Vienna Abstract Machine) [3], where goals and heads were directly unified, with the major advantage that we do not need to create a new abstract machine. We create a new predicate, **append_list_list_var**, whose WAM code is a subset of the code of the clauses of predicate **append/3**, in this case being the code of the second clause, as this is the only clause that has a first argument of type *list*. We now unfold this code, **get_list(1), unify_x_variable(4), unify_x_variable(1), get_list(3), unify_x_value(4), unify_x_variable(3), execute(append/3)**, making use of knowing that register X[1] has type *list*, register X[2] has also type *list*, and register X[3] is a new variable, that is, a variable without any references to it.

In various other systems the way to make use of the information deduced by a phase of abstract interpretation was by creating a new abstract machine, more low level than the WAM, dividing a single WAM instruction into several simpler instructions, and then eliminating some of this instructions in special cases detected by the information derived by abstract interpretation.

We do not have a phase of abstract interpretation, but by just propagating information about types of local and global variables, and unification modes, we can derive almost the same information.

Instead of creating a new abstract machine, the way we make use of such information is by complementing WAM instructions with information about the type of the arguments, like `get_list(1,list)`. The execution of such instruction will be much simplified, as we do not have to dereference arg `1`, switch on the case of being *var* or *nonvar*, in the *nonvar* case check if its *tag* is *list*, and finally set `S` to the value of the cell. In `get_list(1,list)` we simply set `S` to the value of register `1`. In an implementation in C of the WAM instruction `get_list(1)`, while the general code would be:

```
if (IsVar(X[1]) d1 = deref(X[1]);
else d1=X[1];
if (IsVar(d1))
{
   trailbind(d1,MakeList((int) H)); H++;
   mode = write;
}
else if (IsList(d1))
     {
          S = (int *) Value(d1);
          mode = read;
     }
     else fail = 1;
if (fail) backtrak();
```

the code for the complemented instruction `get_list(1,list)` would be:

```
S = (int *) Value(X[1]);
```

Not even the mode flag would have to be set, has it will be propagated while unfolding the code, and it will complement the instructions were mode information is relevant.

The `unify` instructions are also simplified by the propagation of information. After the execution of the `get_list(1,list)` we conclude that the unification mode is *read*, and we propagate this information to the next instructions. Then `unify_x_variable(4)` and `unify_x_variable(1)` become `unify_x_variable(4,read` and `unify_x_variable(1,read)`, and in its execution we don't have to test the current *mode*. Also in an implementation in C, while the general code for `unify_integer(1)` would be:

```
if (mode == read)
```

```
{
   d1 = deref(S);
   if (IsVar(d1))
   {
      *((int *) d1) = MakeInteger(1);
      trail(d1);
   }
   else if (d1 != MakeInteger(1)) fail=1;
}
else
{
   *H = MakeInteger(1); H++;
}
if (fail) backtrak();
```

the code for `unify_integer(1,write)` would be:

```
*H = MakeInteger(1); H++;
```

Another important simplification happens in the next instruction, `get_list(3)`, that becomes `get_list(3,var)` because we know register 3 has type *var*, which means it is an uninitialized variable. In this case, we simply copy to the address register 3 points to a new *list* cell:

```
*((int *) X[3]) = MakeList(H);
```

The `unify_x_variable(3)` that appears next is known to be executed in write mode, and so register `X[3]` will have type *var*. The propagation of such information will cause the `execute(append/3)` instruction to be executed with arguments *any*, *list*, *var*. The reason why register `X[0]` has type *any* is because it was read from the heap. This leads to the creation of a new predicate `append_any_list_var`, with a specialised code that makes a `switch_on_term` on register `1`, and then has all the advantages described above, by knowing that argument `2` has type *list* and argument `3` has type *var*, that is, it is to be used as output.

This paper is organised as follows. We first present three state of the art Prolog compilers. We use the `wamcc` compiler as the system to experiment with our ideas. We then present our unfolding algorithm in detail, and present conclusions and future work.

2 Efficient Prolog compilers

2.1 Aquarius

The Aquarius compiler [5] is currently the most efficient complete system in Prolog execution. Its performance is based in four principles:

1. Reduce instruction granularity

2. Exploit determinism
3. Specialize unification
4. Dataflow analysis

The implementation of these principles is quite complex in the Aquarius compiler. A new intermediate language, the BAM was developed to implement the reduce instruction granularity principle. The other three principles were based on a complex dataflow analysis phase.

2.2 Parma

The Parma [4] system was developed by A.Taylor in Australia in parallel with Aquarius. Many of its ideas are similar to the principles used in Aquarius. It compiles into MIPS assembly code.

Parma compilation proceeds in 10 steps. The most important of these steps is abstract interpretation, which is implemented in about 4500 lines of Prolog. The abstract domain is more complex than the one used by Aquarius.

The way the system was developed allowed Taylor to know what information should analysis derive, in order to support the optimizations of the remaining steps.

Both Parma and Aquarius depend by much on their performance on the global analysis phase.

2.3 `wamcc`

The `wamcc` [1] compiler differs substantially from the two compilers described above. A first difference is the fact that this compiler does not compile Prolog to native code, as do both Aquarius and Parma. It compiles into C code, which can then be compiled using gcc, to generate a executable file.

Another important difference is that it is not as complex. In fact, one of the requirements of this system was extensibility, which implies simplicity in the design of the Prolog engine, without complex optimizations that would excessively enlarge the size of the system. As a consequence, performance is not impressive, as compared with the two systems above.

Because of its simplicity and extensibility, we decided to use the `wamcc` to for our first implementation of the ideas we intended to test. In our usage, `wamcc` was essentally a generic Prolog to WAM compiler.

3 Unfolding WAM code

We now present our approach to obtain an efficient code to Prolog programs, showing that the use of abstract interpretation can be reduced to a minimum, and that only by collecting and propagating information present in WAM instructions we can implement the principles enumerated in the Aquarius compiler.

3.1 Needed information

Before we start unfolding the WAM code, there are three types of information needed:

1. The WAM code for the clauses of the program
2. A list with the output types of the arguments for the predicates (e.g., fib(int,int))
3. A list with the indication of which predicates to unfold

The use of the first information is quite obvious, as it is the subject of our unfolding.

Almost all WAM instructions can give information about their arguments. For instance, after executing an instruction `get_list(1)`, we will know that register `1` will have type *list*, or else execution will have failed. The `call` instruction however can not give any information about influenced variables by its execution, because we don't know what will come out of the execution of a goal. That is why the second information is important, allowing to improve the types of the variables influenced, instead of having to promote all of them to any possible value.

The third and last information is needed because unfolding predicates causes code to enlarge quite importantly, and therefore, to large programs only certain predicates must be unfolded.

The way the second information is derived is by using abstract interpretation on the source program. The algorithm used is quite simple when compared with the ones used in Aquarius or Parma, as it only has to derive information for the outputs. It follows a bottom-up strategy, starting with the facts, and closing the goals in the body of a clause. When a body of a clause has been completely closed, information is propagate to the head, deriving its argument types. This new information will be joined to older information and used in the next passes. The algorithm proceeds until a fix-point is reached.

Third information can be automatically derived, by applying a certain criterium to the predicates. Our criterium was to choose those predicates whose clauses defined cycles. To determine such predicates a graph was created, with the heads of clauses representing points and its goals representing the branches of the graph.

As those clauses define cycles it is more likely that the program will spent more time in its execution, paying off its unfolding. It is sure that this may not happen, but a deterministic criterium could only be based on the execution of the program and in its profiling.

Figure 2 represents the structure of our compiler, and its phases, some of them provided by `wamcc`.

3.2 How unfolding works

When we start to unfold a predicate we do not know anything about its input arguments. It is when we cross the WAM code of a clause that we collect

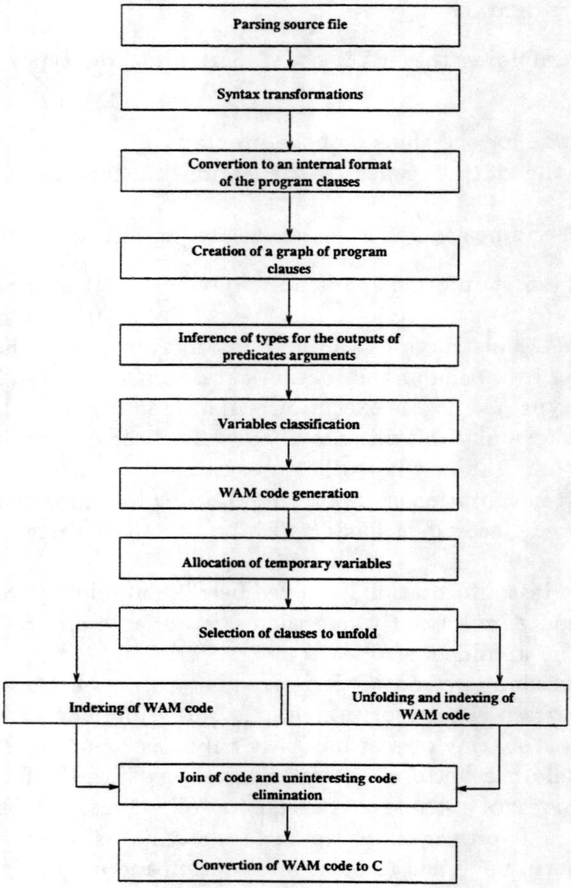

Fig. 2. Structure of the compiler

information. We simply look to the WAM instructions that encode a clause, like `get_list(ArgNo)`, or `put_integer(ArgNo)`, or `get_constant(ArgNo)`, etc. In each case we would conclude that the argument `ArgNo` had type *list*, *int* or *const*, respectively.

As we cross the WAM code of clauses, and if those clauses have body, we will find the instructions `call(P/N)` or `execute(P/N)`. If `P/N` represents a predicate that is also on the list of predicates to unfold, it makes sense to use the information collected so far about global and temporary variables an mode of structures. This information allows the simplification of the execution of the goal, because instead of executing it in its general form, i.e., when we not know nothing about its arguments, we can execute a specialised form to the type of arguments that we know this clause is to be executed with. This is the main idea of unfolding: to expand the WAM code of clauses from a predicate into WAM code of clauses specialised to a certain type of input arguments.

As we know the types of arguments of the calling predicates we can use this information together with the types of arguments of the clauses to decide in which argument to index the code. We select this argument by choosing the one that will create less choice-points.

Not only calling instructions are complemented with the refered information. Every other WAM instruction is complemented with this information, allowing it to be crucially simplified. For instance, if when we were crossing the WAM code for a clause we concluded that `ArgNo` had type *nil*, and if we then find the instruction `get_nil(ArgNo)`, complementing this instruction with information about the argument would result in the instruction `get_nil(ArgNo,nil)`, allowing a lot of simplifications (we don't have to dereference `ArgNo`, switch on tag mode, and compare the constant), because this instruction reduces itself to increment `P`. Similar optimizations are possible in other WAM instructions.

Figure 3 gives the Prolog code to the unfolding of a WAM instruction `get_list(I)`.

```
unfold([get_list(I)|CCode],Status0,Code,UPCode,ECode0,ECode) :-
    get_a_mode(I,ModeI,Status0),
    ( ModeI == list ->
        set_s_mode(read,Status0,Status1),
        unfold(CCode,Status1,Code,UPCode1,ECode0,ECode),
        combine(get_list(I,list),UPCode1,UPCode);
    ( ModeI == var; ModeI == ovar) ->
        set_s_mode(write,Status0,Status1),
        unfold(CCode,Status1,Code,UPCode1,ECode0,ECode),
        combine(get_list(I,ModeI),UPCode1,UPCode);
    ModeI == ? ->
        set_s_mode(read,Status0,Status1),
        unfold(CCode,Status1,Code,UPCode1,ECode0,ECode1),
        set_s_mode(write,Status0,Status2),
        unfold(CCode,Status2,Code,UPCode2,ECode1,ECode),
        UPCode = [switch_on_mode(I,?,UPCode1,UPCode2)]
    ).
```

Fig. 3. Prolog code to unfold the instruction `get_list`.

It is clear that unfolding WAM code will give rise to a major code growth, specially if we can't cut a lot of possible values to the arguments like we can when execution of a programa starts by a directive. It is exponential in the number of arguments and the number of values of our domain. To control this code growth we can do three things:

- To limit the number of predicates to unfold

- To use a small domain of types
- To replace uninteresting specialised forms by the general form of the predicate

4 Early results

Table 1 shows the speed-up and code growth of doing unfolding over four simple Prolog programs. The code growth is an important aspect to evaluate, as it can be very large, because a predicate can be unfolded into a large number of specialised predicates. On the other hand, the C code to implement WAM instructions complemented with the information explained, is considerably smaller than the general version. This is why code growth factor in this examples is not very large, and can even be less than 1, as happens with fib, because this program is only specialised into one predicate, `fib(int,var)`.

Program	non-unfolded	unfolded	C Code growth	Description
append	1	5.1	2.1	append two lists of 30 elements
nreverse	1	4.8	2.8	nreverse a list of 30 elements
qsort	1	4.3	5.1	qsort a list of 50 elements
fib	1	2.1	0.7	calculate fib of 100

Table 1. Performance of unfolding: Speed-up and Code growth

5 Conclusions and further work

Unfolding WAM code is quite a nice way of getting efficient code for Prolog programs. It implements the fundamental principles of efficiency described in Van Roy, without having to perform any complex tasks. Reducing instruction granularity is achieved not by creating a new abstract machine but by complementing WAM instructions with information that is generated.

The exploitation of determinism is achieved by replacing general calls to predicates by specialised calls, and by a more intelligent indexing system.

The fact of having information about variables and structures modes allows the simplification of unification.

The use of abstract interpretation to support these optimizations has been reduced to a minimum, resulting in a quite simple algorithm.

In the future we plan to develop our system so that it will be able to run real applications, evaluating the results of unfolding in the execution of such applications.

Acknowledgments

This work has been partly supported by JNICT under the PROLOPPE project (contract Praxis/3/3.1/TIT/24/94). Michel Ferreira thanks PRAXIS (Grant Praxis/2093/94) for supporting his research.

References

1. Philippe Codognet and Daniel Diaz. wamcc: Compiling Prolog to C. In *12th International Conference on Logic Programming.* MIT Press, 1995.
2. Patrick Cousot and Radhia Cousot. Abstract interpretation and application to logic programs. *The Journal of Logic Programming,* 13(1, 2, 3 and 4):103–179, 1992.
3. A. Krall and U. Neumerkel. The Vienna Abstract Machine. In *International Workshop in Programming Language Implementation and Logic Programming (PLIP'90),* number 456 in Lecture Notes in Computer Science, pages 121–135. Sweeden, Springer-Verlag, 1990.
4. A. Taylor. *High Performance Prolog Implementation.* PhD thesis, University of Sydney, June 1991.
5. P. Van Roy. *Can Logic Programming Execute as Fast as Imperative Programming?* PhD thesis, University of California at Berkeley, November 1990.
6. P. Van Roy. 1983-1993: The Wonder Years of Sequential Prolog Implementation. *The Journal of Logic Programming,* 19/20, May/July 1994.
7. David H. D. Warren. An Abstract Prolog Instruction Set. Technical Note 309, SRI International, 1983.

This article was processed using the LaTeX macro package with LLNCS style

An Extension of the WAM for Uninitialized Variables

Dante Baldan Nicola Civran Gilberto Filè

Dept. of Pure and Applied Mathematics
University of Padova
Via Belzoni 7, I-35131, Padova, Italy
dante@math.unipd.it, cvrncl26@leonardo.math.unipd.it,
gilberto@math.unipd.it

Abstract. An extension of the WAM for handling uninitialized variables is presented. Our modification of the WAM is based on a static analysis designed within the *classical* Cousot's abstract interpretation framework. The main contributions of this work are the simplicity of the domain of the analysis, the WAM-like extension supporting the optimization and the fact that the analysis is provably correct according to the well-known proof-scheme of Cousot's framework.

1 Introduction

We present a static analysis of `Prolog` [7, 3] programs that supports the production of optimized WAM [1, 15] code for these programs. This analysis is designed within the *classical* Cousot's Abstract Interpretation framework [8, 9]. The information that is inferred by this static analysis is that certain program variables are uninitialized. The uninitialized variables are defined at two levels:

- at logical level, an uninitialized variable is unbound and unaliased with other variables;
- at implementation level, an uninitialized variable is a memory location that is allocated to contain an unbound variable, but the location is not given a value.

The binding of an uninitialized variable can be reduced to an assignment. No dereferencing is needed, since the variable is uninitialized. No trailing is needed, since the variable contains garbage up to its binding to a value. The goal of the optimization consists in postponing the initialization of the variables as much as possible. The phenomenon that the analysis aims to avoid is the initialization of a variable as self-referencing memory cell followed by a binding of that variable with another value. This situation is very common as stated in [14].

The uninitialized variable analysis is not new since it has been already proposed for the first time in [4] and then used also in [5, 13, 14].

Beer's approach was to tag uninitialized variables as such and dynamically test for uninitializedness. Van Roy instead detected them at compile-time through a global analysis. Debray et al. relied on declared outputs in the framework of a concurrent logic language. Lindgren proposed a straightforward program transformation that detects uninitialized arguments in predicate calls and rewrites the program to make such arguments obvious to the compiler.

The contribution of this paper are the following. In first place, our analysis is described as a non-standard semantics (of logic programs) that is defined by an abstract domain and by abstract operations that correspond to the concrete domain and operations of the concrete semantics. This leads to the second contribution, that is the proof of correctness of the analysis according to the modular scheme of Cousots' Abstract Interpretation framework. The last contribution is that our analysis is more precise than that of Van Roy and than that of Lindgren.

In the present work we outline the analysis by means of a simple and well-known program that is *append*. The analysis for the introduction of uninitialized variables is performed using GAIA [12]. The GAIA analyzer has been integrated into the SICStus Compiler 2.1. The Emulator of SICStus has been extended with a new set of instructions for handling the uninitialized memory locations. We ran the system on a SparcStation Classic 40Mb RAM powered by a MicroSparc Processor equipped with SunOS 4.1.3.

The paper is organized as follows. Sect. 2 defines some basic notations. In Sect. 3 the well-known *append* program is used for presenting both the concrete and the abstract semantics for our analysis. In Sect. 4 the result of the fixpoint computation is presented and compared with the information computed by the Aquarius dataflow analyzer. The optimized version of *append* is outlined together with performance results.

A short conclusion closes the paper.

2 Preliminaries

In this section we introduce some terminology used in the paper. A complete introduction to lattice theory is in [6] and the theory of Abstract Interpretation can be found in [9].

2.1 Logic programming

We introduce some notation about *logic programming* [11].

Let t be a term in the first order logic.

- $Vars(t)$ is the set of variables of the term t;
- $var(t)$ is true if and only if t is a variable in the first order logic;
- $Dups(t)$ is the set of the variables occurring at least twice in t.

It is well-known that compilers for logic programs are, in most cases, based on an abstract machine that has been introduced by D.Warren [15] and that is called the Warren Abstract Machine (WAM). For reading this paper a good knowledge of the WAM is required. A crystal-clear introduction to the WAM is presented by Hassan [1].

We will consider logic programs in normalized form as illustrated in the following example.

Example Let P be the following logic program.

cl : `p(f(f(X)),Y,Y) :- q(X,g(g(g(Y))),Z), q(Z,Z,Z), functor(X, f, 1).`

The normalized form of P is as follows:

cl : p/3 :- (0) A^0_0=f(f(X_0)) (1) A^0_1=X_1 (2) A^0_2=X_1 (3)
A^1_0=X_0 (4) A^1_1=g(g(g(X_1))) (5) A^1_2=Y_0 (6) q(A^1_0,A^1_1,A^1_2) (7)
A^2_0=Y_0 (8) A^2_1=Y_0 (9) A^2_2=Y_0 (10) q(A^2_0,A^2_1,A^2_2) (11).

To indicate program point i in clause cl we will write (cl, i). This normalized form is convenient for the static analysis because in this way unifications are expressed by the equality built-ins inside the clauses that can be handled one at a time. Few remarks about such programs are useful.

- The body of a normalized clause is logically divided into blocks. In the first clause of the previous example there are two blocks. The first is:
  A^0_0=f(f(X_0))d (1) A^0_1=X_1 (2) A^0_2=X_1 (3) A^1_0=X_0 (4) A^1_1=g(g(g(X_1))) (5)
  A^1_2=Y_0 (6) q(A^1_0,A^1_1,A^1_2)
  and the second is:
  A^2_0=Y_0 (8) A^2_1=Y_0 (9) A^2_2=Y_0 (10) q(A^2_0,A^2_1,A^2_2)
  Each block is called *body goal*. Observe that the built-ins corresponding to the head unifications belong to the first body goal.
- The variables A^i_j are called *argument variables* because they correspond to the argument registers used in the WAM. Clearly, there is an important difference between these variables and the argument registers of the WAM: in the WAM the same registers are used for passing the arguments of all calls, whereas in a normalized clause each atom has argument variables with distinct superscripts. Obviously, this difference is unavoidable: normalized programs are still programs and thus they do not contain registers. However, when later we will describe the concrete semantics of the normalized programs (that is very close to the WAM), it will be very simple to treat the argument variables as registers simply ignoring the superscripts.
- It is easy to see that a clause in normalized form contains one (non argument) variable for each variable of the original (non normalized) clause. As in the WAM we distinguish two types of these non-argument variables: the *temporary* and the *permanent* variables. The temporary variables are those that occur in at most one of the body goals of the clause, whereas the permanent ones are those that occur in at least two distinct body goals of the clause.
  Following the notation used in [1], the argument variables are always indicated with the letter A, the temporary ones with X and the permanent ones with Y, eventually with appropriate superscripts and subscripts.

3 Uninitialized Variable Analysis

Van Roy [14] proposed an uninitialized variable analysis for the BAM implemented in the Aquarius Compiler. The analysis needs two abstract domains: one made of tuples of modes associated with the argument variables of the predicates and one made of 4-tuples of sets of program variables. The elements of the domain of modes are functions that assign a mode to each argument of each predicate. The elements in the domain of the sets of variables are 4-tuple (G, N, U, R) carrying information about the variables that are (bound to) ground terms, structured terms, uninitialized variables and recursively dereferenced terms. Those two domains cooperate in the analysis. The domain of modes is used to perform the least upper bound operation and the clause call-exit operations while the one made of 4-tuples of sets is used to compute the values inside the clause. A first contribution of our work is that we use only one domain to perform all the computation. Our domain is made of 3-tuples of sets of variables (G, N, U) that represent the variables that are (bound to) ground terms, structured terms and that are uninitialized, respectively. A second contribution of our work is that our analysis supports a modification of the WAM without requiring the design of an abstract machine (and then a new compiler). The third contribution is that our analysis is designed in Cousot's abstract interpretation framework that allows to prove the correctness of the analysis according to a well-known proof-scheme.

This section introduces the concrete and the abstract semantics for the uninitialized variable analysis. Both semantics are characterized by a domain and operations (respectively, concrete and abstract). The concrete semantics is an abstraction of the operational semantics of the WAM so as it is presented in [1], thus familiarity with this work is required for following our description. The concrete semantics is illustrated simply sketching the computation of the meaning of the *append* program according to this semantics.

In the WAM setting, a variable is *uninitialized* if either its representation is a self-referencing cell possibly pointed to by argument or temporary variables or its representation is a cell pointing to a self-referencing location possibly pointed to by registers or argument variables. In other words, we define *uninitialized* those variables that we can directly (i.e. within one step) access through an argument or a temporary variable.

3.1 The Concrete Semantics

As uninitialized variable analysis is concerned only with the variables of the clauses of a program, the concrete semantics is obtained from the operational semantics of the WAM [1] focusing only on the heap, on the variables of the local stack, and on the argument and temporary variables and ignoring all the other data structures used in the WAM such as the trail, the choice points etc.. In the following we will follow [1] calling *stack* the memory part of the WAM made of the heap, the local stack and the argument and temporary variables.

The concrete semantics of a given logic program P, computes for each program point (cl, i) of P the set of all stacks that are computed in the executions that reach (cl, i) (starting from some given initial goal). In this semantics the operations are as follows:

- equality built-ins are interpreted as operations that transform these sets of stacks just as the corresponding WAM operations modify them.
- the calls appearing in clause bodies are interpreted as operations that push on the current stack a new environment for the called clause (if necessary).

Append. For illustrating the concrete semantics we will apply it to the *append* program that is shown in Fig. 1. Fig. 2 shows the normalized version of the program and Fig. 3 illustrates the corresponding WAM code produced by the SICStus [2, 10] Compiler 2.1.

cl_0 : `main:-append(X,Y,[a,b,c]).`
cl_1 : `append([],L,L).`
cl_2 : `append([X|L],L1,[X|L2]):- append(L,L1,L2).`

Fig. 1. Non-normalized form of append

cl_0 : main/0:- (0) A^1_0=X_1 (1) A^1_1=X_2 (2) A^1_2=[a,b,c] (3) append(A^1_0,A^1_1,A^1_2) (4).
cl_1 : append/3:- (0) A^0_0=[] (1) A^0_1=A^0_2 (2).
cl_2 : append/3:- (0) A^0_0=[X_3|X_0] (1) A^0_1=X_1 (2) A^0_2=[X_3|X_2]
(3) A^1_0=X_0 (4) A^1_1=X_1 (5) A^1_2=X_2 (6) append(A^1_0,A^1_1,A^1_2) (7)

Fig. 2. Normalized form of append

The Concrete Semantics of *Append*. In what follows we will briefly describe the computation of the concrete values at some of the program points of *append*.

The computation starts from the goal `?-main`, following the style of the benchmarks in [14]. The changes from one point to another will be indicated with $\leftarrow$. Clause cl_0 is called and the situation at program point $(cl_0, 3)$ is depicted in Fig. 4(a).

The call to procedure **append** is executed. Let us first consider the execution of cl_1. The two built-ins of cl_1 produce the following effect:

```
A2versionB121C31902I-1J1J3L-1
clause(main/0/1, [ifshallow, neck(0), else, endif,
    put_list(2), unify_constant(a), unify_list, unify_constant(b),
    unify_list, unify_constant(c), unify_nil, put_x_void(0),
    put_x_void(1), execute(append/3)]).
clause(append/3/1, [get_nil_x0, get_x_value(1,2), neck(3), proceed]).
clause(append/3/2, [ifshallow, get_list_x0, unify_x_variable(4),
    unify_x_variable(3), get_list(2), unify_x_value(4), neck(3),
    unify_x_variable(2), put_x_value(3,0), execute(append/3), else,
    get_list_x0, unify_x_variable(3), unify_x_variable(0), get_list(2),
    unify_x_value(3), unify_x_variable(2), execute(append/3), endif]).
predicate(append/3, [switch_on_term([append/3/1,append/3/2], [append/3/2],
    [[]-append/3/1],[])]).
predicate(main/0, [switch_on_term([main/0/1],[main/0/1],[],[main/0/1])]).
```

Fig. 3. WAM code for append

- A_0^0=[]: it corresponds to executing **get_nil_x0** of the WAM code in Fig. 3 which assigns the empty list to (the location pointed by) the first argument register; the stack obtained after this operation is shown in Fig. 4(*b*).
- A_1^0=A_2^0: it corresponds to executing **get_x_value (1,2)**, (see Fig. 3); Fig. 4(*c*) shows the new stack.

We can see that the location pointed to by A_0^1 is assigned a CON value and that the location pointed to by A_1^1 is assigned a LIS structure. The optimization will show how to exploit this observation.

Let us consider now the call of cl_2 (from $(cl_0, 3)$). The built-ins until program point $(cl_2, 7)$, are handled as follows:

- A_0^0=[X_3|X_0]: this corresponds to executing the sequence constituted by the instructions **get_list_x0**, **unify_x_variable(3)** and **unify_x_variable(0)** (see Fig. 3). The stack it produces is shown in Fig. 5(*a*).
- the built-in A_1^0=X_1 has no correspondent WAM instruction since the second argument is simply read and then reloaded in A_1^1=X_1 with the same content on the same WAM register;
- the built-in A_2^0=[X_3|X_2] corresponds to executing **get_list(2)**, **unify_x_value(3)** and **unify_x_variable(2)** (see Fig. 3).

We describe the stack at $(cl_2, 7)$ in Fig. 5(*b*). The WAM semantics applies and clause cl_1 is called. The output is depicted in Fig. 5(*c*). In a similar way we can continue the computation according to the WAM semantics. We will not show the details of the computation since they are not relevant for the rest of the paper.

As you can see, there are many cases where a self-referencing cell is allocated and then assigned a value. What [14] proposes is the uninitialization of such memory cells since they will be eventually assigned a 'real' value.

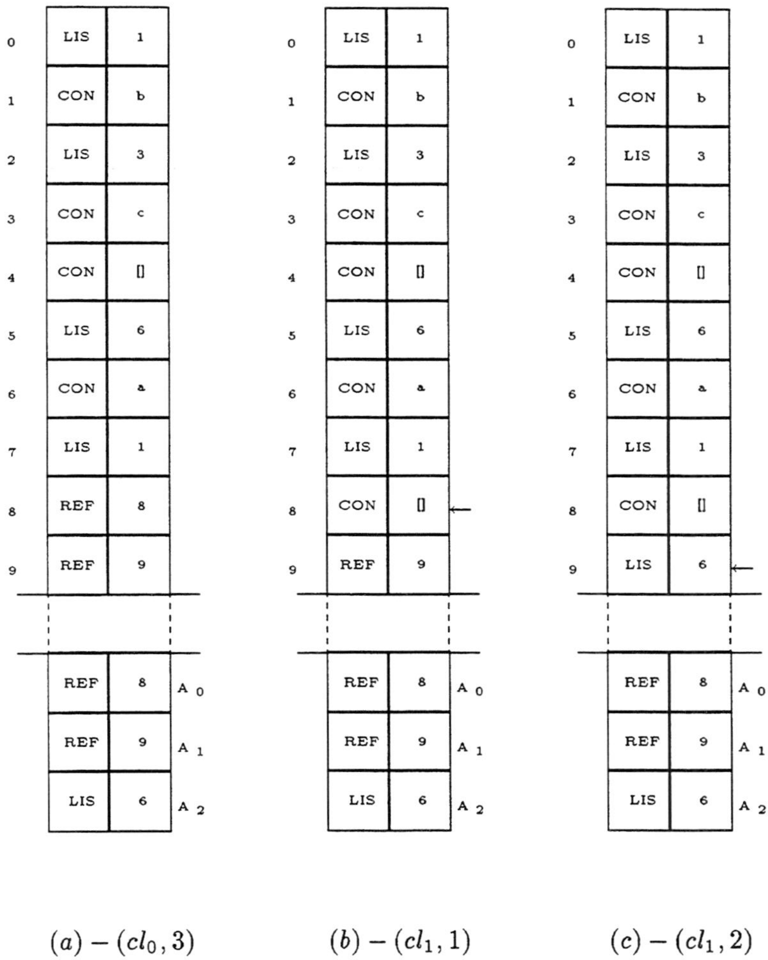

Fig. 4. Stacks at program point $(cl_0, 3)$, $(cl_1, 1)$, $(cl_1, 2)$ for append

3.2 The Abstract Semantics

The analysis in [14] requires two abstract domains: one made of 4-tuples of sets of variables and one made of tuples of modes associated with the argument variables of the predicates. We adopted an abstract domain made of 3-tuples of sets of variables according to the Abstract Interpretation framework. Therefore our domain is simpler than the one in [14] and closer to the Cousot's framework.

3.3 The Abstract Domain

Let, in what follows, *cl* be any clause in normalized form. Recall that *Vars*(*cl*) is the set of the variables of *cl*. We will describe the values of the abstract domain for *cl*.

A (non bottom) value of the domain is a 3-tuple $\Gamma = (G, N, U)$ with the following meaning:

- G and N are subsets of *Vars*(*cl*). G and N are sets of variables bound to *surely* ground and *surely* non variable terms, respectively.
- U is a subset of *Vars*(*cl*). U is a set of *surely* uninitialized variables; recalling the definition of uninitialized variables, we can say that U is the set of variables over which the optimization applies.

The abstract domain $\mathcal{D}$ for *cl* consists in a bottom element $d_\perp$ and in all the 3-tuples $\Gamma = (G, N, U)$ satisfying the following (soundness) condition:

$$G \subseteq N \wedge U \cap N = \emptyset$$

$d_\perp$ is assumed to be the minimum element and the ordering between two 3-tuples is given by the componentwise superset (partial) relation. The top element is $(\emptyset, \emptyset, \emptyset)$.

The least upper bound (*lub*) operation is the componentwise intersection, while the greatest lower bound can be defined as the dual of the *lub* since $\mathcal{D}$ has the minimum element. It is easy to see that $\mathcal{D}$ forms a complete lattice.

3.4 The Abstract Operations

Now we present briefly the definition of the abstract operations. To do that we need an auxiliary partition on the set *Vars*(*cl*) expressing which variables are alias by means of the equations of the form $\mathtt{A}_j^i{=}V$ of *cl*. Given a variable $\mathtt{A}$ and a partition C, $alias_C(\mathtt{A})$ is the element of C that contains $\mathtt{A}$. Moreover, for each program point (cl_i, j) we will need the set of the variables appearing in the part of the body of *cl* coming before (cl_i, j). Let (G, N, U) and (G', N', U') [C and C'] be the abstract values [partitions] associated with the program points preceding and following $\mathtt{A}_j^i = t$, respectively, where t is a first order logic term. The following rules are to be interpreted as follows: next line condition has to be evaluated if the current line condition does not hold. The new abstract value (G', N', U') is the following. Consider the case $\mathtt{A}_i^j = V$.

- $G' \equiv \begin{cases} G \cup alias_{C'}(V) & \text{if } \mathtt{A}_i^j \in G \text{ or } V \in G \\ G & \text{otherwise} \end{cases}$
- $N' \equiv \begin{cases} N \cup alias_{C'}(V) & \text{if } \mathtt{A}_i^j \in N \text{ or } V \in N \\ N & \text{otherwise} \end{cases}$
- $U' \equiv \begin{cases} U \setminus alias_{C'}(V) & \text{if either } V \notin U \text{ or } \mathtt{A}_i^j \notin U \\ U & \text{otherwise} \end{cases}$

Consider the case $\mathtt{A}_j^i = t$ with t non variable.

$$- \; G' \equiv \begin{cases} G \cup \bigcup_{Z \in vars(t)} alias_C(Z) & \text{if } \mathtt{A}_i^j \in G \\ G \cup alias_C(\mathtt{A}_j^i) & \text{if } Vars(t) \subseteq G \\ G & \text{otherwise} \end{cases}$$

$$- \; N' \equiv \begin{cases} N \cup \bigcup_{Z \in vars(t)} alias_C(Z) & \text{if } \mathtt{A}_i^j \in G \\ N \cup alias_C(\mathtt{A}_j^i) & \text{otherwise} \end{cases}$$

$$- \; U' \equiv \begin{cases} U \setminus alias_C(\mathtt{A}_j^i) & \text{if } j > 0 \\ U \setminus (alias_C(\mathtt{A}_j^i) \setminus \bigcup_{Z \in Vars(t) \setminus (Dups(t) \cup Vars(cl[0,\ldots,s-1]))} alias_C(Z)) & \\ & \text{if } j = 0 \text{ and } \mathtt{A}_i^j \in U \\ U \setminus alias_C(\mathtt{A}_j^i) & \text{if } j = 0 \text{ and } \mathtt{A}_i^j \notin U \end{cases}$$

where $cl \equiv \mathtt{q}/m : -(cl, 0), \ldots, (cl, s-1), \mathtt{A}_i^j = t, (cl, s), \ldots$ and $cl[0, \ldots, s-1] \equiv \mathtt{q}/m : -(cl, 0), \ldots, (cl, s-1)$

These are the abstract operations for the built-ins execution. Now we present the abstract operations for the clause entry and exit phases. Let cl_1 and cl_2 be the calling and the called clauses, respectively. Let (G, N, U) be the abstract value holding at the calling point in cl_1 and let $\mathtt{p}(\mathtt{A}_0^i, \ldots, \mathtt{A}_m^i)$ be the calling atom. Then the abstract value associated with the program point 0 in cl_2 is:

- $G' \equiv \{\mathtt{A}_j^0 \in Vars(cl_2) : \mathtt{A}_j^i \in Vars(cl_1) \cap G\}$
- $N' \equiv \{\mathtt{A}_j^0 \in Vars(cl_2) : \mathtt{A}_j^i \in Vars(cl_1) \cap N\}$
- $U' \equiv Vars(cl_2) \setminus \{\mathtt{A}_j^0 \in Vars(cl_2) : \mathtt{A}_j^i \in Vars(cl_1) \setminus U\}$

Finally, we present the clause exit operation. Let cl_1 and cl_2 be the calling clause and the clause just executed, respectively. Let (G, N, U) be the abstract value holding at the calling point in cl_1, let $\mathtt{p}(\mathtt{A}_0^i, \ldots, \mathtt{A}_m^i)$ be the calling atom, and let (G', N', U') be the abstract value holding at the end of cl_2. Then the abstract value associated with the program point following $\mathtt{p}(\mathtt{A}_0^i, \ldots, \mathtt{A}_m^i)$ in cl_1 is:

- $G'' \equiv G \cup \bigcup_{\mathtt{A}_j^i \in Vars(cl_1) \wedge \mathtt{A}_j^0 \in Vars(cl_2) \cap G'} alias(\mathtt{A}_j^i)$
- $N'' \equiv N \cup \bigcup_{\mathtt{A}_j^i \in Vars(cl_1) \wedge A_j^0 \in Vars(cl_2) \cap N'} alias(\mathtt{A}_j^i)$
- $U'' \equiv U \setminus \bigcup_{\mathtt{A}_j^i \in Vars(cl_1) \wedge \mathtt{A}_j^0 \in Vars(cl_2) \setminus U'} alias(\mathtt{A}_j^i)$

It is easily verified that the above described operations returns values in $\mathcal{D}$.

4 Uninitialized Variable Analysis applied to Append

In this section we apply the abstract semantics to the program of Fig. 2. We implemented our domain in GAIA obtaining a modified version of that software. There are two main differences with respect to GAIA: the normalization and the association of abstract values with the program points. Moreover, we adopted a single-input/single-output granularity for the predicates since our goal was not the one of performing multiple specialization of the programs. In the second part we present a comparison with the analysis and with the speed-up obtained by [14].

4.1 The Fixpoint

We present the fixpoint computed by our implementation. Each program point is associated with a 3-tuple (G, N, U).

Clause cl_0				
main:-	G = {} N = {} U = $\{X_1, X_2, A_0^1, A_1^1, A_2^1\}$	$A_0^1 = X_1$	G = {} N = {} U = $\{X_1, X_2, A_0^1, A_1^1, A_2^1\}$	$A_1^1 = X_2$
G = {} N = {} U = $\{X_1, X_2, A_0^1, A_1^1, A_2^1\}$	A_2^1=[a,b,c]	G = $\{A_2^1\}$ N = $\{A_2^1\}$ U = $\{X_1, X_2, A_0^1, A_1^1\}$	append(A_0^1, A_1^1, A_2^1)	G = $\{X_2, A_1^1, A_2^1\}$ N = $\{X_1, X_2, A_0^1, A_1^1, A_2^1\}$ U = {}

Clause cl_1				
append(A_0^0, A_1^0, A_2^0):-	G = $\{A_2^0\}$ N = $\{A_2^0\}$ U = $\{A_0^0, A_1^0\}$	A_0^0 = []	G = $\{A_0^0, A_2^0\}$ N = $\{A_0^0, A_2^0\}$ U = $\{A_2^0\}$	$A_1^0 = A_2^0$	G = $\{A_0^1, A_1^1, A_2^1\}$ N = $\{A_0^1, A_1^1, A_2^1\}$ U = $\{A_0^1, A_1^1, A_2^1\}$

Clause cl_2			
append(A_0^0, A_1^0, A_2^0):-	G = $\{A_2^0\}$ N = $\{A_2^0\}$ U = $\{X_1, X_2, X_3, X_4, A_0^0, A_1^0, A_0^1, A_1^1, A_2^1\}$	$A_0^0 = [X_1 \mid X_2]$	G = $\{A_2^0\}$ N = $\{A_0^0, A_2^0\}$ U = $\{X_1, X_2, X_3, X_4, A_1^0, A_0^1, A_1^1, A_2^1\}$
$A_2^0 = X_3$	G = $\{A_2^0\}$ N = $\{A_0^0, A_2^0\}$ U = $\{X_1, X_2, X_3, X_4, A_1^0, A_0^1, A_1^1, A_2^1\}$	$A_2^0 = [X_1 \mid X_4]$	G = $\{X_1, X_4, A_2^0\}$ N = $\{X_1, X_4, A_0^0, A_2^0\}$ U = $\{X_2, X_3, A_1^0, A_0^1, A_1^1, A_2^1\}$
$A_0^1 = X_2$	G = $\{X_1, X_4, A_2^0\}$ N = $\{X_1, X_4, A_0^0, A_2^0\}$ U = $\{X_2, X_3, A_1^0, A_0^1, A_1^1, A_2^1\}$	$A_2^1 = X_3$	G = $\{X_1, X_4, A_2^0\}$ N = $\{X_1, X_4, A_0^0, A_2^0\}$ U = $\{X_2, X_3, X_4, A_1^0, A_0^1, A_1^1, A_2^1\}$
$A_2^1 = X_4$	G = $\{X_1, X_4, A_2^0, A_2^1\}$ N = $\{X_1, X_4, A_0^0, A_2^0, A_2^1\}$ U = $\{X_2, X_3, A_1^0, A_0^1, A_1^1\}$	append(A_0^1, A_1^1, A_2^1)	G = $\{X_1, X_3, X_4, A_1^0, A_2^0, A_1^1, A_2^1\}$ N = $\{X_1, X_2, X_3, X_4, A_0^0, A_1^0, A_2^0, A_0^1, A_1^1, A_2^1\}$ U = {}

The input mode for append(A_0^0, A_1^0, A_2^0) is (G=$\{A_2^0\}$,N=$\{A_2^0\}$,U=$\{A_0^0,A_1^0\}$), while the output is (G=$\{A_1^0,A_2^0\}$,N=$\{A_0^0,A_1^0,A_2^0\}$,U={}).

Each of the concrete values computed by the concrete semantics is approximated by the abstract value associated with the corresponding program point. The approximation is by the means of the given semantics of the abstract element.

In the following we describe our optimization technique supported by the abstract values computed in the fixpoint. As an example, consider $A_0^1 = X_1$ in clause cl_0. The abstract value associated with the program point $(cl_0, 1)$ (i.e. the following one) carries information stating that X_1 is uninitialized. Thus, we substitute the `put_x_void(0)` with `put_uninit_x_void(0)` whose semantics differs from the one of `put_x_void(0)` only in that it does not initializes the top of the heap (but it simply increments the top pointer by 1). A similar reasoning applies for `put_uninit_x_void(1)` and `put_x_void(1)`.

Since the first and the second arguments of *append* are uninitialized, the `get` instructions have to cope with arguments that cannot be dereferenced. As a side effect, the `switch_*` operations had to be modified, too. The switching operations do not have to dereference the first argument if it is uninitialized.

At program point $(cl_1, 0)$ the fixpoint expresses the fact that the first and the second arguments are uninitialized. Thus, we exploit this information to design two new instructions. We introduced `get_uninit_nil_x0` whose semantics differs from the one of `get_nil_x0` in that it does not perform the dereferencing of the first argument but it simply assigns the empty list to the location pointed to by the first argument variable. Moreover we designed `get_uninit_x_str_value(1,2)` whose semantics is simpler than the one of `get_x_value(1,2)` in that it exploits the knowledge about the uninitialization of the second argument and the knowledge about the compoundness of the third one.

At program point $(cl_2, 0)$ the fixpoint expresses the same information about the append arguments as in $(cl_1, 0)$. Thus we introduced a new instruction `get_uninit_list_x0` whose semantics differs from the one of `get_list_x0` since we know that the first argument is uninitialized.

Finally `unify_uninit_x_variable(I)` and `unify_uninit_x_value(I)`, if executed in write mode, simply make the variable `I` pointing to an uninitialized location, else, if executed in read mode, they perform the binding of `I` with the input value `S` (in the notation of [1]).

The whole optimized code is shown in Fig. 6.

4.2 A Comparison with the The BAM

Now we compare the information computed by Aquarius and by our analysis. First we consider the input values for the predicate `append`. The BAM analysis computes the same information as our analysis about the first argument: the first argument is uninitialized. The information returned by the BAM about the second argument is `uninit_reg` which is a special kind of uninitialized variable. Our analysis returns the information that the second argument is uninitialized. Finally the third argument is known to be a recursively dereferenced structure by Aquarius while it is known to be a structure by our analysis.

As regards the uninitialized variables, Aquarius and our system have the same precision. In addition, our analysis is simpler and its use does not require the definition of a new abstract machine but only a minor extension of the WAM. The extension of the optimization to other benchmarks will be the next part of the work.

5 Conclusion

A static analysis of logic programs has been presented for the introduction of uninitialized variables in the WAM. The concrete domain we proposed is an abstraction of the WAM memory model, that focuses only on the stack and on the registers.

The abstract domain consists of 3-tuples that express information about the groundness of the variables. Moreover it expresses information about the variables bound to non variable term and about the variables that are uninitialized.

The present work is a step of an ambitious project whose aims are the following:

1. The design of a very low-level generic concrete semantics of logic programs that can be instantiated in different ways in order to express different properties of the execution of logic programs.
2. Show that the concrete semantics expressing a particular property can be very useful for defining an abstract semantics for automatically inferring approximations of that property.
3. Use the method described in the previous point for designing correct static analyses for inferring other low-level properties.

We would like to thank Dr. Mats Carlsson for his kindness, timeliness and patience in answering our beginner-like questions about SICStus and the anonymous referees for their precious and interesting advices.

References

1. H. Ait-Kaci. *Warren's Abstract Machine.* The MIT Press, Cambridge, MA, 1991. Prepared with LaTeX.
2. J. Almgren, S. Andersson, L. Flood, C. Frisk, H. Nilsson, and J. Sundberg. *SICStus Prolog Library Manual.* Swedish Institute of Computer Science, October 1991.
3. K. Apt. *From Logic Programming to Prolog.* Prentice Hall, 1997.
4. J. Beer. The occur-check problem revisited. *Journal of Logic Programming,* 5(3):243–261, September 1988.
5. P. A. Bigot, D. Gudeman, and S. K. Debray. Output value placement in moded logic programs. In Pascal van Hentenryck, editor, *Logic Programming - Proceedings of the Eleventh International Conference on Logic Programming,* pages 175–189, Massachusetts Institute of Technology, 1994. The MIT Press.
6. G. Birkhoff. *Lattice Theory,* volume 25 of *American Mathematical Societ Colloquium Publications.* American Mathematical Society, New York, N.Y., third edition edition, 1967.
7. A. Colmerauer, H. Kanoui, R. Pasero, and P. Roussel. Un systeme de comunication homme-machine en francais. Technical report, Groupe d'Intelligence Artificellle, Universit'e d'Aix-Marseille II, November 1973.
8. P. Cousot and R. Cousot. Abstract interpretation: a unified lattice model for static analysis of programs by construction or approximation of fixpoints. In *Fourth ACM Symposium on Principles of Programming Languages,* pages 238–252, Los Angeles, California, January 1977. ACM Press, New York.

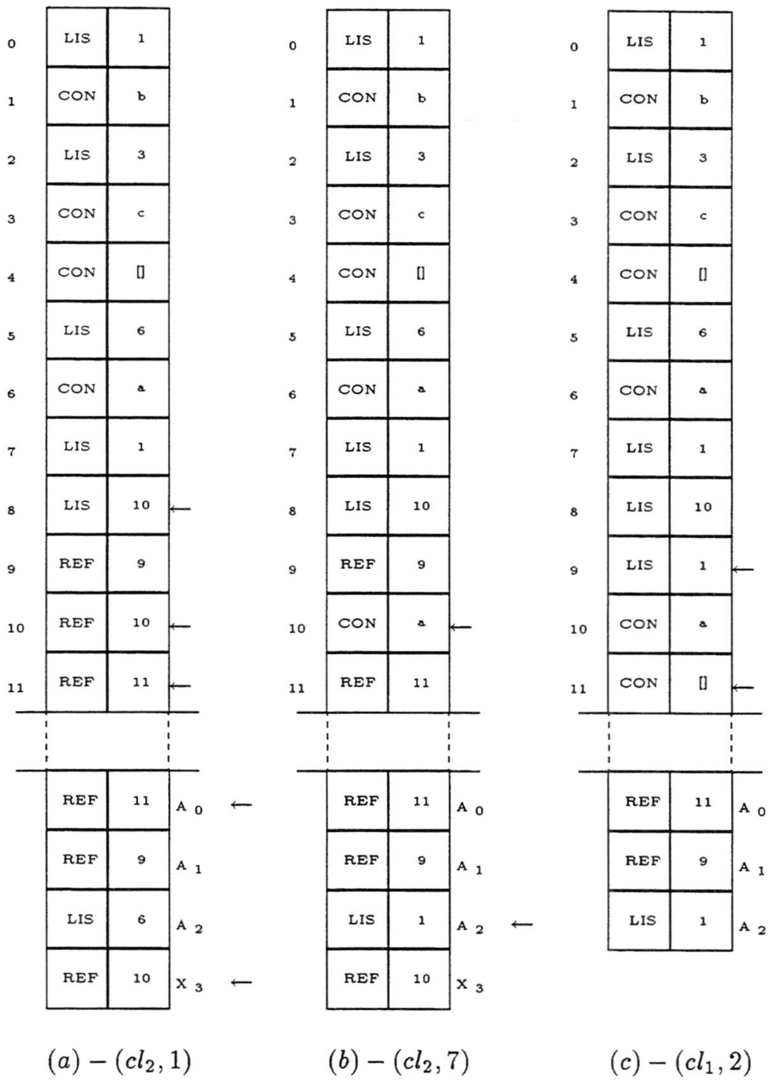

Fig. 5. Stacks at program point $(cl_2, 1)$, $(cl_2, 7)$, $(cl_1, 2)$ for append

9. P. Cousot and R. Cousot. Abstract interpretation and application to logic programs. *Journal of Logic Programming*, 13(2-3):103–179, July 1992.
10. R. C. Haygood. Native code compilation in SICStus Prolog. In Pascal van Hentenryck, editor, *Logic Programming - Proceedings of the Eleventh International Conference on Logic Programming*, pages 190–204, Massachusetts Institute of Technology, 1994. The MIT Press.
11. R. Kowalski. *Logic for Problem Solving.* North-Holland, New York, 4 edition, 1983.
12. B. Le Charlier and P. Van Hentenryck. Experimental evaluation of a generic abstract interpretation algorithm for PROLOG. *ACM Transactions on Programming Languages and Systems*, 16(1):35–101, January 1994.
13. T. Lindgren. Polyvariant detection of uninitialized arguments of prolog predicates. *Journal of Logic Programming*, 28(3):217–229, September 1996.
14. P. L. Van Roy. *Can Logic Programming Execute as Fast as Imperative Programming.* PhD thesis, Computer Science Division, University of California Berkeley, December 1990.
15. D. H. D. Warren. An Abstract PROLOG Instruction Set. Technical Report 309, Artificial Intelligence Center, Computer Science and Technology Division, SRI International, Menlo Park, CA, October 1983.

```
A2versionB121C31902I-1J1J3L-1
clause(main/0/1, [ifshallow, neck(0), else, endif,
    put_list(2), unify_constant(a), unify_list, unify_constant(b),
    unify_list, unify_constant(c), unify_nil, put_uninit_x_void(0),
    put_uninit_x_void(1), execute(append/3)]).
clause(append/3/1, [get_uninit_nil_x0, get_uninit_x_str_value(1,2),
    neck(3), proceed]).
clause(append/3/2, [ifshallow, get_uninit_list_x0,
    unify_uninit_x_variable(4), unify_uninit_x_variable(3), get_list(2),
    unify_uninit_x_value(4), neck(3), unify_uninit_x_variable(2),
    put_uninit_x_value(3,0), execute(append/3),
    else, get_uninit_list_x0, unify_uninit_x_variable(3),
    unify_uninit_x_variable(0), get_list(2), unify_uninit_x_value(3),
    unify_uninit_x_variable(2), execute(append/3), endif]).
predicate(append/3, [switch_on_term([append/3/1,append/3/2], [append/3/2],
    [[]-append/3/1],[])]).
predicate(main/0, [switch_on_term([main/0/1],[main/0/1],[],[main/0/1])]).
```

Fig. 6. Optimized WAM code for append

The CIAO Multi-Dialect Compiler and System: An Experimentation Workbench for Future (C)LP Systems

M. Hermenegildo F. Bueno* D. Cabeza* M. Carro**
M. García de la Banda† P. López G. Puebla**

Abstract

CIAO is an advanced programming environment supporting Logic and Constraint programming. It offers a simple concurrent kernel on top of which declarative and non-declarative extensions are added via libraries. Libraries are available for supporting the ISO-Prolog standard, several constraint domains, functional and higher order programming, concurrent and distributed programming, internet programming, and others. The source language allows declaring properties of predicates via assertions, including types and modes. Such properties are checked at compile-time or at run-time. The compiler and system architecture are designed to natively support modular global analysis, with the two objectives of proving properties in assertions and performing program optimizations, including transparently exploiting parallelism in programs. The purpose of this paper is to report on recent progress made in the context of the CIAO system, with special emphasis on the capabilities of the compiler, the techniques used for supporting such capabilities, and the results in the areas of program analysis and transformation already obtained with the system.

1 Introduction

CIAO is a multi-paradigm compiler, run-time system, and program development environment. It efficiently supports the programming styles of LP, CLP, and CC languages on multiprocessor machines. It also supports distributed execution and Internet/WWW programming. The program development tools in the system include execution visualizers and modular global program analyzers. The latter infer several properties including types, modes, determinacy, non-failure, and independence. Such properties can be checked against user supplied assertions for debugging purposes. Several program transformations (including parallelization) are also performed automatically.

The system offers a simple but versatile kernel language with sequential,

*CS Dept., Technical U. of Madrid. {herme,bueno,dcabeza,mcarro,plg,german}@fi.upm.es

†Dept. of CS, Monash University, Clayton 3168, Australia. mbanda@bruce.cs.monash.oz.au

parallel, concurrent, and distributed execution capabilities. All extensions to this language and support packages are provided as libraries, which are intended to be portable so that they can be used with little modification in other logic and constraint logic programming systems.

The kernel language is directly supported by a comparatively simple abstract machine, mainly based on the parallelism and concurrency capabilities of the &-Prolog parallel abstract machine (the PWAM [Her86, HG91]). The CIAO system is an evolution of &-Prolog [Her86, HG91], which uses the &-Prolog abstract machine as underlying kernel execution mechanism and significantly extends the &-Prolog parallelizing compiler to support several logic programming paradigms.

The implementation of the CIAO system makes use of the observation that the languages and programming styles that it implements share much at both the semantic and the implementation levels [HtCg93, HtCg94]. In that work we discussed several methodological aspects regarding the design and efficiency of a class of future logic programming systems. In particular, we proposed a novel view of parallel and concurrent logic programming systems. We argued that a large number of the actual systems and models can be described through the application of only a few basic principles. We also argued that, in fact, a system supporting several models can be implemented using a comparatively simple, common abstract machine. These principles include determinism, non-failure, independence (also referred to as stability), and task granularity. We also argued for a separation between those principles which have to do with the computation rule (i.e., to performing the least work possible) and those directly related to parallelism (i.e., to performing such work in the smallest amount of time by splitting it among several processors). Finally, and basing our discussion on the convergence of concepts that this view brought, we sketched the design of the CIAO system.

In CIAO the different source-level constructs, and even full sub-languages, are supported by compilation via *source to source* transformations into the kernel language. This allows simplifying the core of the compiler which can then implement a reduced set of analysis and transformation techniques. These techniques are based on novel semantic modeling of CLP and CC program behavior and on the exploitation of fundamental optimization principles (independence/stability and determinism), and techniques based on global analysis (program specialization and abstract executability). This approach allows reusing significant portions of modern Prolog implementation technology. The same philosophy is used in the language syntax design where the better part of the Prolog syntax and language design is used extensively. As a result CIAO subsumes ISO-Prolog (in some cases using a library) and ISO-Prolog programs run in CIAO.

Given the characteristics mentioned above, CIAO can be used quite effectively for developing applications. However, one of its fundamental objectives is to be a tool for easily experimenting with and evaluating language design issues, including program analysis and transformation methods and lower-level implementation techniques.

The main aim of this paper is to offer a general overview of the system and provide references to publications or technical reports where the actual techniques used are described. We hope that the reader will understand in this context the large number of references to CIAO-related publications. A good overview of work in the parallelization of logic programs can be found in [CC94]. Good overviews of recent progress in Constraint Logic Programming and Concurrent (Constraint) Logic Programming can be found respectively in [JM94] and [Tic95]. Most of the papers and technical reports referenced can be obtained from our Laboratory's WWW server `http://www.clip.dia.fi.upm.es/`.

2 Some Design Guidelines of the CIAO System

We now expand on some of the considerations outlined in the introduction, which guide the design of the CIAO system. Such guidelines include:

- *Extensive property inference capabilities, but few compulsory assertions:* The system includes a global analyzer capable of inferring many properties such as types, modes, determinacy, non-failure, freeness, independence, etc. However, in contrast to strongly typed systems such as Mercury [HSC96], none of these annotations are compulsory. In addition, the user can add annotations regarding this properties. Such annotations can optionally be 'checked" by the compiler or "trusted," i.e., used to guide the analysis (for example, when stating the interface of a module). The analyzer communicates the results of analysis in the same assertion language [BCHP96, PBH97, Gro97, BDD+97, HtCG97].

- *Support for ISO-Prolog:* The system provides support for ISO-Prolog. However, this is not done directly but rather via a library. The basic language (when this library is not loaded) can be seen as constructed by first eliminating "unnecessary" impure features in ISO-Prolog (which are put in the library) and adding other features, but keeping the basic syntax. For example, the CIAO system allows constraints, functions, higher order syntax (e.g., `P(X)`), and other Prolog extensions, but all syntactically correct ISO-Prolog programs are also syntactically correct CIAO programs.

- *Versatile compilation options and small executables:* The system provides several different ways of producing executables. These include, in addition to the traditional modes of compilation in Prolog systems, support for the use of CIAO as a scripting language (which avoids any need to use the compiler or top level for program development), compilation to bytecode executables, compilation into C files for linking into C applications, compilation to small native executables, etc.

- *Support for Multiple Models and Paradigms:* The system supports a range of LP, CLP, and CC programming languages. It also supports several computation rules, including standard left-to-right SLD resolution and the determinate-first principle (as in the Andorra model [SCWY90, dMSC93]).

- *Support for Distributed Execution:* In the belief that many distributed applications are a good target for computational logic systems, the CIAO system includes extensive distributed execution capabilities. Such capabilities allow the transparent execution of parallel/concurrent code written for a multiprocessor in a distributed environment (of course, granularity control is an issue here). Furthermore, the system includes the notions of "team" of workers and "active module" (or active object), which conveniently encapsulate different types of functionalities desirable from a distributed system, from parallelism for achieving speedup to client-server applications (the notion of active object is provided as a smooth extension of the built-in module/object system). The distributed capabilities of CIAO are described in [CH95]. In addition, the system also offers several facilities and a library for developing WWW-based applications.[1]

- *Implementation via Compilation into a Simple Kernel Language:* This is based on the belief that medium to high performance implementations of many LP systems can be obtained in this way, with the advantages then that optimizations can be performed via source to source transformations and the low level machinery can be kept minimal. Optimizations, which include parallelization, reduction of concurrency and synchronization, reordering of goals, code simplification, specialization, etc., are performed via source to source transformation. Most analysis phases are performed at the kernel language level, so that the same analyzer can be used for several models. For example, a single analyzer framework can handle Prolog programs with delay and concurrent (constraint) programs.

- *Explicit Control in the Kernel Language:* makes it possible to perform many control-related optimizations at the source level. Such explicit control is performed via operators which include:

  - *Sequential, Parallel, and Concurrent Operators:* the presence of separate sequentiality ("`,`"), concurrency ("`&/1`") and parallelism ("`&/2`", "`&>/2`", "`<&/1`") operators allows performing optimizations such as parallelization (task creation based on dependencies), partitioning and schedule analysis (task coalescence based on dependencies), and granularity control (task coalescence based on task size considerations) as source to source transformations.

    The *parallel operators* allow indicating points where parallelism can be exploited. Their behavior is otherwise equivalent to that of the

[1] See `http://www.clip.dia.fi.upm.es/miscdocs/html_pl/html_pl.html` for details.

sequential operator. Thus, full backtracking is supported. These operators essentially assume independence among goals. Communication of bindings is therefore not guaranteed until the join. No variable locking is performed. The *concurrency operator* allows concurrent programming in the style of CC languages (also, the parallelism in such concurrent execution may be exploited if resources are available). Backtracking is limited to allow a relatively straightforward implementation. In particular, in the current version of the CIAO system no "active shared binding" is allowed to be undone via backtracking. An active shared binding is a binding to a variable that is shared among active (i.e., non-finished) processes. Variable communication (and locking) is performed.

- *Explicit And-Fairness Operator:* based on the observation that and-fairness in concurrent systems is still expensive to implement, a fair concurrency operator ("`&&/1`") is introduced which explicitly requests the (efficient) association of computational resources (e.g., an operating system thread) to a goal. Note that this leaves open the possibility of implementing a fair source language that compiles efficiently into this and the above operators (perhaps via an analysis which can determine the program points where fairness is really needed – to ensure, for example, termination).
- *Explicit Synchronization:* handled in the kernel language by means of "`wait/1`" and "`ask/1`" operators (the latter as in concurrent constraint programming, the former as in &-Prolog), augmented with some meta-tests on the variables (such as `ground/1` or `nonvar/1`).
- *Explicit Placement Operator:* The "`@`" operator allows control of task placement in distributed execution. This operator can be combined with any of the parallelism and concurrency operators mentioned before. Other primitives for controlling distributed execution include primitives for dealing with teams of workers, and for using active modules or active objects.

• *Generic Abstract Machine:* a comparatively simple abstract machine directly supports the kernel language. The design of the abstract machine is based on the belief that there is much in common at the abstract machine level among many of the LP, CLP, and CC models, and thus builds strongly on the parallelism and concurrency capabilities of the PWAM/&-Prolog abstract machine [Her86, HG91] and recent work on extending its capabilities and efficiency [PGT+96]. The abstract machine includes native support for *attributed variables* [Hol92, Hui90, Neu90] [Hol92] which are used in the implementation of constraint solvers (as in other systems such as Eclipse [Eur93] and SICStus 3 [Swe95]) and in supporting communication among concurrent tasks [HCC95]. While the current abstract

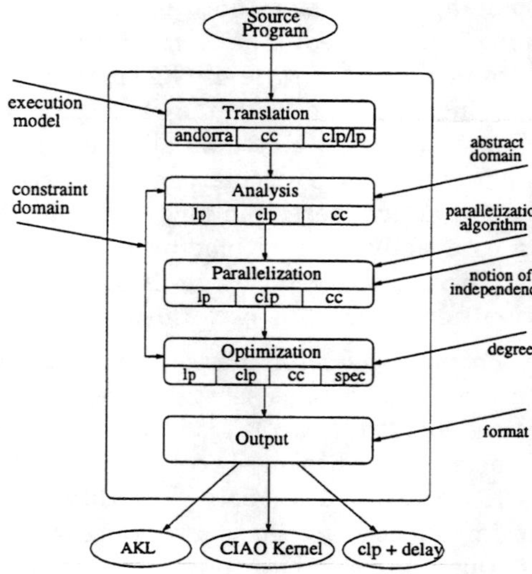

Figure 1: CIAO Compiler Structure

machine supports only ("dependent" and "independent") and-parallelism, it is expected that combination with or-parallelism will be possible by applying the techniques developed in [GSCYH91, GC92, GHPSC94].

3 The CIAO Compiler

The CIAO compiler provides the required support for the different programming paradigms and their optimization. As mentioned before, it is strongly based on program analysis and transformation. The compilation process can be viewed as a translation process from the input language to (kernel) CIAO. The system is able to translate the input source, automatically extracting parallelism, compiling synchronization, and optimizing the final program. Optimizations include simplifying the code to avoid run-time tests and suspensions, and specializing predicates in order to generate much simpler and efficient code in the back end.

This compilation process is depicted in Figure 1, which illustrates the inputs and outputs, as well as the compilation options, which are selected via either menus or program flags. The compilation process is structured into several steps. First, a module in a given input language is translated into the kernel language. Then, analysis is performed if required to support the rest of the compilation process. Some degree of analysis may also be performed to aid in the translation step. After analysis, the program is optionally annotated for parallel execution, simplified and specialized.

The output can then be loaded for execution on the abstract machine. As an alternative, and using the transformational approach, most of the capability of the system is also supported (with sometimes somewhat lower efficiency) on any Prolog system with delay declarations and attributed variables (e.g., SICStus Prolog Version 3 [Swe95]). In that sense, the CIAO compiler can also be viewed as a library package for Prolog systems with these capabilities.

The compiler steps and options are discussed in the following sections. As mentioned before, our aim herein is to offer a general description and provide references for publications or technical reports where the techniques used are described. An extended description of the capabilities of the compiler can be found in the User's Manual [Bue95].

3.1 Source Languages Supported and Transformations Performed

The compiler can deal with several languages and computation rules simultaneously and perform several translations among them. Currently, there are three languages supported: the CIAO kernel language (backwards compatible with Prolog, plus the specific CIAO primitives), languages based on the basic Andorra model, and basic CC languages. Also, for each of these languages several constraint domains can be chosen. Currently, the system supports those of Prolog, CLP(R), and CLP(Q).

The mode of the system can be changed by typing at the top level the commands `ciao(Domain)`, `andorra(Domain)`, or `cc(Domain)`, where the variable `Domain` has to be instantiated to either `h`, `q`, or `r`, indicating the desired constraint domain, i.e. Herbrand, Q, or R, respectively. Programs read from then on will be assumed to have the characteristics associated to the new mode:

- `ciao(Domain)`: CIAO full syntax (backwards compatible with Prolog, plus the specific CIAO primitives) language; left-to-right and (encapsulated) concurrency.
- `andorra(Domain)`: Prolog language; computation rule based on the basic Andorra principle.
- `cc(Domain)`: basic CC language; concurrent computation rule.

Alternatively, the mode can be directly included in the program. This is done in the module declaration, which has one additional argument available for the specification of the mode.

Program transformations bridge the semantic gaps between the different programming paradigms supported. The methods used for translating programs based on the (Basic) Andorra model to CIAO are described in [BDGH94]. The methods used for translating CC languages are an extension of those of [DGB94, Deb93] and are described in [BH95b].

3.2 Analysis

The CIAO compiler includes both local and global analysis of programs. Local analysis of program clauses is usually very simple but not accurate. Nonetheless, it is sometimes partially useful in some optimizations, as in program parallelization [BGH94]. Global analysis is performed in the context of abstract interpretation [CC77, Deb92, CC92]. The underlying framework of analysis is that of PLAI [HWD92, MH90, MH92]. PLAI implements a generic (goal-dependent and goal-independent) top-down driven abstract interpreter. The whole computation is domain–independent. This allows plugging in different abstract domains, provided suitable interfacing functions are defined. PLAI also incorporates incremental analysis [HPMS95] in order to deal with large programs and is capable of analyzing full languages (in particular, full standard Prolog [BCHP96, CRV94]).

A modification of the PLAI framework capable of analyzing dynamically scheduled programs is also provided in order to support the concurrent models. Note that, thanks to the transformational approach, only two frameworks are used (one for simple, left-to-right execution and another for the case when there are dynamically scheduled goals). The compiler automatically decides the framework to be used.

The CIAO analyzer incorporates the following domains, which are briefly explained below: *Sh*, *Sh+Fr*, *ASub*, *Sh+ASub*, and *Sh+Fr+ASub*, which are used in logic programming, and *Def*, *Fr*, *Fd*, which can be used either in logic or constraint logic programming, and *LSign*, which is more specific to constraint logic programming.[2] Programs with dynamic scheduling can be analyzed with the *Sh+Fr* and *Def* domains.

3.2.1 HERBRAND: For the analysis of (classical) logic programs (over the Herbrand domain) the CIAO compiler includes a number of traditional domains proposed in the literature for capturing properties such as variable groundness, freeness, sharing, and linearity information. This includes the set sharing *Sh* [JL89, MH89], set sharing and freeness Sh+Fr [MH91], and pair sharing *ASub* [Son86] domains. Combinations of the *Sh* and *Sh+Fr* domains with *ASub* are also supported, resulting in the *Sh+ASub* and *Sh+Fr+ASub* domains. The combination is done in such a way that the original domains and operations of the analyzer over them are re-used, instead of redefining the domains for the combination [CC79, CMB$^+$95]. Two other domains, a modified version of *Path sharing* [KS95] and *Aeqns* (abstract equations) [MSJB95] are currently being incorporated to the system. In addition the system performs type and determinacy/non-failure analysis [BJ88, GdW94, DLH97].

3.2.2 CONSTRAINT PROGRAMMING: Several domains are available, some of which have been implemented by other users of the PLAI system, notably

[2] Some of these domains have been implemented by other users of the PLAI system, notably the K. U. Leuven, Monash University, and the U. of Melbourne.

the K. U. Leuven, Monash University, and the U. of Melbourne.

The abstract domain *Def* [GHB+96] determines whether program variables are definite, i.e. constrained to a unique value. In doing this it keeps track of *definite* dependencies among variables. The abstract domain *Fr* [GHB+96] determines which variables act as *degrees of freedom* with respect to the satisfiability of the constraint store in which they occur. In doing this it keeps track of *possible* dependencies among variables. The definite and possible dependencies are used to perform accurate definiteness and non-freeness propagation, respectively, and are also useful in their own right to perform several program optimizations. A combined domain *Fd* which infers both definiteness and freeness is also integrated.

A preliminary version of the domain *LSign* [MS94] is also supported. This domain is aimed at inferring accurate information about possible interaction between linear arithmetic equalities and inequalities. The key idea is to abstract the actual coefficients and constants in constraints by their "sign". A preliminary implementation of this domain shows very promising accuracy, although at a cost in efficiency.

3.2.3 DYNAMICALLY SCHEDULED PROGRAMS: CIAO also includes a version of the PLAI framework which is capable of accurately analyzing (constraint) programs with dynamic scheduling (e.g., including delay declarations [Col82, Car87]). Being able to analyze constraint languages with dynamic scheduling also allows analyzing CC languages with angelic nondeterminism.[3] This is based on the observation that most implementations of the concurrent paradigm can be viewed as a computation which proceeds with a fixed, sequential scheduling rule but in which some goals suspend and their execution is postponed until some condition wakes them. Initial studies showed that accurate analysis in such programs is possible [MGH94], although this technique involves relatively large cost in analysis time. The analysis integrated into the CIAO compiler uses a novel method which improves on the previous one by increasing the efficiency without significant loss of accuracy [GMS95]. The approach is based on approximating the delayed atoms by a closure operator.

A direct method for analysis of CC programs has also been developed and is currently being integrated into the compiler. This method is an extension of previous work of Debray [DGB94, Deb93]. It is based on the observation that for certain properties, it is possible to extend existing analysis technology for the underlying fixed computation rule in order to deal with such programs [BH95b]. In particular, this idea has been applied using as starting point the original framework for the analysis of sequential programs. The resulting analysis can deal with programs where concurrency is governed by the Andorra model as well as standard CC models. The advantage with respect to the method above

[3] This is a kind of nondeterminism which does not give rise to an arbitrary choice when applying a search rule.

is lower analysis time, in exchange for a certain loss of accuracy.

3.3 Parallelization

LP, CLP, and CC offer an interesting case study for automatic parallelization. On the one hand these languages pose significant challenges to automatic parallelization, such as a symbolic nature, non-determinism, irregular computations, dynamic control flow, and (well behaved) pointers. On the other hand they offer a clear semantics on which formal program analysis and transformation techniques can be easily based. In the CIAO compiler the information inferred during the analysis phase is used for independence detection, which is the core of the LP and CLP parallelization process [BGH94, GBH96]. The compile-time parallelization module is currently aimed at uncovering goal-level, restricted (i.e., fork and join), independent and-parallelism (IAP). Independence has the very desirable properties of correct and efficient execution w.r.t. standard sequential execution of Prolog or CLP. In the context of LP, parallelization is performed based on the well-understood concepts of *strict* and *non-strict* independence [HR95], using the information provided by the abstract domains. While the notions of independence used in LP are not directly applicable to CLP, specific definitions for CLP (and constraint programming with dynamic scheduling) have been recently proposed [GHM93, Gar94] and they have been incorporated in the CIAO compiler in order to parallelize CLP and CC programs [GHM95]. Additionally, the compiler has side-effect and granularity analyzers (not depicted in Figure 1) which infer information which can yield the sequentialization of goals (even when they are independent) based on efficiency or maintenance of observable behavior.

The actual automatic parallelization of the source program is performed in CIAO during compilation of the program by the so called *annotation* algorithms. The algorithms currently implemented are: `mel`, `cdg`, `udg` [Mut91, Bue94], and `urlp` [CH94]. To our knowledge, the CIAO system is the first one to perform automatic compile-time (And-)parallelization of CLP programs [GBH96].

3.4 Optimization

The CIAO compiler performs several forms of code optimization by means of source to source transformations. The information obtained during the analysis phase is not only useful in automatic program parallelization, but also in this program specialization and simplification phase.

The CIAO compiler can optimize programs to different degrees, as indicated by the user. It can just simplify the program, where simplification amounts to reducing literals and predicates which are known to always succeed, fail, or lead to error. This can speed up the program at run-time, and also be useful to detect errors at compile-time. It can also specialize the program using the versions generated during analysis [PH95a]. This may involve generating different versions of a predicate for different *abstract call patterns*, thus increasing the program size whenever this allows more optimizations. In order to keep the size of the specialized program as reduced as possible, the number of versions of each predicate is minimized attaining the same results as with Winsborough's algorithm [Win92].

As well as handling sequential code, the optimization module of the CIAO compiler contains what we believe is the first automatic optimizer for languages with dynamic scheduling [PH95b]. The potential benefits of the optimization of this type of programs were already shown in [MGH94], but they can now be obtained automatically. These kinds of optimizations include simplification and elimination of suspension conditions and elimination of concurrency primitives (sequentialization).

3.5 Granularity Control

The compiler also performs granularity control using the techniques described in [DLH90, Tic88, LHD94, DGHL94, LH95]. The compiler estimates the granularity of parallel tasks, i.e. the work available under them, by generating expressions that are upper and lower bounds for the computation time of parallel tasks as a function of the size of task input data. These functions are used at run-time to perform granularity control by comparing cost bounds to suitable thresholds. The results so far are encouraging, and we plan to perform much further investigation in this very important area.

3.6 Output

The back end of the compiler takes the result of the previous program transformations and generates a number of final output formats. Normally, the result of the compiler is intended for the CIAO/&-Prolog abstract machine. Output possibilities are then byte-code ("`.ql`") files, C-files (for linking into traditional applications), stand-alone executables, and incore compilation (when the compiler is running inside the system rather than as a stand-alone application). As mentioned before, and as an alternative output, most of the capability of the system can also be handled by any Prolog which supports delay declarations and attributed variables. Alternatively, also AKL [JH91] can be used as a target, using the techniques described in [BH95a].

Finally, it is possible to obtain the results of each of the intermediate compilation phases. This allows visualizing and affecting the transformation, analysis, parallelization, and optimization processes. Because of the source to source nature of the compiler, this output is always a (possibly annotated) kernel CIAO program.

4 Performance Evaluation Tools

Two tools have been developed to complement the environment and help during performance debugging. VisAndOr [CGH93] is a tool for visualizing parallel executions. It supports both conjunctive and disjunctive execution graphs (or- and and-parallelism). It is currently in use by several other researchers in the field and it is distributed with other parallel systems such as Muse [AK90]. IDRA

[FCH94] is a simulator which can quite accurately compute ideal speedups from traces from a sequential execution of a parallelized program. It allows evaluating the performance of the parallel run-time system independently of the quality of the parallelization performed by the compiler, by comparing the obtained speedups with those predicted by IDRA for the given parallelized program.

5 Some Future Directions

We have briefly described the current status of the CIAO system. The current main objective of the system is to be an experimentation and evaluation vehicle for programming constructs and optimization and implementation techniques for the programming paradigms of LP, CLP, CC, and their combinations. The system has already shown itself useful in illustrating the power (or lack thereof) of a number of analysis and optimization techniques (see the referenced papers for details). Additionally, we are developing pilot applications with the system which should provide valuable feedback regarding its capabilities.

While the CIAO system illustrates that analysis and optimization of concurrent programs is possible, much work remains in improving the efficiency and accuracy of the analysis and in improving the performance gains obtained with the resulting optimizations.

As mentioned in Section 3.3, the automatic parallelization currently performed in the CIAO system is at the goal level. However, it is possible to parallelize at finer granularity levels, thus obtaining greater degrees of parallelism. The concept of *local independence* [MRB$^+$94, BHMR94] can be used for this purpose. Although some promising progress has been made in this direction [HCC95], it remains as future work to implement a system fully capable of efficiently exploiting this very fine grained level of parallelism.

While our work in detection of parallelism in the CIAO compiler concentrates on compile-time detection of parallelism, run-time detection also needs to be explored. Significant progress has been made in this area by models and systems such as DDAS [She92], Andorra-I, and AKL.

Some parts of the CIAO system (e.g., the PLAI analyzers, the parallelizers, the WWW libraries, the distributed programming libraries, etc.) have been distributed in the public domain and have been used experimentally by several researchers. Current versions of other parts of the system which are less developed are available for experimentation (please contact the authors; further information can be obtained from `http://www.clip.dia.fi.upm.es/`). Both kernel system and all the libraries are intended to be put gradually in the public domain.

Acknowledgments

The development of the CIAO system is a collaborative effort of several groups and includes work developed at the U. of Arizona (S. Debray's group), New Mexico State University (G. Gupta and E. Pontelli), K. U. Leuven (M. Bruynooghe's group), and Monash and Melbourne U. (M. García de la Banda, K. Marriott, and P. Stuckey), in addition to the CLIP (Computational Logic, Implementation, and Parallelism) group at the Technical University of Madrid. Parts of this work have been funded by ESPRIT projects PRINCE, PARFORCE, and ACCLAIM, and CICYT project IPL-D.

References

[AK90] K. A. M. Ali and R. Karlsson. The Muse Or-Parallel Prolog Model and its Performance. In *1990 North American Conference on Logic Programming*, pages 757–776. MIT Press, October 1990.

[BCHP96] F. Bueno, D. Cabeza, M. Hermenegildo, and G. Puebla. Global Analysis of Standard Prolog Programs. In *European Symposium on Programming*, number 1058 in LNCS, pages 108–124, Sweden, April 1996. Springer-Verlag.

[BDD+97] F. Bueno, P. Deransart, W. Drabent, G. Ferrand, M. Hermenegildo, J. Maluszynski, and G. Puebla. On the Role of Semantic Approximations in Validation and Diagnosis of Constraint Logic Programs. In *Proc. of the 3rd. Int'l Workshop on Automated Debugging–AADEBUG'97*, pages 155–170, Linkoping, Sweden, May 1997. U. of Linkoping Press.

[BDGH94] F. Bueno, S. K. Debray, M. García de la Banda, and M. Hermenegildo. QE-Andorra: A Quiche–Eating Implementation of the Basic Andorra Model. Technical Report CLIP13/94.0, T.U. of Madrid (UPM), September 1994.

[BGH94] F. Bueno, M. García de la Banda, and M. Hermenegildo. Effectiveness of Global Analysis in Strict Independence-Based Automatic Program Parallelization. In *International Symposium on Logic Programming*, pages 320–336. MIT Press, November 1994.

[BH95a] F. Bueno and M. Hermenegildo. An Automatic Translation Scheme from CLP to AKL. Technical Report CLIP7/95.0, Facultad de Informática, UPM, June 1995.

[BH95b] F. Bueno and M. Hermenegildo. Analysis of Concurrent Constraint Logic Programs with a Fixed Scheduling Rule. In *ICLP95 WS on Abstract Interpretation of Logic Languages*, Japan, June 1995.

[BHMR94] F. Bueno, M. Hermenegildo, U. Montanari, and F. Rossi. From Eventual to Atomic and Locally Atomic CC Programs: A Concurrent Semantics. In *Fourth International Conference on Algebraic and Logic Programming*, number 850 in LNCS, pages 114–132. Springer-Verlag, September 1994.

[BJ88] M. Bruynooghe and G. Janssens. An Instance of Abstract Interpretation Integrating Type and Mode Inference. In *Fifth International Conference and Symposium on Logic Programming*, pages 669–683, Seattle, Washington, August 1988. MIT Press.

[Bue94] F. Bueno Carrillo. *Automatic Optimisation and Parallelisation of Logic Programs through Program Transformation.* PhD thesis, Universidad Politécnica de Madrid (UPM), October 1994.

[Bue95] F. Bueno. The CIAO Multiparadigm Compiler: A User's Manual. Technical Report CLIP8/95.0, Facultad de Informática, UPM, June 1995.

[Car87] M. Carlsson. Freeze, Indexing, and Other Implementation Issues in the Wam. In *Fourth International Conference on Logic Programming*, pages 40–58. University of Melbourne, MIT Press, May 1987.

[CC77] P. Cousot and R. Cousot. Abstract Interpretation: a Unified Lattice Model for Static Analysis of Programs by Construction or Approximation of Fixpoints. In *Fourth ACM Symposium on Principles of Programming Languages*, pages 238–252, 1977.

[CC79] P. Cousot and R. Cousot. Systematic Design of Program Analysis Frameworks. In *Sixth ACM Symposium on Principles of Programming Languages*, pages 269–282, San Antonio, Texas, 1979.

[CC92] P. Cousot and R. Cousot. Abstract Interpretation and Application to Logic Programs. *Journal of Logic Programming*, 13(2 and 3):103–179, July 1992.

[CC94] J. Chassin and P. Codognet. Parallel Logic Programming Systems. *Computing Surveys*, 26(3):295–336, September 1994.

[CGH93] M. Carro, L. Gómez, and M. Hermenegildo. Some Paradigms for Visualizing Parallel Execution of Logic Programs. In *1993 International Conference on Logic Programming*, pages 184–201. MIT Press, June 1993.

[CH94] D. Cabeza and M. Hermenegildo. Extracting Non-strict Independent And-parallelism Using Sharing and Freeness Information. In *1994 International Static Analysis Symposium*, number 864 in LNCS, pages 297–313, Namur, Belgium, September 1994. Springer-Verlag.

[CH95] D. Cabeza and M. Hermenegildo. Distributed Concurrent Constraint Execution in the CIAO System. In *Proc. of the 1995*

COMPULOG-NET Workshop on Parallelism and Implementation Technologies, Utrecht, NL, September 1995. U. Utrecht / T.U. Madrid. Available from `http://www.clip.dia.fi.upm.es/`.

[CMB+95] M. Codish, A. Mulkers, M. Bruynooghe, M. García de la Banda, and M. Hermenegildo. Improving Abstract Interpretations by Combining Domains. *ACM Transactions on Programming Languages and Systems*, 17(1):28–44, January 1995. Available from `http://www.clip.dia.fi.upm.es`.

[Col82] A. Colmerauer et al. *Prolog II: Reference Manual and Theoretical Model.* Groupe D'intelligence Artificielle, Faculté Des Sciences De Luminy, Marseille, 1982.

[CRV94] B. Le Charlier, S. Rossi, and P. Van Hentenryck. An Abstract Interpretation Framework Which Accurately Handles Prolog Search–Rule and the Cut. In *International Symposium on Logic Programming*, pages 157–171. MIT Press, November 1994.

[Deb92] S. Debray, editor. *Journal of Logic Programming, Special Issue: Abstract Interpretation*, volume 13(1–2). North-Holland, July 1992.

[Deb93] S. K. Debray. Implementing logic programming systems: The quiche-eating approach. In *ICLP '93 Workshop on Practical Implementations and Systems Experience in Logic Programming*, Budapest, Hungary, June 1993.

[DGB94] S. Debray, D. Gudeman, and P. Bigot. Detection and Optimization of Suspension-free Logic Programs. In *1994 International Symposium on Logic Programming*, pages 487–501. MIT Press, November 1994.

[DGHL94] S. K. Debray, P. López García, M. Hermenegildo, and N.-W. Lin. Estimating the Computational Cost of Logic Programs. In *Static Analysis Symposium, SAS'94*, number 864 in LNCS, pages 255–265, Namur, Belgium, September 1994. Springer-Verlag.

[DLH90] S. K. Debray, N.-W. Lin, and M. Hermenegildo. Task Granularity Analysis in Logic Programs. In *Proc. of the 1990 ACM Conf. on Programming Language Design and Implementation*, pages 174–188. ACM Press, June 1990.

[DLH97] S. K. Debray, P. López García, and M. Hermenegildo. Non-Failure Analysis for Logic Programs. In *1997 International Conference on Logic Programming*, pages 48–62, Leuven, Belgium, June 1997. MIT Press, Cambridge, MA.

[dMSC93] Vítor Manuel de Morais Santos Costa. *Compile-Time Analysis for the Parallel Execution of Logic Programs in Andorra-I.* PhD thesis, University of Bristol, August 1993.

[Eur93] European Computer Research Center. *Eclipse User's Guide*, 1993.

[FCH94] M. Fernández, M. Carro, and M. Hermenegildo. IDRA (IDeal Resource Allocation): A Tool for Computing Ideal Speedups. In *ICLP WS on Parallel and Data Parallel Execution of Logic Programs*, June 1994.

[Gar94] M. García de la Banda. *Independence, Global Analysis, and Parallelism in Dynamically Scheduled Constraint Logic Programming.* PhD thesis, Universidad Politécnica de Madrid (UPM), Facultad Informatica UPM, 28660-Boadilla del Monte, Madrid-Spain, September 1994.

[GBH96] M. García de la Banda, F. Bueno, and M. Hermenegildo. Towards Independent And-Parallelism in CLP. In *Programming Languages: Implementation, Logics, and Programs*, number 1140 in LNCS, pages 77–91, Aachen, Germany, September 1996. Springer-Verlag.

[GC92] G. Gupta and V. Santos Costa. And-Or Parallelism in Full Prolog based on Paged Binding Array. In *Parallel Architectures and Lenguages Europe '92.* Springer Verlag, June 1992.

[GdW94] J.P. Gallagher and D.A. de Waal. Fast and precise regular approximations of logic programs. In Pascal Van Hentenryck, editor, *Proceedings of the Eleventh International Conference on Logic Programming*, pages 599–613. The MIT Press, 1994.

[GHB+96] M. García de la Banda, M. Hermenegildo, M. Bruynooghe, V. Dumortier, G. Janssens, and W. Simoens. Global Analysis of Constraint Logic Programs. *ACM Transactions on Programming Languages and Systems*, 18(5):564–615, 1996.

[GHM93] M. García de la Banda, M. Hermenegildo, and K. Marriott. Independence in Constraint Logic Programs. In *1993 International Logic Programming Symposium*, pages 130–146. MIT Press, Cambridge, MA, October 1993.

[GHM95] M. García de la Banda, M. Hermenegildo, and K. Marriott. Independence and Search Space Preservation in Dynamically Scheduled Constraint Logic Languages. Technical Report CLIP10/95.0, Facultad de Informática, UPM, February 1995.

[GHPSC94] G. Gupta, M. Hermenegildo, E. Pontelli, and V. Santos-Costa. ACE: And/Or-parallel Copying-based Execution of Logic Programs. In *International Conference on Logic Programming*, pages 93–110. MIT Press, June 1994.

[GMS95] M. García de la Banda, K. Marriott, and P. Stuckey. Efficient Analysis of Constraint Logic Programs with Dynamic Scheduling. In *1995 International Logic Programming Symposium*, pages 417–431, Portland, Oregon, December 1995. MIT Press, Cambridge, MA.

[Gro97] The CLIP Group. Program Assertions. The CIAO System Documentation Series – TR CLIP4/97.1, Facultad de Informática, UPM, August 1997.

[GSCYH91] G. Gupta, V. Santos-Costa, R. Yang, and M. Hermenegildo. IDIOM: Integrating Dependent and-, Independent and-, and Or-parallelism. In *1991 International Logic Programming Symposium*, pages 152–166. MIT Press, October 1991.

[HCC95] M. Hermenegildo, D. Cabeza, and M. Carro. Using Attributed Variables in the Implementation of Concurrent and Parallel Logic Programming Systems. In *Proc. of the Twelfth International Conference on Logic Programming*, pages 631–645. MIT Press, June 1995.

[Her86] M. Hermenegildo. An Abstract Machine for Restricted AND-parallel Execution of Logic Programs. In *Third International Conference on Logic Programming*, number 225 in Lecture Notes in Computer Science, pages 25–40. Imperial College, Springer-Verlag, July 1986.

[HG91] M. Hermenegildo and K. Greene. The &-Prolog System: Exploiting Independent And-Parallelism. *New Generation Computing*, 9(3,4):233–257, 1991.

[Hol92] C. Holzbaur. Metastructures vs. Attributed Variables in the Context of Extensible Unification. In *1992 International Symposium on Programming Language Implementation and Logic Programming*, pages 260–268. LNCS631, Springer Verlag, August 1992.

[HPMS95] M. Hermenegildo, G. Puebla, K. Marriott, and P. Stuckey. Incremental Analysis of Logic Programs. In *International Conference on Logic Programming*, pages 797–811. MIT Press, June 1995.

[HR95] M. Hermenegildo and F. Rossi. Strict and Non-Strict Independent And-Parallelism in Logic Programs: Correctness, Efficiency, and

Compile-Time Conditions. *Journal of Logic Programming*, 22(1):1–45, 1995.

[HSC96] F. Henderson, Z. Somogyi, and T. Conway. Determinism analysis in the mercury compiler. In *Proc. Australian Computer Science Conference*, Melbourne, Australia, January 1996.

[HtCg93] M. Hermenegildo and the CLIP group. Towards CIAO-Prolog – A Parallel Concurrent Constraint System. In *Proc. of the Compulog Net Area Workshop on Parallelism and Implementation Technologies*. FIM/UPM, Madrid, Spain, June 1993.

[HtCg94] M. Hermenegildo and the CLIP group. Some Methodological Issues in the Design of CIAO - A Generic, Parallel, Concurrent Constraint System. In *Principles and Practice of Constraint Programming*, number 874 in LNCS, pages 123–133. Springer-Verlag, May 1994.

[HtCG97] M. Hermenegildo and the CLIP Group. Programming with Global Analysis. In *Proceedings of ILPS'97*. MIT Press, October 1997. (abstract of invited talk).

[Hui90] S. Le Huitouze. A New Data Structure for Implementing Extensions to Prolog. In P. Deransart and J. Małuszyński, editors, *Proceedings of Programming Language Implementation and Logic Programming*, number 456 in Lecture Notes in Computer Science, pages 136–150. Springer, August 1990.

[HWD92] M. Hermenegildo, R. Warren, and S. K. Debray. Global Flow Analysis as a Practical Compilation Tool. *Journal of Logic Programming*, 13(4):349–367, August 1992.

[JH91] S. Janson and S. Haridi. Programming Paradigms of the Andorra Kernel Language. In *1991 International Logic Programming Symposium*, pages 167–183. MIT Press, 1991.

[JL89] D. Jacobs and A. Langen. Accurate and Efficient Approximation of Variable Aliasing in Logic Programs. In *1989 North American Conference on Logic Programming*. MIT Press, October 1989.

[JM94] J. Jaffar and M.J. Maher. Constraint Logic Programming: A Survey. *Journal of Logic Programming*, 19/20:503–581, 1994.

[KS95] A. King and P. Soper. Depth-k Sharing and Freeness. In *International Conference on Logic Programming*. MIT Press, June 1995.

[LH95] P. López García and M. Hermenegildo. Efficient Term Size Computation for Granularity Control. In *International Conference on Logic Programming*, pages 647–661. The MIT Press, June 1995.

[LHD94] P. López García, M. Hermenegildo, and S. K. Debray. Towards Granularity Based Control of Parallelism in Logic Programs. In Hoon Hong, editor, *Proc. of First International Symposium on Parallel Symbolic Computation, PASCO'94*, pages 133–144. World Scientific, September 1994.

[MGH94] K. Marriott, M. García de la Banda, and M. Hermenegildo. Analyzing Logic Programs with Dynamic Scheduling. In *20th. Annual ACM Conf. on Principles of Programming Languages*, pages 240–254. ACM, January 1994.

[MH89] K. Muthukumar and M. Hermenegildo. Determination of Variable Dependence Information at Compile-Time Through Abstract Interpretation. In *1989 North American Conference on Logic Programming*, pages 166–189. MIT Press, October 1989.

[MH90] K. Muthukumar and M. Hermenegildo. Deriving A Fixpoint Computation Algorithm for Top-down Abstract Interpretation of Logic Programs. Technical Report ACT-DC-153-90, Microelectronics and Computer Technology Corporation (MCC), Austin, TX 78759, April 1990.

[MH91] K. Muthukumar and M. Hermenegildo. Combined Determination of Sharing and Freeness of Program Variables Through Abstract Interpretation. In *1991 International Conference on Logic Programming*, pages 49–63. MIT Press, June 1991.

[MH92] K. Muthukumar and M. Hermenegildo. Compile-time Derivation of Variable Dependency Using Abstract Interpretation. *Journal of Logic Programming*, 13(2/3):315–347, July 1992. Originally published as Technical Report FIM 59.1/IA/90, Computer Science Dept, Universidad Politecnica de Madrid, Spain, August 1990.

[MRB+94] U. Montanari, F. Rossi, F. Bueno, M. García de la Banda, and M. Hermenegildo. Towards a Concurrent Semantics based Analysis of CC and CLP. In *Principles and Practice of Constraint Programming*, number 874 in LNCS, pages 151–161. Springer-Verlag, May 1994.

[MS94] K. Marriott and P. Stuckey. Approximating Interaction Between Linear Arithmetic Constraints. In *1994 International Symposium on Logic Programming*, pages 571–585. MIT Press, 1994.

[MSJB95] A. Mulkers, W. Simoens, G. Janssens, and M. Bruynooghe. On the Practicality of Abstract Equation Systems. In *International Conference on Logic Programming*. MIT Press, June 1995.

[Mut91] Kalyan Muthukumar. *Compile-time Algorithms for Efficient Parallel Implementation of Logic Programs.* PhD thesis, University of Texas at Austin, August 1991.

[Neu90] U. Neumerkel. Extensible Unification by Metastructures. In *Proceeding of the META'90 workshop*, 1990.

[PBH97] G. Puebla, F. Bueno, and M. Hermenegildo. An Assertion Language for Debugging of Constraint Logic Programs. In *Proceedings of the ILPS'97 Workshop on Tools and Environments for (Constraint) Logic Programming*, October 1997. Available from `ftp://clip.dia.fi.upm.es/pub/papers/assert_lang_tr_discipldeliv.ps.gz`.

[PGT+96] E. Pontelli, G. Gupta, D. Tang, M. Carro, and M. Hermenegildo. Improving the Efficiency of Nondeterministic And–parallel Systems. *The Computer Languages Journal*, 22(2/3):115–142, July 1996.

[PH95a] G. Puebla and M. Hermenegildo. Implementation of Multiple Specialization in Logic Programs. In *Proc. ACM SIGPLAN Symposium on Partial Evaluation and Semantics Based Program Manipulation*, pages 77–87. ACM Press, June 1995.

[PH95b] G. Puebla and M. Hermenegildo. Specialization and Optimization of Constraint Programs with Dynamic Scheduling. Technical Report CLIP12/95.0, Facultad de Informática, UPM, September 1995. Presented at the 1995 COMPULOG Meeting on Program Development.

[SCWY90] V. Santos-Costa, D.H.D. Warren, and R. Yang. Andorra-I: A Parallel Prolog System that Transparently Exploits both And- and Or-parallelism. In *Proceedings of the 3rd. ACM SIGPLAN Symposium on Principles and Practice of Parallel Programming.* ACM, April 1990.

[She92] K. Shen. Exploiting Dependent And-Parallelism in Prolog: The Dynamic, Dependent And-Parallel Scheme. In *Proc. Joint Int'l. Conf. and Symp. on Logic Prog.*, pages 717–731. MIT Press, 1992. To appear in JLP special issue.

[Son86] H. Sondergaard. An application of abstract interpretation of logic programs: occur check reduction. In *European Symposium on Programming, LNCS 123*, pages 327–338. Springer-Verlag, 1986.

[Swe95] Swedish Institute of Computer Science, P.O. Box 1263, S-16313 Spanga, Sweden. *Sicstus Prolog V3.0 User's Manual*, 1995.

[Tic88] E. Tick. Compile-Time Granularity Analysis of Parallel Logic Programming Languages. In *Int. Conf. on FGCS*. Tokyo, November 1988.

[Tic95] E. Tick. The Deevolution of Concurrent Logic Programming Languages. *The Journal of Logic Programming*, 23(1–3):89–125, 1995.

[Win92] W. Winsborough. Multiple Specialization using Minimal-Function Graph Semantics. *Journal of Logic Programming*, 13(2 and 3):259–290, July 1992.

The BEAM
Towards a first EAM Implementation

Ricardo Lopes, Vítor Santos Costa
{rslopes,vsc}@ncc.up.pt

LIACC, Universidade do Porto,
Rua do Campo Alegre, 823, 4150 Porto, Portugal

Abstract. Logic programming provides a high-level view of programming, giving implementors a vast latitude in what techniques to research towards obtaining the best performance for logic programs. One of the holy grails of logic programming has been to design computational models that could be executed efficiently and would allow for both a reduction of the search space and for exploiting all the available parallelism in the application. These goals have motivated the design of the Extended Andorra Model. We report on the design of a first implementation for the Extended Andorra Model with Implicit Control, the BEAM.

1 Introduction

Logic programming provides a high-level view of programming where programs are fundamentally seen as a collection of statements that define a model of the intended problem, and questions may be asked against this model. Prolog is the most popular example of a logic programming language, and has been successfully used in applications such as artificial intelligence, database programming, circuit design, genetic sequencing, expert systems, compilers, simulation and natural language processing. The high-level nature of logic programs gives implementors a vast latitude in what techniques to research towards obtaining the best performance for logic programs. Advanced compilation techniques [10] have been used to obtain performance close to imperative languages for some benchmarks [9]. Parallelism [6] allows logic programs to transparently exploit the advantages of the new parallel machines that are more than ever gaining in popularity. Extensions such as co-routining, constraints, and tabulation allow for substantial reductions in search space over the traditional Prolog selection function, and are a basis on which to build advanced features and support novel applications. Towards obtaining maximum performance, one of the holy grails of logic programming has been to design computational models that could be executed efficiently and would allow for both a reduction of the search space and for exploiting all the available parallelism in the application. These goals have been presented by David H. D. Warren [12] as, in order of priority:

- *Minimum number of inferences*: this is achieved by trying never to repeat the same execution step of one inference in different locations of the execution tree.

– *Maximum parallelism*: this is achieved by allowing goals to be executed as more independently as possible, and by doing the combination of all solutions as late as feasible.

These goals have motivated the design of the Extended Andorra Model. The model originates from the research on the Basic Andorra Model (BAM) [11]. The Andorra-I prototype [7] demonstrated that the BAM can successfully exploit two forms of parallelism, or-parallelism and dependent and-parallelism, and that it can reduce the search space for a large category of programs. On the other hand, Andorra-I depends on finding determinate applications. If determinacy cannot be found efficiently, applications with strong parallelism may need to be run sequentially. The Extended Andorra Model was proposed as an extension of the Andorra Model that could address the major problems of the Basic Andorra Model, and approximate the goals of minimising the search space and maximising the parallelism. The original proposal was based in the concept of rewriting and- and or-boxes. Research then evolved in two directions. David H. D. Warren and researchers at Bristol concentrated on the"1991" *Extended Andorra Model with Implicit Control* [12], where the goal was to obtain the advantages of the Extended Andorra Model with least effort from the programmer. Haridi, Janson and researchers at SICS concentrated on the AKL [3], the Andorra Kernel Language, based on the principle that the advantages of the Extended Andorra Model justified a new programming paradigm that could subsume both traditional Prolog and the committed choice languages. Research in AKL concentrated on including novel features such as ports [2], important for concurrent programming, and on obtaining good performance through sequential [4] and parallel implementations, such as Penny [5], with good results. More recently, the AKL researchers have shifted their interest to Oz [8], a language developed at DFKI which provides similar features to AKL. Research on the Extended Andorra Model with Implicit Control, that will refer to more shortly as *EAM*, followed a rather different approach. Research started by trying to prove the feasibility of the model by developing an interpreter. Gupta's interpreter [1] showed that the EAM was indeed feasible, but demonstrated difficulties in giving the best performance for some programs and queries. Towards obtaining maximum performance, Warren proposed solutions such as lazy copying and eager producers to give finer control over search when required. We report on the design of a first implementation for the EAM. As a first step we concentrate on the original rewriting rules of the EAM. This subset of the EAM will be implemented on our first prototype, the *BEAM*. We present the major data structures and execution algorithms that are required for efficient execution. The paper is organised as follows. We first give an overview of the EAM, and present an example for better understanding of the model. Next, we discuss the basic data structures required to implement the model. Last, we discuss some issues on extending the EAM to avoid infinite computations and present one solution.

2 The Extended Andorra Model

The EAM was designed to generate all answers to problems coded in Horn with a minimum number of inferences. The EAM tries to achieve this goal by performing as many steps in parallel as possible. The EAM extends the Basic Andorra Model in that it allows non-deterministic goals to execute in and-parallel, *as long as they do not bind external variables*. It thus allows the three main forms of parallelism:

- *Or-parallelism*, between alternatives in the search.
- *Independent and-parallelism*, between goals that do not share variables.
- *Dependent and-parallelism*, between goals that communicate via variables, say producer-consumers.

2.1 Execution Principles for the EAM

The EAM is formally defined using rewrite rules which manipulate and-or-trees. These are represented through *and*, *or* and *choice-boxes*.

- **And-box:** $[\exists X_1, ..., X_m : \sigma \& C_1 \& ... \& C_n]$
  And-boxes are created when launching a new clause, the variables X_1 to X_n represent the variables created in the box and σ represents the constraints on external variables imposed by the and-box.
- **Or-box:** $\{C_1 \vee ... \vee C_n\}$
  Or-boxes are created when launching a new goal, each C_i represents an alternative clause for the goal.
- **Choice-box:** $\{G_1 \% C_1 \vee ... \vee G_n \% C_n\}$
  Choice-boxes are special or-boxes created when the clauses defining a procedure include a pruning operator, %. Each G_i represents the guard of the goal and each C_i represents the remainder of the clause. The original EAM supports two pruning operators, cut, !, and commit, |. We shall not discuss choice-boxes further here.

There are four main operations in the Extended Andorra Model:

- **Reduction:**
$$G \rightarrow \{[\exists Y_1 : \sigma_1 \% C_1] \vee ... \vee [\exists Y_n : \sigma_1 \% C_n]\}$$
  Reduction expands a goal G in an and-box into an or-box.
- **Promotion:**
$$[\exists X : A \& [\exists Y, W : Z = \theta(W) \& C] \& B] \rightarrow [\exists X, W : X = \theta(W) \& A \% [\exists Y : C] \& B]$$
  Promotion promotes constraints from a inner-box to the outer and-box.
- **Substitution:**
$$[X, Z : Z = \theta(W) \& C] \rightarrow [\exists X : C\theta]$$
  Substitution applies a constraint on a variable.
- **Forking:**
$$[\exists X : \{(C_1 \vee ... \vee C_n) \& G] \rightarrow \{[\exists X : C_1 \& G] \vee ... \vee [\exists X : C_n \& G]\}$$
  Forking distributes a conjunction across a disjunction.

2.2 Control in the EAM

The EAM uses a control scheme where an and-box suspends if it constrains an external variable. Figure 1, taken from Gupta's report [1], shows the control scheme used in the EAM interpreter. The systems tries to apply reduction and promotion steps as much as possible. *Simplification* steps are also used in the interpreter to maintain the data structures.

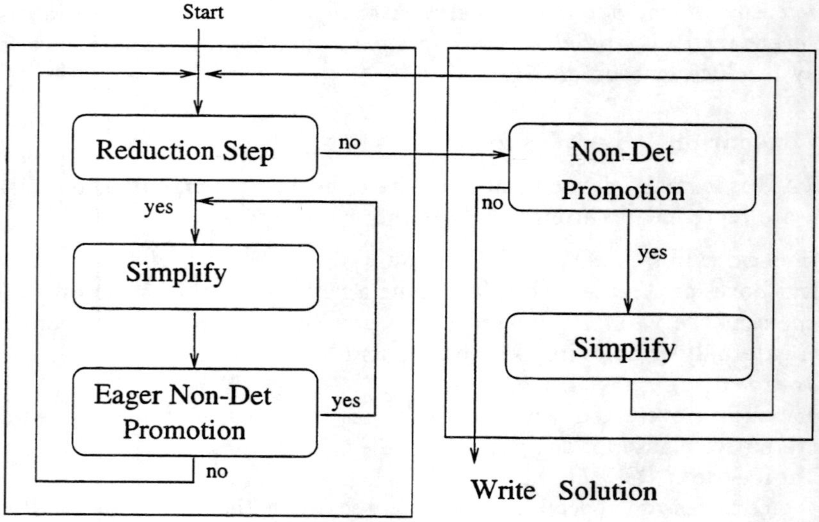

Fig. 1. Execution.

Forking is the operation that can lead to duplication of work, and it thus is only applied when all the other operations cannot be applied further. In the EAM interpreter, if several goals can produce a non-determinate binding for a variable, the leftmost one will be chosen. Notice that, before forking is started, a binding for variable X has to be generated by one of the C_i. After forking, this binding can be promoted in the newly created and-box. A forking step followed by a promotion is called *global forking*. The EAM allows the parallel early execution of non-determinate goals. In some cases, this may create speculative and-work, as some other goals might fail. This may result in a larger search space or even lead to non-termination, as the EAM allows any computation to go ahead as long as it does not bind variables. Ideally one would like to provide an implicit control mechanism to prevent this problem. Unfortunately detecting speculative work depends on knowing a priori whether the computation will terminate, which is in general undecidable. Section 5 discusses this problem in more detail. One of the aims of the Extended Andorra Model is to perform the least number of reductions to obtain the solutions for a goal. To obtain this effect one often wants to do computations for different goals as independently as possible. Notice that in order to obtain maximum independence between goals it is necessary to limit the number of goals that can be allowed to delay global forking. That is, global forking should happen as soon as the goals that can bind the variable, and only this goals, cannot apply any other operations. A solution to classify these goals as used in the interpreter is to give scope to variables, possibly obtained through rewriting clauses in mini-scope form [1].

2.3 An Example of EAM Execution

This section presents an simple example that shows the essential ideas of how the computation of an Prolog program proceeds in EAM. Consider the very simple Prolog program:

```
g(X):- a(X),b(X).     b(4).               a(1).     c(1).
                      b(X):- c(X).        a(2).     c(3).
```

Figure 2 shows several execution steps for this program and the query:

```
?- g(X).
```

Or-boxes are represented as a black dot. And-boxes are represented as a rectangle divided in 3 areas. The left area is reserved to the local variables, the middle area to the conjunction of goals, and the right one is for the external vars. On the first step, after starting execution, the EAM would perform a reduction on `g(X)` followed immediately by a promotion since `g(X)` only has one alternative. On the second step, we perform a reduction on both `a(X)` and `b(X)`. Notice now there are two alternatives to `a(X)`. The first one tries to make `X=1`, leading to suspension because `X` is an external variable. The second alternative will also suspend when trying to make `X=2`. Again there are also two alternatives to `b(X)`. The first one suspends when trying to make `X=4`. The next step (3) can only work on `c(X)` because all the others are suspended. A reduction is applied, creating two more alternatives. Both of them suspend immediately because they also try to assign a value to `X`. At this point, all possible alternatives are suspended, which leaves only execution strategy, applying a nondeterminate promotion. We choose the or-box that is the leftmost on the tree. After forking, we can see the tree divided in two, with a or-box on top. The left side has `X` bound to 1. The right side has `X` bound to 2. After reactivating all the suspended and-boxes, most of them fail immediately, leaving just one solution, which is `X=1` on the left side of the tree. As you can conclude from this very simple example, the representation of and-boxes plus or-boxes are very important in a EAM implementation, because all the EAM operations are to be applied on and-boxes and or-boxes. Another important point is the representation of variables, because before any assignment is necessary to know if a variable is local or external.

2.4 Lazy Copying

In the original EAM a goal will always suspend when nondeterminately trying to bind an external variable, irrespective of whether it is the producer (the goal

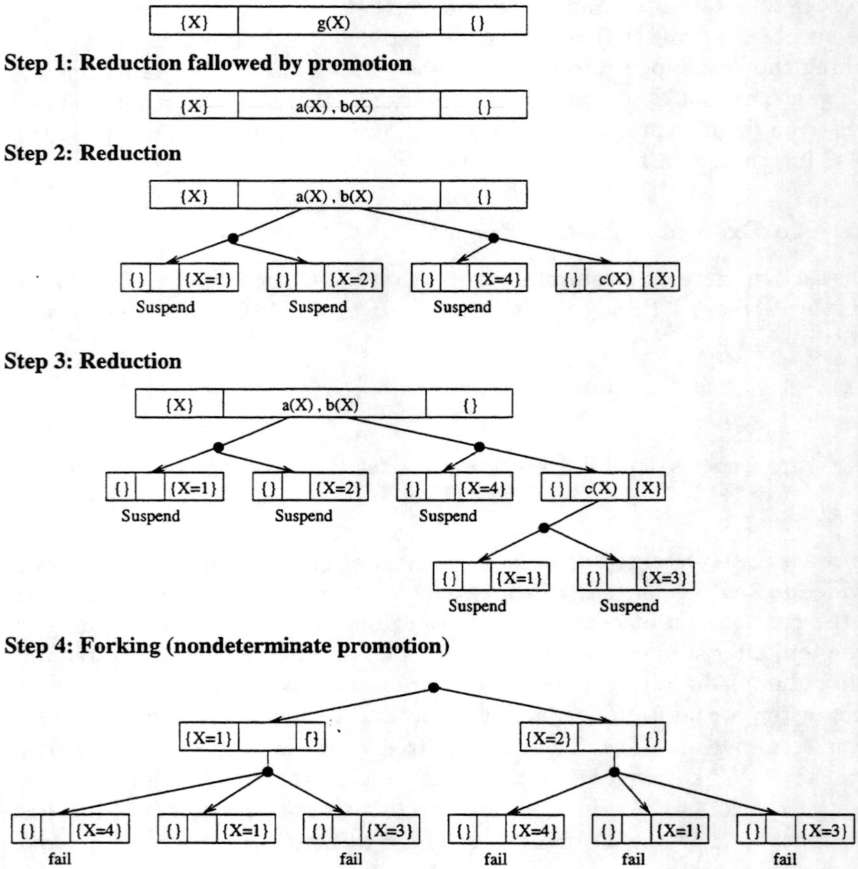

Fig. 2. Execution in EAM.

that generates bindings for) or the consumer (the goal that reads bindings for) that variable. One important observation is that if the goal is the producer, there is no need for it to suspend. The EAM does in fact try to obtain extra parallelism by letting the producer continue. To avoid duplicating work, this is implemented by creating pointers from the producer to the consumer goal and not by creating a physical copy for every alternative of the producer. This copy of the consumer is now done in lazy fashion, hence the name *lazy copying*. The forking rule now becomes:

$$[\exists X : \{C_1 \vee ... \vee C_n \& G] \rightarrow \{[\exists X : C_1 \& G_p] \vee ... \vee [\exists X : C_n \& G_p]\}$$

where G_p is a reference to a single goal. One can do even better, by copying parts of G_p as soon as they suspend. To support this scheme the EAM now includes a classification scheme for variables as guessable or non-guessable. This classification might be provided by the programmer, or generated automatically.

A variable is annotated as *guessable* if the annotator is certain it is going to be guessed non-determinately. In this case, as soon as a binding is generated by a producer for a guessable variable, global forking with lazy copying is performed. In contrast, global forking on non-guessable variables is only performed if there is no other way to restart the computation.

3 Data Structures

An efficient implementation of the EAM requires data structures capable of performing the four main operations of the EAM quickly and efficiently. We next present a first design for the data structures that we intend to use on the BEAM.

3.1 Local Variables

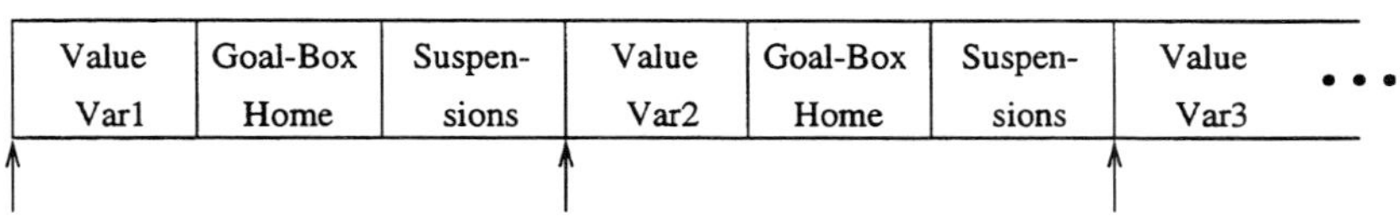

Fig. 3. Local Vars representation.

Each and-box may create several local variables, corresponding to each individual subgoal. Local variables are represented with the attributes shown in Figure 3:

- *Value*: the actual value of the variable, may be bound or unbound. The representation is done with the help of tags as used in WAM. Unbound variables are represented as self-pointing references.
- *Goal-Box_home*: pointer to the goal-box on the and-box where the variable was created.
- *suspensions*: pointer to a list of goals-boxes (inside and-boxes) that have suspended on this variable.

For each Goal we have a collection of Local variables. These variables are organised sequentially, in a vector, as in Figure 3.

3.2 External Variables

Accesses to variables external to the current and-box require special data structures. Each external variable has the attributes shown in Figure 4:

- *Value*: the value that has been assigned to the variable by the local and-box.
- *Var_Home*: pointer to the home of the local variable (as example consider one of the pointers in Figure 3)

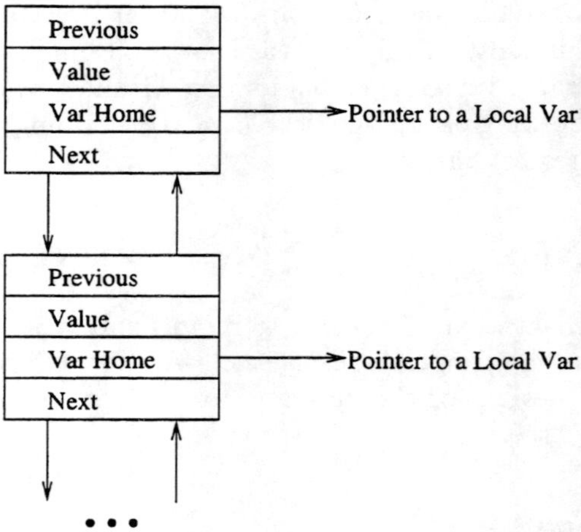

Fig. 4. External Vars representation.

If a goal changes a value to a variable that is not local, the assignment is recorded in an external variable struct and on the local variable. This way, whenever a descendent and-box wants to use the value of this external-variable, it can do it simply by accessing to the local variable directly. The external_variables structure is very important, as it allows to save possible assignments to variables that will be used ahead to know if the execution should proceed or not. They also work as an advanced kind of trail. If a assignment is made to a variable that belongs to a upper and-box, it's recorded in the External_Vars structure. If later the computation fails, or if the computations needs to suspend, the external struct will be used to recover all assignments made to non-local vars.

3.3 Or-Box

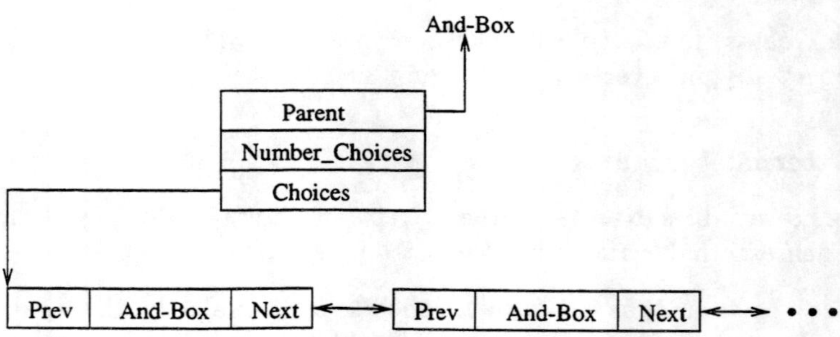

Fig. 5. Or-Box representation.

Figure 5 shows how to implement an or-box. Each or-box has the following attributes:

- *Parent*: a reference to the parent goal that is represented in the upper level and-box.
- *Number_choices*: an integer that has two functions. The first is to indicate the number of alternatives that have been expanded. The second function is to, after all alternatives have been expanded, keep track of the number of choices still available. It works like this, imagine a clause with 4 choices. The field Number_choices is initialised with -4. Each time an alternative is expanded, the counter is incremented. When all alternatives have been expanded, this counter reaches 0. At this point it moves to the second function, and it's value goes to 4. When each alternative is removed, the counter is decremented.
- *Choices*: a pointer to a double-linked list of and-boxes

Note that each or-box contains a pointer, the Choices pointer, to a doubly-linked list of alternatives, each one being an and-box. This list must be double-linked because it has to support arbitrary insertion and deletion of and-boxes. Despite the fact that the integer *Number_choices* can be deduced from the doubly-linked list, it's representation is very important because it allows a quick access whenever we need to know the number of existent alternatives. For example, whenever the Number_choices field decreases to one, there is no need to keep the or-box. In this case, a promotion can be applied to that (only) choice so that the or-box disappears and the choice and-box goes up one level to be combined with the parent's and-box. The parent goal that was pointing to the or-box can be eliminated.

3.4 And-Box

And-boxes require a more complex structure, as they must store information on what goals are active, and on external and internal variables. Figure 6 shows an and-box with the following attributes:

- *Parent* : a reference to an or-box
- *Level* : a integer that indicates the level in the tree of the current and-box. If a and-box has level `n`, then the parent has level `n-1`, and the descendents have level `n+1`. This field is used to find the nearest and-box common to two and-boxes. For example, suppose that you have two and-boxes, A and B. Suppose that A is in level 4 and B in level 6. Then B can't be parent of A. Going up two levels in the tree of B, we get to know if A is parent of B. If not we can go up in the tree once in a time to find the common parent to both of the and-boxes.
- *External_Vars*: a pointer to a double-linked list of external variables as shown in Figure 4. These are the external variables used in the and-box. Note that all variables that are external in this and-box are necessarily local variables in some upper and-box.

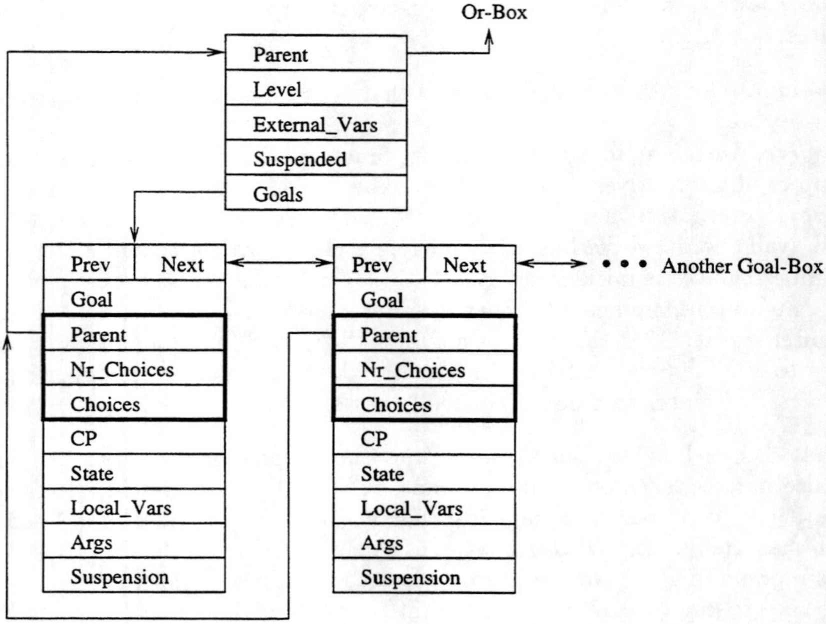

Fig. 6. And-Box representation.

- *Suspended*: this field is used to indicate when the and-box is suspended. If this value is false, then it means that it still exists work to be done in the current and-box. If this value is true, then it means that the current and-box has suspended.
- *Goals*: a pointer to a double-linked list of structures that represent the goals created in clause, and have information about a goal or one or-box with several alternatives. This structure, that we call goal-box, is divided in the following attributes:
  - *Goal*: pointer to the goal structure.
  - *Parent, Number_Choices, Choices*: these 3 fields represent an Or-Box that is created for the goal.
  - *CP*: sometimes the goal-boxes aren't all expanded at the same time. This field is used in conjunction with the pointer to the and-box to create the next goal-box.
  - *state*: can be:
    - *ready*: when the goal is ready to start execution
    - *active*: the goal is running
    - *fail*: the goal has failed
    - *success*: the goal has succeed
    - *suspended*: the goal has suspended in some point
    - *suspended_on_end*: the goal has suspended on the end. This is a special case of the suspended case. The general suspended case needs to

try to continue the goal execution. This special case knows that the execution has already ended, so if the suspension can be activated, the goal can skip immediately to a success state.

- *Local_Vars*: pointer to the start of a vector with the Local Vars, as shown in Figure 3.
- *Args*: pointer to the start of the vector of arguments.
- *Suspension*: pointer to a doubly-linked list of continuation record, each one with info about in which variable a goal suspended, and in which part of the goal.

Whenever there are goal-boxes suspended the and-box is not necessarily suspended. The and-box is only suspended when the field suspended is true. This field can only be true when at least one of the goal-boxes has suspended. Note that the Or-Box is physically included on the goal-box. This way the arguments can be accessed by the or-box directly.

4 Execution Model

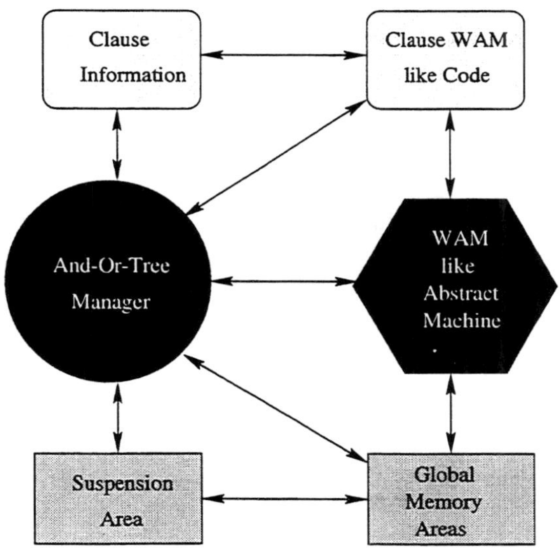

Fig. 7. Execution Model.

There are six main components in the execution model of BEAM, as shown in Figure 7. They are:

- *And-Or-Tree Manager*: This module manipulates the and-boxes plus the or-boxes using the EAM rewriting rules, and starts WAM-like execution for the selected goal.

- *WAM like abstract machine*: This module runs WAM-like instructions. These include WAM instructions such as `puts`, `gets` and `unifys`. Instructions such as `calls` and `trys` may need to call the And-Or-Tree manager area if complex rewriting is necessary or if the current expansion must suspend.
- *Clause Information*: This area contains all the information related to the program's code. It contains all the information about the clauses available in the program. It includes the next area.
- *Clause WAM like Code*: It contains the clauses WAM like code.
- *Suspension Area*: This area is responsible for managing the suspended clauses or boxes of the EAM trees. The decision to wake suspended boxes is responsibility of the And-Or-Tree manager.
- *Global Memory Areas*: It operates like the heap in the WAM. Is used for saving variables values, compound terms like lists and structures, and even Prolog atoms. It is also used for advanced unification and most important, this area serves the and-or-boxes memory requests.

The execution model presented has two main areas. The first and most complex, is responsible for managing the and-or-box tree. It uses the Clause information area to know how many alternatives one clause have and how many goals one clause calls. Using this information it constructs the tree and uses the EAM rewriting rules to manage it. It request memory for the boxes in the Global Memory Areas, and it uses the Suspension Area if one of the boxes needs to suspend. The WAM like Abstract Machine is called by the And-Or-tree Manipulation to execute and unify the arguments of the goals and clauses. As an example consider the clause: `p(X,Y):- g(X), f(Y).`. When running this clause the And-Or-Tree Manipulation transforms the `p(X,Y)` into one and-box with `g` and `f` as goals-boxes. During this creation it calls the WAM like Abstract Machine to manage the arguments of `g` and `f`.

The And-Or-Tree Manipulation area uses the EAM rewriting rules to work with the constructed tree. The most important rewriting rules are: the **`Reduction`**, the **`Promotion`** and **`Forking`**. Their implementation is explained individually in the following sections.

4.1 Reduction

The reduction operation expands a goal `P` into an or-box where each component of the or-box is the body of a clause whose head unifies with the goal. See example in Figure 8.

Note that in the example presented all the alternatives to `P` were expanded after the reduction, but in a real execution this could become very expensive. Sometimes to avoid overheads, the reduction first expands only the left alternative, and only when needed, it expands the second one, and so on.

4.2 (Deterministic) Promotion

If an and-box contains a or-box with only one alternative, then all the constraints within the lower and-box can be promoted to the upper and-box and finally the

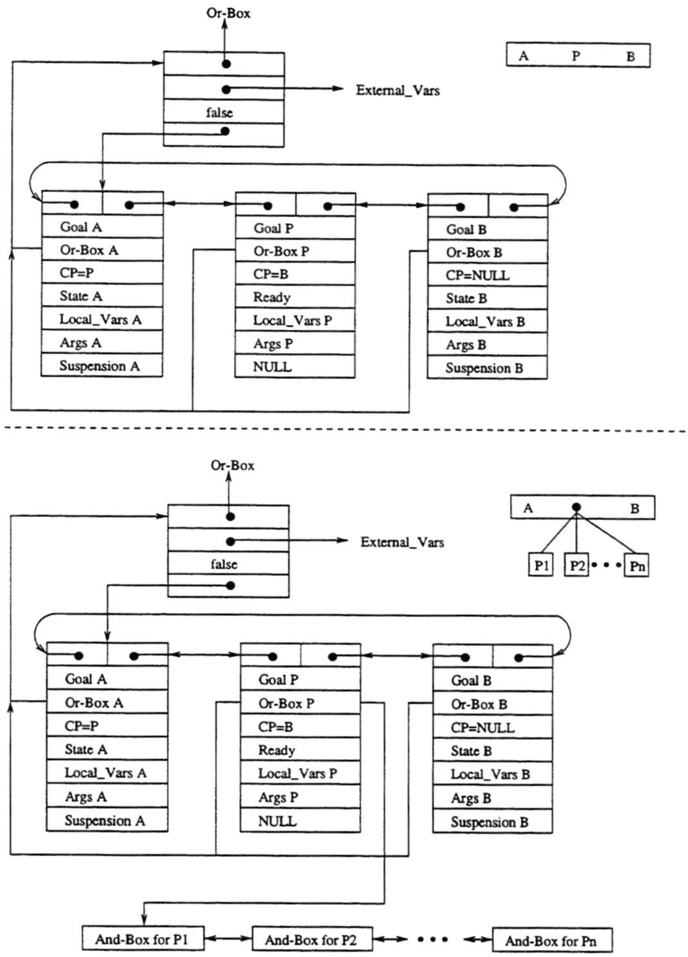

Fig. 8. Applying Reduction.

or-box can be removed. See example in Figure 9.

Note that some of the external variables to `P` (represented as `External_Vars2`) could be local in the parent and-box. So after the promotion this kind of variables wouldn't be in the external variables structure.

4.3 Forking (Non-Deterministic Promotion)

This operation consists of distributing a goal across a disjunction. See example in Figure 10.

Note that some of the external variables to `P1` or `P2` could be local in the parent and-box. So after the forking this variables wouldn't be in the external

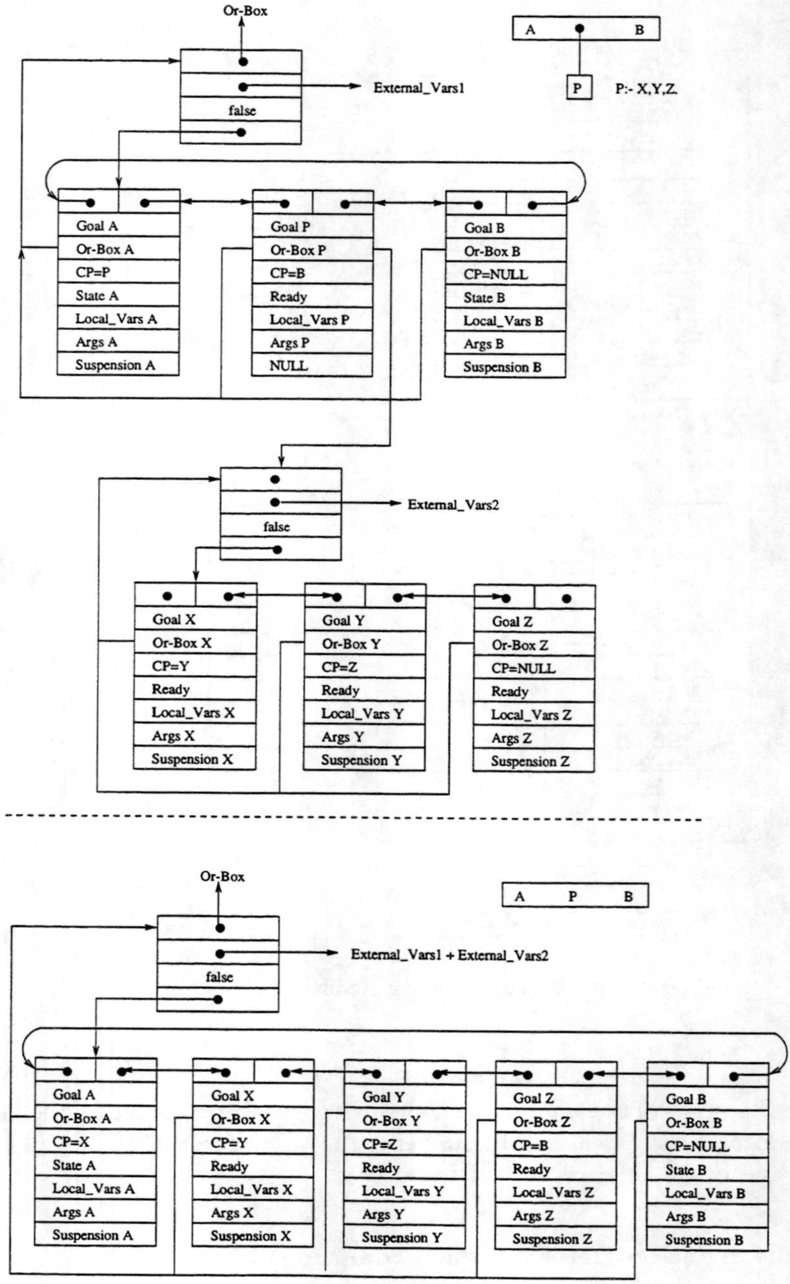

Fig. 9. Applying Promotion.

variables structure. Note also that `A` and `B` are suspended, but after forking they can become ready if eventually they were suspended on variables that would change because of `P1` or `P2`.

5 Dealing with Non-Termination

In most cases the EAM should be able to significantly reduce the execution space for logic programs. Unfortunately, this is not always the case. In this section we present an example that shows this problem in the current definition of the EAM, and we propose a solution to avoid non-termination without the need for expensive global analysis or for user intervention. Consider the following Prolog program:

```
    ancestor(X,Y):- parent(X,Y).
    ancestor(X,Z):- parent(X,Y), ancestor(Y,Z).
    parent(a,fa).      parent(a,ma).      parent(b,fb).     parent(b,mb).
    parent(ma,mma).    parent(ma,fma).    parent(mb,c).     parent(mb,d).
    parent(fa,c).      parent(fa,d).      parent(fb,mfb).   parent(fb,ffb).
?- ancestor(a,Z), ancestor(b,Z).
```

To simplify the notation we use `a(X)` for `ancestor(X)` and `p(X)` as `parent(X)` in Figure 11 and the following discussion. Figure 11 shows how the EAM leads to non-termination in this example.

When the goal `p(X,Y)` is called, its execution is always suspended because an non-determinate assignment is needed. The only call that does not suspend is the goal `a(X,Y)`. This will lead to non-termination, since no value will ever be assigned. Warren and Gupta proposed a solution to this problem using Eager Non-Determinate promotion [1]. However, to use this solution, one must classify variables as *guessable*, *non-guessable* or *others* before execution. This annotation can be generated by means of compile time analysis, or it can be supplied by the programmer explicitly. Unfortunately, their solution is not complete since in some problems it may be very difficult to mark a variable as guessable. It is also not very elegant since one of the aims of EAM is to obtain the maximum performance with the minimum control information from the user (Implicit Control). The solution that we propose to solve these problems is the combination of Eager Non-Determinate promotion with tabling. This solution seems to be ideal in two contexts. First it guarantees that the computation ends in programs that have finite solutions. In second it allows the reuse of goals. This would be particularly useful in exploiting independent and-parallelism. With the Eager forking and tabling the execution would change this way. On the level 3, the call `a(X2,Z)` would suspend because in level 2 was already made a similar call `a(X1,Z)`. Then, an eager forking could be made on `p(a,X1)`, assigning `X=fa` on one side and `X=ma` on the other side. This assignments would be sufficient to make the computations step out of the cycle, and eventually would lead to the solutions `Z=c` or `Z=d` (see Figure 12).

Note that termination analysis should still be useful in detecting which goals would be required to tabulate.

6 Conclusions

In this paper we have presented a feasible data structures to be used in the BEAM, a first implementation of the EAM. We have also presented a novel solution to deal with Non-Termination on the EAM. We believe that this solution can also be useful to implement reuse of goals in the EAM. Implementation work has already started on the implementation of a sequential version of the BEAM.

Acknowledgments

The authors would like to acknowledge and thank the contribution and support that Fernando Silva gave to this work. Our work has been partly supported by Fundação da Ciência e Tecnologia and JNICT under the Melodia project (JNICT contract PBIC/C/TIT/2495/95). Ricardo Lopes thanks Fundação da Ciência e Tecnologia and PRAXIS (Praxis Grant BD/9277/96) for supporting his research.

References

1. G. Gupta and D.H.D. Warren. An Interpreter for the Extended Andorra Model. Internal report, University of Brsitol, 1991.
2. Sverker Janson. *AKL – A Multiparadigm Programming Language.* SICS Dissertation Series 14, Uppsala University, 1994.
3. Sverker Janson and Seif Haridi. Programming Paradigms of the Andorra Kernel Language. In *Logic Programming: Proceedings of the International Logic Programming Symposium*, pages 167–186. MIT Press, October 1991.
4. Sverker Janson and Johan Montelius. Design of a Sequential Prototype Implementation of the Andorra Kernel Language. Sics research report, in preparation, Swedish Institute of Computer Science, 1992.
5. Johan Montelius and Khayri A. M. Ali. An And/Or-Parallel Implementation of AKL. *New Generation Computing*, 13(4), 1995.
6. V. Santos Costa. *Compile-Time Analysis for the Parallel Execution of Logic Programs in Andorra-I.* PhD thesis, University of Bristol, August 1993.
7. V. Santos Costa, D. H. D. Warren, and R. Yang. Andorra-I: A Parallel Prolog System that Transparently Exploits both And- and Or-Parallelism. In *Third ACM SIGPLAN Symposium on Principles & Practice of Parallel Programming PPOPP*, pages 83–93. ACM press, April 1991. SIGPLAN Notices vol 26(7), July 1991.
8. Gert Smolka. The Oz programming model. In Jan van Leeuwen, editor, *Computer Science Today*, Lecture Notes in Computer Science, vol. 1000, pages 324–343. Springer-Verlag, Berlin, 1995.

9. P. Van Roy. *Can Logic Programming Execute as Fast as Imperative Programming?* PhD thesis, University of California at Berkeley, November 1990.
10. P. Van Roy. 1983-1993: The Wonder Years of Sequential Prolog Implementation. *The Journal of Logic Programming*, 19/20, May/July 1994.
11. David H. D. Warren. The Andorra model. Presented at Gigalips Project workshop, University of Manchester, March 1988.
12. David H. D. Warren. The Extended Andorra Model with Implicit Control. Presented at ICLP'90 Workshop on Parallel Logic Programming, Eilat, Israel, June 1990.

This article was processed using the LaTeX macro package with LLNCS style

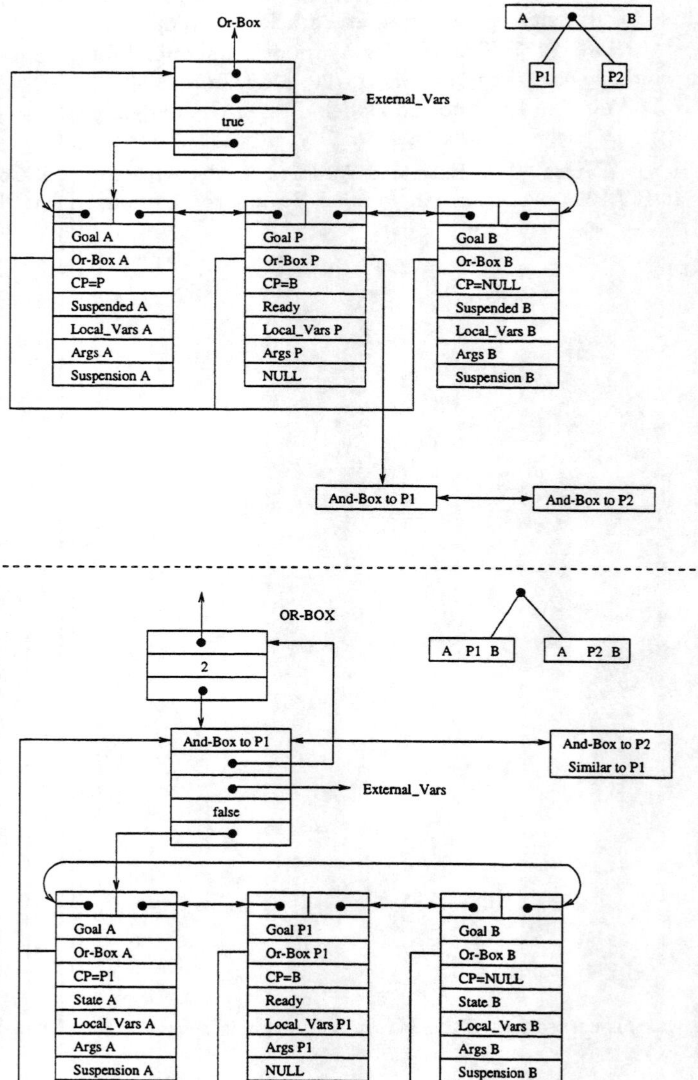

Fig. 10. Applying Forking.

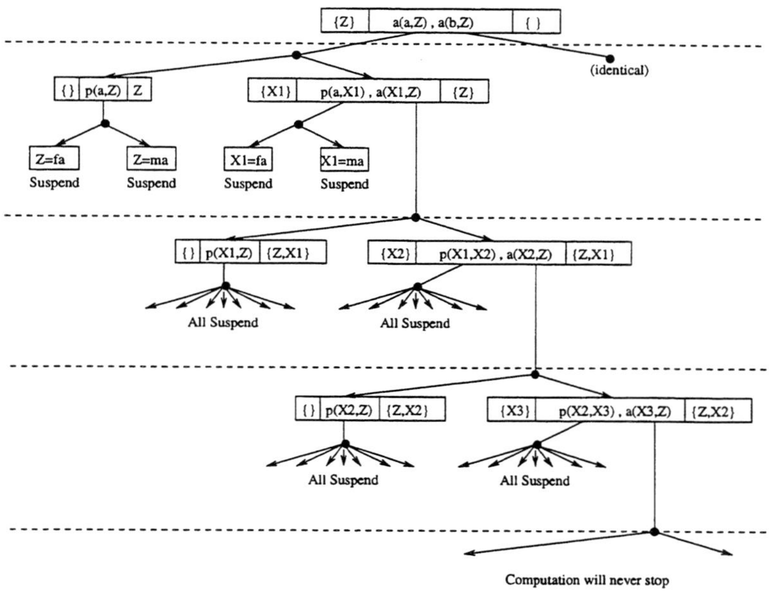

Fig. 11. The ancestor example that leads to Non-Termination in EAM.

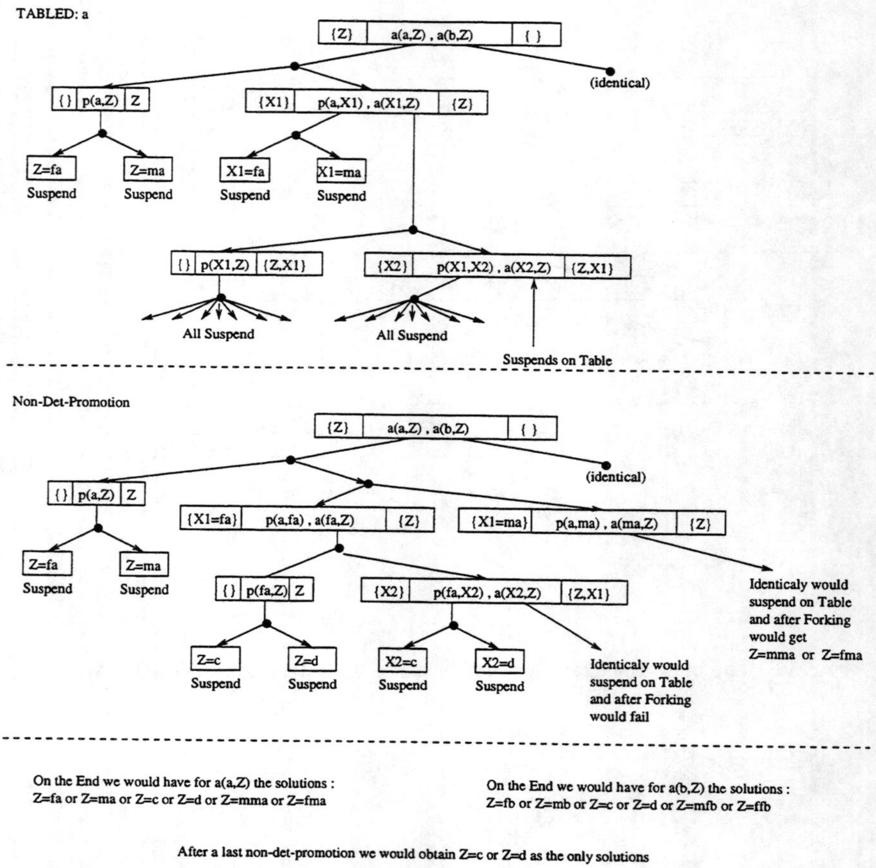

Fig. 12. The ancestor example with tabulated goal.

Last Alternative Optimization for Or-parallel Logic Programming Systems

Gopal Gupta & Enrico Pontelli

Laboratory for Logic, Databases, and Advanced Programming
New Mexico State University
Box 30001, Dept. CS
Las Cruces, NM 88003
{gupta,epontell}@cs.nmsu.edu
http://www.cs.nmsu.edu/lldap

Abstract. We present a new optimization for or-parallel logic programming (Prolog) systems, called *Last Alternative Optimization (LAO)*. The LAO follows from the *Flattening Principle* and the *Principle of Duality of or-parallelism and and-parallelism.* Originally LAO was conceived as the dual of the *Last Parallel Call Optimization* [7] an optimization developed by us for and-parallel systems. LAO enables Prolog programs that have *data-or parallelism* to execute more efficiently. It also enables more efficient (parallel) execution of *Constraint Logic Programs over finite domains.* LAO is a fairly general optimization and can be readily applied to virtually any parallel system that exploits non-determinism (e.g., parallel search based artificial intelligence systems). The Last Alternative Optimization has been implemented in the ACE parallel Prolog system. The performance results presented in this paper indeed prove the effectiveness of LAO.
We also present a second optimization based on the flattening principle, called the *Balanced Nesting Optimization (BNO)*, that is related to LAO, and that also leads to reduction of parallel overhead.
Keywords: Prolog, Or-parallelism, Data or-parallelism, Parallel Constraint Logic Programming.

1 Introduction

Logic programming is a popular computer programming paradigm that has been used in wide variety of applications, ranging from Artificial Intelligence, Database programming, Genetic Sequencing, Expert Systems, Natural Language Processing, Constraint based Optimization, to general purpose programming and problem solving. The most popular logic programming language is *Prolog.*

An advantage of logic programming languages over traditional programming paradigms is that parallelism implicitly present in program constructs can be *automatically* exploited, resulting in faster execution. Thus, programs coded for sequential machines, can be run in parallel without much intervention from the user. This approach differs considerably from the approaches in which parallelism is explicitly programmed by the user. Three main types of (implicit) parallelism have been identified and successfully exploited in logic programs:

1. *Or-parallelism:* arises when more than a single rule defines some relation and a procedure call unifies with more than one rule head—the corresponding bodies can then be executed in or-parallel fashion. Or-parallelism is thus a way of efficiently searching for solution(s) to the top-level query, by exploring in parallel the branches of the solutions space tree. Or-parallelism has been efficiently implemented in the Aurora [13] and MUSE [1] systems.
2. *And-parallelism* arises when more than one goal is present in the query or in the body of a procedure, and these (multiple) goals are solved in parallel with each other.

In this paper we are mainly concerned with or-parallelism. Logic programming systems execute a program by building a *search tree.* Or-parallelism is exploited when different branches of this search tree are explored in parallel. Considerable overhead is incurred while exploiting or-parallelism, as multiple processors traverse the branches of this search tree during *forward execution* (resolution and unification) as well as *backward execution* (backtracking). In this paper we present two optimizations that *simplify* the structure of the Prolog search tree allowing for more efficient traversal. These optimizations are based on the *principle of flattening* that we have successfully used for speeding up execution of and-parallel programs, and the *principle of duality.* The principle of flattening simply states that a reduction in the number of levels of nesting of an execution tree, generally results in improved performance. The principle of duality is based on our insight that, given a technique that has been developed for an and-parallel logic programming system, its dual can be successfully applied to an or-parallel system (and vice versa)

Based on these two principles we present two optimizations for or-parallel systems: the *Last Alternative Optimization (LAO)*, and the *Balanced Nesting Optimization* (BNO). In the rest of the paper, we explain these two optimizations, and the principles on which they are based. We also show how these optimizations can be applied for: (i) exploiting *data or-parallelism* more efficiently, and (ii) exploiting parallelism from constraint logic programming systems based on *finite domains* [11,4]. The results of implementing these optimizations in the ACE system, a high performance parallel Prolog system are also presented.

The rest of the paper is organized as follows: Section 2 presents a high level description of or-parallel systems, and the main problems encountered in implementing them. The *flattening principle* and its application to and-parallel system is also discussed in Section 2. Section 3 present the Last Alternative Optimization and the motivation for it, while Section 4 presents implementation details and performance results for LAO. Section 5 and Section 6 describe how LAO leads to better exploitation of data or-parallelism. Section 7 describes the Balanced Nesting Optimization and presents performance figures for it, while Section 8 presents our conclusions.

2 Or-parallel Execution: An Abstract View

2.1 Introduction

Or-parallelism arises when multiple clauses match a subgoal, and the bodies of these clauses are tried in parallel. Each clause gives rise to an execution path that may potentially lead to a solution. An or-parallel execution can be depicted using a tree, called the *search tree* or the *or-tree*. The or-tree has a node for each subgoal solved during execution and a branch for each clause matching that subgoal. Figure 1 shows an example or-tree.

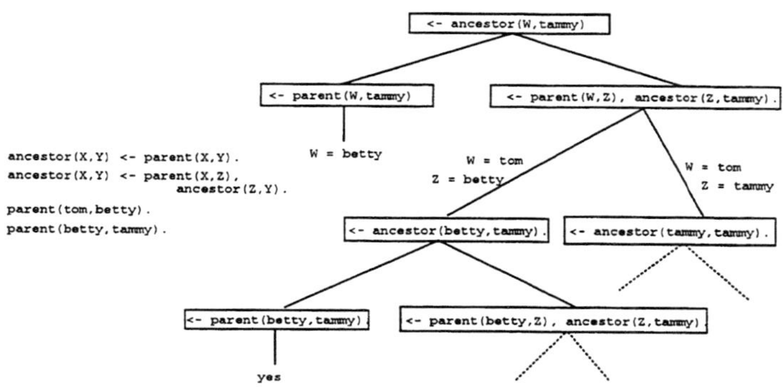

Fig. 1. An Example Or-tree

In a sequential system the or-tree is visited in a predetermined order (for Prolog a depth-first order of traversal is adopted, with goals at each node being explored left-to-right). Whenever a leaf of the tree is reached (corresponding to a success or a failure) and a new solution is desired, a node with an unexplored branch is selected, backtracked to, and traversal of that unexplored branch started. Nodes in an or-tree with multiple branches are termed *choice-points*. In an or-parallel system different processors concurrently explore different branches of the or-tree. Building logic programming systems that exploit or-parallelism implicitly is a challenging task. Most of the complexity comes from: (i) the management of non-determinism (i.e., multiple search paths), and (ii) the management of variable bindings.

- *Management of variable bindings:* Management of variable bindings becomes considerably more complex in an or-parallel system. Variables generated before a choice point may receive different bindings along the different branches emanating from the choice point. These variables are termed *conditional variables*, and proper mechanisms are needed to maintain the "multiple" bindings that they may receive [8]. For example, in Figure 1 the variable `W` gets conditionally bound to different values in different branches.
- *Management of non-determinism:* Goals in logic programming are non-deterministic, i.e., they can have multiple solutions. Non-determinism is generally handled through *backtracking*. Incorporation of backtracking implies that a

computation should be restorable to every point where a choice was made. At the implementation level this means saving extra information and allocation of extra data-structures (choice points) on the runtime stack. In the event of backtracking, the state of the computation will be restored by recalling the information stored in this additional data structures. The problem is further exacerbated when parallelism is exploited as the size of the saved state and its complexity become considerably larger.
The tree structure of the computation needs to be repeatedly traversed in order to search for multiple alternatives and/or cure failure of goals, and such traversal often requires synchronization between processors. These traversal and synchronization activities are absent from a sequential computation (in which the management of non-determinism is reduced to a linear and fast scan of the branches in a predetermined order). If execution is to remain efficient, the tree structure developed should be as simple as possible. In fact, the simpler the tree structure, the more efficient will be the execution. With this observation in mind we have developed the *Flattening Principle* to improve the efficiency of execution.

We next describe the principle of flattening and the principle of duality, that played a pivotal role in our development of the Last Alternative Optimization.

2.2 Flattening Principle

As mentioned before, the main source of overhead in parallel execution of logic programs arises due to the need to repeatedly traverse a deeply nested tree structure. This traversal is needed for two reasons: for management of parallel work (e.g., scheduling) and the management of non-determinism (e.g., searching for multiple solutions). This traversal is absent in sequential systems, where the whole computation can be encoded as a simple linear structure (e.g., sequence of choice points on a control stack). In parallel systems, by contrast, the computation structure gets distributed across the control stacks of multiple processors, so traversal is more involved. One way to improve the execution performance is to simplify the structure of the computation tree, in order to make its traversal cheaper and faster. This observation inspires the *Flattening Principle.*
The **Flattening Principle** can be simply stated as follows:

> *"Flattening the tree structure, i.e., reducing the levels of nesting whenever possible while preserving the operational semantics, leads to more efficient parallel execution."*

The flattening principle helps in reducing the levels of nesting of or-parallelism thereby reducing overhead. Of course, the flattening principle should be applied in such a way that program semantics are unaltered—i.e., the external behaviour of the execution is unchanged w.r.t. a standard sequential execution. In the case of logic programming systems, preserving operational semantics boils down to guaranteeing that the order in which backtracking points are selected is unchanged.

The flattening principle manifests itself in many situations both in nondeterministic as well as deterministic systems:

- The tail recursion optimization (and its logic programming counterpart, the last call optimization [24]) is an instance of the flattening principle, where nested recursive calls get flattened into one single call.
- In parallel implementation of flat committed choice languages [23] the nested goals created are held in a single large pool resulting in faster implementation. In fact, flat versions of committed choice languages evolved so that levels of nesting of processes could be eliminated to obtain faster implementations.
- The flattening principle has also been used for efficient implementation of nested data-parallel operations in languages such as Paralation Lisp [20], C*, etc. Guy Blelloch was the first one to advocate the use of flattening in implementing data-parallel languages [3]. Recently it has also been incorporated in other data-parallel systems [15].
- The flattening principle is also employed in optimizing parallel code that has nested *barriers*. Parallel programs with nested barriers are transformed so as to merge the multiple barriers into one, resulting in improved performance [19].

The flattening principle has been successfully applied by us in the design of the Last Parallel Call Optimization (LPCO) [17]. The LPCO is applied while exploiting and-parallelism, and is the parallel analog of the *Last Call Optimization* [26] found in sequential systems. The intent of the LPCO is to merge, whenever possible, distinct *parallel conjunctions* (or *parcalls*), which are nested one inside the other (see figure 2). The final aim of this optimization is to reduce as much as possible the depth of nesting of parallel conjunctions.

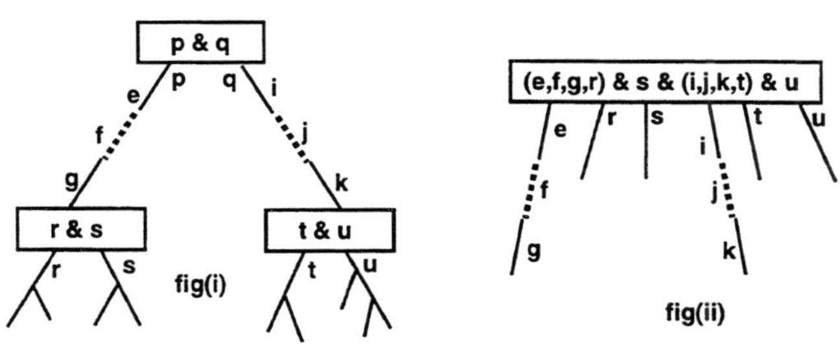

Fig. 2. Reusing Parcall Frames

LPCO cannot be applied every time a nested and-parallel conjunction arises inside another and-parallel call, since doing this in an unrestricted way may change the operational semantics, especially in presence of backtracking over parallel conjunctions. However, under certain restrictions, the operational semantics is preserved. To illustrate LPCO, consider a parallel conjunction of the form *(p & q)* ("&" denotes a potentially parallel conjunction), where p and q are defined by the following clauses (see figure 2(i)):

p :- e, f, g, (r & s). *q :- i, j, k, (t & u).*

LPCO will apply to p (resp. q) if:

1. there is only one (remaining) matching clause for p (resp. q), i.e., p (resp. q) is determinate;
2. all goals preceding the parallel conjunction in the clause for p (resp. q) are determinate;
3. the parallel call *(r & s)* (resp. *(t & u)*) is at the end of the clause for p (resp. q).

These conditions can be more easily understood by considering the layout of the information on the stacks: conditions 1 and 2 are equivalent to the absence of choice points between the current point of execution and the logically preceding parallel conjunction. It is important to observe that these conditions are met in a large variety of programs (e.g. programs expressing a data-parallel behaviour), making the optimization applicable very frequently. We have also shown elsewhere [17] how to considerably simplify these conditions without any additional overhead. If these conditions are satisfied then a new descriptor is not needed for the parallel conjunction in the clause. Rather the descriptor for *(p & q)* can be extended with an appropriate number of *subgoal descriptors* (each parallel conjunction has a descriptor associated, containing in turn a descriptor for each subgoal belonging to the conjunction) and execution continues as if clause for p was defined as *p :- ((e,f,g,r) & s)*[1], if we determine at the time of the parallel call *(r & s)* that e, f, and g are determinate. This is illustrated in Figure 2(ii).

Note also that the conditions for LPCO do not place any restrictions on the nature of the parallel subgoals in the clause for p (resp. q). Clearly, the goals r, s, etc. can be non-deterministic.

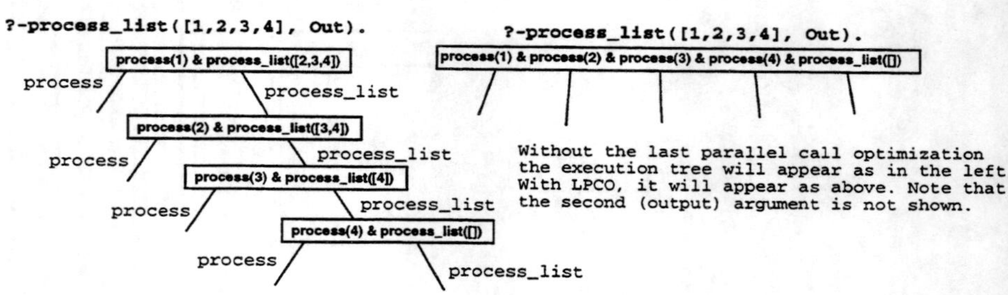

Fig. 3. Reuse of Parcall Frames for Recursive Programs

The benefits of LPCO become even more evident when a failure causes backtracking over a parallel call: the expensive traversal of the tree structure in search

[1] In reality though, the variable bindings generated by e, f, g are produced *before* the execution of r is started.

of a new alternative is replaced by a simple linear scan of the subgoals descriptors inside a single parallel conjunction descriptor.

One could argue that the improved scheme described above can be accomplished simply through compile time transformations. However, in many cases this may not be possible. For example, if *p* and *q* are dynamic predicates or, more simply, if there is insufficient static information to detect the determinacy of *p* and *q*, then the compile-time analysis will not be able to trigger the application of the optimization. Also, for many programs the number of parallel conjunctions that can be combined into one will only be determined at run-time. For example, consider the following recursive clause:

```
process_list([H|T],[Hout|Tout]) :-
      process(H,Hout) & process_list(T,Tout).

process_list([],[]).
```

In this case, compile time transformations cannot unfold the program to eliminate nesting of parallel conjunctions because it will depend on the length of the input list. However, using our runtime technique, given that the goal `process_list` is determinate, nesting of parallel conjunctions can be completely eliminated (figure 3). As a result of the absence of nesting of parallel conjunctions, if the *process* goal fails for some element of the list, then the whole conjunction will fail in one single step.

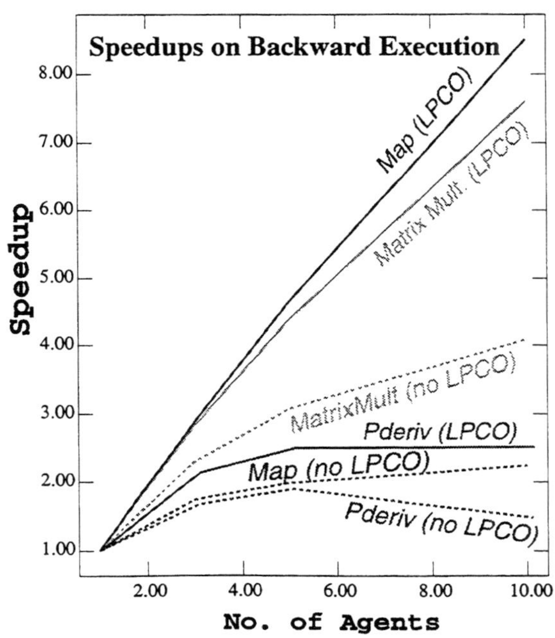

Fig. 4. Speedup Curves for exec. with backtracking

On applying the LPCO in a situation such as the one shown in Figure 3, control parallelism that is deeply nested transforms itself into data-parallelism resulting in improved efficiency. Performance improvement for selected programs due to LPCO are shown in Figure 4. In fact, our data-parallel version of Prolog, based on LPCO is comparable in performance with dedicated data-and parallel Prolog systems such as Reform Prolog [2].

2.3 Principle of Duality

Table 1 compares and contrasts items of interest for and-parallelism and or-parallelism. The first two lines of the table relate and- and or-parallelism. Thus, while or-parallelism is obtained by parallel execution of *multiple alternatives in a choice point*, and-parallelism is obtained by executing *multiple subgoals in a parallel conjunction.* In both cases the parallel threads originate from a data structure containing a certain number of alternative executions (choice points vs. parallel conjunctions' descriptors). Likewise, or-parallel execution produces multiple bindings for conditional variables, while and-parallel execution may do the same for shared variables. In both cases, during the execution of parallel threads, common variables can be concurrently accessed and/or bound. This creates possible *dependencies* that need to be resolved by adopting proper synchronization techniques.

Characteristic	Or-Parallelism	And-Parallelism
object of parall.	alternatives in a choice point	subgoals in a goal
dependency	on conditional variables	on shared variables
additional work	on failure	on success
speculativeness	on success	on failure
continuation	independent computations	join of computations

Table 1. Comparison and-parallelism vs. or-parallelism

The duality between or-parallelism and and-parallelism can be noted immediately in the way in which alternative executions are handled, since in or-parallelism we are looking for *one* alternative to succeed (i.e., $\exists$), while in and-parallelism we are forced to verify that all the alternative executions are successful (i.e., $\forall \equiv \neg\exists$).

This observation manifests itself, for example, in the design of schedulers for parallel logic programming systems. In or-parallelism a lot of effort has been spent in building *smart* schedulers, capable of selecting the alternative that is more likely to succeed as soon as possible—i.e., finding, as quickly as possible, the ($\exists$) branch leading to a solution. In and-parallelism the typical schedulers are quite simple (e.g., just push and pop and-parallel subgoals on goal stacks) due to the fact that ($\forall$) all the alternatives need to be tried[2].

[2] Nevertheless, in [16], the duality principle has been applied to develop arguably more effective scheduling techniques for and-parallel systems.

Based on the above discussion, the **Duality Principle** can be formulated as follows:

> *"If an implementation technique benefits or-parallel systems, its dual will benefit and-parallel systems and vice versas"*

3 Last Alternative Optimization

The last alternative optimization is based on the principle of flattening. After we developed the LPCO, an optimization for and-parallel systems described above, the principle of duality led us to believe that the dual of LPCO should work for or-parallel systems. That is how the idea of LAO was born.

We illustrate the Last Alternative Optimization with an example. In a majority of or-parallel applications, or-parallelism arises because a variable can be given one of many possible values. This is typically coded as a call to `member` or `select` predicate. For example, given a variable `V`, we want it to assume values from the list `[1,2,3,4]`, and for each possible value of `V` we want to perform some computation (almost all non-deterministic search problems and constrained optimization problems are programmed in this manner). The query will look as follows:

```
?- member(V,[1,2,3,4]),compute(V,R).
```

where `R` will hold the result of the computation with a given value for `V`, and `member` is defined as follows.

```
member(X,[X|T]).
member(X,[Y|T]) :- member(Y,T).
```

The search tree structure created is shown in figure 5(i).

Notice that or-parallelism will be exploited when processors move to choice points (shown as dark circles in Figure 5) and pick the `compute` goals for execution. A possible scenario is shown in figure 5(i) itself where processors P1, P2, P3, and P4 are exploring the four branches created for solving `compute(`i`,R)` where $1 \leq i \leq 4$.

Note that the intent in the program is to fire off a `compute` goal for every element in the list `[1,2,3,4]`. However, because a repetitive action can be programmed in a logic programming language only via recursion, we are forced to use the recursive `member` predicate for firing off all the `compute` goals. Thus, the various calls to compute, one for each element of the list, can only be generated in a recursive manner. Ideally, we would like to have all calls to `compute` generated all at once as shown in Figure 5(ii).

The tree structure shown in figure 5(i) is nested, thus processors have to traverse larger distances to move around the tree, and obtain work (the various `compute` goals). In contrast, in Figure 5(ii) all `compute` goals are clubbed at one choice points from where they can all be picked by processors with less traversal.

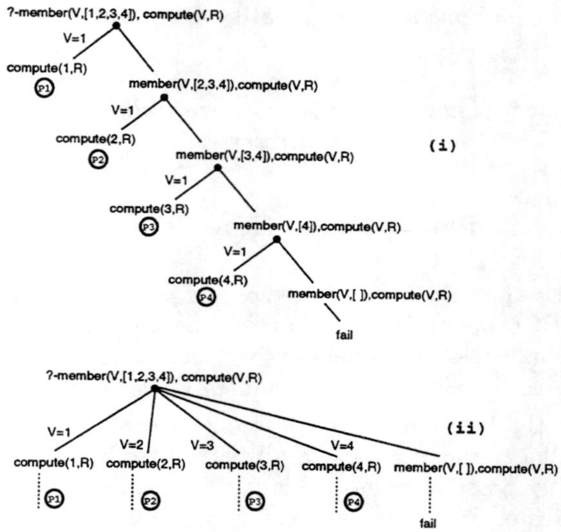

Fig. 5. Search tree created for member

The same discussion applies to the `select` predicate that, like the `member` predicate, is also traditionally used to spawn or-parallelism:

```
select(X,[X|T],T).
select(X,[Y|T],[Y|R]) :- select(X,T,R).
```

Several researchers have proposed ways for making the work distribution operation more efficient. For example, Smith, in his Multilog system [21, 22], has proposed the addition of a *disj* primitive to Prolog, that the programmer should place before call to member. Thus, the query is of the form:

?- *disj* `member(X,[1,2,3,4]), compute(X,R).`

The *disj* is handled by the Multilog system in a special way: the `compute` predicate is iteratively called for each element in the list. Thus, intuitively, the list structure is converted into an array like structure, on which a data-parallel `compute` call is made.

Our goal is to avoid the overhead of having to traverse the extra nestings created due to recursive unfolding of the member function, but without requiring any help from the programmer. The solution thus is to recognize the case in Figure 5(i) and somehow transform it at runtime to the situation shown in 5(ii). This is indeed what the Last Alternative Optimization accomplishes.

When the last alternative in a choice-point B_1, further creates a choice-point B_2, then there is no need to allocate this new choice-point, rather B_1 can be *updated* with the information that will be stored in B_2. The information in B_1 is no longer needed as the last alternative has already been picked up for execution. (We do assume that when processors pick work in the form of untried alternatives from a choice-point, they do it in the Prolog order, i.e., left to right, so that the rightmost alternative is always the last alternative to be selected). Of course, while reusing the existing choice point, we have to make sure that we will not change the meaning of the program. Thus, we have to ensure that the all the alternatives have access to the correct environment, the correct arguments, etc. Note that while we have illustrated LAO with the `member` example, where the two choice points merged (B_1 and B_2 above) correspond to the same predicate, in the general case, they may correspond to different predicates (however, in such a case special action will be needed if predicates corresponding to the two choice points have different number of arguments; see later).

The LAO can be thought of as a generalization of the last call optimization (LCO) found in sequential Prolog system for or-parallel systems. The last call optimization itself is a generalization of the familiar tail recursion optimization for sequential Prolog systems. The last alternative optimization not only saves execution time but also space. Execution time is saved in two ways:

- the search tree is simplified (its depth is reduced); as a consequence, the processors have shorter paths to traverse to get to choice-points that contain work in the form of untried alternatives.
- since an existing choice-point is used instead of allocating a new one, time is saved—various fields of the older choice points can be re-used without any update.

The LAO demonstrates another implementation principle—the principle of reuse—that leads to greater efficiency when applicable. The **Reuse Principle** [18] states

"Reuse a data-structure or computation whenever possible."

An interesting point to note about LAO is that, although it is applicable to sequential implementations of Prolog [14], it does not bring much benefit to sequential execution. This is because in sequential execution, when the last alternative is picked, the corresponding choice point is already deallocated (however, the fact, that some of the fields in the old choice point may be reused may bring some marginal savings if LAO were to be applied). However, for parallel implementations of Prolog, the efficiency gains can be enormous as our performance figures indicate. Unlike a sequential system, in an or-parallel implementation when the last alternative from a choice point is picked, that choice point cannot be deallocated as alternatives before the last one may still be active (i.e., they are still being explored by other processors). Thus, reuse of choice point can lead to considerable savings in memory and time. Also, because of the simplification of the tree structure due to flattening, the need for processors to synchronize with each other is reduced, resulting in not only a simple to implement model but also a more efficient one.

Parallel logic programming systems that incorporate or-parallelism system will considerably benefit from LAO, as the simplification of the structure of the tree leads to fewer constraints on the scheduling algorithm, and thus to more efficient scheduling. For instance, in the DNA sequencing program [6], one of the largest or-parallel program that has been ever tried, or-parallelism is obtained from the following two rules

```
find_match([C|Right],Left) :-
   find_a_matching_pattern(C,Right,Left).
find_match([C|Right],Left) :-
   find_match(Right,[C|Left).
```

A `find_match` query will create a right-recursive tree that is explored in parallel. Lusk et al switch the order of rules, due to the scheduling policy used in their Aurora or-parallel system, in order to generate a left recursive tree, so that work is more evenly distributed. With LAO such considerations become moot, since all the untried alternatives become available in a single choice-point. (Lusk et al extensively discuss how to make the scheduler work the way they want it to in their paper [6]). It is our conjecture that incorporation of LAO in Aurora will considerably improve the performance of Lusk et al's program (LAO provides exactly the effect that Lusk et al are seeking) as well as of other or-parallel programs run on the Aurora system.

LAO will also improve the performance of programs that use failure driven loops based on Prolog's `repeat` builtin. The repeat builtin (defined below) creates an infinite number of choice points from where work gets picked up (a cut is usually necessary later to destroy the infinite choice-points and terminate the computation). Applying LAO will merge the multiple choice points created by the recursive repeat into one single choice point.

```
repeat :- repeat.
repeat.
```

4 Implementation of LAO in ACE

4.1 Or-parallelism in ACE

ACE [10, 9] is a high performance implementation of parallel Prolog based on the SICStus WAM engine that exploits both and- and or-parallelism. The Last Parallel Call Optimization (LPCO) has already been incorporated in the ACE system and the results reported elsewhere [17, 7]. We have also incorporated the LAO in the ACE system and results are reported in section 4.3. In this section we describe the changes that had to be made to the ACE system in order to implement LAO.

The ACE system uses the *stack copying* environment representation technique (originally developed for the MUSE or-parallel system [1]) for representing *multiple environments* that arise during or-parallelism. In traditional sequential implementations only one branch of the or-parallel tree resides on the control stack at any given time. As a result bindings for conditional variables can be stored in-place. These bindings are undone on backtracking with the help of the *trail stack*, so that if the next branch also produces a binding for the conditional variable then it can be safely stored. As indicated in figure 6, in the presence of or-parallelism alternative executions arising from a choice point may be active simultaneously and may potentially generate different bindings for variable allocated in environments created before the branching point (the choice point where or-parallelism originated). Thus, multiple environments can exist at run-time, and these have to be carefully maintained so that each branch sees only the bindings that it created.

```
q( ... ) :- ... Y = a ... p(Y,X).
p(Y,X) :- X = b ....
p(Y,X) :- X = c ...
?- q(...)
```

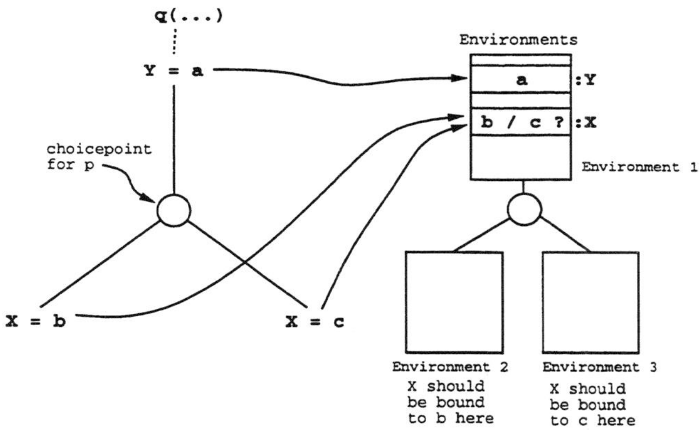

Fig. 6. Environment Representation Problem

Stack copying is based on the idea of creating different copies of the existing environments when branching takes place (i.e., when an idle processor selects an alternative from a choice point to start a parallel computation). Thus, in Figure 7, if processor P2 selects the second alternative from choice point c2, then before starting execution it will copy all choice points and environments from the root node up to choice point c2 on its local stack[3]. The existence of local copies of the "shared" environments allows to overcome the previously described binding management problem, since each processor will have a local space to store the locally generated binding.

In the stack copying model the whole state of computation is copied; this requires copying not only the environments created before the choice point, but

[3] Note that stack copying requires that each processor's address space be mapped in such a way that it is identical to all other processors' address space, so that on copying of stacks, no pointer relocation is required.

also the choice points themselves (and other data areas, e.g. the trail stack), in order to allow each processor to perform its execution as independently as possible from the others. However, choice points hold control information and, thus, need to be shared data-structures. Connection between the different copies of the same choice point is maintained through a *shared frame*. The shared frame contains those parts of the choice point that are shared and that may be modified during the parallel execution (see figure 7).

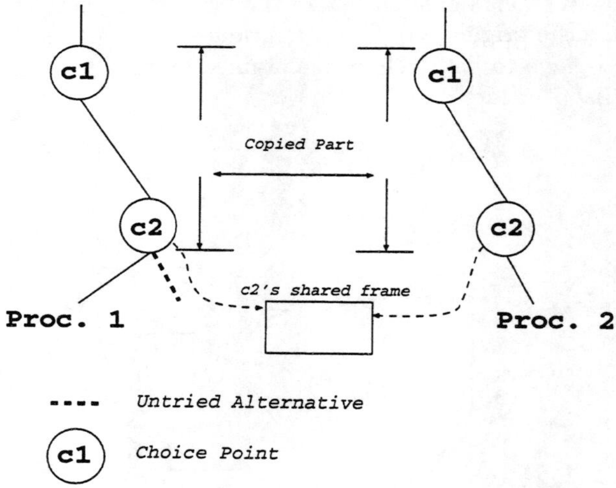

Fig. 7. Stack Copying management of choice points

The process of selecting a choice point and copying the computation state up to such choice point (and creating the needed shared frames for each copied choice point) is termed a *sharing operation* [1].

4.2 Implementation of LAO in ACE

The current implementation of LAO in ACE is quite simple. The opportunities for applying the optimization are automatically identified. A test is performed before creation of new choice points. If the current execution is the rightmost alternative of the previously created choice point, and both the previous choice point and the new one are "parallel"[4], then no new choice point will be created. Instead the previous choice point is reused.

The "reuse" of the choice point is simply realized by avoiding allocation of the new choice point and by using the fields of the old choice point to store

[4] Note that in most or-parallel systems whether a choice point is parallel or sequential is indicated by the user. Only a parallel choice point can give or-parallel work to other processors. Restricting the application of the LAO to parallel choice points is necessary in order to limit the influence of the optimization on the behaviour of the scheduler.

the various state information. This gives the advantage that certain fields of the choice point may already contain the right value and their initialization may be avoided (e.g., pointer to the heap). Reuse of choice point also involves attaching the alternatives of the choice point being created to the existing choice point, and storing in the same choice point the relevant state information (e.g., value of the arguments of the associated subgoal).

Some changes to the design of the data structures are required to accommodate the new features of LAO. As discussed earlier, a parallel choice point that has been shared actually replicates itself into (i) a number of *private* copies of the choice point (one for each processor that took work from that choice point), and (ii) the shared frame, with each private copy having a pointer to it. Intuitively, the private copies are meant to store the "static" part of the state (the information that will not change between execution of the different alternatives), while the shared frame is used to maintain the part of the state that will be modified during execution (and modification performed by one processor need to be visible to the others).

Given that implementation of LAO requires modification of certain fields of an existing choice point, these fields need to be transferred from the choice point to the shared frame, in order to allow communication of the changes to the other processors. In particular, two relevant parts of the choice point that need to be *"globalized"* or transferred to the shared frame are:

- the arguments of the subgoal;
- the pointer to the trail stack[5].

The general structure of the choice point and of the shared frame is depicted in figure 8.

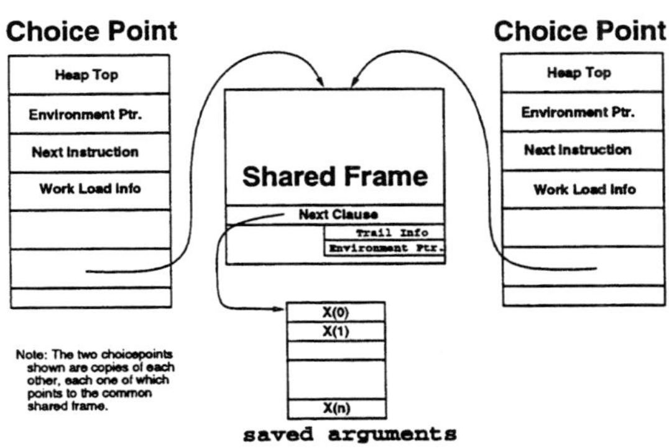

Fig. 8. Choice Points and Shared Frames

The current prototypical implementation of LAO is mainly aimed at taking advantage of recursive generators like those described in the previous examples (`member`, `select`, etc.). LAO can be easily generalized to situations where the

[5] The trail stack keeps track of the bindings that need to be undone on backtracking.

choice point created along the last alternative of another choice point corresponds to a different predicate. The price of this generalization is the requirement of further globalizing some more fields of the choice point (in particular the environment pointer needs to be moved to the shared frame). Furthermore, the more general scheme should take care of the following two situations:

1. the different procedures may have different number of arguments (see figure 8).
2. various environments may have been allocated between the two choice points being merged. If the alternatives of the latter choice point are promoted to the former one, then these environments need to be "communicated" to the other processors (otherwise they will not be able to correctly execute the new alternatives). This means that a further copying phase may be needed upon backtracking over an optimized choice point.

Nevertheless, the savings guaranteed by LAO easily overcome the additional expenses for the above overheads.

4.3 Performance Figures

Table 2 describes the results obtained by running some benchmarks on the ACE systems with and without LAO. Each entry in the table indicates the unoptimized execution time (in milliseconds), the time obtained using LAO, and the corresponding percentage of improvement. All the figures have been obtained on a Sequent Symmetry multiprocessors[6]. Figure 9 compares the speed curves with and without optimization, while figure 10 represents the improvement in execution time obtained using LAO.

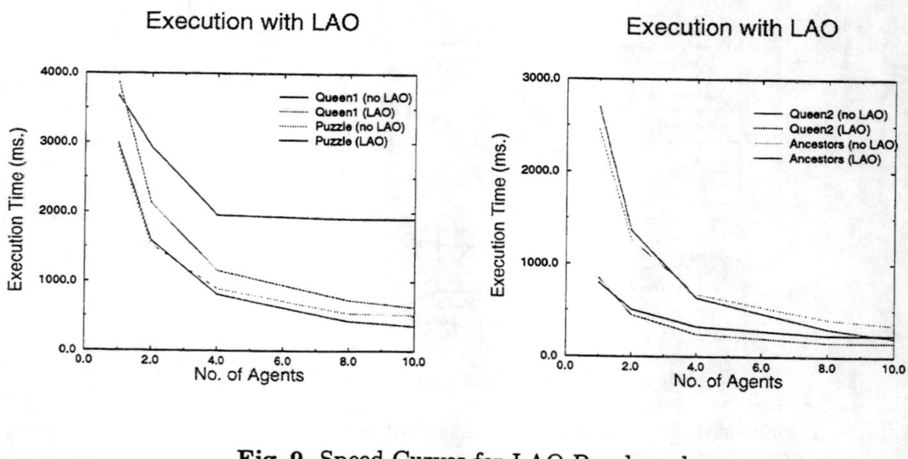

Fig. 9. Speed Curves for LAO Benchmarks

[6] Analogous improvements have been observed on a Sun Sparc multiprocessor machine.

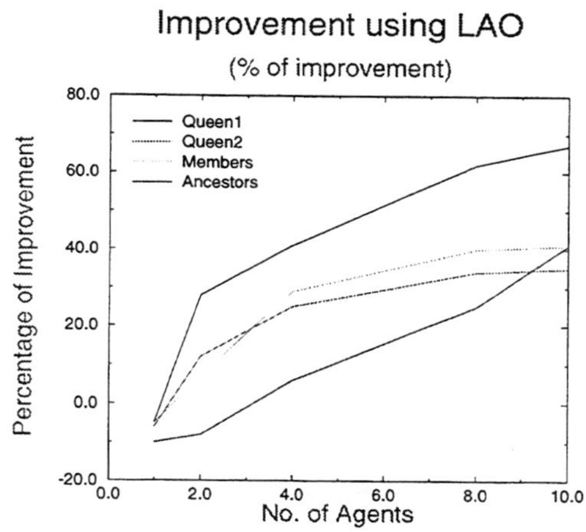

Fig. 10. Improvement in Exec. Time

Even though the current implementation of LAO is still a prototype, the numbers produced are quite impressive. Especially with larger number of processors, the reduction in execution time is frequently over 30%. These good results are consequence of the particularly good interaction between LAO and stack copying. The application of LAO allows to "promote" new alternatives created by a processor, storing them directly in a choice point that has already been copied by other processors (i.e., it has already a shared frame associated with it). In this way the new alternatives become immediately visible to the other processors, without the need of performing further sharing activities. As a consequence the number of sharing operations performed during execution is considerably reduced (in some benchmarks this number decreased from over 100 to less than 10). Considering that each sharing activity may be quite expensive, a good reduction in execution time can be expected.

Briefly, the benchmarks analyzed are

- *Queen*[1], a generate&test version of the queens problem;
- *Queen*[2], a smarter solution to the queens problem;
- *Puzzle*, a solver for a crypto-arithmetic puzzle;
- *Ancestors*, a program performing a search in a genealogical tree;
- *Members*, a generate&test solution to an optimization problem.

All these programs use either the `member` or the `select` predicate to generate alternative paths to the solution(s).

It must be noted that, in the current implementation, the presence of LAO tends to produce a slight degradation in execution time on a single processor (as can be observed from the execution times on one processor). This is due to the additional cost of testing, at each choice point creation, whether LAO can be applied or not. We expect to be able to considerably reduce this overhead by using a more careful implementation of these tests and by taking advantage of the information supplied by the compiler (e.g., distinction between sequential and parallel nodes).

Program	No. of Agents				
	1	2	4	8	10
Queen[1]	3689/3889 (-5%)	2939/2129 (28%)	1959/1159 (41%)	1910/730 (62%)	1909/629 (67%)
Queen[2]	799/850 (-6%)	510/450 (12%)	320/240 (25%)	229/150 (34%)	229/149 (35%)
Puzzle	2939/3001 (-2%)	1529/1589 (-4%)	890/809 ((9%)	540/429 (21%)	519/360 (31%)
Ancestors	2460/2706 (-10%)	1269/1370 (-8%)	669/629 (6%)	399/299 (25%)	340/201 (41%)
Members	8029/8450 (-5%)	4021/3731 (7%)	3733/2667 (29%)	3480/2080 (40%)	3400/2011 (41%)
Maps	35420/36240 (-2%)	21079/19879 (6%)	11620/12189 (-10%)	9290/8329 (10%)	6100/7100 (-16%)
Zebra	3730/3779 (-1%)	2120/1970 (7%)	1120/1750 (22%)	879/1150 (31%)	789/870 (37%)

Table 2. Improvements using LAO (unoptimized/optimized)

In one of the benchmark tested, the *Maps* program (which solves the map coloring problem for a map of West Europe), we observed abnormal behaviour. On increasing the number of processors used the improvements produced by LAO vary significantly. For selected number of processors LAO leads to a definite improvement over unoptimized execution, while for other instances unoptimized execution seems to be more efficient. We believe that it is due to the quirkiness of our scheduler. We are working on modifying our or-parallel scheduler so as to eliminate this anomalous behavior.

5 Data Or-parallelism

The Last Alternative Optimization *transforms control or-parallel computations into data-or parallel ones.* This is especially obvious from the `member` example, where all the calls to `compute` (one for each element of the list) get clubbed into one choice-point as a result of the LAO. All these `compute` goals execute identical instructions but on different data. The effect of LAO is thus, similar to the *disj* operator in Smith's Multilog, except that the runtime system automatically exposes data or-parallelism from data or-parallel computations that have been programmed using a control parallel construct (recursion in the case of logic programming). A comparison with performance of Multilog is not possible because Multilog has not been implemented on a Sequent Symmetry. However, we believe that performance of data-or parallel programs on ACE augmented with LAO will be comparable to their performance on MultiLog, a dedicated data-or parallel system.

The disadvantage that our system suffers w.r.t. the Multilog system is that the time taken to distribute all the data-parallel work is $O(n)$ in our case, while in case of Multilog, theoretically, it can be reduced to $O(\lg n)$. This is because in our system, the data-parallelism is exposed by unfolding of recursion, an inherently linear process. In Multilog, data-parallelism is exposed by the user, and thus all of it is visible all at once and can be distributed to multiple processors with an $O(\lg n)$ overhead.

The main advantage that LAO has over approaches such as Multilog is that it is applicable to more general parallel logic programming systems. No special machinery for data-parallelism needs to be built in. Also, LAO is much more general as the two choice points that get merged may not necessarily correspond to the same call. Thus, if a call `p` creates a choice-points and then calls `q` in its last clause which also leads to creation of a choice point, then `q`'s choice-point can reuse `p`'s. Thus, the two choice-points being merged do not have to correspond to a call to the same predicate. In this case, the transformation does not really exploit data-parallelism, but improves execution's efficiency and leads to better speed-ups that result from simplification of the execution tree. Thus, LAO is a more general technique for exploiting parallelism efficiently than Smith's.

6 Parallel Constraint Logic Programming

A parallel constraint logic programming system, based on finite domains, such as CHIP [11] or CLP(FD) [4] can take substantial advantage of LAO. A typical CLP problem can be characterized as follows: given a collection of variables, each of which ranges over a finite domain (set of values), the task is to find out an assignment of values for these variables from their respective domains such that certain user stated constraints are satisfied. In traditional logic programming this will be stated as a *generate and test* problem, where all possible assignments of values for the variables from the domains will be considered and then tested for consistency under the given constraints. CLP over finite domains makes this process efficient, by setting up the constraints first, which significantly prunes the domains of variables (any constraints that cannot be solved in this phase are suspended), and then performing a generate and test, where the generation phase considers values from the pruned domain (programmed by using builtins like `labeling` or `indomain`) and the test phase consists of testing the assignments generated in the `generate` phase for the remaining suspended constraints.

The predicate `indomain` is nothing but a call to a member predicate, where the variable in question is assigned successive values from the pruned domain.

In a parallel CLP system that incorporates LAO, the `indomain` predicate unfolds into a data-parallel call due to LAO, thus, automatically improving the efficiency of parallel execution. Thus, with the incorporation of LAO, one can incorporate data-parallelism automatically into a parallel CLP system.

7 Balanced Nesting Optimization

The Last Alternative Optimization was inspired by our observation of duality between and-parallel implementation techniques and or-parallel ones. This lead us to believe that the principles of flattening and reuse that have been applied to and-parallelism can also be applied to or-parallelism. Thus, LAO is the dual of LPCO. The dual of other optimizations devised on and-parallelism can similarly be conceived of. In this section we present one such optimization.

It is well known that in order to exploit parallelism programmers should write their algorithms in such a way as to expose parallelism. Thus, an inherently sequential program cannot be parallelized. Consider for example the following logic program for computing the factorial of a number:

```
fact(0,1).
fact(N,M) :-
    N > 0, N1 is N-1
    fact(N1,M1),
    M is M1 * N.
```

Significant amount of and-parallelism or or-parallelism cannot be exploited from this program due to the way it is written. Clearly, and-parallelism does exist in the program for computing factorial, since to compute the factorial of n, the n multiplications can be done in parallel. However, the way the program above is written this parallelism is not "exposed". It is well known that programs with certain characteristics, such as the factorial above, can be transformed automatically to expose more parallelism (see for instance [8, 12]; a more comprehensive treatment can be found in [5]). This transformation essentially consists of transforming a linear recursive computation into a structure that is more balanced. This transformation relies on the associativity and commutativity of the multiplication operator. The transformed program appears as follows:

```
fact(N, M) :- fact(1, N, M).

fact(N, N, N).
fact(L, H, M) :- L < H,
      Mid1 is (L + H) div 2,
      Mid2 is Mid1 + 1,
      fact(L, Mid1, M1),
      fact(Mid2, H, M2),
      M is M1 * M2.
```

Essentially a linearly recursive program has been transformed into a doubly recursive divide-and-conquer program that can be easily parallelized (the two recursive calls to `fact1`) are independent of each other and can be executed in parallel. This transformation (either done by the programmer or by a smart compiler) can result in program becoming parallelizable, and thus capable of being speeded-up on a parallel computer. Experiments done by Debray [5] have indeed shown that considerable speed-ups can be obtained by thus transforming the program.

The same idea can be applied to or-parallel systems, and linearly recursive structured programs. Let's consider the member predicate again. The query `member(X, [1,2,3,4])` will produce a search tree shown in Figure 11(i). The objective of the member predicate is to act as the generator and launch the compute goal for every element of the list. A better way of doing this is to convert the list into a balanced binary tree, and then use tree-member as a generator. The effect of the program is the same except that tree-member produces a more balanced (flattened tree), so that the overhead of getting the work arising out of elements in the list that come later is not unnecessarily more. Figure 11 illustrates this situation.

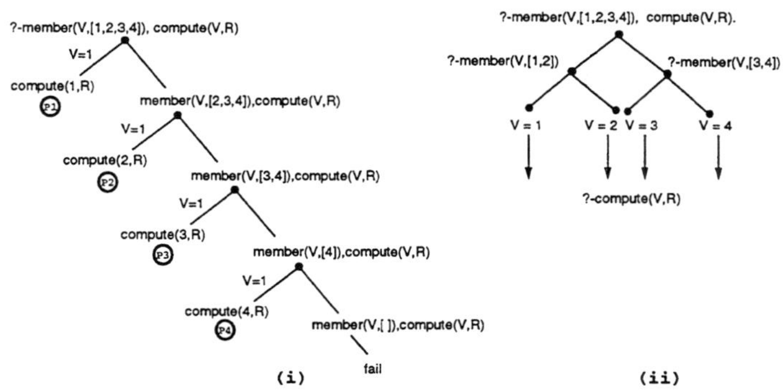

Fig. 11. From Linear List to Binary Tree

When ordinary member is used, essentially the choice points that get unfolded are shaped as a linear tree, traveling to one of whose nodes requires an overhead that is $O(n)$. With tree-member they get unfolded into a log-structured tree, traveling to one of whose nodes involves only a $O(\lg n)$ overhead. One will not see much difference in performance when a program with this transformation is run in a sequential environment, however, in a parallel environment, considerable improvement is observed as our performance figures show. This performance improvement comes about because with a more balanced, flatter tree the overhead incurred in picking work (untried alternatives) is simplified. Processors have to traverse shorter distances to reach choice-points. In case of MUSE, it also means less amount of copying, and in case of Aurora[7] less work at the time of task-switching. In both cases because task-switching distances are reduced, there is less contention for choice-points that have to be locked while traversing the tree.

Note that LAO and the balancing transformation are competing transformations in many cases. Of course, if both are applicable, we will prefer to apply LAO. The balancing transformation is done automatically by our compiler (with some help from the user), and if the compiler figures that applicability of LAO may be destroyed as a result of this transformation, then the transformation is not applied at all. However, there are several other situations when LAO is

[7] Aurora is an or-parallel system based on a different environment representation scheme [25].

not applicable and the balancing transformation can be applied. For example when the computation structure produced is left-recursive. So, for instance, if the order of the member rules was switched, then LAO will cease to apply, while the balancing transformation can still be applied.

7.1 Performance Figures

Development of automatic compile-time techniques to perform the previously described transformation are currently undergoing. To test the efficacy of the balanced nesting optimization we have applied it to the Queens problem. Table 3 illustrates the execution times obtained with and without the transformation. Figure 12 compares the execution times with and without BNO.

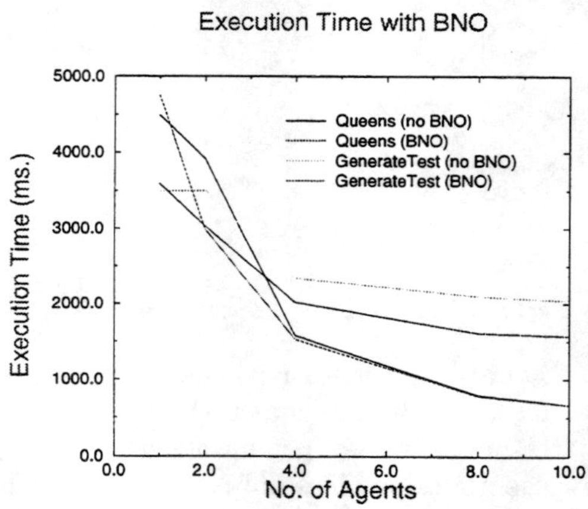

Fig. 12. Execution with BNO

As we can observe from the results, the improvement in execution time is considerable especially for small number of processors, since it allows to obtain a better distribution of work and reduces synchronization activity between different processors. The difference in execution time tends to fade with higher number of processors, as the execution behaviour in the two case becomes almost equivalent.

More interesting results were obtained when this transformation was applied to a typical *generate and test* solution to a search problem. As we can see from table 4, the transformed version of the program manages to achieve constantly better execution times and better speedups than the unoptimized version. It is interesting to note how the system is unable (due to the way in which scheduler works) to achieve parallelism from an execution with 2 processors on the unoptimized program, while the transformed version produced an improvement in execution. The balanced nesting optimization can also be applied to parallel constraint logic programming systems based on finite domains. Essentially, the finite domains should be represented as a binary tree rather than as a simple list, and the builtin `indomain` predicate should be defined as a tree-member predicate instead of as the regular member predicate.

Execution	No. of Agents 1	2	4	8	10
Unoptimized	4490	3919	1580	789	659
Optimized	4750	2990	1529	779	659
Improvement	-6%	24%	3%	1%	0%

Table 3. Application of Transformation to Queens Problem

Execution	No. of Agents 1	2	4	8	10
Unoptimized	3490	3500	2340	2100	2040
Optimized	3590	3029	2019	1610	1570
Improvement	-3%	13%	14%	23%	23%

Table 4. Application of Transformation to Generate&Test Problem

8 Conclusions

In this paper we presented two fairly general transformations for or-parallel systems—the last alternative optimization and the balanced nesting optimization. Both are inspired by the *flattening principle* which states that the structure of the search tree developed during parallel execution should be as simple (flat) as possible. Both the LAO and BNO are very general optimizations and are applicable to any type of or-parallel system. Another feature of these optimizations is that they produce only marginal benefits for sequential implementations, however, for parallel implementation, the savings can be enormous. Both optimizations have been incorporated in the ACE and-or parallel Prolog system running on a Sequent Symmetry. The performance results of both optimization on various benchmarks was presented and shown to be quite good. Our results prove that LAO and BNO are very useful optimizations that can considerably reduce the parallel overhead in or-parallel systems.

Acknowledgements

The research presented here benefited from discussions with M. Carro, E. Correia, M. Hermenegildo, D. Ranjan, V. Santos Costa, and K. Shen, all of whom we would like to thank.

This work is supported by NSF Grants CCR 96-25358, HRD 96-28450, INT 95-15256, and by NATO Grant CRG 921318.

References

1. K.A.M. Ali and R. Karlsson. The Muse Or-parallel Prolog Model and its Performance. In *1990 N. American Conf. on Logic Prog.* MIT Press, 1990.
2. J. Bevemyr, T. Lindgren, and H. Millroth. Reform Prolog: the Language and its Implementation. In *Proc. of the 10th Int'l Conf. on Logic Progr.*, MIT Press, 1993.
3. G.E. Blelloch. *Vector Models for Data-parallel Computing.* MIT Press, 1990.
4. P. Codognet and D. Diaz. A Minimal Extension of the WAM for `clp(fd)`. In *Int'l Conf. on Logic Progr.*, MIT Press, 1993.
5. S. Debray and M. Jain. A Simple Program Transformation for Parallelism. In *Proc. of the 1994 Symp. on Logic Progr.*, MIT Press, 1994.
6. S. Mudambi et al. E. Lusk. Applications of the Aurora Parallel Prolog System to Computational Molecular Biology. In *Int'l Logic Progr. Symp.*, MIT Press, 1993.
7. E.Pontelli and G. Gupta. Data And-parallel Logic Programming in &ACE. In *Proc. of 7th IEEE Symp. on Parallel and Distributed Processing*, 1995.
8. G. Gupta. *Multiprocessor Execution of Logic Programs.* Kluwer Academic Press, 1994.
9. G. Gupta, M. Hermenegildo, and E. Pontelli. &ACE: A High-performance Parallel Prolog System. In *IPPS 95.* IEEE Computer Society, 1995.
10. G. Gupta, M. Hermenegildo, E. Pontelli, and V. Santos Costa. ACE: And/Or-parallel Copying-based Execution of Logic Programs. In *Proc. ICLP'94*, MIT Press, 1994.
11. P. Van Hentenryck. *Constraint Handling in Prolog.* MIT Press, 1988.
12. M. Hermenegildo and M. Carro. Relating Data-Parallelism and (And-)Parallelism in Logic Programs. In *EuroPar'95.* Springer Verlag, 1995.
13. E. Lusk and al. The Aurora Or-parallel Prolog System. *New Generation Computing*, 7(2,3), '90.
14. M. Meier. Recursion vs. Iteration in Prolog. In *Int'l Conf. on Logic Progr.*, MIT Press, 1991.
15. D.W. Palmer, J.F. Prins, and S. Westfold. Work-Efficient Nested Data-Parallelism. In *Frontiers of Massively Parallel Computing*, 1994.
16. E. Pontelli and G. Gupta. On the Duality Between And-parallelism and Or-parallelism. In *Proc. of Euro-Par'95.* Springer Verlag, 1995.
17. E. Pontelli and G. Gupta. Nested Parallel Call Optimization. In *IPPS96*, IEEE Computer Society, 1996.
18. E. Pontelli, G. Gupta, and D. Tang. Determinacy Driven Optimizations of Parallel Prolog Implementations. In *Proc. of the Int'l Conf. on Logic Progr.*, MIT Press, 1995.
19. V. Ramakrishnan, I.D. Scherson, and R. Subramanian. Efficient Techniques for Fast Nested Barrier Synchronization. In *Seventh ACM Symposium on Parallel Algorithms and Architectures*, 1995.
20. G.W. Sabot. *The Paralation Model: Architecture Independent Parallel Programming.* MIT Press, 1988.

21. D.A. Smith. Why Multi-SLD beats SLD (even on a uniprocessor). In *LPAR*. Springer Verlag, 1994.
22. D.A. Smith. Multilog: Data or-parallel logic programming. In *International Conference on Logic Programming*. MIT Press, 1993.
23. E. Tick. Concurrent Logic Programs *a la mode*. In E. Tick and G. Succi, editors, *High Performance Logic Programming Systems*. Kluwer, 1994.
24. D. H. D. Warren. An Improved Prolog Implementation Which Optimises Tail Recursion. Research Paper 156, Dept. of Artificial Intelligence, University of Edinburgh, 1980.
25. D. H. D. Warren. The SRI Model for OR-Parallel Execution of Prolog—Abstract Design and Implementation. In *Proc. IEEE Int'l Symp. on Logic Prog.*, pages 92–102, 1987.
26. D.H.D. Warren. An Improved Prolog Implementation Which Optimises Tail Recursion. In *Proc. of the 2nd ICLP*. Academic Press, 1984.

Side-effects in PloSys OR-parallel Prolog on distributed memory machines*

É. Morel, J. Briat, J. Chassin de Kergommeaux, C. Geyer
Projet CNRS-INRIA APACHE
{Eric.Morel, Jacques.Briat,Jacques.Chassin,Claudio.Geyer}@imag.fr
Tl : +33 76 51 46 63, +33 76 51 45 72, +33 76 51 45 75
Fax : +33 76 51 48 46

LMC-IMAG, B.P. 53, F-38041 Grenoble Cedex 9 France

Abstract. The aim of the logic programming system PloSys is to offer most Prolog functionalities on distributed memory parallel computers as well as networks of personal computers. The PloSys computational model exploits OR-parallelism. It is designed to implement cut and side-effects while keeping low the number of messages exchanged between processors. It is a multi-sequential model based on copying. Scheduling is centralised as is the management of cut and side-effects. The scheduler keeps up to date the knowledge of the left-most worker in the scope of each cut. A PloSys prototype was implemented and its first results, on IBM SP-1, are promising.
Keywords: Logic programming, OR-parallelism, Distributed Memory, Side-effects, Multi-sequential.

1 Introduction

Logic programming is one of the best suited paradigms to parallel processing and has given rise to a large number of parallel models of wich several were implemented efficiently [7]. By efficiently it is meant here that efficient parallel logic systems execute some programs more rapidly than the most efficient sequential Prolog systems and that, in the worst case (intrinsically sequential programs), parallel execution is not slower than sequential execution. Most OR-parallel logic programming systems were implemented on shared-memory symmetric multiprocessors [2, 16]. Some prototypes were also implemented on distributed memory systems but they do not include the usual Prolog side-effects [13, 3].

The objective of PloSys is to build a "Prolog-like" OR-parallel logic programming system for distributed memory parallel architectures. "Prolog-like" means that PloSys will implement Prolog cut and side-effects. This will ease the parallelisation of applications since applications will be debugged on a sequential Prolog system before being executed in parallel.

* This work is subject to a cooperation agreement with KFKI-MSZKI, sponsored by the Balaton project No. 95021 of the French ministeries of Foreign Affairs and of Education

The PloSys computational model is multi-sequential: each worker importing work copies the state of the worker exporting work. Scheduling is centralised. The management of cut and side-effects aims at limiting the number of messages exchanged during the execution. A PloSys prototype is currently being tested on distributed memory parallel computer IBM SP-1.8. Its first results are promising. Another research stream, not described in this paper, is concerned with the evaluation of scheduling strategies [14].

The organisation of this paper is the following. This introduction is followed by a general description of the PloSys system. The management of PloSys side-effects is described in the next section. The PloSys prototype is then outlined before a comparison with other OR-parallel logic programming systems.

2 Overview of the PloSys system

The PloSys computational model is a multi-sequential model tailored to distributed memory parallel architectures. Special care was given to keep low the number of messages exchanged during the parallel execution of logic programs. The reason is that, in distributed memory parallel systems, the latency of communications becomes increasingly important relatively to the speed of processors and it becomes more important to reduce the number of messages than their size. The scheduler must on the one hand allocate work to the workers executing the program and on the other hand manage the Prolog cut and side-effects (see section 3). In the existing prototype, scheduling is centralised although it will be distributed in the future. Each worker was designed so that the management of the cut and side-effects was kept separated from the inference engine. A PloSys prototype is currently being tested (see section 4.1).

2.1 Computational model

The PloSys computational model is inspired from OPERA [4], without implementing some optimisations tailored for the Supernode architecture used in OPERA. In PloSys, a Prolog program is executed in parallel by several workers, including each an inference engine as well as an exporter and an importer process. The inference engine is a sequential Prolog inference engine, as efficient as possible and therefore based on an implementation of the Warren Abstract Machine (WAM) [21] which executes compiled Prolog programs. An idle worker obtains work from an active one by developing one or several unexplored choices originating from one or several choice points of this worker. To import work, a worker copies the state (mainly the stacks) of the exporter worker up to the choice point (or to the most recently created one) used to provide work. Copy is only possible when the exporter worker is modifying its choice points, in order to simplify the management of the coherency of the bindings of the exported variables. Similarly, the inference engine of the exporter worker remains idle during the export phases.

When receiving work from an active worker, a previously idle worker processes first unbinds non valid bindings[2] using its trail stack, before simulating a fail to execute the most recent untested alternative of the copied state.

2.2 Architecture and functionalities of the scheduler

The design of the scheduler is modular to ease its future evolutions: it includes a skeleton and several independent units. The first unit is dedicated to the distribution of work. The process associated to the work distribution unit collects periodically the state of the workers and distribute work according to a scheduling policy. As in OPERA [4], idle workers search work from "over-loaded" workers whose load is over some pre-defined threshold[3]. Matching idle and over-loaded workers is performed by the scheduler, which keeps an approximate global state of the system using the load information sent by the workers. An idle worker gets from the scheduler the location of an over-loaded worker. The idle worker then requests work from this over-loaded worker, this work consisting of the unexplored alternatives of one or several choice-points. A work request may fail if the requested worker is not any more in the over-loaded state when the request is received (see figure 1).

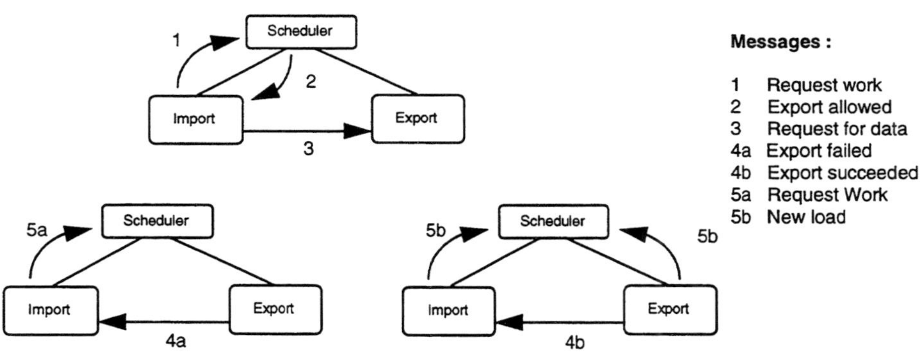

Fig. 1. Exchange of work in PloSys

The other units are in charge of coordinating the side effects with each other and load balancing (see section 3.5). Each unit can be modified independently of the others so that several scheduling strategies can be made available or several side-effect management strategies can be tested or matching of work to workers can be changed (distributed for example).

---

[2] that is bindings that were done by the exporter worker in the development of another, non exported, alternative of the exported state

[3] The determination of this threshold will be subject of future work

2.3 Architecture of the PloSys workers

Each worker includes at least three processes : one inference engine, one exporter and one importer. In addition, there exist several processes, specialised for the management of side-effects. Not like in OPERA, the inference engine and the exporter cannot be simultaneously active. Exporting is only possible in some of the states of the inference engine. This limit has a minor consequence on the execution but saves many synchronisations between the exporter and the inference engine processes[4]. Information of the scheduler by the worker is done by regular calls of the inference engine and not by a specialised spy process as in OPERA. As for the scheduler, the implementation of the workers is modular to ease experiments and evolutions (see figure 2).

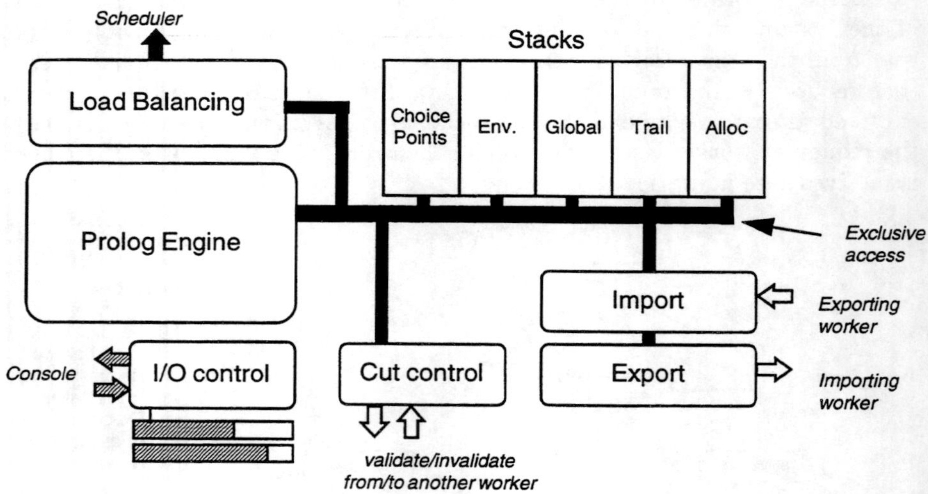

Fig. 2. Architecture of the Plosys workers

3 Management of side effects in PloSys

Prolog includes two types of side effects:

- the cut which prunes the branches on the right of the "cut clause" in the AND/OR search tree of the program.
- the other side-effect operators which modify or depend on the environment (I/Os, Prolog data-base, etc.).

[4] Also, DMA being not possible in the SP-1.8 prototype (see section 4.2), exporting and executing the inference engine can not be done at the same time in one worker

Management of side-effects There are two possible approaches. Either the semantics of the side-effect operators includes the execution order of these operators. Or, this execution order is determined by the sequential execution order of the Prolog program. The second approach was adopted to keep the programming language untouched. The most simple implementation differs the execution of a side-effect until the processor becomes "left-most" in the execution tree of the program. Another possible solution is to record the operation so that it can be executed when it is correct and meanwhile either to continue the computation (output to a file for example) or to suspend (input operation).

Management of the cut One possible solution is to process sequentially all the branches originating from an OR-node, under the scope of a cut. To avoid the inhibition of parallelism caused by this solution, parallel execution of such "speculative" OR-nodes [10] is continued. When a cut is executed, speculative computations are undone; otherwise if the cut is not executed, these computations are validated.

Interaction between cut and side effects Some branches of the search tree, under the scope of a cut, can therefore be computed in parallel executions while this would not have been the case sequentially. Side-effects performed in such branches ought to be undone. Therefore, side-effects executed in such conditions should be "reversible" either by restoring the previous state of computation, or by performing the side-effect in some cache that will be cleared if the side effect is not to be validated.

3.1 Maintenance of the sequential order

Solutions adopted in shared-memory systems [10, 2] cannot be used in PloSys. These solutions demand the exploration of the Prolog search tree to identify the left-most worker of the tree. This approach would require the use of a large number of messages in a distributed memory architecture. Instead, our approach is based on keeping the sequential order in the scheduler and using dedicated processes to control each side effect on each worker. This solution is not costly since the scheduler can keep track of the sequential execution order by computing the position of the workers in the search tree from the work transfers between workers. A list is used to point the relative positions of the workers in the program execution tree. When a worker exports work, it exports the highest (oldest) ones in the tree. Therefore the importer worker will be located at the right of the exporter and will be its successor in the list (see figure 3). Idle workers are removed from the list, until they benefit from new transfers. Although the list needs to be slightly complicated to support the management of side-effects, it is the basis for keeping the sequential order of side-effects (see section 3.4).

3.2 Identification of speculative work

The management of the cut by the workers include two phases. The first one, associated to compilation, is the maintenance of the knowledge of the specula-

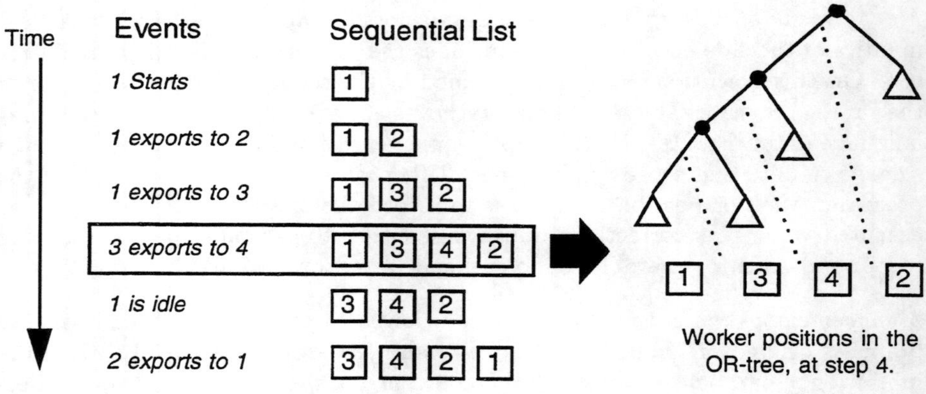

Fig. 3. Maintenance of the sequential order

tive nature of some choice points. The second phase is the control of exported speculative choice-points and their associated work.

In a sequential system, a dedicated variable is used to store the top of the execution stack before calling a predicate including a cut. In an OR-parallel system, part of this stack portion may have been developed by another worker which needs to be identified to validate or unvalidate its work. Similarly, a worker importing choice points under the scope of a cut, needs to be informed of the "speculativity" of this work in order to manage correctly its side-effects. This requires a slight modification of the WAM instructions managing choice-points. A global variable indicates the current cut level during the execution and two fields are added to each choice point to store and restore this level (see figure 4). These modifications do not change the sequential behavior of the Prolog inference engine and the associated overhead remains very low.

3.3 Management of cuts

In order for the scheduler process to take cuts into account, it is sufficient to know the "speculativity level" of the available work, to limit as much as possible the number of messages. Only the load information message needs to be modified to represent speculative loads. Specific scheduling problems raised by the management of speculative work are addressed in section 3.5.

When several workers execute a program, exported choice points need to be marqued and their new (worker) owner memorised in order to be able to propagate the execution of a cut (validation or invalidation of work). An exported choice point will thus hold a special mark (such as a negative cut level, see figure 5) so that its previous "owner" can take appropriate decisions upon backtracking or executing a cut. The new "owner" identification needs also to be stored in a specific field of the choice point.

When a worker backtracks across an exported choice point, the cut management process of the worker (see figure 2), will check the choice point stack

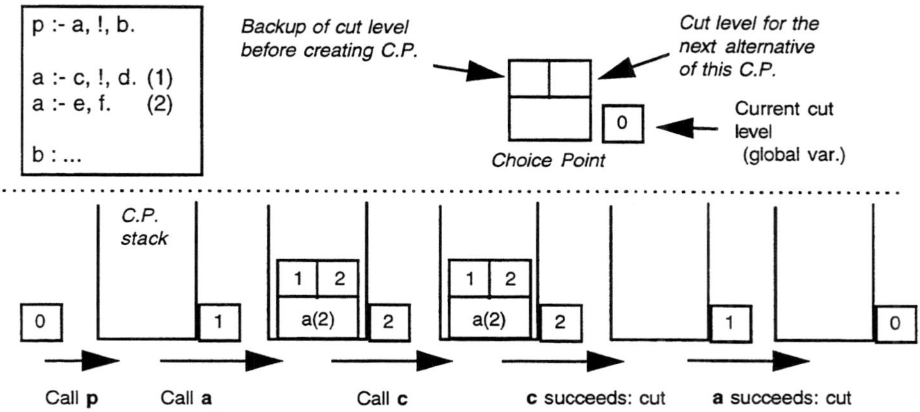

Fig. 4. Cut management with no work exported

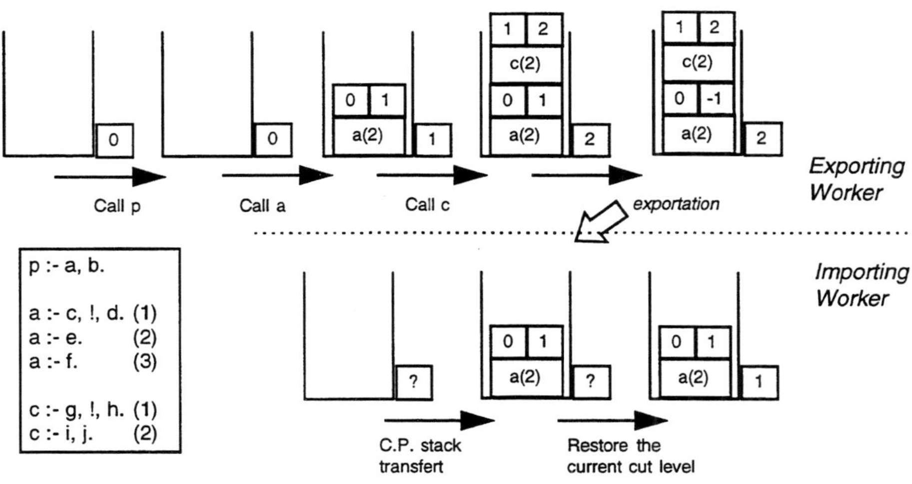

Fig. 5. Management of cuts and work exportation

to identify all the workers developing branches issued from speculative choice points. A validation message has to be sent to each of these workers before the backtracking worker can resume its work. Similarly, if a worker executes a cut, its cut management process will send an invalidation message to each worker having imported work from one of the choice points concerned by the cut (see figure 6). It may occur that a worker has exported several choice points, previously imported or developed from previously imported ones. In this case if the exporter process receives a validation/invalidation message, it must forward it to the cut management process of the importer worker. Last, if a worker receives a validation message, it must update the cut levels stored in its choice points as well as its global cut level.

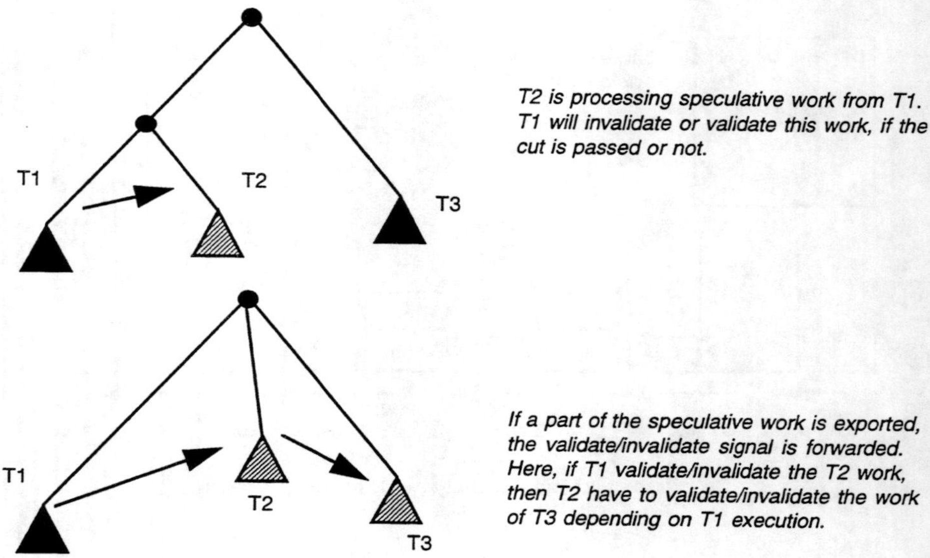

Fig. 6. Cut messages propagation

It is possible to avoid speculative work by using a "cavalier cut" [10] whose execution prunes all other solutions of a predicate. However, interactions with other side effects need to be taken into account to avoid mixing two different solution flows (see [17] for example). Another possibility is to prohibit the exportation of choice points under the scope of a cut (see a simple possible solution in section 3.5).

3.4 Inputs and Outputs management

The input case is the most simple since it is necessary, for a worker to read a data, to be left-most. The management of inputs thus amounts to a simple test to check whether the worker is left-most. If this is not the case, it will be suspended until it is notified by the scheduler that it has become left-most.

In PloSys, the inputs/outputs are managed by a dedicated server called "console" process. This process interacts between a specialised process within each worker and the outside world. A worker performs all its outputs in a local buffer. When the worker is the first one in the worker list of the scheduler (see section 3.1), outputs are transfered to the "console" process and the buffer is reset. If a worker runs out of work and it has pending outputs, these must be preserved to be placed correctly in the output flow and respect the sequential Prolog order. The worker list of the scheduler includes a special marker, associated to each output buffer containing a pending output done by a worker before becoming inactive (see figure 7). When this marker becomes the first element of the list, the scheduler notifies the inputs/outputs management process of the associated worker to perform the output. One consequence of using buffered outputs is a reduction of the amount of communications to the "console" process.

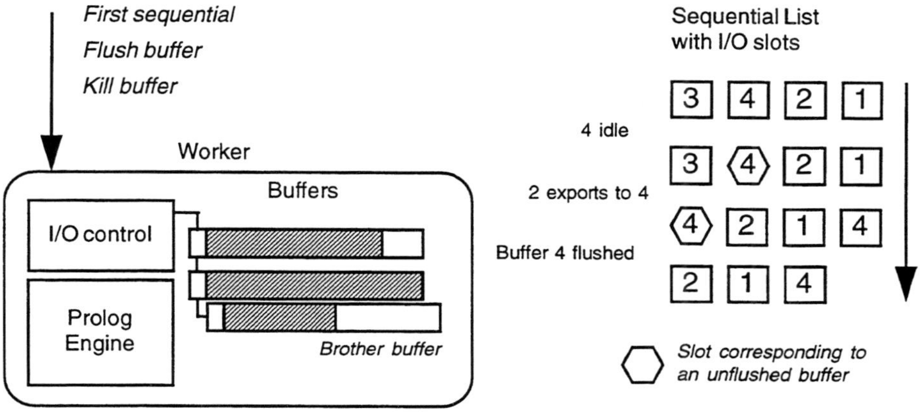

Fig. 7. Management of inputs/outputs

3.5 Influence of side effects on the scheduling

The management of side-effects as described above, introduces new constraints on the scheduling. We describe here the main solutions but there remains still a lot of experimental work to be performed.

Cut: there exist several possibilities to take into account speculative work in the scheduling [10]. The first is to make no distinction between speculative and non speculative work. Scheduling is then easier but this solution may be inefficient if a large number of workers execute speculative work which proves later unuseful. Another possiblity is to give a lower weight to speculative work in order to favor the dispatching of non-speculative work. The last possibility is to favor the allocation of work in the left part of the Prolog execution tree in order to reduce the amount of speculative work available.

Inputs/Outputs: when many workers are blocked, waiting for inputs, the scheduler should allocate work to the left of these workers. A similar situation may occur when the output buffer space of some workers is full.

4 Implementation and preliminary results

4.1 Prolog engine and parallel programming environment

A portable PloSys prototype was implemented using the *wamcc* [8] inference engine and the ATHAPASCAN [5] parallel programming library. The *wamcc* system includes a compiler which translates Prolog programs into Warren Abstract

Machine (WAM) [21] instructions and then translates WAM instructions into C. The main interest of using *wamcc* is that the inference engine is not "too" big and can thus be "easily" modified, although the amount of modifications required to implement PloSys remains limited. Another interest of *wamcc* is that it represents a good compromise between performances and portability: its performances are close to the performances of the compilers generating native code while it only requires a GCC compiler to be ported to a new target processor[5]. *wamcc* is 1.5 times faster than SICStus emulated and 1.5 times slower than SICStus "native code" .

PloSys uses also the ATHAPASCAN parallel programming library developed within the APACHE research project. In ATHAPASCAN, a parallel application is executed by a set of identical virtual processors executing asynchronously. Parallelism is triggered by blocking or non blocking remote procedure calls which hide the communication protocols used to transmit parameters and results.

4.2 Preliminary results

A PloSys prototype is partially running on workstation (SUN OS4), personnal computer (Linux) and distributed memory multiprocessor IBM SP-1.8. The benchmark results given in the sequel were obtained on this latter prototype. In the SP-1.8 prototype, inter-process communications use the Ethernet connection instead of the communication switch of the machine, for technical reasons which are out of the scope of this paper. In addition, cut and side-effects being currently tested, existing results were obtained with programs which do not use these instructions.

The overhead arising from the (limited) modifications done to *wamcc* to implement PloSys depend on the frequency of load transmission from the workers to the scheduler. It is limited to 1 % of the execution time of benchmarks if workers do not send any load information. However it may rise to 20 % if load information is transmitted every 0.1 s., because of the inefficiency of Ethernet communications and of the problems related to the use of ATHAPASCAN. In parallel, performances are good for "large" sized problems and when the number of processors is limited (see figure 8).

The use of ATHAPASCAN to implement PloSys raises a number of problems. Because of the lack of preemption and the impossibility to transmit signals, it is not possible to react rapidly to load variations and manage side-effects efficiently. Most of these problems are currently taken into account in the definition of a new version of ATHAPASCAN.

Most benchmarks used in the past to measure OR-parallel logic systems (see for example [1]), cannot be used to test PloSys because of their "too" small size: for example, it only takes 110 milliseconds to compute the whole set of solutions to the classical eight queens problem, using *wamcc* running on a 133 Mhz

[5] *wamcc* exploits the GCC possibility of generating *jumps* between functions to reduce the size of the stacks necessary to the computation.

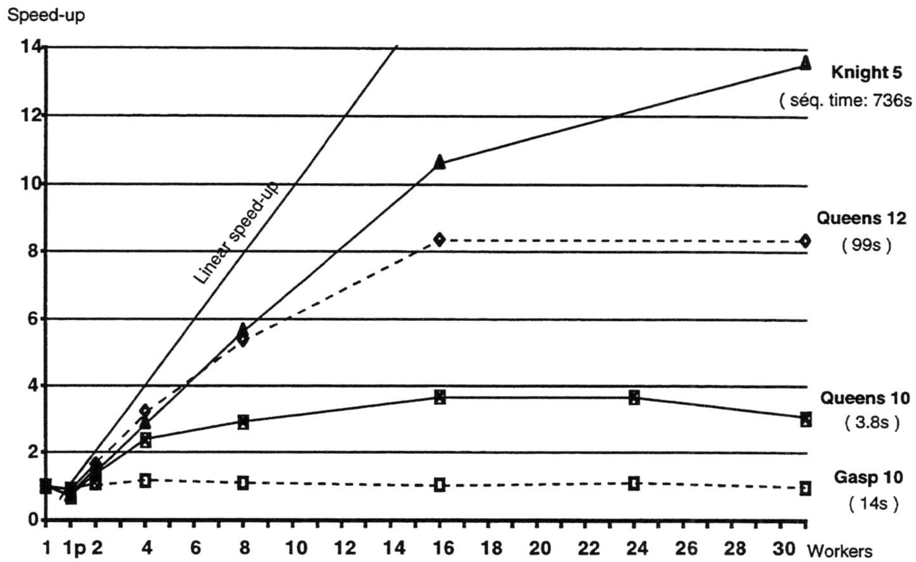

Fig. 8. Benchmark results of the PloSys SP-1.8 prototype

Pentium processor. Defining a new set of benchmarks, better suited to the performances of modern micro-processors, was undertaken jointly by LMC-IMAG and KFKI and is currently in progress.

5 Related work

The PloSys system derives directly from the OPERA system [4]. Compared to OPERA, the computational model has been simplified since some OPERA optimisations, targeted to the Supernode parallel architecture used in OPERA, cannot be used in PloSys. This is the case in particular of the possibility for workers to carry on computing while exporting work. The most important difference with respect to OPERA is the management of side effects, integrated from the design of PloSys. Other differences with OPERA come from different design decisions which favor portability and modularity in PloSys, to make experimentations and evolutions easier. The OR-parallel system of the Malaga university [3] is also multi-sequential and implemented on a distributed memory computer. However it does not yet include any side-effect.

Several computational models avoid inter-workers communications, where each worker recomputes the entire path leading from the root of the Prolog search tree to its branch. Branch allocation to workers is done either by the application of a tree exploration rule by each worker [15], or by a centralised scheduler [6]. This type of model makes it difficult to implement Prolog cut and side-effects. One solution was proposed to adapt the cavalier cut to this type of model [11].

Muse [2] is an OR-parallel logic programming system based as PloSys on copying. However, the Muse system assumes some shared memory between workers, to implement the sharing of choice points. This shared memory area is also used to manage Prolog cut and side-effects. Unlike Muse, PloSys assumes that workers do not share any memory at all. Indeed it could be interesting to adapt Muse to distributed memory architectures, using some ideas of PloSys: the shared memory area would then be managed by the centralised scheduler, while accesses to this area would be done by message exchanges between the workers and the scheduler.

A lot of work was dedicated to the implementation of Prolog cut and side-effects in Aurora [16, 10] but all solutions assume the existence of a shared memory such as in a symmetric shared memory multiprocessor including a limited number of processors. The techniques developed for Aurora seem difficult to adapt to the type of parallel systems aimed by PloSys.

6 Conclusion and future work

PloSys is an OR parallel logic programming system offering most Prolog functionalities on distributed memory parallel systems. The programming model includes a novel solution to implement cut and side effects on this type of parallel system. A PloSys prototype was implemented on network of personal computers and workstation as well as on a IBM SP-1.8.

In the short term, tuning of the prototype will be continued, in particular to test the cut and side-effects implementation and their relation with the scheduling policies. In the longer term, the prototype will be entirely distributed. The distributed scheduling algorithm will use some of the techniques developed in the LOGFLOW system [19, 12] for which there already exists an animation tool [18] that can be used to tune load-balancing strategies. Another foreseen extension is to combine constraint propagation techniques, already available in the inference engine *wamcc* [9] with OR-parallelism. Such a combination was already proven to be very effective [20].

Acknowledgements

All APACHE project research reports are available by *ftp* at *ftp.imag.fr* in the directory *pub/APACHE/RAPPORTS*.

References

1. K. A. M. Ali and R. Karlsson. The Muse Or-Parallel Prolog Model and its Performance. In Saumya Debray and Manuel Hermenegildo, editors, *Proc. of the 1990 North American Conference on Logic Programming.* MIT Press, 1990.
2. K.A.M. Ali and R. Karlsson. Full prolog and scheduling or-parallelism in muse. *International Journal of Parallel Programming*, 19(2):445–475, december 1990.

3. V. Benjumea and J.M. Troya. An or parallel prolog model for distributed memory systems. In *Programming Language Implementation and Logic Programming*, LNCS 714. Springer Verlag, August 1993.
4. J. Briat, M. Favre, C. Geyer, and J. Chassin de Kergommeaux. OPERA: OR-Parallel Prolog System on Supernode. In Kacsuk and Wise [13], chapter 3, pages 45–63.
5. M. Christaller. Athapascan-0a sur PVM3: définition et mode d'emploi. Rapport APACHE 11, IMAG, Grenoble, February 1994. Disponible sous ftp.imag.fr:imag/APACHE/RAPPORTS.
6. W.F. Clocksin and H. Alshawi. A Method for Efficiently Executing Horn Clause Programs Using Multiple Processors. *New Generation Computing*, 5:361–376, 1988.
7. J. Chassin de Kergommeaux and P. Codognet. Parallel logic programming systems. *ACM Computing Surveys*, 26(3):295–336, september 1994.
8. D. Diaz. wamcc prolog user's manual. Rr inria, INRIA-Rocquencourt, Domaine de Voluceau, 78153 Le Chesnay, July 1994.
9. D. Diaz and P. Codognet. A minimal extension of the wam for clp(fd). In *Proc. of ICLP'93, 10th International Conference on Logic Programming*, Budapest, Hungary, 1993. MIT Press.
10. B. Hausman. *Pruning and Speculative Work in OR-Parallel Prolog.* PhD thesis, Royal Institute of Technology, Stockholm, Sweden, 1990. SICS research report D-90-9001.
11. P. Kacsuk. Or-parallel prolog on distributed memory systems. In *Proc. of PARLE'94*. Springer-Verlag, 1994.
12. P. Kacsuk. Wavefront scheduling in logflow. In *Proc. of the Euromicro Workshop on Parallel and Distributed Processing*, pages 503–510. IEEE Computer Society Press, 1994.
13. Peter Kacsuk and Michael Wise, editors. *Implementations of Distributed Prolog.* John Wiley and Sons, 1992.
14. S.E. Kannat, E. Morel, J.P. Kitajima, and J. Briat. A platform to study dynamic load balancing functions for parallel logic systems. In *IEEE First International Workshop on Parallel Processing*, Bangalore - India, 1994.
15. Z. Lin. A distributed fair polling scheme applied to or-parallel logic programming. *International Journal of Parallel Programming*, 20(4), August 1992.
16. E. Lusk et al. The Aurora Or-Parallel Prolog System. In ICOT, editor, *Proc. of the International Conference on Fifth Generation Computer Systems 1988*. ICOT, 1988.

17. E.L. Lusk, S. Mudambi, Overbeek R, and P. Szeredi. Applications of the aurora parallel prolog system to computational molecular biology. In *Proc. of the JICSLP'92 Post-Conference Joint Workshop on Distributed and Parallel Implementations of Logic Programming Systems*, Washington DC, November 1992.
18. Zs. Nemeth and P. Kacsuk. Performance measuring facilities in logflow. In *Proc. of European School on Parallel Programming Environments, ESPPE'96*, Alpe d'Huez, 1996.
19. Zs. Puskas and P. Kacsuk. Distributed token scheduler for the ws-logflow. submitted to DAPSYS'96.
20. P. van Hentenryck. Parallel Constraint Satisfaction in Logic Programming: Preliminary Results of Chip within PEPSys. In *Proc. of the Sixth International Conference on Logic Programming*, pages 165–180. MIT Press, 1989.
21. D. H. D. Warren. An Abstract Prolog Instruction Set. Technical Report tn309, SRI, October 1983.

This article was processed using the LaTeX macro package with LLNCS style

Combining Scheduling Strategies in Tabled Evaluations

Juliana Freire* David S. Warren

Department of Computer Science
State University of New York at Stony Brook
Stony Brook, NY 11794-4400
{juliana,warren}@cs.sunysb.edu

Abstract. Tabled evaluations such as SLG have proven to be efficient and elegant to evaluate logic programs. Given the flexibility tabling provides in the choice of when to schedule answers, efficiency of evaluation can be further improved by choosing an appropriate scheduling strategy. Several scheduling strategies have been devised for SLG. Empiric results have shown that, even though a specific strategy might perform well in general, there may be cases where it leads to unacceptable inefficiency. Because different strategies have advantages in different situations, when addressing practical problems, one would expect a fully mature tabling system to take advantage of these different strategies within the same evaluation. In this paper we discuss the issues involved in intermixing different strategies in a tabled evaluation and describe an SLG-WAM implementation which provides engine-level support for a multiple-strategy evaluation at the predicate level.

1 Introduction

Tabled evaluations ensure termination for Datalog programs by distinguishing calls to tabled subgoals. Given several variant subgoals in an evaluation, only the first (the generator) uses program clause resolution, the rest (consumers) must perform answer resolution using answers computed by the original invocation. This use of answer resolution prevents the possibility of infinite looping for Datalog programs, which sometimes occurs in SLD. As variant subgoals can be called at different stages of the evaluation, in tabled evaluations there is an intrinsic asynchrony between the generation and consumption of answers. Given this asynchrony, implementations of tabled logic programs face an important scheduling choice not present in traditional top-down evaluation.

Experience has indicated that tabled evaluations can be highly sensitive to the scheduling strategy used. Previous work [8, 7] has shown that different scheduling strategies can radically affect memory usage, execution time, and disk access patterns. Strategies that have been evaluated in the XSB [11] system include:

* Current address: Bell Laboratories, 600 Mountain Ave., Murray Hill, NJ 07974; *juliana@research.bell-labs.com*.

- *Single Stack Scheduling* [12]: the original scheduling strategy for XSB. As the name implies, it uses a stack to control the scheduling of program and answer resolution steps.
- *Batched Scheduling* [8]: improves on Single Stack Scheduling both in running time and in memory usage.
- *Local Scheduling* [8]: has applications to non-monotonic reasoning, and it can arbitrarily improve the performance of some programs that benefit from answer subsumption, such as many aggregate computations [15] and program analyses [2].
- *Breadth-First Scheduling*: performs a breadth-first (set-at-a-time) search. Experimental results [7] have shown that Breadth-First Scheduling can efficiently evaluate queries that involve relations in external databases without incurring any significant overheads for in-memory data.

Even though a specific strategy can result in considerable speedups for some applications, for others it may add overheads or even lead to unacceptable inefficiency. Since different applications have different requirements, the ability to use multiple strategies in an evaluation is likely to be beneficial. The ideal would be to use a strategy or set of strategies that results in the best performance for a desired application. The importance of providing this kind of flexibility has been identified in deductive databases. In bottom-up systems, the search can be controlled through the use of different rewriting techniques [1]. In Aditi [14], for instance, users may specify at the predicate level not only which transformation to use, but also the evaluation algorithm (e.g., variations of semi-naive [13]).

Here, we propose combining multiple scheduling strategies in a tabled evaluation as a means to control the search and achieve the best possible performance. In the following sections, we will show how this can be realized in the context of SLG [4] and implemented in the SLG-WAM [12].

This paper is organized as follows. We start in Section 2 with a brief overview of SLG and the SLG-WAM. In Section 3 we explain how different scheduling strategies can be defined for an SLG evaluation. In Section 4, we discuss the issues involved in providing engine support for combining different scheduling strategies at the predicate level, and describe a prototype implementation of this multiple-strategy evaluation. Finally, in Section 5 we give some preliminary performance results.

2 SLG: A Brief Overview

SLG resolution is a partial deduction procedure that is sound and search space complete with respect to the well-founded partial model for all non-floundering queries. This section provides a brief (and informal) overview of SLG; for a more detailed discussion see [4].

Example 1. Consider the following program

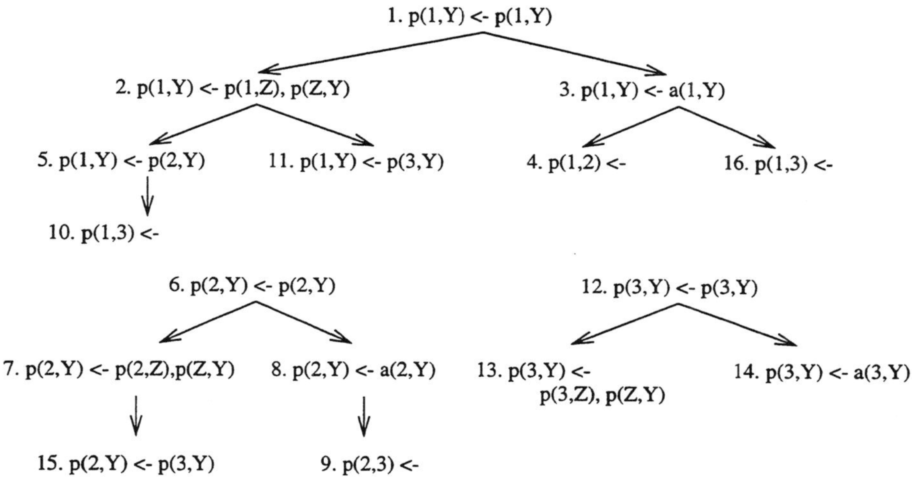

Subgoals	Answer
p(1,Y)	p(1,2), p(1,3)
p(2,Y)	p(2,3)
p(3,Y)	

Fig. 1. *An SLG evaluation*

```
:- table p/2.
a(1,2). a(2,3). a(1,3).
p(X,Y) :- p(X,Z), p(Z,Y).
p(X,Y) :- a(X,Y).
```

and the query `?- p(1,Y)`, which seeks to find all nodes in the graph defined by the relation `a/2` that are reachable from node `1`.

SLG evaluations are conveniently modeled as forests of trees as in Figure 1, which represents the transitive closure query of Example 1 at the end of its evaluation. The nodes in these trees have the form *AnswerTemplate* $\leftarrow$*GoalList*, where *AnswerTemplate* accumulates the bindings during the evaluation, and *GoalList* contains the list of literals to be resolved. Consider the operations performed by an SLG evaluation. The first time a subgoal S is encountered during a tabled evaluation, S is registered in the table, and a new tree created with root S. Figure 1 contains trees rooted at nodes `1`, `6` and `12` (we will also refer to these roots as *generator nodes*). Program clause resolution is then used to obtain the immediate children for each root node. In addition, the node calling S becomes a *consuming node*, so named because it will consume answers produced by S's tree. Alternatively, if S is not new to the evaluation (S is contained in the table), no new tree is required for S. However, a *consuming node* is still created for S as in the previous case (in Figure 1 the consuming nodes are 2, 7 and 13). Processing of answers is as follows: the first time an answer to a subgoal is derived during an evaluation it is added to the table and returned to relevant consuming subgoals; any subsequent derivations of the answer are failed. In this manner, redundant subcomputations (including loops) are prevented by tabling. Of course, tabled resolution can be mixed with the program clause resolution of SLD. In this case, we refer to tabled predicates and non-tabled predicates depending on the form of resolution used for each. In an SLG tree, nodes that correspond to non-tabled predicates are termed as *interior nodes*. In Figure 1, nodes 3, 8 and 14 are interior nodes.

In a tabled evaluation, groups of mutually dependent subgoals are called *strongly connected components* or SCCs. When all program and answer clause resolution has been performed for the subgoals in an SCC, the subgoals are termed *completely evaluated* or *completed*. At completion time, all trees for subgoals in the SCC can be disposed since at this point the table contains all answers for the subgoals. The notion of completion is necessary for evaluating programs with negation, as well as being useful for space reclamation.

To summarize, for definite programs, SLG resolution has four operations:

1. SUBGOAL CALL: creates a consuming node, and if the subgoal is not present in the evaluation a new tree for the subgoal is created.
2. PROGRAM CLAUSE RESOLUTION: used for all non-tabled (SLD) subgoals, and for immediate children of the root of each tree.
3. ANSWER CLAUSE RESOLUTION: resolves the selected literal of a consuming node against an answer from a table.
4. COMPLETION: determines when a set of subgoals is completely evaluated, and disposes of their trees.

In order to handle normal programs, SLG needs the ability to delay ground calls which are involved in negative loops. Accordingly, the notation for nodes in an SLG forest is extended. A non-root node is represented by $AnswerTemplate \leftarrow DelaySet|GoalList$, where $DelaySet$ contains a set of delayed literals. Besides, if the truth value of a delayed literal DL becomes known, the clause where DL appears needs to be simplified. Thus, besides the operations described above, SLG needs two other operations to handle programs with negation:

1. DELAY: delays negative literals involved in a negative loop.
2. SIMPLIFICATION: simplifies delayed literals whose truth values are known to be true or false.

The following example illustrates how SLG handles programs with negation.

Example 2. Consider the following program

```
:- table_all.
(C1) p(X) :- ~q(X).
(C2) q(X) :- r(X).
(C3) r(X) :- ~t(X).
(C4) t(X) :- r(X), u(X).
(C5) u(X) :- t(X).
```

and the query `?- p(a)`. Figure 2 shows the SLG evaluation of this query.

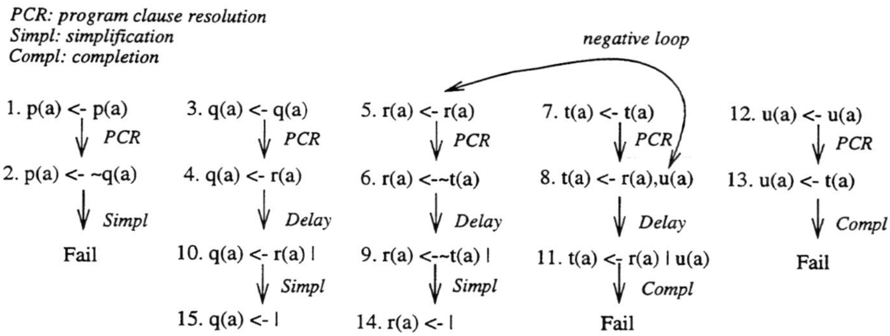

Fig. 2. *SLG evaluation of a program with negation*

Evaluation starts with the initial query in node 1 of Figure 2.[2] When `r(a)` is called in the clause for `t(a)` in node 8, a negative loop is created between `r(a)` and `t(a)`. The action of SLG is to delay any negative literal involved in a negative loop, accordingly, DELAY is applied and `~t(a)` is delayed in the clause `r(a)` $\leftarrow$ `~t(a)` | (in node 9). Since there are no more literals to be selected in that clause, node 9 becomes a *conditional answer*, that is, `r(a)` is true if `t(a)` is false. This answer can then be returned to the consuming nodes 4 and 8 (via ANSWER CLAUSE RESOLUTION). When this conditional answer is returned to the clause for `q(a)` in node 4, the literal `r(a)` is (positively) delayed and another conditional answer `q(a)` $\leftarrow$ `r(a)`| is created (in node 10); and when `r(a)` is returned to the clause for `t(a)` in node 8, the literal `r(a)` is delayed and the next literal in the clause, `u(a)` is selected (see node 11). A call to `u(a)` is made which in turn calls `t(a)` (in node 13). At this point, there is a positive loop between `u(a)` and `t(a)`. Since both subgoals have been completely evaluated and have no answers, they can be failed. Note that the answer for `r(a)` is conditional on `~t(a)`, and as at this point `t(a)` is known to be false, SIMPLIFICATION can be applied. This answer can be made unconditional by *simplifying* away the literal `~t(a)` in node 9. This step will trigger further simplification: as `r(a)` is now known to be unconditionally true, the answer `q(a)` $\leftarrow$ `r(a)`| in node 10 can also be made unconditional (i.e., q(a) succeeds); and as a consequence, in node 2, the answer `p(a)` which is conditional on `~q(a)` fails.

The SLG-WAM

The data structures and instruction set used by the SLG-WAM are described in [12]; here we briefly summarize aspects of the SLG-WAM needed to describe scheduling strategies.

---

[2] Note that the numbers in the nodes of Figure 2 reflect the order in which the nodes are created.

As mentioned above, there are several types of nodes: *generator*, *consuming*, *interior* and *answer*. Interior nodes are represented in the SLG-WAM by Prolog-style (or interior) choice points. Special choice points are used to represent generator and consuming nodes (information in the consuming choice point will be used to reconstitute the environment in which the subgoal was called, so that answers can be returned to this environment as they are derived). Using these choice points, tabling operations of are reflected more or less directly in SLG-WAM virtual machine instructions.

- TableTry: (implementing SUBGOAL CALL) If a subgoal S is already in the subgoal table, this instruction creates a *consuming choice point*. Otherwise it creates a *generator choice point* for S.
- RetryActive and AnswerReturn: (implementing ANSWER CLAUSE RESOLUTION) RetryActive resolves the selected literal of a consuming node against a set of answers present in a table, whereas AnswerReturn returns a newly created answers to a set of consuming nodes.

Answer nodes are maintained in an explicit table by the instruction NewAnswer:

- NewAnswer: This instruction checks whether an answer is in the table. If so the instruction fails, otherwise the answer is added to the table.

Two other changes must be made to the WAM [16] to support these tabling operations. To see the first change, note that children of a consuming node in one SLG tree may be derived using answers produced by other trees. Indeed, trees may be mutually dependent so that an answer in $tree_1$ is consumed by a node in $tree_2$, which allows the production of a new answer by $tree_2$ to be consumed by $tree_1$. We may thus speak of an asynchrony between the production of answers by one tree and its consumption by nodes in another. To handle this asynchrony, the SLG-WAM must be able to move back and forth between different consuming nodes. This is achieved by *freezing* the various WAM stacks at the point a new consuming node is created. In fact, the SLG-WAM keeps a *linearized* version of the search space in its stacks (similar to the cactus stacks of OR-parallel implementations such as Aurora [9]). Switching from one environment to another is performed by backtracking to a common ancestor, and then using a forward trail to reconstitute the environments of consuming nodes.

The second change arises from the need to keep a subgoal dependency graph (SDG), and thus provide incremental completion. The SLG-WAM adds a new memory area to the WAM, the *completion stack*, which (for efficiency reasons) maintains an approximation of the dependencies among subgoals. Throughout this paper we will distinguish between the SCCs of an SLG system and their (safe) approximation by the completion stack, ASCCs (approximate SCCs). Another instruction, CheckComplete is responsible for making sure subgoals are completely evaluated.

- CheckComplete: (implementing COMPLETION) This instruction uses the completion stack to determine whether a set of subgoals is completely evaluated.

An important difference between the WAM and the SLG-WAM is that the trust instruction sets a CheckComplete instruction onto the instruction field of the generator choice point, rather than disposing of the choice point as in the WAM. A CheckComplete instruction is thus not invoked until after all program clause resolution is performed for a subgoal.

3 Scheduling in SLG

SLG allows an arbitrary computation rule for selecting a literal from a rule body and an arbitrary control (scheduling) strategy for selecting transformations to apply. In our discussion we fix the literal selection (from left to right), and execute clauses in the textual order. The following example illustrates how different control strategies can be devised for SLG.

Example 3. Consider the program of Example 1 and the corresponding SLG forest in Figure 1. Let us examine the possible actions of SLG for this query. When `?- p(1,Y)` is called, the applicable SLG operations are PROGRAM CLAUSE RESOLUTION of the initial query against the two clauses for `p/2`. When the first clause is resolved, node 2 is created with selected literal `p(1,Z)`, a variant of the original query. Node 2 becomes a *consumer*. Since there are no answers for node 2, at this point the only operation left to apply is PROGRAM CLAUSE RESOLUTION of node 1 against the second clause of `p/2`, which results in the creation of node 3. Since the selected literal in node 3 is non-tabled, SLD (or program clause) resolution is used. The resolution of the first clause for `a/2` results in a new answer for `p(1,Y)` in node 4 — which makes available ANSWER CLAUSE RESOLUTION of this new answer against the selected literal of node 2. Note that at this point there is a choice of either returning the newly derived answer in node 4 to the consumer in node 2 (the action taken by Single Stack Scheduling), or resolving the next available clause for `a/2` (the action taken by Batched Scheduling).

Single Stack Scheduling schedules answers eagerly, as soon as they are created, whereas Batched Scheduling *delays* the return of answers — favoring the execution of PROGRAM CLAUSE RESOLUTION and batching the return of answers until no more program clauses are available. Different strategies have different performance behaviors. In [8] we compared implementations of Single Stack Scheduling and Batched Scheduling (for definite programs), and not only Batched Scheduling has proven to be faster, but it also uses significantly less memory than Single Stack Scheduling for a representative set of benchmarks.

Other strategies are possible. For instance, Local Scheduling can be seen as a variant of Batched Scheduling that tries to completely evaluate subgoals as soon as possible. Evaluation is done one SCC at a time: while an SCC S is not completely evaluated, Local Scheduling prevents answers from being returned to the calling environment of the *leader* of S, the subgoal in S that was first called in the evaluation. By doing this, the exact dependencies among subgoals are preserved during the evaluation. The following example illustrates the actions of Local Scheduling.

Example 4. Consider the following program

```
p(X) :- subsumes(min)(q,X),long_computation(X).
q(X) :- r(X).
q(1).
r(X) :- q(X).
r(3). r(2).
```

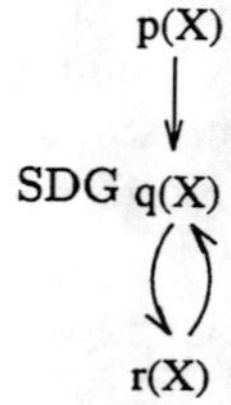

where subsumes(min) is a tabled HiLog [3] predicate that performs answer subsumption and deletes non-minimal answers every time a new answer is added to the table.[3] The subgoal dependency graph (SDG) for this program and query `:- p(X)` is depicted above. Under Local Scheduling, the SCC {`q(X), r(X)`} is completely evaluated before the minimal answer for `q(X)` (`q(1)`) is returned to `p(X)`.

If this query is evaluated under Batched Scheduling, each answer for `q(X)` (`q(3), q(2) and q(1)`) is propagated to `p(X)`, as each of them was minimal at the time it was created. As a result, *long_computation/1* is executed for `X=2` and `X=3` unnecessarily.

As can be seen from the example above, Local Scheduling can perform arbitrarily better than Batched Scheduling. Evaluating SCC by SCC, and following the exact dependencies of subgoals may be beneficial for a number of applications that use answer subsumption, such as program analyses and aggregate computations. At the SLG-WAM level, by completing subgoals as early as possible, Local Scheduling may ensue better performance: since accesses to completed tables tend to be more efficient than to non-completed ones, running times can be improved; and by early reclaiming space for completed subgoals, memory usage can be reduced as fewer frames are likely to get trapped on the stacks.

Local Scheduling can also benefit the evaluation of programs with negation. In order to avoid unnecessary delaying, the SLG-WAM needs to know the exact dependencies among subgoals so that it only delays negative literals involved in (real) loops through negation. But, as we have mentioned in Section 2, the SLG-WAM approximates the dependencies between subgoals in the completion stack. For some programs with negation, this can lead to false negative loops. So, during the CheckComplete instruction, if negative dependencies are present, the engine explicitly builds the *exact* SDG of the program to rule out false negative loops [10]. In contrast, under Local Scheduling, this step can be avoided: since SCCs are preserved during the evaluation, the completion stack keeps exact dependencies, that is, negative dependencies are only created if there are actual loops through negation. For a more detailed discussion on this issue, the reader is referred to [5].

---

[3] XSB provides an efficient implementation aggregates using HiLog syntax. For more information on these aggregate predicates, consult the XSB Manual [11].

4 Integrating Different Scheduling Strategies

In the previous section we have mentioned a number of advantages of Local Scheduling over Batched Scheduling. One might then ask: why not always use Local Scheduling? There are a couple of reasons. First of all, even though Local Scheduling may be better for "all-solutions" problems, that might not be the case when all you want is a single answer (e.g., for existential queries). The other reason stems from the cost of delaying the return of answers within an SCC in our particular implementation of the SLG-WAM. In Batched Scheduling variable bindings are shared between the calling environment and the root of an SLG tree: when a new answer is derived in the tree, its bindings are automatically propagated to the calling environment. Since Local Scheduling has to delay answers within an SCC, it cannot allow this optimization, and after the SCC is completed these delayed answers have to be *explicitly* returned, incurring extra costs to copy the answer out of the table, and also requiring extra environment switches. Thus, for programs that do not benefit from answer subsumption, Local Scheduling is likely to perform worse than Batched Scheduling. Similarly, other scheduling strategies have advantages and disadvantages in different situations, as Table 1 summarizes.

Table 1. *Advantages and disadvantages of different scheduling strategies*

Strategy	Advantages	Disadvantages
Single Stack Scheduling [12]	conceptually simple	expensive in terms of trailing and memory consumption
Batched Scheduling [8]	reduces trailing and memory consumption	requires fixpoint checks
Local Scheduling [8]	efficient for programs that benefit from answer subsumption, and for normal programs with negation	slow for existential queries, and adds overheads for programs that do not benefit from answer subsumption
Breadth-First [7]	good for accessing external relations	adds overheads for in-memory queries, and may result in high memory consumption for some programs

To fulfill the requirements and needs of different applications, we propose a hybrid strategy that combines multiple scheduling strategies in an evaluation at the predicate level. In what follows, we describe how such an evaluation can be formulated for SLG, and implemented as an extension of the SLG-WAM.

Multiple-Strategy SLG

In a multiple-strategy SLG evaluation, a scheduling strategy is defined for each predicate. In the course of evaluation, depending on the strategy defined for a subgoal, SLG operations might be scheduled at different times. In what follows we describe the main issues involved in combining scheduling strategies in an SLG evaluation. For simplicity, we restrict our discussion to Batched Scheduling and Local Scheduling.

In the previous section we introduced Local Scheduling, a strategy that evaluates one SCC at a time, following the dynamic dependencies between subgoals. Effectively, Local Scheduling can be seen as variation of Batched Scheduling that adds a barrier at each SCC leader to prevent answers from being returned out of the SCC before it is completely evaluated. Note that non-leader subgoals propagate their answers to their respective calling environments, so that the SCC they lie in can be completely evaluated.

In order to combine Local Scheduling and Batched Scheduling at the predicate level, the multiple-strategy evaluation needs to enforce the barriers at leader subgoals defined as *local*. Thus, ANSWER CLAUSE RESOLUTION for answers of a *local* leader subgoal LS against its calling environment can only be scheduled after LS's SCC is completed. On the other hand, ANSWER CLAUSE RESOLUTION for answers of any subgoal BS declared as *batched* can be scheduled to the calling environment of BS as soon as the answers are created. This distinction is evident in Algorithm 4.1, which describes the AnswerReturn[4] instruction for the multiple-strategy evaluation.

Algorithm 4.1 AnswerReturn(*answer*,*subgoal*)

If *answer* is not in the table for *subgoal*
    Add *answer* to the table;
    If the scheduling strategy for *subgoal* is Batched
        Execute the forward continuation to return *answer* to the
        calling environment of *subgoal*;
    Else if the scheduling strategy for *subgoal* is Local
        / The return of this answer is delayed until the subgoal is known*
        ** to be completely evaluated, or not to be the leader of an SCC */*
        Fail;
Else fail;

The multiple-strategy evaluation can then be thought of as a variation of Local Scheduling where sets of subgoals (SCCs or ASCCs) are evaluated under a specific strategy, the strategy defined for the leader of each set. Since SCCs

[4] The SLG-WAM AnswerReturn instruction is executed every time an answer is created.

Algorithm 4.2 Find Fixpoint(Subgoal S)

```
SchedChain = Null;
For each subgoal S' in the ASCC of S
    If S' has a consuming node with unresolved answers
        TmpSchedChain = Schedule Answers(S');
        SchedChain = SchedChain ∪ TmpSchedChain;
    If S' ≠ S
        SchedStrat(S') = Batched;
Return SchedChain;
```

are dynamic entities that may change at run-time, an issue to be considered is which actions should be taken when SCCs merge during the evaluation, and some subgoals cease to be leaders. For instance, when from within an SCC SCC_{young} a call is made to an earlier SCC SCC_{old}, these two SCCs as well as all SCCs between them are collapsed into a single SCC SCC_{new}. If an SCC SCC_{local} which was previously being evaluated under Local Scheduling is among the collapsed SCCs, its answers, which are currently being accumulated at the leader LS of SCC_{local}, must be returned to the calling environment of LS to ensure completeness of the evaluation.[5]

Algorithm 4.3 Schedule Answers(Subgoal S)

```
SchedChain = Null;
While there exists a consuming node Cons_S
whose selected literal is S
    If Cons_S has unresolved answers
        Add Cons_S to SchedChain;
If the scheduling strategy of S is Local and S is not the
leader of its SCC
    Add the generator-consuming choice point of S to SchedChain;
Return SchedChain;
```

It is during the CheckComplete operation that the SLG-WAM checks whether fixpoint has been reached, that is, if all answers have been returned to the existing consuming nodes. The fixpoint procedure is given as in Algorithm 4.2. During the fixpoint check, the engine iterates through the subgoals in the ASCC SCC_S,

[5] Note that no special actions are needed for SCCs whose leaders are defined as *batched*, as in Batched Scheduling answers are immediately propagated to the calling environments of generator nodes.

whose leader is the subgoal S, and for each subgoal S' in SCC_S it checks whether there is any available ANSWER CLAUSE RESOLUTION for the consuming nodes of S', and if that is the case, these answers are scheduled (lines 3-4). Under the multiple-strategy, besides unresolved answers for consuming nodes, the engine must schedule any answers for non-leader local subgoals (line 6-8 of the Schedule Answers procedure described in Algorithm 4.3). It is worth pointing out that all the non-leader subgoals, regardless of the strategy originally defined for them, must propagate their answers to their calling environments — effectively their strategy is set to *batched*. Thus, statically defined strategies may be overridden at run-time.[6]

A final issue to consider for the multiple-strategy evaluation is how to handle programs with negation. In a pure Local Scheduling evaluation, as exact dependencies are followed, negative dependencies are only created in the completion stack if there is a negative loop. When Local Scheduling is combined with Batched Scheduling, this property no longer holds. Therefore, when negative dependencies involve subgoals defined as *batched*, before these subgoals are delayed, checks are needed to verify whether the dependencies are indeed part of a negative loop. Accordingly, the SLG-WAM CheckComplete instruction for the multiple-strategy evaluation is defined in Algorithm 4.4.

Algorithm 4.4 CheckComplete(Subgoal S)

```
If S is the leader of an approximate SCC ASCC_S
    FixpointSchedChain = Find Fixpoint(S)
    If FixpointSchedChain is empty
        If there are negative dependencies within ASCC_S
            If SchedStrat(S) == batched
                Build the SDG for the ASCC of S;
                If the SDG has cyclic negative dependencies
                    Delay subgoals involved in negative loops;
            Else delay subgoals involved in negative loops;
        else
            Mark all subgoals in ASCC as completed;
            Reclaim stack space for the subgoals in ASCC_S;
            If SchedStrat(S) == Local
                return the answers to the generator-consuming of S
    Else backtrack to return unresolved answers;
Else backtrack to previous tabled subgoal;
```

The multiple-strategy evaluation has been implemented on top of the SLG-

[6] As an optimization, the strategy for any non-leader subgoal may be set to batched (lines 6-7 of Algorithm 4.2).

WAM of XSB. As a first approach, we provide compiler directives so that users can specify for each predicate or set of predicates which scheduling strategy to use. As we have indicated in Algorithms 4.1–4.4, dynamic tests have been added to SLG-WAM operations that take different actions according to the scheduling strategy. Given the dynamic nature of SCCs, some of these checks must be performed at run-time, but others can be compiled away. For example, the AnswerReturn instruction for a subgoal S could be specialized with respect to the scheduling strategy of S.

5 Experimental Results

In this section we compare the performance of the following engines, which differ only in the scheduling strategy used:[7]

- XSB v. 1.7: uses Batched Scheduling [8].
- XSB-Local: uses Local Scheduling [8].
- XSB-Integ: combines Batched Scheduling and Local Scheduling at the predicate level (Section 4).

We consider both execution time and memory usage of SLG-WAM engines. Benches were run on a SPARC2 with 64MB RAM under SUNOS. We will show that, even though the preliminary prototype implementation of XSB-Integ adds some overheads over the single-strategy engines, it can be arbitrarily better for some applications.

Combining Strategies

The implementation of XSB-Integ described in Section 4 incurs the cost of dynamically checking the strategies defined for subgoals at some SLG operations. In order to measure this cost, we compared the running times of XSB-Integ using Batched Scheduling as default against XSB v. 1.7, and XSB-Integ using Local Scheduling as default against XSB-Local. The bench program used was left-recursive transitive on linear chains and complete binary trees. As Figure 3 shows, for these examples the overheads of XSB-Integ range between 5 and 25%.

A question then arises as to whether it is worthwhile to combine these two strategies given the added overheads. Below we argue that: 1) even with added overheads, there are situations in which XSB-Integ can be arbitrarily better than either single-strategy engine; and 2) the overheads of the current implementation of XSB-Integ can be significantly reduced.

In Section 4 we mentioned a couple of situations where either Local Scheduling or Batched Scheduling would lead to unacceptable inefficiency, below we give concrete examples.

---

[7] XSB v. 1.7 and XSB-Local are freely available at `www.cs.sunysb.edu/~sbprolog`. XSB-Integ is available upon request.

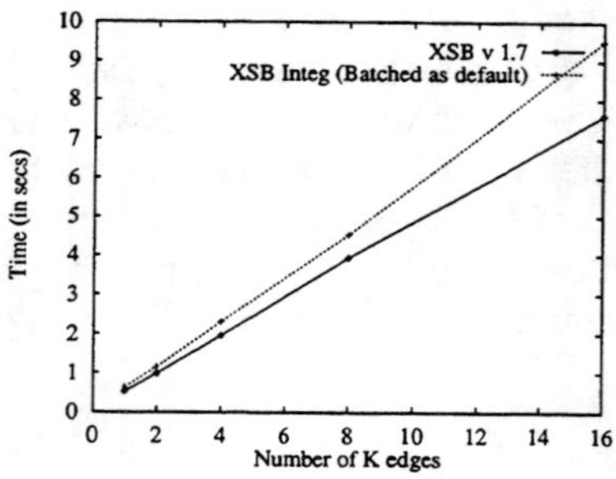

(a) Linear chains

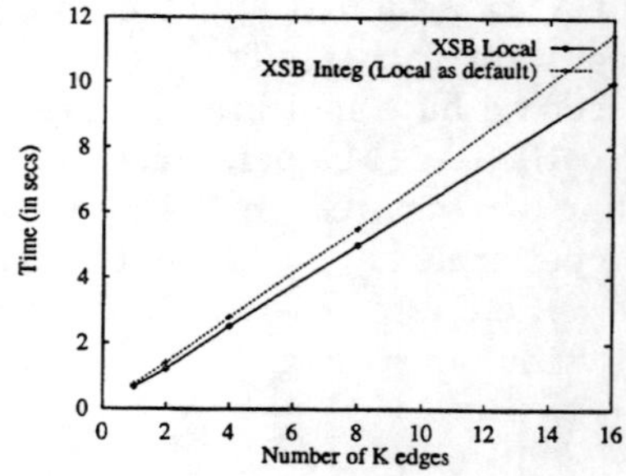

(b) Linear chains

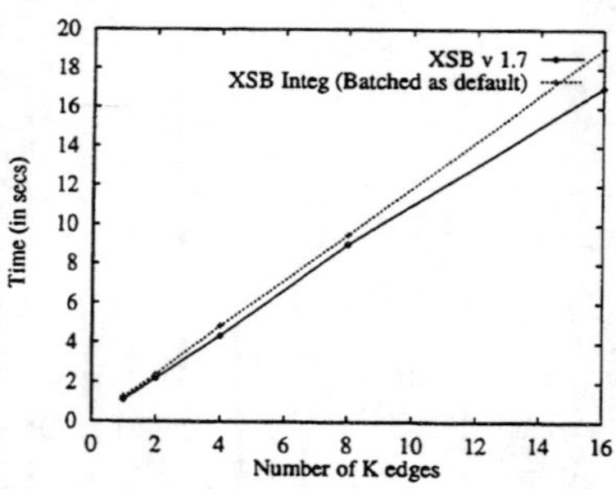

(c) Binary trees

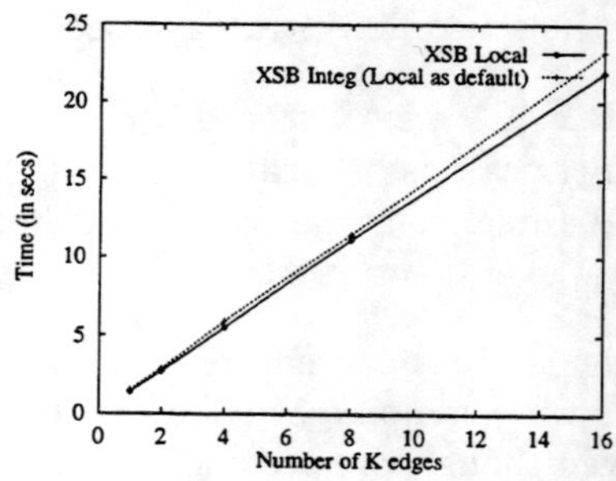

(d) Binary trees

Fig. 3. *Running times for transitive closure on chains and trees of varying size*

Example 5. Consider the following variation of the same generation program which finds the smallest distance between two people in the same generation:

```
sgi(X,Y)(I) :-
      ancestor(X,Z),
      subsumes(min)(sgi(Z,Z1),I1),
      ancestor(Y,Z1),
      I is I1+1.
sgi(X,X)(0).
```

Figure 4(b) shows the running times of XSB-Integ, XSB-Local and XSB v. 1.7 for finding the shortest-path between *n-1* and *n* for varying *n* in graphs such as the one in Figure 4(a). Note that XSB-Integ and XSB-Local perform asymptotically better than XSB v. 1.7: the times for XSB v. 1.7 vary between 0.08 and 4142.82 secs, whereas for the other two engines they vary between 0.07 and 16.21 secs.[8]

[8] Note that the times for XSB-Local and XSB-Integ are very similar in this example.

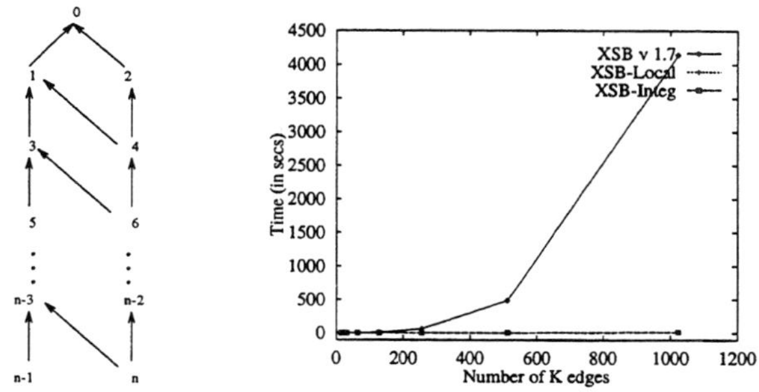

(a) (b)

Fig. 4. *(b) shows the execution time for the query* `subsumes(min)(sgi(n-1,n),I)` *on graphs of the form depicted in (a) for varying* `n`

Example 6. Given a graph, suppose we want to find out whether there exists a path between any two nodes (e.g., we issue the query `path(X,Y)`). If we use XSB-Local to answer such a query, it will compute all the existing paths before returning the first answer. Just to give an idea, for a linear chain with 1024 nodes, XSB-Local takes 63.45sec to return the first answer, whereas both XSB v. 1.7 and XSB-Integ return it *immediately* (in less than a hundredth of a second).

The examples above demonstrate that a multiple-strategy evaluation can be as efficient as its single-strategy counterparts. Now suppose there is an application where the queries from both examples are needed:

```
:- path(X,Y), subsumes(min)(sgi(n-1,n),I).
```

For this query, as the graphs grow larger, XSB-Integ can be arbitrarily better than either single-strategy engine. The times for the different engines to compute the three queries described above are given in Table 2.[9] These times indicate that a multiple-strategy evaluation can indeed be the best alternative for applications that benefit from both Local and Batched Scheduling.

Table 2. *Times (ins secs) for different engines*

	XSB-Integ	XSB v. 1.7	XSB-Local
1. `path(X,Y)`	0.001	0.001	61.909
2. `sgi(255,256,D)`	1.1	65.4	1.13
3. `path(X,Y),sgi(255,256,D)`	1.121	65.09	64.94

[9] Note that for XSB-Integ `path/2` is declared as batched and `subsumes(min)/2` as local.

6 Conclusions and Future Directions

Different scheduling strategies have been devised for SLG. Each of these strategies was shown to have specific characteristics in terms of memory usage, execution time, and disk access patterns. Even though a particular strategy can have very good performance for a certain class of applications, for others it might add overheads or even lead to unacceptable inefficiency.

In order to address this problem, we propose a multiple-strategy evaluation that combines different scheduling strategies at the predicate level, letting the user control the tabled search in order to obtain the best performance possible. As we have shown in Section 5, even though our preliminary implementation of a multiple-strategy engine adds some overheads due to dynamic checks needed to support this new strategy, it can be arbitrarily faster than its single-strategy counterparts.

It is likely that there is room for optimization in our implementation, and we intend to pursue that. We also intend to add strategy-specific SLG-WAM instructions, which combined with compile-time analysis, might reduce the current overheads even further. Another important problem we intend to investigate is the possibility of automatically inferring for each predicate the most appropriate scheduling strategy.

References

1. C. Beeri and R. Ramakrishnan. On the Power of Magic. *Journal of Logic Programming*, 10(3):255–299, 1991.
2. M. Bruynooghe. A practical framework for the abstract interpretation of logic programs. *Journal of Logic Programming*, 10:91–124, 1991.
3. W. Chen, M. Kifer, and D.S. Warren. HiLog: A foundation for higher-order logic programming. *Journal of Logic Programming*, 15(3):187–230, 1993.
4. W. Chen and D.S. Warren. Tabled Evaluation with Delaying for General Logic Programs. *JACM*, 43(1):20–74, January 1996.
5. J. Freire. *Scheduling Strategies for Evaluation of Recursive Queries over Memory and Disk-Resident Data.* PhD thesis, SUNY at Stony Brook, 1997.
6. J. Freire, T. Swift, and D.S. Warren. Beyond depth-first: Improving tabled logic programs through alternative scheduling strategies. In *8th International Symposium PLILP*, pages 243–258. Springer-Verlag, 1996.
7. J. Freire, T. Swift, and D.S. Warren. Taking I/O seriously: Resolution reconsidered for disk. In *Proceedings of the International Conference on Logic Programming (ICLP)*, pages 198–212, 1997.
8. J. Freire, T. Swift, and D.S. Warren. Beyond depth-first: Improving tabled logic programs through alternative scheduling strategies. *Journal of Functional and Logic Programming*, 1998. To appear (An earlier version appeared in [6]).
9. E. Lusk et al. The Aurora or-parallel Prolog system. In *Proceedings of the International Conference on Fifth Generation Computer Systems*, pages 819–830. ICOT, 1988.
10. K. Sagonas, T. Swift, and D.S. Warren. An abstract machine for computing the well-founded semantics. In *Proceedings of the Joint International Conference and Symposium on Logic Programming (JICSLP)*, pages 274–289, 1996.

11. K. Sagonas, T. Swift, D.S. Warren, J. Freire, and P. Rao. The XSB programmer's manual. Technical report, Department of Computer Science, State University of New York at Stony Brook, 1997. Available at http://www.cs.sunysb.edu/~sbprolog.
12. T. Swift and D.S. Warren. An Abstract Machine for SLG Resolution: Definite Programs. In *Proceedings of the International Symposium on Logic Programming (ILPS)*, pages 633–654, 1994.
13. J. Ullman. *Principles of Data and Knowledge-base Systems Vol I.* Computer Science Press, 1989.
14. J. Vaghani, K. Ramamohanarao, D.B. Kemp, Z. Somogyi, P.J. Stuckey, T.S. Leask, and J. Harland. The Aditi deductive database system. *The VLDB Journal*, 3(2):245–288, 1994.
15. A. van Gelder. Foundations of Aggregation in Deductive Databases. In *Proceedings of the International Conference on Deductive and Object-Oriented Databases (DOOD)*, pages 13–34, 1993.
16. D.H.D. Warren. An Abstract Prolog Instruction Set. Technical Report 309, SRI, 1983.

Structure Sharing and Structure Copying Revisited

Xining Li

Department of Computer Science
Lakehead University
Thunder Bay, Canada
E-mail: xli@thunder.lakeheadu.ca

Keywords

Unification, Term Representation, Abstract Machine

Abstract

Various Prolog systems can be classified into two categories: *Structure Sharing* (SS) and *Structure Copying* (SC). The fundamental distinction of SS and SC is the way of representing structures. SS represents a structure instance by a two-pointer molecule with one to the structure skeleton and the other to a binding environment. On the other hand, SC makes a concrete copy of a structure whenever the structure is matched against a variable. SS was used in earlier Prolog implementations while SC has been accepted as the *de facto* standard in modern Prolog implementations. However, analysis and practical comparison of SS and SC shown that programs can be written which make any one method almost arbitrarily worse than the other. In this paper, I propose a new Prolog implementation approach - *Program Sharing* (PS). The major contribution of this work is that PS has the advantages of both SC (representing terms of different types to fit in the size of a machine word) and SS (low overhead in constructing a dynamic structure instance), and the concept of program sharing could be used to realize all special-case instruction-driven unification. PS has been adopted in the design of a new Prolog abstract machine - the LAM$^{\frac{1}{2}}$. I have implemented an experimental LAM$^{\frac{1}{2}}$-emulator in C. Benchmarks show that this new approach is very promising in both performance and memory utilization.

1 Introduction

For more than twenty years, two very different methods - Structure Sharing (SS) and Structure Copying (SC), have been used to implement term unification in various Prolog systems. SS was first introduced by Boyer and Moore [1] and used in earlier Prolog implementations, such as DEC-10 Prolog [2] and MProlog [3]. The first report of SC implementation came from Bruynooghe [4] and has been accepted as the *de facto* standard in modern Prolog implementations. The abstract machines dedicated to Prolog, such as the WAM [5][6] and the VAM [7], adopt SC as the fundamental component to implement efficient unification. Most of the high performance Prolog systems, such as Aquarius, Parma, BIM, Quintus, SICStus and wamcc, are based on the WAM or the WAM data structure with refined instructions for further efficiency [8][9][10][11].

The principal distinction of SS and SC is the way of representing structures. SS represents a structure instance by a two-pointer molecule with one to the structure skeleton and the other to a binding environment. On the other hand, SC makes a concrete copy of a structure whenever the structure is matched against a variable. Analysis and practical comparison of SS and SC shown that programs can be written which make any one method almost arbitrarily worse than the other. In this paper, I will propose a new term representation method - *Program Sharing*. The idea of PS is originated from SS. The significant differences, however, are that PS only needs one pointer to represent a dynamic instance of a structure, and the shared resources are no longer structure skeletons but executable code. The major contribution of this work is that PS has the advantages of both SC (representing terms of different types to fit in the size of a machine word) and SS (low overhead in constructing a dynamic structure instance), and the concept of program sharing could be used to realize all special-case instruction-driven unification.

This paper is organized as follows. In section 2, I briefly compare SS and SC, revisit the principle of SS. In section 3, I present PS - its term representation, memory allocation, pair-wise instruction-driven unification - in detail. Section 4 gives a comparison of memory utilization of different methods and a brief performance analysis. The performance evaluation came from a PS-based Prolog abstract machine - LAM$^{\frac{1}{2}}$. An experimental C-emulator of the LAM$^{\frac{1}{2}}$ has been implemented. I will present the empirical results of the emulator on a small set of hand-translated benchmarks (the translator of Prolog to LAM$^{\frac{1}{2}}$ instructions is in progress). Two existing Prolog systems, SICStus 2.1 (emulated) and BIN-Prolog 3.30, have been compared under the same environment. Performance evaluation shows that the LAM$^{\frac{1}{2}}$ emulator is at least as efficient as the WAM-based systems in general while exhibits much better performance to those tasks involving large, complex data structures.

2 SC and SS Revisited

The performance and memory utilization of a Prolog system are greatly influenced by the way of how logic terms are represented. In a SC system, terms of different types fit in the size of a machine word/register. Non-structure terms can be handled quite efficiently in most cases. Their unification operations could be simplified into matches and assignments. When a variable comes to stand for a structure, however, a concrete *instance* of the structure must be created on the heap, which includes copying the ground description of the structure and allocating a heap cell for every argument in the structure. Copying a complex structure consumes not only time, but also space because superfluous memory cells must be allocated to constants and pointers to shared variables. Furthermore, SC conceals the knowledge about structures. As soon as a structure has been copied onto the heap, the information about its arity and argument types becomes indirectly accessible. Only the instance pointer can be carried around in the future unification. The efficient special term treatments are no longer applicable to a structure instance and its arguments. Therefore, when two terms to be unified are both structure instances, a general unification procedure will be invoked to carry out the stack-based full unification. This procedure forces each pair of terms to go through a sequence of unavoidable operations: push, pop, dereferencing, tag-checking and unification.

On the other hand, a SS system takes advantage of the fact that different instances of the same term could share a single prototype and differ only in their variable bindings. The cost of constructing a new structure instance is quite low: it only needs an environment allocation plus a *molecule* assignment. Why has this scheme been abandoned in the latter Prolog implementations? A major reason is that a molecule, which is used to represent a dynamic instance of a structure, consists of two components: a pointer to the skeleton of the structure together with a pointer to a global stack frame which contains the variable instances of the structure. There are three commonly used methods for handling molecules: to embed these two components in a single machine word, to allocate two machine words to each variable catering to the contingency that it might be bound to a structure instance, or to allocate a single machine word to each variable which either refers to a non-structure binding or points to a two-cell molecule created on the heap. The problems involved with these methods are that the first scheme makes it impossible to cope with large address space on 32-bit machines, the second method wastes half of the local/global space on non-structure bindings, while the third increases the usage of the global space.

Let us consider the following Prolog example:

A structure creation and unification example

```
?- p(A), q(B), A = B.
p(t(X, q(X, Y, a), Y)).
q(t(r(Z), W, f(a, b, c))).
```

The execution of the query will create two structure instances carried by variables A and B and unify A and B afterwards. Fig. 1 and Fig. 2 illustrate term representations of SC and SS, before and after A = B. In Fig. 1, two structure instances are copied onto the heap as flattened records. Each record starts with a main functor followed by an array of cells identifying its arguments. Multiple occurrences of a shared variable are equated by pointers to a self-referential cell which represents a single occurrence. Pointers to a shared variable are superfluous and increase dereferencing level. Fig. 2 gives the SS term representation by the third molecule handling method, implemented in MProlog. A molecule is represented in two successive machine words delimited by a dotted line. When a structure becomes the binding of a variable, a molecule is created on the heap and its address with a tag MRF is assigned to the variable. Each molecule is constructed by a skeleton pointer and an environment pointer. A special molecule

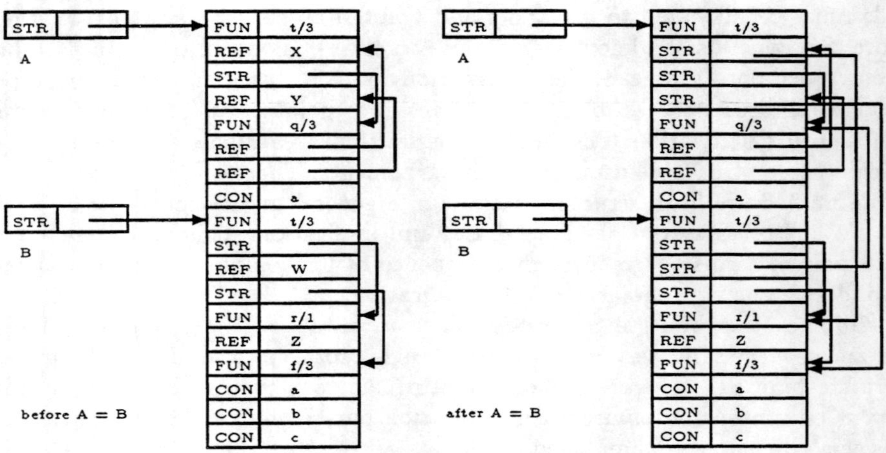

Fig. 1. Term Representations of Structure-Copying

with a nil environment pointer indicates that the structure is ground (environment independent). In addition, Fig. 2 also shows the structure skeletons in directed graphs, where *off:i* indicates the offset of the *i*th variable in its environment. For this example, SC needs 18 global cells while SS requires 14 global cells to carry out the query.

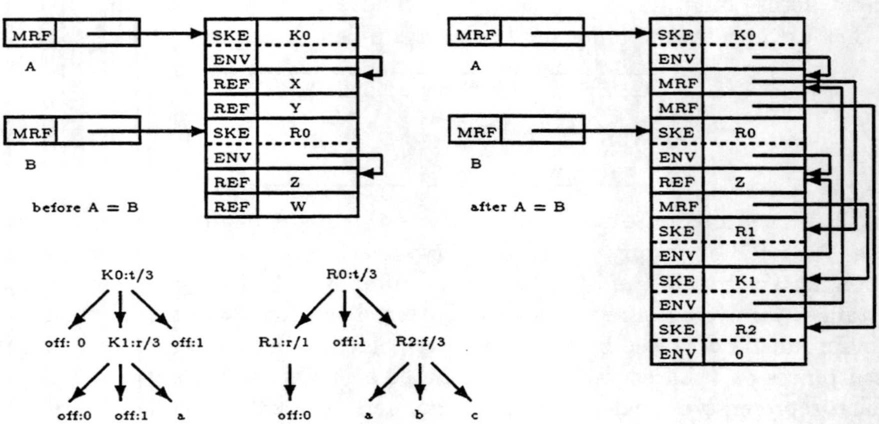

Fig. 2. Term Representations of Structure-Sharing

SC and SS have been thoroughly investigated in [13] [14]. It is faster to create terms in a SS system while it is faster to access (unify) terms in a SC system. Comparison between them shown that programs can be written which make any one method almost arbitrarily worse than the other. As Mellish remarked: "the comparison between structure sharing and its alternative is not a simple one, and no quick answer can be given as to which approach is best. It is interesting, however, that a significant factor in the decision is the relationship between the word size and address size of the machine on which the system is implemented. Unfortunately, neither of the systems discussed is optimal in its use of the local and global stacks. It remains to be seen whether mixed approach can be devised that have the advantages of both" [13]. David Warren also indicates that "Although the WAM is a distillation of a long line of experience in Prolog implementation, it is by no means the only possible point to consider in the design space. For example, whereas the WAM adopts *structure copying* to represent Prolog terms, the *structure sharing* representation used in the Marseille and DEC-10 implementation still has much to recommend it" [12].

3 Program Sharing

Prolog is a dynamic typing language in the sense that variables may hold dynamically created data objects of any type. The creation and manipulation of dynamic data objects cost both time and space during execution. For example, when a variable is unified with a complex structure, SC duplicates the whole structure no matter it is a ground or a partially ground structure. In contrast with SC, SS tries to extract static information from a structure during compilation. Consequently, the static information, *i.e.*, the structure skeleton, could be shared by all instances of the structure, if only care is taken to let them have different dynamic variables. I adopt the same idea in my proposal - Program Sharing. The significant differences, however, are that PS only needs one pointer to represent a dynamic instance of a structure, and most importantly, the shared static information is no longer structure skeletons but executable code.

With PS, a Prolog program is compiled into separate code segments for control and unification. The core of PS is the way of implementing unification. It mirrors the pair-wise term unification algorithm cost-effectively. Informally speaking, Prolog terms consists of three basic types: variable, constant and structure. Correspondingly, for a pair of given terms, its unification could be simplified into one of three basic operations: assignment, matching and structure expansion. ¿From PS point of view, there is virtually no *data* in a pure Prolog program. All terms are compiled into and handled as instructions. Like SC, PS represents terms of different types to fit the size of a machine word. Unlike SC, PS sees terms as executable instructions instead of tagged data. Unification (term) instructions have a single format: <opcode, operand>, and they are executed in pair-wise, that is, a unification operation is determined by the combination of a pair of opcodes. Let V denote a variable offset (it could be a register variable, a local variable or a global variable, however, the usage of global variable - indicated by G, is emphasized in this paper), E a memory address and C a constant,

Table 1 gives the unification instructions.

opcode	operand	meaning
VAR	V	an uninitialized variable
VAL	V	a variable's value
SCD	E	a selector†
CCD	G	a constructor
FUN	C	a functor
CON	C	a constant†
REF	E	a unbound variable‡
DCD	E	a constructor‡

Table 1: Unification Instructions

Unification instructions can be divided into two classes: static and dynamic. Static instructions are used to encode terms during compilation while dynamic instructions are constructed during execution. In Table 1, instructions marked by ‡ are dynamic instructions, by † are dynamic/static instructions, and the rest are static instructions. A dynamic instruction is one which can become the binding of a variable. Dereferencing operation terminates when a dynamic instruction is reached.

Since PS is originated from SS, they face a same question: how many structure instances will be created during execution. Here I take remarks from [3] to answer this question: " In general it is impossible to know when, and how many molecules are created - this considerably complicates the management of the global stack. We have noticed, however, that in many cases (which occur frequently in Prolog programs) it is in fact possible to know about the molecules that will be created during execution and therefore the space for molecules can be allocated during compile time. This is the case for structures appearing in head arguments in an *output* position and for all structures in call arguments."

For reasons of efficiency and minimizing memory usage, PS supports and encourages *mode declaration*. The mode information can be obtained by user-declaration or through global analysis during compilation, where the latter has become a practical tool in some high performance Prolog implementations[8][9]. Based upon the mode declaration (*in*/+, *out*/$\wedge$), structure arguments can be classified into *selectors* and *constructors*. A structure is a selector if it cannot, under any circumstances, be used to form bindings of variables outside the clause; or a constructor otherwise. A special type of constructors is the kind of statically ground structures. They are handled as selectors for a reason to be explained later. Let Ci be a constructor and Si be a selector. In compiling a clause, structure arguments are classified by the following algorithm (assume that all non-ground structures in goal arguments are constructors):

1. Scan arguments of the clause from left to right. For each structure argument, flatten the structure and identify each flattened (sub)structure by a unique name Ci;

2. Scan the flattened structures in reverse order:

i) change Ci to Si if Ci's mode is +, or

ii) change Ci to Si if Ci's arguments consist of ground terms and Sj's only.

Mapping Prolog terms to PS code is straightforward. The following is a simple example of how to generate unification code, where the offset calculation will be discussed later.

Mode: $\{\wedge\}$
Term: {f(a, g(X, h(b, j(c, d))), Y)}
Flattening: C1 = f(a, C2, Y), C2 = g(X, C3), C3 = h(b, C4), C4 = j(c, d)
Scanning: change C4 to S4, then C3 to S3; C2 and C1 remain as constructors.
Results: C1 = f(a, C2, Y), C2 = g(X, S3), S3 = h(b, S4), S4 = j(c, d).

Unification code		
P1:	FUN	f/3
	CON	a
	CCD	offset(C2)
	VAL	offset(Y)
P2:	FUN	g/2
	VAL	offset(X)
	SCD	P3
P3:	FUN	h/2
	CON	b
	SCD	P4
P4:	FUN	j/2
	CON	c
	CON	d

Selectors can be handled very efficiently in PS. A selector code is identified by an instruction <SCD, code-entry>. In general, a selector code is executed under the current environment without delay - this is guaranteed by its input mode. A special case that a selector could be carried by a variable is that the selector is a statically ground structure. To *construct* such a structure, we simply assign the selector instruction to that variable. In this case, we say that the execution of the selector is delayed. Such a selector can be carried to and invoked at any place, because its code is environment independent.

The problem of using two-cell molecules in SS is that we do need a structure skeleton pointer (structure code entry in PS), and an environment pointer for a constructor, since a constructor instance might be carried by a variable to an arbitrary place and the delayed execution of the constructor code needs to access global variables which were allocated in some environment different from the current one. How do I handle these two pieces of information without using molecules? I use a so called *constructor code stub* mechanism to solve the two-pointer problem. When a procedure is called, an integral global frame is allocated to hold global variables as well as the constructor code entries occurred in the matched clause. I call the global cell holding a constructor code entry as the constructor code stub, or just the *stub* in our latter discussion. A static constructor is identified by an instruction <CCD, stub-offset>. When a free variable is matched against a CCD instruction, it is assigned by a dynamic constructor instruction of the form <DCD, stub-address>. A stub will serve on two purposes: its address is the environment base for executing the constructor code, and its content gives the code entry. For example, if a variable's binding is a DCD instruction, then by accessing the stub we have the entry to the code segment which defines the necessary instructions for the structure unification,

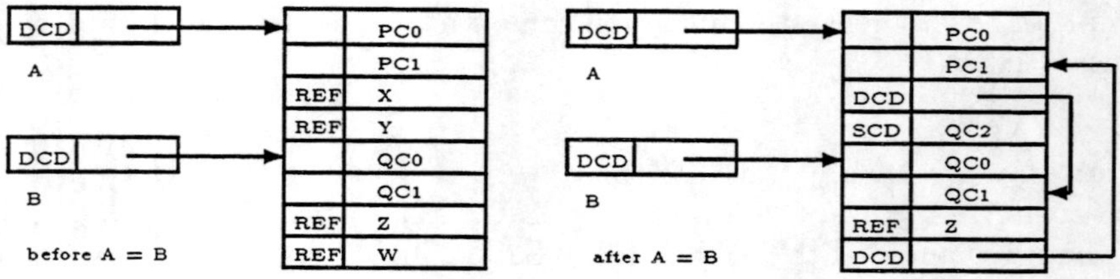


```
PC0: FUN t/3          QC0: FUN t/3
     VAL G2                CCD G1
     CCD G1                VAL G3
     VAL G3                SCD QC2
PC1: FUN q/3          QC1: FUN r/1
     VAL G1                VAL G1
     VAL G2           QC2: FUN f/3
     CON a                 CON a
                           CON b
                           CON c
```

Fig. 3. Term Representations of Program-Sharing

and by the stub-address we get the environment which will be consulted during unification to access global variables occurred in the structure.

With this setup, Fig. 3 shows the term representation of PS for the example presented in the previous section. When procedure p/1 is called by goal p(A), four global cells are allocated as an integral heap frame to hold global variables and stubs occurred in p/1, where the first two cells are initialized by stubs (PC0 and PC1) and the next two cells are unbound variables (X and Y). The execution of p/1 will assign the address of stub PC0 plus an opcode DCD to variable A. The similar behavior happens for the call of q(B). The goal of A = B thus involves four basic pair-wise operations: a functor matching and three assignments. For this example, PS requires only 8 heap cells to carry out the query, while SC and SS need 18 and 14 heap cells respectively.

In SS, variable indices are calculated against a common frame base. If a variable is allocated at the ith cell of the frame, then *off:i* will be used in all structure/substructure skeletons where this variable occurs. For example, *off:0* refers to the same variable X in both skeletons of K0 and K1. On the other hand, PS introduces a scope rule to compute the offsets of variables/stubs occurred in each code segment. Let P1, P2, ..., Pm be constructor entries and V1, V2, ..., Vn be global variables occurred in a clause, Fig. 4 shows the global frame allocated upon the invocation of the clause and illustrates the access scopes of different code segments, where the first m cells represent stubs of P1 to Pm, and the next n cells are allocated to global variables. Let G_i represent the ith frame cell against a stub address, then G_{m+1}, G_{m+2}, ..., G_{m+n} refer to V1, V2, ..., Vn in code P1, whereas G_1, G_2, ..., G_n refer to V1, V2, ..., Vn in code Pm. In other words, each constructor code segment uses the scoped index calculation to decide the offsets of its arguments. The code segments in Fig. 3 have revealed such a fact, for example, G_2 denotes variable X in PC0 whereas G_1 represents

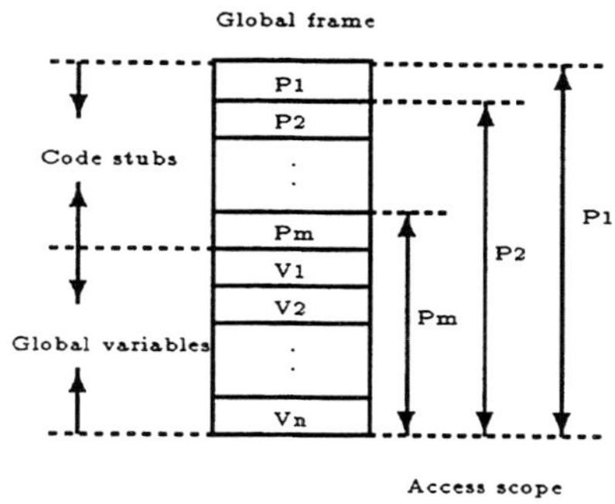

Fig. 4. Frame Allocation and Access Scope of PS

the same variable in PC1. It is worth to note that the number of stubs, global variables as well as their indices can be calculated during compilation.

To illustrate the index calculation and global frame allocation, let us examine another simple example:

Constructing a variable list

```
:- vlist(∧).
vlist([X0, X1, X2, X3]).
```

Fig. 5 shows the term representations of different schemes upon the execution of a goal *vlist(L)*. For this example, PS and SC require the same amount of heap cells to construct list L. Although it seems that SS needs fewer heap cells, three more molecules (six heap cells) will probably be created when L is accessed in the execution of successive goals. An interesting phenomenon in PS representation is that the code labeled by P0 is shared by three stubs. This is because the first three flattened lists, *i.e.*, C0 = [X0, C1], C1 =[X1, C2], and C2 =[X2, C3], happen to use the same instructions and the same (scoped) indices to encode their arguments. Sharing a code pattern is not just on rare occasions in PS, and is of benefits to code locality.

4 Memory Utilization and Performance Analysis

It is certain that both PS and SS consume less local space than SC, this has been discussed by [13]. As regards global space utilization, PS is clearly better than SS, because it uses one-cell stubs to replace two-cell molecules. Now, I will compare the global space utilization of PS and SC by two typical examples.

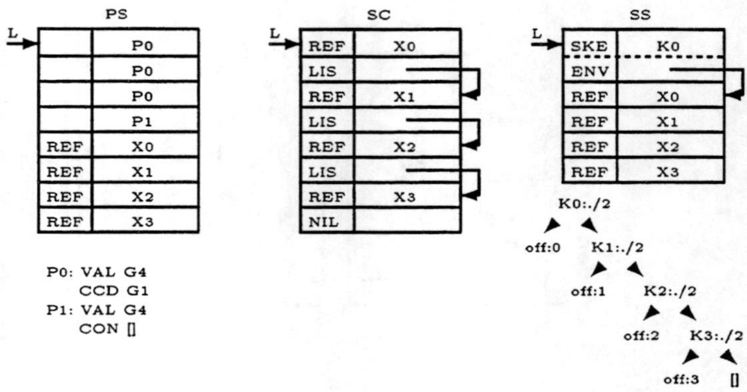

Fig. 5. Variable List Representations of PS, SC and SS

A worst case example of SC

```
?- construct([k1, k2, ...], L).
:- construct(+, ∧).
construct([], []).
construct([K|T], [G|L]):- record(K, G), construct(T, L).
:- record(+, ∧).
record(k1, f(a1, a2, a3, a4, a5)).
record(k2, f(b1, b2, b3, b4, b5)).
....
```

The first example collects a list of records from a database through a list of given keys. On this example, PS will gain by arbitrary amounts. Suppose that the total number of records to be collected is N, then PS will use $3 * N$ global space to construct the record list, where N cells for stubs and $2 * N$ cells for global variable instances extracted from [G|L]. On the other hand, SC will use $2 * N + (5 + 1) * N + 2 * N$ global cells where the first $2 * N$ for the record list, $(5 + 1) * N$ for N records and the last $2 * N$ for constructing the input key list. If the arity of the database records is an arbitrary M instead of 5, SC will use $(M + 2) * N$ more heap cells than PS for this particular example.

A worst case example of PS

```
?- nreverse(L, [1,2,3,4,5,6,7,8,9,10,11,12,13,14,15,16,
        17,18,19,20,21,22,23,24,25,26,27,28,29,30]).
:- nreverse(∧, +).
nreverse(L, [X|L0]) :- nreverse(L1, L0), concatenate([X], L, L1).
nreverse([], []).
:- concatenate(_, ∧, +).
concatenate(L1, [X|L2], [X|L3]) :- concatenate(L1,L2,L3).
concatenate(L, L, []).
```

By running the second example, we found that nreverse/2 is called 30 times and concatenate/3 is called 435 times. PS uses 2 cells to construct an instance of [X] (one for a stub and another for X), and 3 cells to construct an instance of [X|L2]. The total amount of heap cells consumed by PS is $435*3+30*2 = 1365$. SC also needs 2 cells for each [X] (X and []), but only 2 cells for each [X|L2]. Furthermore, SC requires additional $30*2$ cells for constructing the input integer list. Thus the total is $435*2+30*2+30*2 = 990$.

For a given Prolog program, the number of structure instances to be created in execution is somehow independent of term representation methods (assuming mode analysis as a practical tool). However, different term representation methods require a variable amount of global space for constructing an individual instance. In general, to construct a structure instance $\mathcal{T}$ of the form $f(T_1, T_2, ..., T_m)$, the global cells required by PS and SC are shown in Table 2.

	selector($\mathcal{T}$)	constructor($\mathcal{T}$)	constructor($\mathcal{T}$ == [X|L])
SC	$m+1$	$m+1$	2
PS	0	$\leq m+1$	3

Table 2: Global cells required in constructing a structure instance

If $\mathcal{T}$ is a constructor, it must contain variable arguments. However, it is possible that some of T_i's are ground terms and some are repeated variables, thus the global cells required by PS is less than or equal to $m+1$. We use $m+1$ to indicate the number of global cells, the 1 in SC represents the cell allocated to the functor of $\mathcal{T}$ whereas in PS it represents the cell assigned to the stub of $\mathcal{T}$. The worst case of PS is to construct a list structure of the form [X|L]. Three cells are needed where one cell for its stub and two cells for X and L. An interesting point is that if SC did not offer a special treatment to a list structure (different tags are used to distinguish structures and lists such that a list is constructed as a special structure without a main functor), then it should also need three cells for creating an instance of [X|L]. ¿From this analysis, we conclude that PS will take no more than 1.5 times of global space as much as SC in the worst case whereas SC will lose by arbitrary amounts in its worst case.

PS not only bridges the gap between SS and SC, but also provides a novel basis for designing new Prolog abstract machine. The LAM$^{\frac{1}{2}}$ is a PS-based Prolog abstract machine (space limit does allow a detailed discussion). I have implemented a LAM$^{\frac{1}{2}}$ C-emulator which copes with a small set of builtin predicates and without stack overflow checking. The LAM$^{\frac{1}{2}}$ emulator is compiled using gcc 2.7.2 with the -O option. Timings of a small set of hand-translated benchmarks are in millisecond measured on a SUN SPARC IPC with 8 megabytes of memory. Table 3 gives the LAM$^{\frac{1}{2}}$ benchmark statistics which include the number of logic inferences (procedure calls), control instructions and unification instruction-pairs executed, average instructions per logic inference, maximum global and local space (words) consumed, execution time and KLIPS. Table 4 compares the performances of the LAM$^{\frac{1}{2}}$ emulator, SICStus 2.1 (emulated) and BIN-Prolog 3.30.

	nrev30	qsort50	tak(18,10,6)	queen8	serialise	mu	puzzle	zebra
Logic Inferences	496	373	8889	1680	227	605	4693	15708
C-instructions	1550	2331	75556	12219	1530	4036	25709	80828
U-Instr-pairs	2475	2069	35556	9252	2706	6055	48542	247403
Instr-per-LI	8.11	11.8	12.5	12.8	18.7	16.7	15.8	20.1
Max global	1365	816	0	89	364	84	258	35
Max local	215	59	201	147	549	119	502	168
Execution time(ms)	3.67	3.85	121	19.3	4.43	11.36	80.0	332
KLIPS	135	97	73	87	51	53	58	47

Table 3: LAM$^{\frac{1}{2}}$ Benchmark Statistics

	nrev30	qsort50	tak(18,10,6)	queen8	serialise	mu	puzzle	zebra
LAM	3.67	3.85	121	19.3	4.43	11.36	80	332
SIC	4.00	7.00	241	35.2	5.68	9.80	140	551
BIN	5.50	8.00	250	37.0	7.50	12.16	140	700

Table 4: Performance Comparison

Here I should point out that my experimental results only give a rough performance evaluation. First, the LAM$^{\frac{1}{2}}$ emulator is not a complete system. It does not perform stack-overflow checking. Adding this function could influence the empirical results. However, an idea proposed by [11] suggests to use UNIX memory manager to raise an exception signal in case of stack overflow, and therefore eliminates costly software tests. Secondly, benchmarks are small and hand-translated with optimizations based on annotated mode. This is unfair towards the compared systems because mode information helps to generate better code. Despite these factors, the performance evaluation suggests that the LAM$^{\frac{1}{2}}$ emulator is as efficient as the WAM-based systems in general while exhibits much better performance to those tasks involving large, complex data structures.

As evidenced by our discussion, to create a structure instance in execution, SC turns static information to dynamic; SS maintains static information but involves great overhead for handling molecules; whereas PS takes the advantages of both SC and SS, *i.e.*, it makes logic terms to fit the size of a machine word, represents static/dynamic terms as bytecode instructions and spends much less overhead for handling dynamics. PS is very promising in memory utilization and reasonably close to very good SC-based systems in performance.

5 Conclusion

In this paper, I have briefly compared two commonly used term representation methods in implementing Prolog, and proposed a new approach - Program Sharing. The major contribution of this research is that PS has the advantages of both SC (representing data object in a single machine word) and SS (low overhead in constructing a dynamic structure instance). PS could be viewed as a superior alternative to SC and SS in implementing high performance logic programming systems.

Based on PS, a Prolog abstract machine - the LAM$^{\frac{1}{2}}$ has been designed. Generally speaking, a Prolog program is translated into a set of LAM$^{\frac{1}{2}}$ code which specify the control and unification. The control instructions similar to the WAM's counterpart, however, unification instructions are defined and implemented in a totally different style. All terms are compiled into and handled as executable instructions. Dynamic objects stored in execution environment (local stack and global stack) are no longer tagged data but either directly executable unification instructions or code segment entries. Unification is purely pair-wise instruction driven. Performance evaluation shows that this new approach is very promising in both time and space utilization, especially for applications which intensively access structured database and manipulate large, complex data structures.

Study on this subject is now being concentrated on the refinement of the instruction set, completing the emulator to cope with full Prolog, and the design of a LAM$^{\frac{1}{2}}$-based compiler. Next, due to efficiency consideration, most Prolog implementations perform unification without the occur-check. I have found that the LAM$^{\frac{1}{2}}$ behaves with respect to occur-check similar to the extended WAM of [15] with no or reduced efforts on occur-check. Strategies for this problem are under investigation. Finally and most importantly, as the LAM$^{\frac{1}{2}}$ uses a different heap-allocation scheme, the traditional garbage collection algorithms [16][17] do not always allow an optimal compaction of the heap. A new algorithm which I called the *Chronological Garbage Collection* has been developed and is under testing.

Acknowledgments

I would like to express my appreciation to the Natural Science and Engineering Council of Canada for supporting this research. Thanks to anonymous referees for valuable comments and suggestions. Special thanks to Dr. Bart Demoen for providing benchmark statistics with SICStus.

References

1. R. S. Boyer and J. S. Moore. The Sharing of Structure in Theorem Proving Programs. *Machine Intelligence 7 (B. Meltzer and D. Miche, eds.)*, Edinburgh University Press, 1972, pp. 101-116.
2. D. H. D. Warren. Logic Programming and Compiler Writing. *Technique Report: DAI 44, University of Edinburgh*, 1977.
3. Z. Farkas, P. Koves and P. Szeredi. MProlog: An Implementation Overview. *Implementations of Logic Programming Systems, Kluwer Academic Publishers*, 1994, pp. 103-117.
4. M. Bruynooghe. An Interpreter for Predicate Programs: Part 1. *Technique Report CW 16*, Katholieke Universiteit Leuven, 1976.
5. D. H. D. Warren. An Abstract Prolog Instruction Set. *Technical Note 209*, SIR International, 1983.
6. H. Ait-Kaci. Warren's Abstract Machine: a Tutorial Reconstruction. *MIT Press*, 1991.
7. A. Krall and U. Neumerkel. The Vienna Abstract Machine. In *PLILP'90, LNCS. Springer*, 1990.

8. P. Van Roy and A. M. Despain. High-Performance Logic Programming with the Aquarius Prolog Compiler. *IEEE Computer*, Vol. 25, No. 1, 1992, pp. 54-68.
9. A. Taylor. LIPS on a MIPS: Results from a Prolog compiler to RISC. In *6th ICLP, MIT Press, Cambridge* , 1990, pp. 174-185.
10. E. Tick and G. Succi. Implementations of Logic Programming Systems. *Kluwer Academic Publishers*, 1994.
11. P. Codognet and D. Diaz. wamcc: Compiling Prolog to C. *PLILP'95, The MIT Press*, 1995.
12. D. H. D. Warren. Foreword in *Warren's Abstract Machine: a Tutorial Reconstruction. MIT Press*, 1991, pp. xiii-xiv.
13. C. S. Mellish. An Alternative to Structure Sharing in the Implementation of a Prolog Interpreter. *Logic Programming, Academic Press*, 1982.
14. M. Bruynooghe. The Memory Management of Prolog Implementations. *Logic Programming, Academic Press*, 1982.
15. Beer, J., The Occur-Check Problem Revisited, *J. Logic Programming 5(3)*, 1988, pp. 243-261.
16. Bruynooghe, M., Garbage Collection in Prolog Interpreters, *Implementation of Prolog, Ellis Horwood Ltd.*, 1984, pp. 259-267.
17. Jones, R. and Lins, R., Garbage Collection: Algorithms for Automatic Dynamic Memory Management, *John Wiley and Sons.*, 1996.

This article was processed using the LaTeX macro package with LLNCS style

A Static Implementation of the Basic Andorra Model for Distributed Memory Systems*

V. Benjumea J.M. Troya
{vicente,troya}@lcc.uma.es

Dpt. Lenguajes y Ciencias Computación
Universidad de Málaga
Spain

Abstract. The paper shows an implementation model to support the execution of the Basic Andorra Model on distributed memory systems. A model for exploiting dependent AND parallelism in Prolog programs on distributed systems is also proposed, as well as the way in which it has to be combined with an OR parallel model. A mechanism for dealing with unbound variables in a distributed environment is proposed. In the current implementation, the arrangement of workers in the system in order to mix both models is done in a static way at the beginning of computation.

Keywords: Distributed Systems, Parallelism, Logic Programming, Andorra Model.

1 Introduction

The exploitation of parallelism in Prolog programs has been studied for the last years. Many models have been proposed in order to exploit OR parallelism [15, 20], independent AND parallelism [7, 11], dependent AND parallelism [5, 18, 19], and combinations among them [3, 10, 12]. However, most of them are focused on shared memory systems, but only a few of them have been oriented towards distributed memory systems [1, 2, 4, 13]. Nevertheless, distributed memory systems are becoming more and more important in modern parallel systems.

The Basic Andorra model [16, 17] modifies the Prolog execution model in order to transparently exploit OR parallelism combined with dependent AND parallelism. The latter has been the basis on which committed-choice languages [5, 18, 19] have been developed, thus providing a natural way of combining Prolog with this kind of languages.

In this paper we present model to support the implementation of the Basic Andorra Model on distributed memory systems. We also propose a model for the exploitation of dependent AND parallelism in Prolog programs on distributed memory systems, on which our implementation of the Basic Andorra Model is

* This work was supported by the project CICYT-TIC 340/90

based. The OR parallel model for distributed systems is based on the model proposed in [4], therefore, and due to space limitations, it will not be explained here. At this stage of development, the arrangement of workers in the combination of both models is achieved in a static way in order to exploit both kinds of parallelism. That is, processors in the distributed system are arranged in a fixed way at the beginning of computation, and they are coordinated in order to exploit both kinds of parallelism. Moreover, side-effects predicates are not supported in the current implementation.

The problem that arises when dealing with unbound variables in parallel execution is addressed. Moreover, a mechanism for dealing with such an unbound variables in parallel computations, and more precisely in distributed environments is also proposed. This mechanism is defined as an extension to the Basic Andorra execution model (it is embedded in it), besides an extension to the Foster's *distributed unification scheme* [9] in order to deal with unbound variables in distributed systems, making it more suitable for our extension of the Basic Andorra execution model.

The paper is organized as follows. Section 2 shows the model on which the combination of both kinds of parallelism is made possible. Section 3 explains the model on which we have based the exploitation of dependent AND parallelism. The model is divided into a model for supporting determinacy detection and goal suspension in sequential Prolog, and a model for parallelizing suspended goals in a distributed environment. Section 4 presents how the AND parallel model and the OR parallel model can be combined. Section 5 analyzes the proposed model.

2 The Basic Andorra Model

The Basic Andorra model [16, 17] arises as an alternative to the Prolog execution model in order to be able to exploit dependent AND parallelism in addition to the intrinsic OR parallelism in Prolog programs. OR parallelism arises in a natural way in the Prolog execution model, since a Prolog program normally defines several alternative paths to be traversed, and during the traversing of a determinate path, some information will be recorded in order to be able to traverse different paths at later stages. It is the traversing of the different alternative paths defined by a Prolog program that makes the exploitation of OR parallelism possible by allowing different *workers*[2] to traverse different paths in parallel.

However, exploitation of dependent AND parallelism is a lot more difficult to manage in Prolog execution. Thus, the Basic Andorra model was proposed to solve this drawback by modifying the Prolog execution order. The Basic Andorra execution model defines two different phases in which Prolog goals are executed. In the *deterministic phase*, execution of non-deterministic goals[3] is suspended and only deterministic goals[4] are executed. It can happen that due

[2] A worker is an entity able to achieve a task.

[3] A non-deterministic goal is such that matches with several clauses.

[4] A deterministic goal is such that matches just with one clause.

to the execution of deterministic goals, some goals that were suspended because of their non-determinacy, now become deterministic, and so, their execution will be resumed within this phase. When all the deterministic goals have been executed, i.e. each suspended goal is non-deterministic, a non-deterministic goal will be selected, according to the Prolog execution order, to be reduced within the *non-deterministic phase.* It will start a new *deterministic phase* where new deterministic goals will be reduced, and so on. The alternating of both phases will go on until the end of computation when all goals have been reduced.

It is during the *deterministic phase*, when dependent AND parallelism can be exploited, since executed goals are deterministic and just one flow of data exists. Therefore, those goals can be executed in any order, and even in parallel, being synchronized by the flow of data.

During the *non-deterministic phase*, a non-deterministic goal will be executed, which will create a choice-point that will make it possible to restart the computation state at that point in order to follow a different alternative path at a later stage. These choice-points are the key points in the exploitation of OR parallelism, since they define different alternative paths that can be traversed in parallel by different workers.

3 Dependent AND Parallelism Exploitation of Prolog Programs in Distributed Systems

In this section we will look at some general concepts related to the exploitation of *dependent AND parallelism* in distributed systems. Thus, *dependent AND parallelism* is characterized by small grain task creation, which is not a great drawback in shared memory systems. However, in distributed systems this becomes an important source of inefficiency, due principally to the high cost of remote task creation in relation to its small lifetime. This fact justifies one of our main design goals, to increase the parallel task granularity.

The other main design goal consists on achieving a suitable and efficient sharing of work. In order to get this, not every parallel task has to be shared out, but we try to keep all workers working for as long as possible with the least amount of task sharing as possible, favoring in this way local work and therefore decreasing the accesses to remote data, which is another important source of inefficiency.

3.1 Goal Suspension in Sequential Prolog

Goal suspension is the key point that supports the exploitation of AND parallelism in the Andorra model. It modifies the WAM execution model to allow the postponement of some goals to be executed at a later stage. This goal postponement can be due to two main reasons. In order to support the Andorra model, which firstly executes deterministic goals and postpones the non-deterministic ones, the execution of goals that have not been proved to be deterministic will be suspended[5], and they will be executed when no deterministic goal remains available. The second reason for goal postponement consists in dividing the computation in smaller parts, this is achieved by avoiding the execution of some suitable goals at the time they should be executed, suspending them for a later execution. This suspension of goals can be seen as the creation of work, which will be carried out later at a convenient stage (or it could be shared with another *worker* to exploit AND parallelism). Thus, the resolution of a Prolog program can be roughly seen as the execution of an initial work that can create more work (deterministic and non-deterministic), which will be executed when the current work has been carried out. Part of the created work will be selected for execution, which could create more work, and so on. The computation will finish when the current work has been carried out and no work remains to be executed.

However, in general, the suspension of goals degrades the performance of the efficient sequential WAM execution model (an exception to the rule consists in the reduction of the search space, which will be described below), therefore it should be only used in cases where creation of work could be useful, such as the exploitation of AND parallelism where created work can be shared between system workers. Due to the degradation of the system performance, the work division has to be done carefully trying to keep as much of the original sequential WAM execution of goals as possible, increasing so the task granularity.

Checking for Determinacy The Basic Andorra Model relies in the fact that deterministic goals are executed before the non-deterministic ones. Thus, the first thing we have to do is to distinguish, in a Prolog program, which goals are deterministic, and which ones are non-deterministic. However, this feature, most cases, can not be detected completely at compile-time, therefore, in order to minimize the overhead that introduces, most of analysis will be done at compile-time and it will left the execution of small tests to run-time. Therefore, the WAM instruction set has to be extended to support run-time checking to detect deterministic goals. Thus, during compilation of a Prolog program, in addition to the WAM code, code for "goal determinacy checking" and "guards" will be generated by the determinacy analyzer. So, during the execution of a goal, it will be taken as deterministic if the checking code proves it, otherwise the goal will be taken as non-deterministic (although it can be taken as a deterministic goal later, if proved).

Execution of deterministic goals earlier than non-deterministic ones brings about a possible reduction of the search space with respect to the Prolog left-to-right execution order, since some failures can be detected earlier, pruning branches in the search space, this feature is an important speed-up factor for suitable Prolog programs.

Creating Work The basic Andorra model support relies in the suspension of non-deterministic goals and their later execution as it was seen in the latter section (Sect. 3.1). However, if we want to improve the performance of our system

[5] A goal is suspended by storing enough information to allow its later execution.

by sharing the computation between system workers, we need a way to divide this computation in parts suitable for sharing. Thus, suspension of goals (deterministic and non-deterministic) is the used mechanism to divide the work in smaller parts suitable for sharing. However, our system is focused on exploiting parallelism in distributed memory systems, where remote task creation is expensive, therefore remote task lifetime have to be big enough to make its sharing worthy, so we can not make a correspondence between a goal and a task as JAM [6] can, but a task will be rooted in a goal, and it will comprise all computation deriving from that goal, unless such a work is divided. Thus, a task is a partial resolution, following the sequential WAM execution model, of a goal. We say partial because this sequential execution can create more tasks by suspending some goals. Though our system tries to follow the sequential WAM execution model as close as possible to support the Basic Andorra Model. This creation of tasks can be led by program analysis [14] or by user annotations.

The Execution Model In order to support the Basic Andorra Model, The WAM sequential execution model has been modified to have two main phases, which alternate each other until the end of computation. The first phase is the *deterministic phase*, which follows a sequential execution, including determinacy checking code, of involved goals (a task). If during this phase a goal can not be proved to be deterministic, it will be suspended. Moreover, a goal can be suspended, too, as a consequence of a sequence breaking instruction (Sect. 3.1). When the current task has finished, another task will be selected for execution. This selection will be achieved within a sub-phase where a deterministic task (a deterministic goal points to a deterministic task) will be searched. Therefore, within this sub-phase, deterministic checking code of goals is executed to know whether some available goal is deterministic. Found non-deterministic goals are suspended again, the first found deterministic goal is selected to be the current task and its sequential execution is started within the *deterministic phase*. When the current task execution has finished and no deterministic task can be found, which means that there is no deterministic goal available in the system, then the system falls into the second phase (the *non-deterministic phase*), where a non-deterministic goal, according to the Prolog execution order, will be selected for non-deterministic execution. If there is no non-deterministic goal available when it has to be selected, then a solution for the initial query will have been found. When a non-deterministic goal is executed in the non-deterministic phase, it creates the correspondent *choice-point* and the phase changes to the *deterministic phase*.

Backtracking Support This section will explain the extensions to the WAM backtracking mechanism in order to support the suspension of goals and the two execution phases in sequential Prolog.

The main change is with respect to the logic variable unique assignation property, which externally remains unaltered, but internally, variables, goal record fields, etc. now hold many different values depending on the computation path.

The WAM trail mechanism is based on the unique assignation property, where it is only necessary to keep the addresses of conditionally bound variables[6] in order to unbind them when backtracking occurs. In our model, whenever an object is bound for the first time, the trail mechanism acts like in WAM, but if the object is bound again to new values, the trail mechanism is modified by storing the object old value and its address in a new area (*Trail_Values*). Thus to restore the object values to a determinate state of computation, the untrailing mechanism is modified to use this information.

Dealing with Unbound Variables As it was explained in Sect. 3.1, when the determinacy of a goal depends on the value of some variables, and any of them is unbound, then the goal is suspended. The same behavior can be applied to built-in predicates. However, sometimes, determinacy of a goal depends on the fact that a variable is unbound, so let us take a look at the following code inspired by [21]:

```
1.1) send_msg(M, Msg) :- var(M), !, M = [Msg|_].
1.2) send_msg([_|M], Msg) :- send_msg(M, Msg).

2.1) get_word(W, [], []) :- !, W = [].
2.2) get_word(W, [X|Rest], Rest) :- X == ' ', !, W = [].
2.3) get_word([X|W], [X|T], Rest) :- X \== ' ', !,
                                      get_word(W, T, Rest).
```

In this example, the *'send_msg/2'* predicate will be always deterministic, thus if the first argument is "unbound" the first clause will be selected, and otherwise the second one. With respect to the *'get_word/3'* predicate, if the second argument is unbound, its determinacy can not be proved, but if it is bound, then the predicate will be deterministic, choosing the first clause if it is bound to the empty list, the second one if it is bound to a list which head is bound to the space (' ') and the third one if it is bound to a list which head is "unbound" or is bound to anything different from space.

In such cases, if the execution order is fixed (like in Prolog), the program will have a known behavior, but if the execution order is not fixed (like in Andorra during the *deterministic phase*) the program will have an unpredictable and non-deterministic behavior. Moreover, in parallel executions, results can be worse.

This problem seems reasonable since if a clause has to be selected depending on the value of a variable, or even if the variable is unbound, and there is no a strict execution order, the time when the variable gets bound will affect to the computation. Thus, this execution model has a non-deterministic behavior in case of dealing with unbound variables.

Andorra-I [17] overcomes this problem by mean of its preprocessor, which makes a preliminary analysis of the Prolog program through *abstract interpretation*, and establishes a sequential ordering in *sensitive* and related predicates.

---

[6] A variable is conditionally bound if since it is created until it gets bound to a value, some choice-point has been created.

We propose to extend the execution model in order to define a deterministic behavior even in such cases. Thus, when the determinacy of a goal depends on a variable that is unbound, the goal will be taken as *non-deterministic* (while the variable remains unbound) even if the goal is deterministic for the case of the unbound variable. Therefore its execution will be delayed up to the *non-deterministic phase*, sequencing so the non-deterministic access to unbound variables. Thus if any deterministic goal bind the variable to any value, the non-deterministic goal will become now deterministic. However, if the variable remains unbound, then the goal will be executed in the *non-deterministic phase* and will select the clause related to the unbound variable. The model can be seen as follows: if the determinacy of a goal depends on a variable that is unbound, the execution of the goal will be delayed until no other goal could bind it. If any goal binds the variable, then its value will be taken to select the deterministic clause (if exists), and if no one binds the variable, then it will be taken as unbound for the delayed goal.

The same behavior can be applied to any built-in predicate that dealt with unbound variables, it will be delayed until the variable became bound or up to the *non-deterministic phase*.

This extension to the execution model guarantees a deterministic behavior in the execution of an Andorra program, and it will conform the execution order of Prolog in most cases.

3.2 Exploiting Dependent AND Parallelism in Prolog

Exploitation of dependent AND parallelism is based on the goal suspension mechanism seen above, which allows the division of the computation into smaller parts (tasks) suitable for sharing between system workers, exploiting so AND parallelism. However, it is important to take into account that our system is oriented to run on distributed memory machines, therefore task division and its sharing have to follow several guidelines to take advantage of distributed execution.

In distributed systems, remote task creation is an expensive operation. For this reason, it is only worthwhile if the task execution time is high enough with respect to its remote creation cost. Most of systems that exploit dependent AND parallelism follow an execution model similar to JAM [6], where in general each goal corresponds to a process, in this way having a big amount of little processes, exploiting so small grain parallelism. Our model follows a different approach in order to exploit medium/coarse grain parallelism, thus a task is executed internally following the modified WAM sequential execution model explained above (which can create more tasks), and the creation of tasks will be controlled by the *sequence breaking instructions*. These instructions will be generated by program analysis [14], user annotations, etc. and it can be used in conjunction with *extended instructions* for a higher control of parallel tasks.

Our system can be seen as a *multisequential* AND parallel machine made up of workers, each one executing a task in a sequential way similar to WAM execution model, and possibly with some tasks waiting to be executed.

Sharing Parallel Work In this section we will see how tasks are shared between systems workers in order to exploit dependent AND parallelism, and how these workers synchronize each other to share work in a suitable way.

The first thing to take into account is that sometimes it could be convenient to break the sequential execution flow in order to postpone the execution of a task or to anticipate the creation of another task, etc., and it could happen that the new created task is not suitable for sharing with other system workers. Therefore our model divides tasks into two main classes, *parallelizable tasks*, which are suitable for sharing between workers in a distributed system, and *local tasks* which are not convenient for sharing, but they are useful for breaking the sequential execution flow.

Another important thing to take into account is that the execution of a task normally will need data produced by other tasks and it will produce data for other tasks[7]. This behavior is quite different from the exploitation of OR parallelism, where tasks are coarse grained and interaction between them is at creation task time. Thus, one of our more important design goals is to get an efficient sharing of AND work, therefore creating tasks suitable for parallelizing (medium/coarse grained task) is not sufficient, but such tasks have to be shared in an efficient way between all system workers. To achieve this goal, we try to keep workers working for as long as possible, but minimizing the amount of task exportation[8]. In this way we get to reduce remote task creation costs and remote data access costs, but we still exploit dependent AND parallelism in an efficient way.

At the time of designing a parallel system on a distributed architecture, abstraction and independence with respect to the underlying architecture is the right approach and has numerous advantages. However if we want to get the best possible performance from the underlying architecture, we need to know some additional information to help us in our work. Thus, in a distributed environment, communication costs vary from some processors to others (depending on the network topology), and this information can be useful, keeping abstraction and independence, for our purposes. Therefore, in our system each worker is surrounded by *levels of neighborhood*, where each level will hold workers that have the same communication costs (Fig. 1). This means that workers have to be ordered by levels depending on their communication costs. Thus this information will be used by our system during the sharing of work to select the most suitable workers with which to do it.

The sharing of tasks is controlled by the state machine in fig. 2 which synchronizes the operation between involved workers. Normally a worker will be in the *"working"* state, which means that it has got enough work to be running but it has not got enough parallel work to share, or in the *"available work"* state, which means that it has got enough parallel work for sharing. When a worker is in this latter state and knows that another worker needs work, it will share a part of its work with it. Whenever the amount of work of a worker is below a

[7] We are exploiting *dependent AND parallelism.*

[8] Task exportation follows a lazy approach.

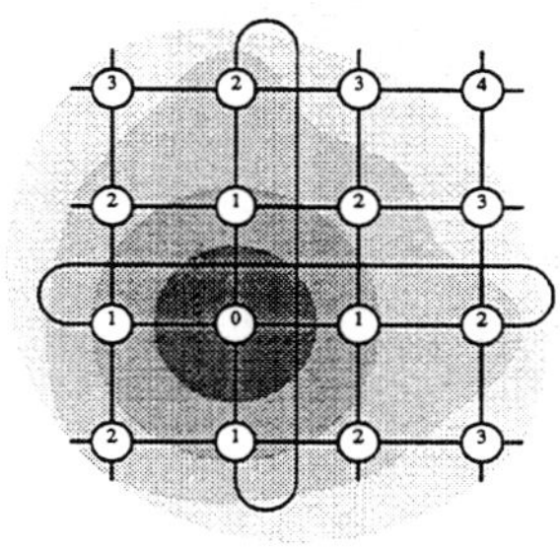

Fig. 1. Levels of neighborhood

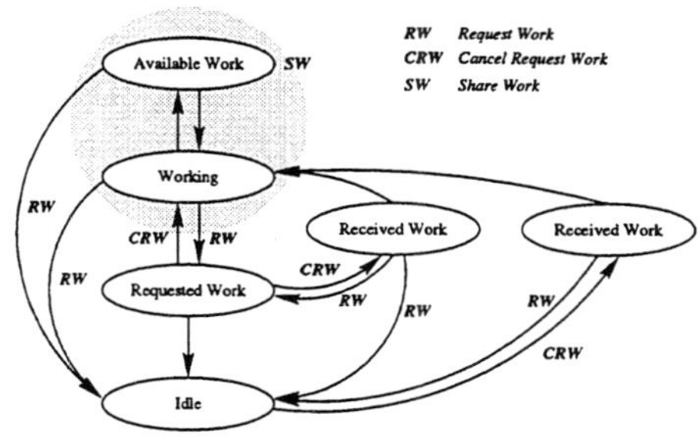

Fig. 2. State machine

determinate level, it will request work from the neighbor workers and will move to the *"requested work"* state. If a worker runs out of work, it will move to the *"idle state"* and it will have to wait to get some work from neighbor workers. When a worker receives some work, it will move to the *"received work"* states. Moving between states is governed by thresholds that mark the amount of work needed to stay at a determinate state, and the amount of shared work is defined by the ratio of sharing.

A state machine is defined for each level of neighborhood, and only neighbor workers belonging to such a level will be involved in the sharing of work, getting so a finer control depending on its communication costs. Thus, each level of neighborhood will have defined suitable thresholds and ratios to produce an efficient sharing of work. The choosing of suitable thresholds and ratios can be done by mean of program analysis.

Thus, the sharing of work can be seen as follows: when the amount of work in a worker is under a determinate threshold (the worker gets into the *"requested work"* or *"idle"* state), it requests work from the neighbor workers from the distance[9] specified by the state machine. When a worker has got enough work to share (it is in the *"available work"* state), it will select a worker that has requested some work within the distance specified by the state machine. Then it selects the most suitable piece of work (the amount of tasks specified for the ratio of sharing for that distance) to send it to the worker that requested it.

The way in which the tasks are selected for sharing is, in order of precedence, as follows:

1. A task imported from the same worker which is now requesting work.
2. A task imported from another worker.
3. A parallelizable task created by the worker that is going to share its work.

It is important to note that this behavior tries to keep as many tasks as possible located at workers where they were created, with the minimum amount

[9] The level of neighborhood.

of task exportation, since sharing of work is achieved in a lazy way by demand when the amount of work is below a specified threshold.

Sharing Data between Parallel Tasks. Extended Distributed Unification This section is based on Foster's distributed unification model for committed choice languages [9], which has been extended to support the mechanism for dealing with unbound variables in a distributed environment. Communication between tasks is achieved by mean of shared logical objects, which are stored in WAM memory areas. These shared objects will be distributed, or in some cases replicated, between the system workers (each worker holds its own memory areas). Thus, communication of tasks will be achieved by accessing a variable to unify it with some value (variables keep their property of unique assignment), or by accessing an object in order to get its value. So in this way, the tasks within a worker communicate with each other by means of objects residing in the same shared WAM memory areas. However, a more sophisticated mechanism is needed in the case of tasks residing in different workers, which need to access remote objects in order to achieve reading and unification operations.

The way in which distributed data are related each another is by means of *remote references.* These are a means of relating a variable residing in a worker local memory to an object residing in a remote worker memory. This is done simply by referring the worker where the object resides and the object with which the remote reference is related.

Whenever a task needs to access to a variable value, if the variable is bound to some object, it just takes it. If the variable is unbound and its value is necessary to know whether a goal is deterministic or not, the goal will be suspended in a suspension list attached to the variable. If the variable value is necessary for the execution of a built-in predicate, this will be suspended in the variable suspension list. It can happen that the variable was a remote reference to an object in a remote worker. In such cases, a message to get the value from the remote object will be sent to the worker that owns the object. Meanwhile, the goal will be suspended in suspension lists attached to variables on which its determinacy depends.

When a worker receives the message asking for the value of an object, if the object is available, it just sends it to the worker that requested it. If the object is a reference to another remote object, the requesting message is forwarded up to get to the worker that owns that object. However if the object is an unbound variable, it will attach a note to the suspension list of the variable, in such a way that when the variable becomes bound, its value will be sent to the worker that requested it.

The other way of accessing a variable is its unification with another object. If both objects are local to the task that wants to unify them, the operation is achieved as in WAM. If the unification involves a local object with a remote one, the local object is sent to the worker where the remote object resides in order to unify the local object with the received one. When both objects are remote, it will send a message to the worker where one object resides to achieve the remote unification operation with the other worker as seen above.

It is important to note that remote references only can be done in one direction, in order to avoid remote circular references. Thus, in our system, worker identifiers are ordered, and only remote references from higher to lower worker identifier are allowed. Thus, operations explained above and remote object creation must be achieved according to this rule.

There are, however, several built-in predicates[10] which achieve *non-strict tests*, that is, they can sometimes proceed even though their input arguments are unbound [9]. However Foster's *non-strict read algorithms* are oriented to *committed choice languages*, which have a very poor treatment of unbound variables. Therefore, in our model, the *non-strict read algorithm* is modified in order to support the *Basic Andorra Model* extended with the *unbound variable treatment* on distributed systems.

As it was said in sect. 3.1, goals which determinacy depended on unbound variables were taken as non-deterministic ones, and so, executed at *non-deterministic phase*. Foster's distributed unification algorithm guarantees that if the value of a variable is needed for any goal in the distributed system, and the variable become bound before the *non-deterministic phase* start, then the value of the variable will get to the goals that need it before the beginning of the *non-deterministic phase*. What we have to get by extending the distributed unification mechanism is to guarantee that whenever a goal needs the *"last"* reference of an "unbound" variable[11], such a last reference will be available at the start of the *non-deterministic phase*, since execution of such goals will be delayed up to then. It is important to note that not every non-strict predicate (such as 'var/1', etc.) needs the last reference of the unbound argument, therefore the next discussion will not be applied to them.

The way in which the right (and last) reference for an unbound variable is guaranteed to be available when needed at *non-deterministic phase* can be roughly seen as follows:

> When a goal needs the *last-reference* from a variable for a non-strict test, a *note*, holding information about the variable whose last-reference is needed, will be attached to the current last-reference, and whenever the last-reference gets bound to another variable, the goal is notified[12] and the *note* is forwarded to the new last-reference. If the last-reference becomes bound to a value, the goal is notified and the note is discarded.

From Deterministic to Non-Deterministic Phase. Detection and Control In this section we will see how the change from *deterministic* to *non-deterministic* phase is controlled by the system workers in order to maintain the Prolog execution order for non-deterministic goals.

---

[10] '==/2', '\==/2', 'var/1', 'nonvar/1', etc.

[11] Some built-in predicates such as '==/2' and '\==/2' compare terms even if they are unbounds. If such predicates appear within the determinacy code or guards of a Prolog predicate, then the Prolog predicate needs their values in the same way.

[12] It must be taken into account that such messages can arrive in an unordered way.

Whenever a task is exported, it is marked as such and records a remote reference to the created remote task. On the other hand, when a task is imported, it is marked as such and records a remote reference to the original task. We have seen that imported tasks can be re-exported to other workers (sect. 3.2), so it is necessary to keep a reference count in each task in order to synchronize the reference messages with the origin.

As it was seen in Sect. 3.1, the alternating of phases will be done until the end of computation. In the AND parallel model, this alternating will have to be achieved in a synchronized way. At a determinate moment, all workers will be in the *deterministic phase* executing tasks in parallel. When there is no available task in the whole system, i.e. every worker in the system is in the "idle" state, then in a synchronized way all workers change to the *non-deterministic* phase. One of them[13] will execute a non-deterministic goal, and will start a new *deterministic* phase by executing the task generated by the non-deterministic goal. Every worker will now change to the same phase and will execute their tasks[14]. Thus, we have seen that it is one worker that starts a new *deterministic* phase, we will call it the *initial worker* for each phase.

Let us go to the start of the Prolog computation. There will be an *initial worker* that will start the *deterministic phase* by executing the *initial Prolog query*. During the execution of the initial task, some tasks could have been created, from which, when it gets to the *non-deterministic phase*, the deterministic ones will have been executed, and the non-deterministic ones will remain waiting for their execution following the Prolog execution order. Processing will go on with phase alternating as explained above up to the point when the selected goal for non-deterministic execution was an exported task. Then a message has to be sent to the worker that owns that task in order to start the non-deterministic execution of that goal or, in the case of it had already been executed, the first non-deterministic goal created by such a task. The worker that sent the message will wait for the beginning of the new *deterministic phase* and non-deterministic goals in such a worker will be executed when all non-deterministic descendents from the exported goal have been executed. The worker that receives the message to execute a non-deterministic goal, will push in the *"non-deterministic execution control stack"* the reference to the remote original goal (in order to return the non-deterministic control to that worker). It will execute the selected non-deterministic goal (or one of its descendents) and will start a new *deterministic phase* (being now the *initial worker* for that phase). It will return the non-deterministic control when all the imported goal descendents have been executed. However, if some of these goals are exported, the process will go on as explained, giving workers the non-deterministic control and returning it at many levels in order to keep the Prolog execution order.

We have seen that it is the *initial worker* that will change to the *non-deterministic phase* by selecting the next non-deterministic goal to be executed,

---

[13] According to the Prolog execution order

[14] Which will have been imported from other workers or will have been awakened by mean of shared logical variables.

which could have been exported. However, to start a new *non-deterministic phase*, all available deterministic goals must have been executed, i.e. there must not remain any available deterministic task in the system workers without being executed. Therefore it is the initial worker for that deterministic phase that has to detect when all workers are in the "idle" state in order to start the new *non-deterministic phase*.

It has to be taken into account that in distributed systems, not all computation is done inside the workers, but some messages can be travelling around the interconection network. So, in order to know if a determinate worker is in the idle state, the workload is not the only important value to be taken into account, but the messages which it is waiting for have to be taken into account too. That is, a worker will move to the "idle state" if it has not got any work available to be executed and it has received an acknowledgment for every message that it has sent, in which case there will not be messages travelling around the network.

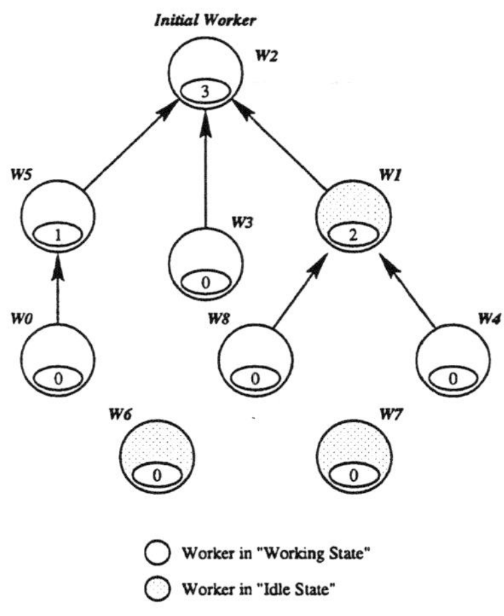

Fig. 3. Detection of the End of the Deterministic Phase

Detection of the End of the Deterministic Phase The algorithm for the *detection of the end of the deterministic phase* is based on the *diffusing computation* termination detection method proposed by Dijkstra and Scholten [8], but it has been oriented to workers instead of tasks[15]. In it, each worker is controlled by the worker which has given it work, and each worker controls the workers to which it gave work. Thus, each worker keeps the worker that controls it, and the

[15] The main difference resides in the fact that in the original method, a task waits for termination of its children in order to finish its computation and to notify this fact to its father. In our environment, a worker can receive work from many workers and can become idle even if its children are working.

count of workers that it controls, following a tree hierarchical structure (fig. 3). The algorithm is as follows:

- When a worker gets some deterministic tasks from other worker and it is not controlled by any worker, the control is established between both workers.
- When a worker has not got any available deterministic task to be executed (it is in "*idle* state"), and it does not control to any worker, then the control from its controller worker is removed .
- If the *initial worker* is in the "*idle* state" and does not control to any worker, that means that there is no available deterministic task in the whole system, and, therefore, the non-deterministic phase must begin.

Backtracking Support In addition to backtracking support for sequential execution explained in Sect. 3.1, our model has to be extended in order to support backtracking in dependent AND parallelism exploitation in a distributed environment.

It is known that *choice-points* are a key piece in the WAM backtracking mechanism, and we have seen that a non-deterministic goal is executed just by one worker (the *initial worker* for a deterministic phase) and it will create a choice-point in its local memory. Then a message for creating a *dummy choice-point* is broadcasted to all system workers[16] in order to allow every worker to backtrack to that state of computation in case of *failure*. After the *initial worker* creates its choice-point and broadcasts the *dummy choice-point* creation message, the *initial worker* will go on executing its new task, however, it can not send any remote work creation message[17] until it has received confirmation from every worker of having created their correspondent dummy choice-points. This is achieved by having a *'queue'* where such a messages will be enqueued. This synchronization is necessary for the choice-points to reflect the same global computation state.

In the same way, when the *initial worker* discards a choice-point, it broadcasts a message to every worker in the system in order to act in the same way. Synchronization as explained above is required. Moreover, after the deallocating of a choiceponit and in case of an early failure, and if due to this failure the *initial worker* changes, then the failure has to be synchronized with the confirmation from every worker of having discarded the dummy choice-point.

When a failure occurs in a worker, a failure message is broadcasted to every worker in the system. However, workers are working asynchronously most of time[18], therefore many failures can happen in different workers over the system, and many obsolete messages can be traveling over the network. Thus, in order to control this asynchrony chaos, a failure level counter is used. Whenever a

[16] Every worker is at this moment at *"idle state"*, since the change of phases is done in a synchronized way.
[17] Remote task creation, requested object value/reference or remote unification.
[18] Workers are only synchronized at change of phases.

failure occurs in a worker, the failure level counter is incremented. Moreover, every message is tagged with the worker's failure level count, in such a way that when a message is received, if the message failure level count is lower than the worker's current failure level count, then the message is discarded as obsolete. However if the message failure level count is higher than the worker's current failure level count, the worker has to fail so many times to get to the message failure level count, and then the message will be processed.

4 Mixing OR Parallelism with Dependent AND Parallelism

This section shows the way in which the system is arranged in order to exploit both kind of parallelism in distributed systems. It is based on the dependent AND parallelism model explained above and in the OR parallel model explained at [4] which is based on the *incremental copy mechanism* [1] for distributed environments. It will not be explained here due to space limitations.

4.1 Static Teams

The structure that governs the whole system in order to exploit both kinds of parallelism is arranged as follows: systems workers are divided into fixed size teams, each one made up of the same number of workers. Workers have identifiers internal to the team and teams have their own identifiers. The system can be seen from two points of view. From the outer level point of view, the system is made up of a set of *teams* which collaborate one another exploiting *OR parallelism* by traversing in parallel different alternative paths from the search space. From the inner level point of view, each team consists in a set of workers which collaborate one another exploiting *dependent AND parallelism* within the traversing of a search space path. This two level approach can also be applied to the levels of neighborhood defined for both models. Hence workers within a team can be organized by levels of neighborhood, and teams within the system can be organized in such a way too.

Let us look at some definitions and restrictions that system team division must fulfill.

- Definitions:
  1. Let d_{ij} be the distance between worker i and worker j within a team. Then let us define the *internal distance* for a team T_t with N workers as
  $$ID_t = \sum_{i=0}^{N-1} \sum_{j=0}^{i-1} d_{ij}$$
  2. Let us call the worker's *counterpart* for a team T_j to the worker which has the same identifier as it within such a team, and let D_{wij} be the distance between worker w from team T_i and its

counterpart from team T_j in the system network. Then let us define the *external distance* between two teams T_i and T_j with N workers as

$$ED_{ij} = \sum_{w=0}^{N-1} D_{wij}$$

- Restrictions:
  1. The team *internal distance* must be minimum, that is, division of workers in teams which internal distance is not minimum is not allowed.
  2. The *global external distance* between all teams must be minimum, that is, team layout and the arrangement of workers within a team must be achieved in order to minimize

$$\sum_{i=0}^{NTeams-1} \sum_{j=0}^{i-1} ED_{ij}$$

These restrictions are in order to decrease the communication costs within a team while exploiting Dependent AND parallelism and while the sharing of work in OR parallel exploitation respectively.

4.2 Mixing both Models

Now we will see how the proposed models have to be modified in order to adapt themselves to the system arranged in fixed size teams.

The *Dependent AND parallel model* is lightly modified in order to allow the mixing of both models. In previous discussion, all workers in the system were involved in the same AND parallel computation. In order to exploit both kinds of parallelism, only workers within a team will be related in the same AND parallel computation, and workers from different teams will be involved in different computations. The model is modified as follows: a team is a subset of workers from the whole system, and worker identifiers are now relative to the subset, hence the model must reflect the relative worker identifiers and the subset of workers as a whole AND parallel system.

The *OR parallel model*, however needs deeper modifications. It has to be modified to support the teams, instead of workers, as the core to exploit the OR parallelism. Now a team plays the same role as a single worker in the OR model. These teams are made up of small pieces that will have to be coordinated in order to achieve the sharing of OR work in the correct way (now the OR work is not a monolithic piece, but it is made up of small parts distributed among the workers belonging to a team).

Therefore, it is the sharing of OR work, and the corresponding coordination of workers within a team and inter-teams on which our attention must be focused.

The way in which the sharing of work was synchronized in the *pure OR parallel model* can roughly be seen as follows [4]:

- When a worker ran out of work, it sent to its neighbors a request for work, and moved to the "idle state".
- When a worker had got enough work to share, it selected the most suitable idle worker with which to share part of its work.
- When an idle worker was selected for sharing work, it chose the most suitable work for sharing and rejected the other ones.
- If *overlapping*[19] occurs before the commitment of the work[20], then the sharing of work is aborted.

This simplified protocol to synchronize two workers for sharing OR work becomes more complex in the case of the mixed models, since now two teams (made up of several workers running most of time asynchronously) have to be synchronized. It can roughly be seen as follows:

> Within a team, there will be a distinguished worker, the *"main worker"*, which will be a fixed one for each team. If a team has enough work to share, this worker will deal with the detection of work and the selection of the idle team with which to share out such work. When the work to share has been detected, another worker will deal with the control of the sharing of work and overlapping, we will call it the *"work controller worker"*, and it will be the worker that created the *"real choice-point"* just over the work to be shared.
>
> If a team is in the "*idle* state", the *"main worker"* will select the most suitable work between the offered ones, and will reject the others. The *"work controller worker"* will be notified of the work request/rejection, the work will be shared between every worker and its counterpart from both teams, and the *"work controller worker"* will be again notified of the end of such an operation.
>
> If overlapping occurs before the work has been committed, then the sharing of work will be aborted, but if it occurs after such commitment and before the end of the sharing of work, then the overlapping will be blocked until its end.

5 Conclusion and Future Work

We have presented a model for implementing the Basic Andorra Model on distributed systems. The model is based on a model for exploiting OR parallelism on distributed systems presented in an earlier paper and in a model for exploiting Dependent AND parallelism on distributed systems explained above. The latter is based on a goal suspension mechanism for WAM with granularity control support embedded in the execution model. Moreover, levels of neighborhood

[19] Overlapping occurs when after several failures the worker that had got work to share has to backtrack to the area selected for sharing.

[20] Work is committed when the worker that owns the work receives the confirmation for sharing the work before overlapping occurs.

and a state machine for each level are defined in order to get a fine control over the sharing of work. Also A mechanism for dealing with unbound variables in the distributed Basic Andorra Model has been also proposed, which is an extension to the Foster's *distributed unification mechanism* for committed choice languages. A model for mixing both kinds of parallelism has been proposed, however at current stage, workers are arranged in a fixed way, being our next step to extend it using a flexible scheduler.

References

1. K. A. M. Ali and R. Karlsson. The Muse Or-parallel Prolog model and its performance. In *North American Conference on Logic Programming*, pages 757–776, 1990.
2. L. Araujo and J. J. Ruz. PDP: Prolog Distributed Processor for Independent-AND/OR parallel execution of Prolog. In *Logic Programming: Proceedings of the 11th International Conference*, pages 142–156. MIT Press, 1994.
3. R. Bahgat. *Pandora: Non-Deterministic Parallel Logic Programming.* PhD thesis, Imperial College. London, February 1991.
4. V. Benjumea and J. M. Troya. An OR parallel Prolog model for distributed memory systems. In M. Bruynooghe and J. Penjam, editors, *Fifth International Symposium on Programming Language Implementation and Logic Programming*, volume 714 of *Lecture Notes in Computer Science*, pages 291–301. Springer-Verlag, August 1993.
5. K. Clark and S. Gregory. Parlog: Parallel programming in logic. *ACM Transactions on Programming Languajes and Systems*, 8(1):1–49, January 1986.
6. J. Crammond. The abstract machine and implementation of parallel Parlog. Technical report, Imperial College. London, June 1990.
7. D. DeGroot. Restricted AND parallelism. In *Proceedings of the International Conference on Fifth Generation Computer Systems*, pages 471–478. ICOT, 1984.
8. E. W. Dijkstra and C. Scholten. Termination detection for diffusing computations. *Information Processing Letters*, 11(1):1–4, August 1980.
9. I. Foster. Parallel implementation of Parlog. In *International Conference on Parallel Processing.* University Park, 1988.
10. G. Gupta and M. Hermenegildo. ACE: And/Or-parallel copying-based execution of logic programs. In A. Beaumont and G. Gupta, editors, *ICLP'91 Pre-Conference Workshop on Parallel Execution of Logic Programs*, volume 569 of *Lecture Notes in Computer Science*, pages 146–158. Springer-Verlag, June 1991.
11. M. V. Hermenegildo. *An Abstract Machine Based Execution Model for Computer Architecture Design and Efficient Implementation of Logic Programs in Parallel.* PhD thesis, University of Texas, August 1986.
12. S. Janson and S. Haridi. Programming paradigms of the Andorra Kernel Language. In *Proceedings of the International Logic Programming Symposium*, pages 167–186. MIT press, October 1991.
13. H. F. Leung. *Distributed Constraint Logic Programming.* PhD thesis, Imperial College. London, November 1991.
14. P. López, M. Hermenegildo, and S. Debray. Towards granularity based control of parallelism in logic programs. In *Proceedings of PASCO'94*, 1994.

15. E. Lusk, D. Warren, S. Haridi, and et al. The Aurora Or-parallel Prolog system. Technical Report 07, University of Bristol, 1990.
16. V. Santos Costa, D. Warren, and R. Yang. The Andorra-I engine: A parallel implementation of the Basic Andorra model. In *Logic Programming: Proceedings of the 8th International Conference*. MIT Press, 1991.
17. V. Santos Costa, D. Warren, and R. Yang. The Andorra-I preprocessor: Supporting full Prolog on the Basic Andorra model. In *Logic Programming: Proceedings of the 8th International Conference*. MIT Press, 1991.
18. E. Shapiro. Concurrent Prolog: a progress report. *IEEE Computer*, 19:44–58, 1986.
19. K. Ueda. Guarded horn clauses. Technical Report 102, ICOT, Tokyo, 1986.
20. D. Warren. Or-parallel execution models of Prolog. In *TAPSOFT*, volume 250 of *Lecture Notes in Computer Science*. Springer-Verlag, 1987.
21. R. Yang. Solving simple substitution ciphers in Andorra-I. In G. Levi and M. Martelli, editors, *Logic Programming: Proceedings of the 6th International Conference*, pages 113–128. MIT Press, June 1989.

This article was processed using the LaTeX macro package with LLNCS style

ParTy — A Parallel-Types Analyser

Luís Fernando Pias de Castro
Cláudio Fernando Resin Geyer
{lfcastro,geyer}@inf.ufrgs.br

Universidade Federal do Rio Grande do Sul
Caixa Postal 15064
Porto Alegre - RS

Abstract. Abstract This work presents a type inference system aimed at the parallel exploitation of logic programs. It emphasizes the determination of costs related to the exportation of goals on distributed memory parallel machines, so types are based on the actual storage model of terms in Warren's Abstract Machine. The proposed type domain introduces a novel notion of type interval, which provides a greater accuracy on type analysis.

1 Introduction

Prolog [1] [2] is a declarative programming language based on first-order logic. It provides the programmer ways to express problems in a high level of abstraction. One important characteristic of this language is its clear distinction between the logic description of a problem and the control needed to solve it.

Parallelism has been widely used as a means of improving the performance of programs. Under imperative programming paradigms a programmer has to be aware of the issues related to parallelism, since he must code the control of the execution of the program. Since Prolog is a declarative language, a programmer doesn't have to deal with the control of the execution. This implies that Prolog is a well suited language for automatic exploitation of parallelism.

There are several parallel implementations of Prolog. However, most of them are based on shared memory machines. Opera [3] [4] is a project aimed at building a parallel Prolog system based on distributed memory machines.

The inclusion of parallelism in the control of a languages such as Prolog adds some overhead due to the issues related to managing the distribution of work among several processors. This overhead is even greater in the case of distributed memory machines where processors don't share memory and, thus, any communication between processors must be done via messages.

There are cases in which the parallel execution of a task may be even slower than the usual sequential execution. That's because the cost of transferring the arguments for the task may be greater than the execution cost of the task.

This work describes a type inference system based on abstract interpretation aimed at providing information to the runtime system to determine the cost related to sending a task to some other processor. This may be used by the runtime system when deciding about the parallel or sequential execution of a task.

The type system described reflects the actual storage of information in Prolog systems based on Warren's Abstract Machine. It introduces a novel notion of type intervals. A type interval denotes the situation in which a variable may be linked to different terms at runtime. It mantains the lesser and the greater types the variable may be linked to, according to a given order relation.

The rest of this paper is divided into four sections. Next section describes the basic concepts used througout the remaining text.

Section 3 defines the static analysis model, along with the parallel type domain proposed. Section 4 provides some description about possible uses of the parallel-type system. The final section describes the conclusions of the work.

2 Basic Concepts

In this section we are going to describe the basic concepts needed to understand the proposed type inference system, that will be used throughout the remaining of the text.

2.1 Abstract Intepretation

Abstract interpretation is a static analysis technique developed by Cousot and Cousot [5]. It's based on the idea of obtaining an approximate semantics of a program, by abstracting the domain over which this program works. In order to do this, first we have to define an abstract domain which reflects the kind of information we want to infer. Also, it's necessary to create equivalent abstract functions for every primitive function of the language in which the program has been written.

An analysis, according to abstract interpretation, involves a fixpoint calculus in order to obtain the abstract semantics of a given program.

Creating a static analyser, based on abstract interpretation, involves three steps:

(i) defining an abstract domain based on the information we want to infer;
(ii) creating the corresponding abstract functions for the primitive operations of the language and
(iii) defining an execution model for the fixpoint calculus.

2.2 Logic Programming

The logic programming paradigm provides the user a way to express problems at a high level of abstraction. Prolog is the most well-known logic programming language used nowadays, and it's based on two independent works of Colmerauer [1] and Kowalski [2].

Prolog's main characteristic is the clear distinction between logic and control. It means that, when a programmer wants to describe a problem, he only has to be concerned about its logic. The underlying system will be responsible for providing a control system to solve the problem.

On one hand, this characteristic makes program development easier, since the programmer doesn't have to specify the control of the program. On the other hand, it allows the underlying runtime system to implement different control systems.

Most of Prolog implementations are based on the Warren Abstract Machine (WAM) [6]. WAM is a stack-oriented abstract machine specially developed for the execution of Prolog programs.

2.3 Parallel Processing

Parallel processing is, nowadays, a widely accepted technique to provide high performance for several kinds of programs. But the introduction of control for parallel processing in existing programs written in imperatives languages is considerably hard. This has led to research on applying parallel processing to other programming paradigms.

Prolog is very well suited for parallel processing, since the user has (at least in theory) no control on how a problem is going to be solved. There are two main kinds of parallelism in Prolog:

- **Or-parallelism**, when two or more clauses of a given predicate are executed in parallel and
- **And-parallelism**, when several goals of a given clause are executed at the same time.

And-parallelism can, still, be split in two categories:

- **Independent And-parallelism**, which exploits the parallel execution of goals which don't share variables and
- **Dependent And-parallelism**, where goals are executed in parallel if they share one or more variables.

There are several implementations of parallel Prolog systems. For example, **Muse** [7] or-parallel system, the independent and-parallelism **&-Prolog system** [8], and **Andorra-I** [9], which exploits both or-parallelism and dependent and-parallelism. However, most of the existing systems are based on shared-memory machines.

2.4 Opera Independent And-Parallelism

Opera is a parallel Prolog system, which exploits or-parallelism and independent and-parallelism. Opera is aimed at exploiting parallelism on distributed-memory machines.

Opera's or-parallelism is based on a multi-sequential model [3]. When a processor asks for work it receives a clause, which must be completely executed by this processor. Each processor executes a WAM-based abstract machine called TWAM.

The independent and-parallelism model used in Opera is called restricted and-parallelism. According to this model, conditional graph expressions are used to denote situations when parallel execution of goals may be exploited. The WAM-based abstract machine used for and-parallelism is the RAP-WAM [10], which has been adapted to work on distributed-memory machines [11].

3 Type Inference for Distributed-Memory Parallel Machines

3.1 Static Analysis Model

The static analysis model presented here includes the execution model for the fixpoint calculus and the abstraction of the primitive operations of Prolog. Also, it's parameterized by domain-dependent functions in such a way that makes it a domain-independent static analysis model.

This model is based on a three levels algorithm. In the first level, a function called compute_fixpoint coordinates the several iterations that have to be done over the program, in order to execute the fixpoint calculus. On a second level, functions exec_rec_pred and exec_nrec_pred are responsible for executing recursive and non-recursive predicates, respectively. These functions also manipulate a memory structure called *Memo Table*, which is used to hold the partial solutions obtained on each iteration. In a third level, function exec_clauses assures that every clause of a predicate will be analysed when analysing that predicate.

In order to instantiate this model for a given abstract domain, there must be defined four domain-dependent functions: calc_in_subst, calc_succ_subst, calc_call_subst and calc_ret_subst.

calc_in_subst is called at the start of the analysis of a clause. Its in-arguments are the variables of the call, a substitution over these variables, and the arguments of the clause. It performs the unification between the variables of the call and the variables of the clause, and returns the clause entrance substitution.

Before returning from the analysis of a clause, function calc_succ_subst is called. It takes as its arguments the arguments for the clause, the arguments for the call, and the exit substitution. It performs the unification between the clause- and the call-arguments, and returns the success substitution over the arguments of the call.

calc_call_subst is called before each goal of a clause is analysed. It takes as arguments the current substitution and the arguments for the next goal. It returns the current substitution restricted to the variables that appear in the arguments for the next goal.

The function calc_ret_subst is called after a goal has been analysed and it takes the substitution prior to the analysis of the goal and the success substitution for the goal as arguments. It, then, applies the changes described in the success substitution for the goal to the previous substitution, returning a new current substitution.

Example This section aims to provide an example of how the domain-specific functions work during an analysis.

Suppose the analysis of the second clause of the *append/3* predicate shown in figure 1. Also, suppose the query shown at the same figure is given with the following abstract substitution:

$$\phi_{call} = \{A \rightarrow list(5, int), B \rightarrow list(8, atom(10)), C \rightarrow \$bottom\$\}. \quad (1)$$

```
append([ ], L, L).
append([H|L], L1, L2) :- append(L, L1, L2).

?- append(A, B, C).
```

Fig. 1. Predicate *append/3* and the query

The analysis starts by calling calc_in_subst, in order to unify the variables of the call to the arguments of the head of the clause. The result of this unification is the substitution

$$\Phi_1 = \{H \rightarrow int, L \rightarrow list(4, int), L2 \rightarrow list(8, atom(10)), L3 \rightarrow \$bottom\$\}. \quad (2)$$

The second step of the analysis is to prepare a substitution to be used when calling the first (and only) goal of the clause. This is the job of the function calc_call_subst. It creates a new substitution with only the variables which appear in the next goal.

$$\Phi_{in1} = \{L \rightarrow list(4, int), L2 \rightarrow list(8, atom(10)), L3 \rightarrow \$bottom\$\}. \quad (3)$$

Then, the goal is called, with the last given substitution. The result of executing a goal is another substitution. In this example, let's suppose we have already reached a fixpoint. So, the result of recursively calling *append/3*, in this case, should be the substitution

$$\Phi_{out1} = \{L \rightarrow list(4, int), L2 \rightarrow list(8, atom(10)),$$
$$L3 \rightarrow list(12, interval(int, atom(10)))\}. \quad (4)$$

This substitution has to be joined to the substitution given in equation 2. This is done by the function calc_ret_subst. Again, the result of this action is given by a new substitution.

$$\Phi_2 = \{H \rightarrow int, L \rightarrow list(4, int), L2 \rightarrow list(8, atom(10)),$$

$$L3 \rightarrow list(12, interval(int, atom(10)))\}. \tag{5}$$

As there are no more goals to be called, the last function to be executed is calc_succ_subst, which applies the last substitution to the variables of the call. It then gives the success substitution for this clause (according to the given query).

$$\phi_{succ} = \{A \rightarrow list(5, int), B \rightarrow list(8, atom(10)),$$
$$C \rightarrow list(13, interval(int, atom(10)))\}. \tag{6}$$

3.2 The Parallel Type Domain

The abstract domain shown here has been specially designed to infer types for Prolog. Its goal is to provide information for the runtime system to be able to decide when the parallel execution of a goal will increase the overall execution time of a program.

In distributed memory machines, the parallel execution of a goal involves transferring the arguments for the goal from one processor to another, usually via messages. This transfer time has to be considered when deciding if a goal should be executed in another processor, since the cost of transferring the arguments from one processor to the other, and the results back to the first one, may be even greater than the cost of executing the goal sequentially. Also, the cost of calculating the size of the messages may decrease the performance of the system.

In order to try to decrease the decisions that have to be taken at runtime and to decrease the cost of calculating the size of the messages, the type system has been designed to reflect the actual storage of Prolog terms in the stacks of WAM-based abstract machines.

A new aspect of type systems for Prolog introduced in this work is the notion of intervals of types. A type interval is used to describe variables that assume different types in runtime. It holds the smaller and the bigger types a variable can assume, according to an appropriate ordering function. The use of intervals provide for a greater accuracy of the analysis.

The Parallel-Types domain is composed by the following types:

- **\$bottom\$** — represents the absence of information about the type of a variable;
- **int** — represents integer numbers;
- **float** — describes floating pointing numbers;
- **atom(Size)** — represents an atom, which is composed by *Size* characters;
- **struct(Size,Arity,[Type_List])** — describes a structure, which has a functor (name) composed by *Size* characters, has arity *Arity*, and each argument has a corresponding type, described in *[Type_List]*.
- **list(Size,Type)** — describes a list, which has *Size* elements of type *Type*;
- **\$top\$** — denotes variables for which the analyser hasn't been able to determine a type; and
- **[minor_type, major_type]** — denotes a type-interval, whose smaller type is *minor_type*, and bigger is *major_type*.

This domain has two characteristics that have to be noted. First, *struct* and *list* are two types that may be recursively defined. It means that one may say, for example, that a list has elements of the type *list*. In order to guarantee that the domain is finite, a depth restriction has to be defined. In fact, the depth restriction is a parameter of the analyser.

Second, the notion of type-interval presumes the existance of an order relation over the simple (punctual) types. This relation is given by the sizeof function which will be described below.

The Order Relation The order relation defined for this domain over the simple (non-interval) types is based on the storage model of term on WAM-based Prolog abstract machines.

Definition 1 (Total Order Operator) *A given type T_1 precedes another type T_2 if and only if the storage size (given by the* sizeof *function) of T_1 is lesser or equal to the size of T_2.*

$$T_1 \sqsubseteq^{\mathcal{T}} T_2 \Leftrightarrow sizeof(T_1) \leq sizeof(T_2) \tag{7}$$

The size of a type is calculated according to the way terms represented by the given type are stored in the stacks of the WAM. The sizeof function returns the size of a type. It's defined as follows.

Definition 2 *Sizeof*

$$sizeof(bottom) = \mathsf{MAX\_SIZE} \tag{8}$$

$$sizeof(int) = 4 \tag{9}$$

$$sizeof(float) = 8 \tag{10}$$

$$sizeof(atom(size)) = size \tag{11}$$

$$sizeof(struct(...)) = 1 + size + arity + \sum_{i=1}^{arity} sizeof(type[i]) \tag{12}$$

$$sizeof(list(...)) = 1 + 3 \times size + size \times sizeof(type) \tag{13}$$

$$sizeof(top) = \mathsf{MAX\_SIZE} \tag{14}$$

Note that these formulas have been optimized for the Opera system. This way, some constants have been used, denoting that an integer is stored using 4 bytes and a floating point number requires 8 bytes to be stored. These values must be adapted according to the Prolog system desired.

The two most complex cases are those for the size of a list and for the size of a structure. The formulas are defined according to the storage of these types, as shown below.

Figure 2 shows the storage of two different structures. The storage of the structure $f(a, b)$ starts at cell 1 and the structure $f(c, d, e)$ is stored from cell 8. From that stack representation, we note that each argument of a structure

1	STR	2
2	f/2	-
3	REF	5
4	REF	6
5	CON	a
6	CON	b
7	...	.
8	STR	9
9	f/3	-
10	REF	13
11	REF	14
12	REF	15
13	CON	c
14	CON	d
15	CON	e
..	...	.

Fig. 2. WAM storage of $f(a, b)$ and $f(c, d, e)$

needs one REF cell, besides the cells needed to store the argument itself. Also, it's necessary one STR cell to describe the type of term stored (a structure), plus the number of cells needed to store the name of the structure. Therefore, the storage requirement of a structure is given by equation 12.

Even though a list may be represented by means of binary structures, this storage model requires too much space. As lists are very common in Prolog, the WAM uses a more optimized way to represent them. Figure 3 shows the storage of two lists. The first one is a list with two elements, which starts at cell 1. The other list has three elements, and starts at cell 11. As we can see, each new element of a list requires one LIS cell and two REF cells, plus the cells required to represent the element itself. Besides, there must be always a *nil* cell, to terminate the list. Therefore, it's straightforward to come up with equation 13 to determine the size of a list.

4 Applications of Parallel Types

There are several applications for the type system described in this work. Here we describe two of the most important applications, that will be used in Opera.

4.1 The Unification Process

The most important primitive operation of Prolog is unification. At the same time, it's the most complex operation of Prolog. This is partially due to the fact that, as Prolog lacks type annotation, the unification algorithm must test for several cases, when unifying two terms.

Using the type inference system describe in this paper, it's possible for the compiler to generate specialized code for the unification process, according to the types of the terms that are being unified.

1	LIS	2
2	REF	7
3	REF	4
4	LIS	5
5	REF	8
6	REF	9
7	CON	a
8	CON	b
9	CON	nil
10	...	.
11	LIS	12
12	REF	20
13	REF	14
14	LIS	15
15	REF	21
16	REF	17
17	LIS	18
18	REF	22
19	REF	23
20	CON	c
21	CON	d
22	CON	e
23	CON	nil

Fig. 3. WAM representation of $[a, b]$ and $[c, d, e]$

4.2 Determination of Costs

One of the main characteristics of and-parallelism is its small granularity [12]. It means that the cost of (sequential) execution of a goal is usually small.

On distributed memory machines, this may cause a great problem, since the cost for exporting a goal to other machine involves transferring WAM stacks via messages. So, the scheduler in such a system has to be prepared to decide whether or not the parallel execution of a goal will bring benefits to the overall execution time of the program.

The parallel-type inference system described may be used to provide information to the scheduler in order to make this decision easier.

Two naive implementations of schedulers may be provided by an optimistic and a pessimistic schedulers. The first one would aim to execute in parallel any goal which **may** provide speedup to the system. So, it would use the minor element of any interval provided by the analyser, when comparing the cost of exportation to the cost of execution of the goal.

On the other hand, a pessimistic scheduler would execute in parallel only those goals which will **surely** provide speedup to the system. This way, it would compare the cost of execution of the goal to the major element of any intervalar type provided by the analyser.

A more sophisticated scheduler should be based on experimentations in order to statistically find an optimal point between the two limits of intervalar types.

5 Conclusions

This work presents a type inference system designed to be used at the cost evaluation of the parallel execution of goals under distributed-memory machines.

The notion of type inference isn't new to logic programming systems. Azzoune [13] defines an inference system based on generating and solving inequations on type variables. Corsini e Musumbu [14] define a type analysis system based on abstract interpretation, allowing for the inference of partially instantiated terms. Codish and Lagoon [15] presents an interesting directional-types inference system based on the use of program abstraction and ACI-unification.

The parallel type system presented in this work is unique in introducing a notion of interval of types. This notion provides for a more accurate analysis.

This work contributes to the Opera system in two ways. First, it allows the introduction of specialized unification algorithms, improving the parallel and sequential execution of programs.

Second, it provides information about the storage size of the arguments of a goal. This information can be used to calculate the cost of the parallel execution of a given goal, thus providing the scheduler a way to determine whether or not the execution of the goal in another processor will improve the performance of the program.

References

1. COLMERAUER, A. et al. **Un Système de Communication Homme-Machine en Français**. GIA: Université d'Aix-Marseille II, 1972.
2. KOWALSKI, R. **Logic for Problem Solving**. New York: Elseviér, 1979.
3. BRIAT, J.; FAVRE, M.; GEYER, C. et al. **Opera**: a Parallel Prolog system and its Implementation on Supernode. Grenoble: Laboratoire de Genie Informatique de Grenoble/CAP-Gemini-Inovation, 1990. (Technical Report).
4. GEYER, C.; YAMIN, A.; WERNER, O. Projeto Opera: Um Modelo E/OU para Prolog. In: CONGRESSO DA SOCIEDADE BRASILEIRA DE COMPUTAÇÃO, 12., 1992, Rio de Janeiro. **Anais...** Rio de Janeiro: SBC, 1992.
5. COUSOT, P.; COUSOT, R. Abstract Interpretation: A Unified Lattice Model for Static Analysis of Programs by Construction or Approximation of Fixpoints. In: ACM SYMP. ON PRINCIPLES OF PROGRAMMING LANGUAGES, 4., 1977. **Proceedings...** ACM Press, 1977.
6. WARREN, D.H.D. **An Abstract Prolog Instruction Set**. Manchester:SRI International: AI Center: Computer Science and Technology Division, 1983. (Technical Note 309).
7. ALI, K.; KARLSSON, R. **The Muse Or-Parallel Prolog Model and Its Performance**. Kista:Swedish Institute of Computer Science, 1990.
8. HERMENEGILDO, M. &-Prolog and its Performance: Exploiting Independent And-Parallelism. In: INTERNATIONAL CONFERENCE ON LOGIC PROGRAMMING, 1990. **Proceedings...**, MIT Press, 1990.
9. COSTA, V.S.; WARREN, D.H.D.; YANG, R. The Andorra-I Engine: A Parallel Implementation of the Basic Andorra Model. In: INTERNATIONAL CONFERENCE ON LOGIC PROGRAMMING, 8., 1991. **Proceedings...**, MIT Press, 1991.

10. HERMENEGILDO, M. **An Abstract machine Based Execution Model for Computer Architecture Design and Efficient Implementation of Logic Programs in Parallel**. Austin: University of Texas at Austin, 1986. Ph.D. Thesis.
11. WERNER, O. **Uma Máquina Abstrata Estendida para o Paralelismo E na Programação em Lógica**. Porto Alegre: CPGCC da UFRGS, 1994. Master Thesis.
12. BARBOSA, J. **GRANLOG: Um Modelo para Análise Automática de Granulosidade na Programação em Lógica**. Porto Alegre: CPGCC da UFRGS, 1996. Master Thesis.
13. AZZOUNE, H. Type Inference in Prolog. **9th. International Conference on Automated Deduction**, Argonne, USA, May 1988.
14. CORSINI, M.-M. e MUSUMBU, K. Type Inference in Prolog: a New Approach. **Theoretical Computer Science**, Elseviér, v. 119, 1993.
15. CODISH, M. e LAGOON, V. Type Dependencies for Logic Programs Using ACI-Unification **From: ftp://132.72.40.8/pub/people/codish/aci-type.ps**, Ben-Gurion University of the Negev, 1996.

This article was processed using the LaTeX macro package with LLNCS style

An implementation of Or-Parallelism based on direct access to the MMU

Laurent Perron
perron@aloes.ens.fr
http://www.ens.fr/users/perron/

Ecole Normale Supérieure
45 Rue d'Ulm,
75005 Paris, France

Abstract. In this article, we propose a new scheme to implement or-parallelism and independent and-parallelism in a concurrent constraint language. Based on a low-level use of the Memory Management Unit of the workstation, this novel approach offers the fastest possible access to variable and constraint values while preserving a small task switching overhead.

Keywords: Non-determinism, or-parallelism, and-parallelism, Logic, Concurrency, Constraints, Compilation, Shared Memory, Execution Model

1 Introduction

Non-determinism is the ability to travel freely through a tree of hypotheses. It allows the programmer to try different hypothesis independently. This capacity is found in Logic Programming (aka Prolog), Constraint Logic Programming and Concurrent Constraint Logic Programming. It is fundamental for instance in the goal resolution in Prolog. But its implementation is complex and costly. There are essentially two opposite implementation schemes.

Trailing is an efficient sequential implementation scheme on a uni-processor computer. Trailing means that when trying an hypothesis, every change which happens to the database is stored, which allows to undo the changes (backtrack) before trying another hypothesis. In practice, changes are pushed on a stack. Every time a hypothesis is tried, a marker is positioned on the stack, thus allowing nested hypotheses and multi-level undoing. This technique is used in the Warren Abstract Machine implementation of Prolog[27].

Encapsulated search is another implementation scheme. It is found for instance in the Oz system [21, 22]. Instead of considering a unique *store* where results of computations are written, encapsulated search develops the notion of local stores. This means that different hypotheses will be tried on independent local stores. Using this technique, backtracking is replaced by a dropping operation which consists in removing the local store and reclaiming the allocated memory. These two implementations offer drastically different performances. In a railing system, accessing the database or the value of a variable is very fast, but switching from one branch of the tree of hypothesis to another is very costly since it requires backtracking. In encapsulated systems, there is no backtracking but this improvement is balanced by the cost induced by the management of local stores.

On parallel architectures, there is no such optimal implementation as the trailing mechanism which is fundamentally sequential (two agent must not interfere on the trailing stack). There exist different solutions to help parallelize logic languages and their derivatives.

In *Prolog and in CLP languages*, various execution models have been proposed. The first one relies on **and-parallelism**[11, 17, 18]. It consists in exploring subgoals in parallel. This technique is interesting because it is compatible with the trailing mechanism since only one node of the tree of hypotheses is explored at a time. But it requires some control since two cooperative workers may lead to inconsistent computations. Two possible execution models have been proposed, *Independent and-parallelism*[10, 11, 18] which parallelize independent goals (goals which do not share variables) and *Stream and-parallelism*[24] which orders subgoals in a producer-consumer way.

The second execution model relies on **or-parallelism** [2, 23, 1, 9, 8, 4, 3, 29, 7]. It consists exploring different branches of a choice point in parallel. In this case, since multiple agents coexist, the same variable may be used in different places with different values. Thus the system has to cope with multiply bound variables and multiple environment[6].

Concurrent Constraint Programming[20, 19, 12, 25] is an elegant merging of CLP and of Concurrent programming. It allows a better control of the execution of processes and it incorporates parallel composition in its design. In this paradigm, the notion of independent and-parallelism and streamed and-parallelism is irrelevant as in CLP languages with a parallel $\wedge$ operator. And parallelism is explicit in CCLP languages. But the availability of both parallel composition and non-determinism forbids an implementation based on trailing since nothing can restrict an agent from backtracking while another is pushing some changes on the trailing stack. Thus the implementation of non-determinism has to use methods inherited from or-parallel languages. For instance, AKL[12] and Oz[13] use techniques inherited from or-parallelism languages.

The CC($\mathcal{M}$) [14, 15, 16] project is aimed at a generic implementation of the Concurrent Constraint class of languages[20, 19]. The CC($\mathcal{M}$) language is a kernel language and constraint domains are implemented as libraries of this language. The CC($\mathcal{M}$) language is designed as a concurrent object language. The contribution of this article is that the implementation of or-parallelism in the CC($\mathcal{M}$) project relies on hardware functionalities (direct programmation of the Memory Management Unit of the CPU) for helping and speeding up the management of multiple environment. Since, with these functionalities, we are able to manage local stores for agents in an efficient way both for accessing variable values and for task switching.

The rest of the paper is sectioned if the following way. In section 2, we will define a constraint domain and the CC class of languages. Section 3 will present the state of the art in the implementation of or-parallelism. In section 4, we will give an overview of the CC($\mathcal{M}$) project, its motivations and its multi-layers architecture. Section 5 will focus on the implementation of or-parallelism within the CC($\mathcal{M}$) language and its use in the implementation of or-parallelism for any CC(X) language. Section 6 will then justify the implementation choices by comparing the resource consumptions of the management of or-parallelism between the CC($\mathcal{M}$) system and other existing systems. It will then present a small running application which will show the scalability of the CC($\mathcal{M}$) language. We will then conclude and present future direction of research.

2 Preliminaries

In this article, $\mathcal{V}$ will denote a finite or countable set of variables. Elements of this set will be written using capital letters X or Y.

A *Constraint Domain*[20, 19] is a structure $\langle X, \vdash \rangle$ where $\vdash$ is a monotonic entailment relation. This structure X is closed under existential quantification and conjunction. It contains two distinguished elements **true** and **false**.

We give the constructors of deterministic CC.

Deterministic CC:

Program	::= Decl . Agent	*Declaration and initial agent*
Decl	::= Decl . Decl	*List of declarations*
	| p :: Agent	*Declaration of a function*
	| .	*Empty declaration*
Agent	::= *tell*(c)	*Adding of a constraint*
	| *ask*(c) → Agent	*Asking of a constraint*
	| Agent || Agent	*Parallel composition*
	| Agent ⊕ Agent	*Non-determinism*
	| $\exists_X$ Agent	*Local variable*
	| p(X)	*Function call*
	| True	*Dummy agent*

We will simplify the notations by using $c\downarrow$ instead of *tell*(c) and by using $c \rightarrow$ A instead of *ask*(c) $\rightarrow$ A.

Let us briefly sketch the semantics of these operators. $c\downarrow$ first checks if the constraint c is compatible with the current store. In this case, the constraint c is added to the store. Otherwise, the *tell*fails and nothing is added to the store. This is done atomicaly. $c \rightarrow$ A will check if either c or $\neg$(c) is entailed by the store. If c is entailed, the *ask*is reduced to the agent A. If $\neg c$ is entailed by the store, the *ask*fails. If neither c not $\neg c$ is entailed by the store, the *ask*stops until either c or $\neg c$ is entailed. The semantic of *parallel composition* is clear. *Non-determinism* implies independent computations, and local stores. *Local variables* imply a notion of hiding as a local variable is independent from the rest of the store. When a *function call* is evaluated, it is reduced to the agent body in the declaration of the called function.

3 Related Works

3.1 Two sequential implementation schemes of non-determinism

The notion of non-determinism implies the ability to try a hypothesis and then to restore the values of the variables to their former state before trying another hypothesis. On uni-processor sequential computers, there exists two major implementation scheme for non-determinism: *trailing* and *encapsulated search.*

In a trailing implementation with cppying , there exists a unique store. When the resolution of a given goal implies a choice point, a marker is positioned on a trailing stack and every time a change happens in the database, a couple ⟨variable, old value⟩ is pushed on the stack. Thus, when the program needs to restore the old state, it just pops old values and variables from the trailing stack and overwrites the new values with the old ones.

In an encapsulated search implementation or backtracking without copying, the idea is different. Instead of storing negative information (from the current store to an old store), one stores positive information (from the old store to the the new one). As a consequence, each choice point contains elements like ⟨variable, new value⟩. In fact, the store is replaced by the original store (at the beginning of the computation) and by a list of choice points containing the new values for the local store.

The performances of these two implementation schemes are very different. In a trailing implementation, accessing the variables is very fast (in constant time in fact) but backtracking time is proportional to the number of changes which happened after the last choice point. On the contrary, in a encapsulated search implementation, there is no backtracking, just a dropping operation, but reading the value of a variable may require accessing a arbitrarily long ascending chain of list of differences.

3.2 Parallelization of trailing and encapsulated search

Many proposals have been made to implement or-parallelism for logic languages. These proposal were primarly motivated by hardware considerations. There are basically two kind of parallel computers which are *shared* memory and *non shared* memory computers. From these two categories of computer derives two categories of parallel implementation.

The first category relates to **non-shared** memory computers. It involves either *copying* of data when a new agent is launched or *recomputing* every changes which appeared before the fork. The advantage of such models is that the problem of multiply bound variables is completely solved by the memory *gap* between processors. Since each processors has its own memory completely separated from the rest of the computer memory, its own references to variables cannot interfere with references on other processors. But the cost of launching a new agent is very high because the whole data needed by the agent are to be copied from the parent agent to the child agent.

Conery's *closed environments*[9] reduce the copying cost by reorganizing the stack frame and by keeping every needed information on the same stack frame. This is achieved by a *closing* operation which implies a selective copying of the stack after each call. Ali's *BC-machine*[1] do not use this algorithm and incrementally copy parts of the WAM stacks when creating a new worker. Clocksin's *Delphi model*[8] is a model using recomputation.

In these models, the good aspect is that the execution of an agent is as efficient as in a sequential implementation but the cost of creating a new agent is very high as it requires copying or recomputing the whole database.

The second category of models relates to **shared** memory computers. In such models, since the difficulty of representing multiple bindings to the same variable cannot be solved by hardware considerations, each agent must be able to find the correct instance of any variable. The alternative here is whether of not each agent maintains a full set of references to the correct values of every variables.

If the answer is no then each agent stores the differences which happened during its own computation. In this case, the usual solution is that each agent has its own hash table which stores the results of local computation. This approach offers a fast task switching overhead since no extra computation is required during the context switch.Bbut it slows down writing to a variable since this is implemented by a writing to an hash table. It slows down even more the reading a variable value since this may require the exploration of any number of ascending hash-windows in order to find the exact location of the variable definition. We will call these models the *hashing* models. Here are some examples: works by Ciepielewski and Haridi[6, 7], the Argonne model [4], the PEPSys system[3], AKL[12] and Oz[25, 26].

If the answer is yes, then reading or writing the value of a variable requires only two more indirections (one to the current process and one to the variable array of this process) than direct access. This is a lot faster than accessing the hash table. But this set of references has to be maintained during the context switch. We will call these models the *vector* models. Various implementations have been proposed. In the SRI model[28], there is one array of references for the whole system. This model suffers from a very high task switching cost since it requires following the path from the old task to the new one and removing references as we go up in the tree[1] and adding references as we go down. The Muse model[2] or the ACE model[17, 18] is very different. Each node contains the memory segment which differs from their parent node, thus task switching involves overwriting the stack. This could be worse than the SRI model but selective copying reduces this overhead. And since variables keep the same address, constraint handling is as fast as sequential prolog. Another model is the *Version Vector model* where each processor has one slot per variable. This model has

[1] the root is at the top of the tree

worse memory performance and has never been implemented.

In these *shared memory* models, it is difficult to find the best implementation either accessing variables or context switching are very expensive. This is where the CC($\mathcal{M}$) implementation will be interesting as it will combine a low task switching overhead and a very fast access to variables.

4 The CC($\mathcal{M}$) project

4.1 Presentation of the CC($\mathcal{M}$) project

The notion of a generic implementation of constraint domain is not new and it can be found for instance in the AKL project[12]. In this project, a few overloaded functions implement the interface between the generic constraint solver and specific constraint domain. These functions deal with the installation, the removal, the entailment test, the garbaging ... of a constraint in the constraint domain. The approach in the CC($\mathcal{M}$) project is very similar.

The CC($\mathcal{M}$) project is a project aimed at the implementation of CC(X) languages where X is an admissible constraint domain as defined by Saraswat. In order to implement different constraint domains and possibly to mix different constraint solvers within the same application, the CC($\mathcal{M}$) project relies on a kernel language. This language should present two different aspects. The first one is that it must encode complex structures representing constraints. Our choice is that it will be an object-oriented language. As object languages offer a class hierarchy to encode complex objects and overloading to reuse generic parts of code, an object language is a good choice for the implementation of generic constraint solvers. Moreover, this language must offer the same primitives of the CC class of languages, i.e. parallel composition, non-determinism.

Therefore the kernel language should be a *concurrent object language.*

As shown in a previous paper[14], implementing a constraint domain over an object-like language is a multi-stage process. This is summarized in figure 2.

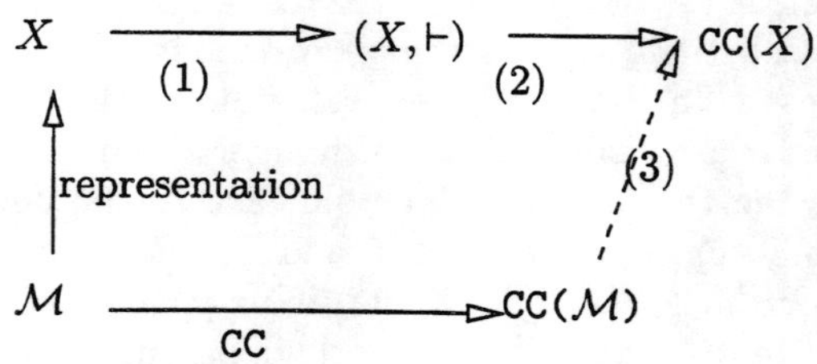

Fig. 1. Implementation scheme of CC(X)

The first stage is the encoding of constraints in a class structure. This is the *representation* arrow. Then the implementor needs to program *entailment* over this new structure. This is the (1) arrow of the figure. The rest is automatic, adding the CC constructs to $(X, \vdash)$ is just using the same constructs in CC($\mathcal{M}$). Thus, with minimal efforts, we are able to implement CC (X) over CC($\mathcal{M}$). This is the (3) arrow.

The architecture of CC($\mathcal{M}$) is based on three independent layers.

1. The first layer implements the interface to the system resources. It provides parallelism (real or simulated) and a database implementation (internal or external). This layer integrates general C libraries (QuickThread provides the thread library), the external database being any stand-alone database.
2. The second one implements the CC($\mathcal{M}$) primitives (*ask*, *tell*, parallel composition, or-parallelism ...). It is programmed in C and interacts with the previous level in two ways: first it issues request to the C libraries and second, it shares with the parallelism libraries the internal description of an agent.
3. The third one provides CC($\mathcal{M}$) with various extensions. These libraries implement constraint domains, an optimizing compiler, ...

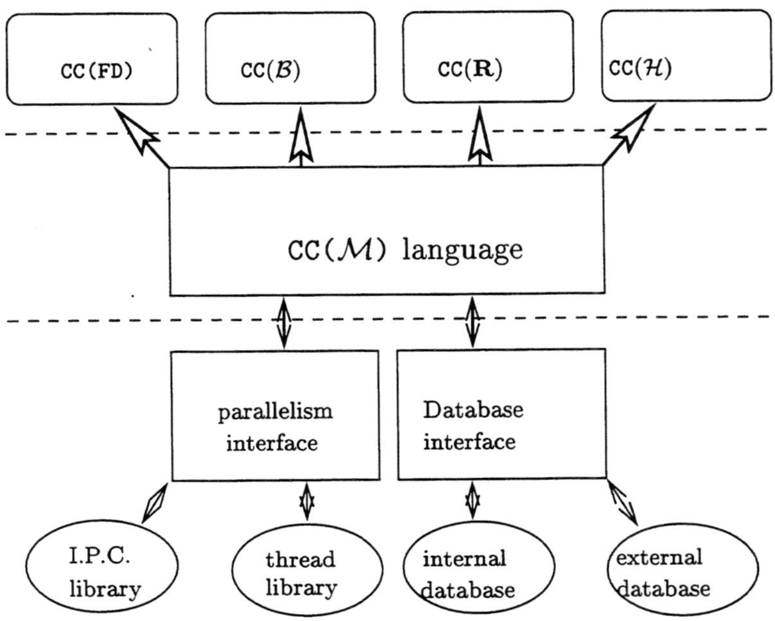

Fig. 2. The CC($\mathcal{M}$) architecture

4.2 Overview of the CC($\mathcal{M}$) language

This section briefly presents the first two layers of the CC($\mathcal{M}$) architecture.

Our memory model Works on *non shared* memory models and *vectors* models have demonstrated many facts. First of all, it is inefficient to duplicate the whole memory during an agent creation. This was shown by the competitivity of models using recomputation on non shared memory computers. Moreover, the size of the area involved during a choice point is critical both from the point of view of memory consumption and from that of time consumption during an agent creation and during a task switching.

Conery's *closed environments*[9] have shown that it was worthy reorganizing the stack after each function call in order to keep the mutable data area as small and as compact as possible. In the ACE system[17], selective copying has shown that keeping variable access as fast as in sequential prolog is profitable even if it means overwriting the stack during each context switch.

The CC($\mathcal{M}$) memory model is inspired by all these experiences. But with a radical approach. Instead of examining the program code in order to find the mutable memory area, the CC($\mathcal{M}$) language implements a two level memory model (figure 3) consisting of

1. A common memory segment shared by all agents. It contains the system definition, the functions and every ground terms of the database.
2. A pool of local memory segment. When an agent becomes active, the local memory segment of the new agent is installed at the *same* address. This address is defined once for all in the system, thus every local memory segment appears at the same address.

Thus it is up to the programmer to define which variables are global and which are local. This approach has many benefits: It allows the mutable memory area to be as small as possible; it also allows some shared variables between agents[2].

Then the CC($\mathcal{M}$) system runs a preemptive scheduler which executes the following imperative code:

```
New <- NextThread()          (* Get next waiting thread  *)
if (New != Nil) then         (* New = Nil -> No waiting thread *)
   Old <- CurrentThread()    (* Old <- preempted thread *)
   EnqueueThread(Old)        (* Put back thread on pool *)
   InstallLocalMemory(New)   (* arrow on figure *)
   Switch(Old, New)          (* switch from Old to New *)
   Continue(New)             (* Resume execution of New *)
endif                        (* Never reached *)
```

Classes and objects in the CC($\mathcal{M}$) language Class and objects can be defined in the CC($\mathcal{M}$) language with the following syntax.

```
<new_class_name>  <: <superclass_name> ( feature : type , ...)
<new_object_name> :: [local] <class_name> ( feature <- value, ...)
```

[2] This possibility is used when transforming the *branch and bound* algorithm into a *parallel cost* algorithm

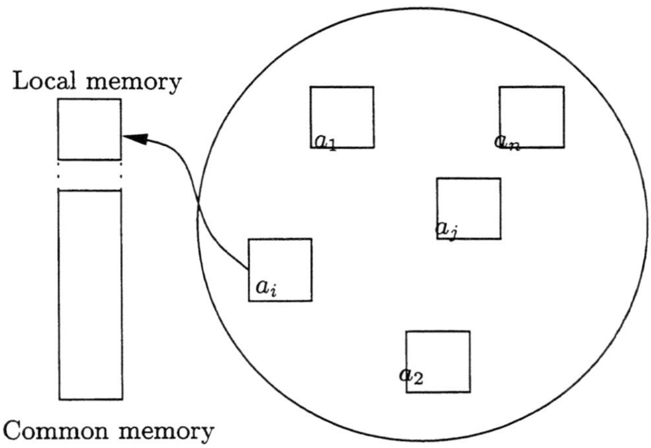

Fig. 3. The CC($\mathcal{M}$) memory model

The optional `local` modifier specifies that the next term is to be allocated on the local heap and not on the global one.

This `local` modifier is of course available each time some memory is allocated (variables, anonymous objects, arrays ...).

When comparing $\mathcal{M}$ with ψ-terms, it turns out that $\mathcal{M}$ implements a two level heirarchy (classes - objects) where ψ-terms implements a single level hierarchy (there is no distinction between classes and objects). Moreover, $\mathcal{M}$ is typed (each attribute of each class has a type decided at compile time) and ψ-terms are totally untyped. Apart from these differences, the two systems offer quite the same expressive power.

The parallelism primitives of CC($\mathcal{M}$) These primitives relate to the calculus of processes and threads:

```
detach [local] <function call>
<variable> <- catch [local] <function call>
raise <exception>

CurrentThread ()          ThreadAbort ()
ThreadSleep ()            RestartThread ()
```

`detach` evaluates the function call in parallel. `catch` does the same, but it also puts a signal handler which catches exceptions raised by the `raise` instruction and returns the raised exception. The `local` modifier specifies if the local memory is to be duplicated during the fork.

`ThreadSleep` freezes the current thread which can be restarted by the `RestartThread` primitive.

5 Implementation of or-parallelism

5.1 The memory management of a workstation

In this section, we describe the functionment of the M.M.U. in a computer, how it can be accessed.

A brief presentation of the M.M.U. On Unix workstations, one important aspect of the operating system is virtual memory. This means that each process lives in its own memory space and cannot see anything else. This behaviour is the key of general protection, identification and rights since a process is trapped in a virtual space without the possibility to escape[3].

This feature is essentially implemented by the hardware which provides the Memory Management Unit (MMU), a chipset located on the memory bus, which performs most of the job as described in figure 4.

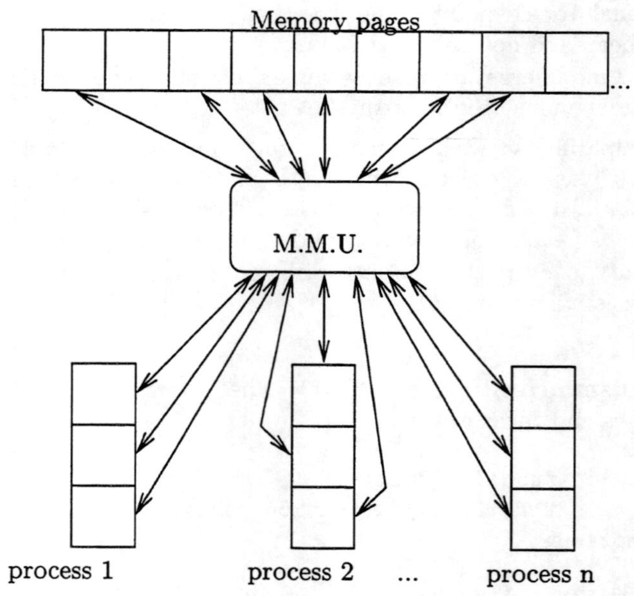

Fig. 4. Description of the M.M.U.

Thus, the MMU uses translation tables and maps virtual memory pages to physical ones. This scheme allows the kernel to (1) map different pages at the same address (for different processes) and (2) to share a physical page among processes (as used in shared libraries).

[3] This is of course an utopia

O.S. and I.P.C. libraries A common library in modern unices is the Inter Process Communication (IPC) library which offers various system calls to implement shared memory, semaphores and messages between processes. We will mainly use the first part of the library.

This library offers three primitives:

```
shmget ( key, size, shmflag )
shmat  ( shmid, shmaddr, shmflag )
shmdt  ( shmaddr )
```

`shmget()` creates a new memory segment of length `size` bytes and returns and identifier `shmid`. This identifier is then used by `shmat()` to map the designated memory segment at the virtual address `shmaddr`. The segment can be unmapped with the `shmdt()` system call.[4].

These system calls directly modify the translation pages of the MMU.

5.2 Implementation of the CC($\mathcal{M}$) memory model

Implementation using the I.P.C. library Using the I.P.C. primitives, we are able to allocate a small memory segment for every agent. This memory segment is mapped at a predefinite address when a agent becomes active. Thus installing the local memory of an agent consists in removing an old local memory segment is done by a `shmdt` system call and then using the `shmdt` system call to map a previously allocated segment at the same address.

Therefore, we are able to implement the ACE model or the Muse model without actually copying the local data.

Distribution of the CC($\mathcal{M}$) execution model As shown in figure 1 and figure 3, CC($\mathcal{M}$) relies on a multi-threading library. But using the I.P.C. facilities for shared memory between processors, the common memory segment can be shared between processes. Furthermore, since the local memory pool is visible from every process, threads (and local memory segments) can be executed by any process. Thus threads can migrate easily from process to process without any additionnal cost. And since the operating system and the hardware allow it, processes can be executed by different processors. The result is then true parallelism and the use of the whole computing power of the workstation.

Each process then runs a preemptive round-robin scheduler called by a timer whose code is the previous scheduler code modified to take into account the I.P.C. primitives and the distribution of threads.

```
New <- GetNewThread()       (* Get Waiting thread from pool *)
if (New != Nil) then        (* New = Nil -> No waiting thread *)
   Old <- CurrentThread()  (* Old <- preempted thread *)
   UnmapLocalMemory(Old)   (* arrow (2)  on figure *)
```

[4] Further details are available by `man shmop` and `man shmget`

```
   PutBackThread(Old)      (* Put back thread on pool *)
   MapLocalMemory(New)     (* arrow (1) on figure *)
   Switch(Old, New)        (* switch from Old to New *)
   Continue(New)           (* Resume execution of New *)
endif                      (* Never reached *)
```

This scheme which implements the migration of threads on different processes and processors is summarized in Figure 5.

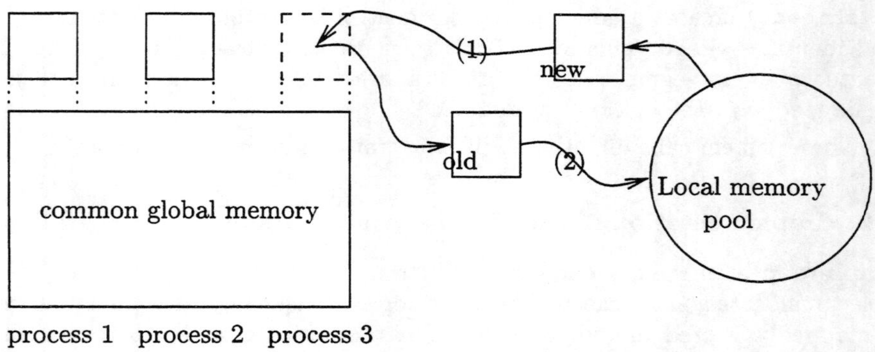

Fig. 5. multi-processing environment

5.3 Implementing multiple environment

In order to implement multiple environments, we need to store logical and constraint variables in the local memory.

Internally, such a variable is a reference to a C structure. In order to keep the local memory as small as possible, only the last reference to the variable is to be local. This last reference is in fact the pointer to the C structure itself. The result is shown in figure 6.

5.4 Or workers and independent And workers

Using the CC($\mathcal{M}$) primitives, launching a new cooperative agent is simply done by using the `detach` instruction.

Launching an Or-Parallel worker is slighty more complex. The implementation changes if the programmer wants every solutions or just the first one.

In case only the first solution is wanted, the following code is enough to implement a choice point:

```
Result <- catch ChoiceFunction ()
```

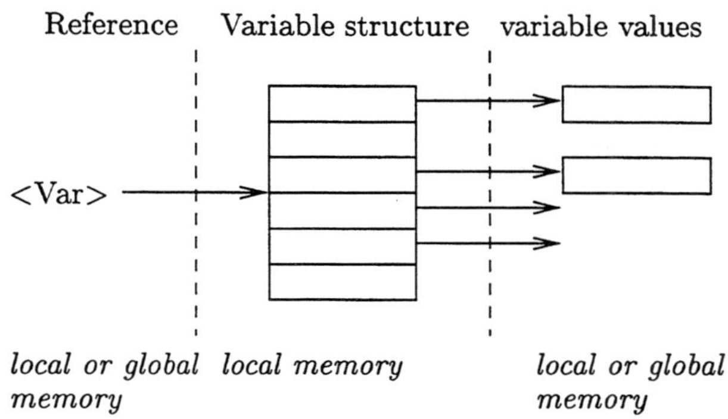

Fig. 6. A variable implementation

where the `ChoiceFunction` detaches every branches of the choice point.

```
foreach H in ChoicePoint
  detach local EvalBranch(H)
```

Each branch `EvalBranch` is then implemented as follows

```
(* CommitHypothesis *)
...
(* rest of the agent code *)
...
(* in case of success *)
raise ResultException ( result <- <found result>)

(* in case of failure *)
ThreadAbort ()
```

Thus `Result` is assigned the first found solution and `Nil` when every agent has failed, since a `catch` instruction returns a `Nil` value when all the sub-processes have aborted.

To keep all the solutions , the implementor needs a shared variable where every agent will enqueue its result before aborting.

6 Comparison with other systems

In this section, we analyze the resources consumption of our execution model and we compare it to other existing models.

6.1 Performance considerations

Typical benchmarks We have run different benchmarks to evaluate the average cost of basic operations used in constraint programming languages. These costs will help us in the comparison of the CC($\mathcal{M}$) project with other systems. These tests were made on a Sun SparcStation 5 with code compiled with gcc without any optimization.

The results are the followings:

Operation	costs
read/write from and to memory, no indirections	0.8 μs
read/write, with 1 indirection	2.4 μs
read/write, with 2 indirections	3.6 μs
unmap a memory segment, map a new one	178 μs
read a value from a partially filled hash table	20 μs
write a value to a partially filled hash table without test	8 μs
copy a memory block of 4096 bytes	204 μs

Comparison with vectors models The implementation of or-parallelism requires three basic operations which are the agent creation, agent switching and accessing (reading or writing) a variable. For vector models[28, 2, 17, 18], an important notion is the distance between two tasks. Accessing variable is as fast in vectors models than in the CC($\mathcal{M}$) language (In fact, it is a bit faster in the CC($\mathcal{M}$) language because there is one less indirection) and the cost of copying a 4 Ko memory segment is comparable with the cost of unmapping-mapping a shared memory segment. Furthermore the overhead induced by the context switch is independent of the mutable area size in the CC($\mathcal{M}$) project and linear in vectors models like the ACE system[17, 18].

Comparison with hashing models When comparing the CC($\mathcal{M}$) language to hashing models[6, 7, 4, 3, 12, 25, 26], the access time of a variable is so high that it justifies easily the overhead of the context switch. In fact, 9 (178 / 20) read operations (and read operations which succeed by using the first hash window) have the same cost than the unmap-map operation. And it is clear that between two context switches, the program will perform much more than 9 read operations. Therefore, the CC($\mathcal{M}$) implementation is much more efficient than implementations of hashing models.

6.2 A running CC(FD) example

We have tested our language on the bridge problem. Using a naive implementation, we have obtained the following results for the optimum (104 days) and its proof of optimality.

Number of processors	1	2	3	4
Optimality proof	3.32 s	1.67 s	1.15 s	0.86 s
Speedup	1	1,98	2,88	3,86
Optimal solution	0.27	0.27	0.27	0.27
Number of backtracks	7600	7600	7600	7600

When comparing with a fast sequential implementation on Claire [5]

Claire implementation	**Naive**	**Smart**
Optimal solution	106 ms	30 ms
First solution	10 ms	30 ms
Optimality proof	660 ms	10 ms
Number of backtracks	4008	0

This preliminary benchmarks show that the speed of the CC($\mathcal{M}$) language is correct (3.32s for finding the solution of the bridge is a very good speed in a naive implementation which explores more than 7600 backtracks) and that the CC($\mathcal{M}$) language scales up well.

We can see that the parallel version is somewhat 2.5 slower than the sequential code, which is not bad after all.

7 Conclusion

Using low-level techniques, we have implemented in the CC($\mathcal{M}$) project a hybrid system which inherits from many different implementation schemes of or-parallelism. The result is very promising, accessing variables is as fast in the CC($\mathcal{M}$) language as in fast prolog implementations (even the address of given local objects may be decided at compile time, to help the C compiler to optimize more the resulting code). Furthermore, the CC($\mathcal{M}$) memory model allows many interesting extensions of the standard prolog resolutions. The extensions come from the mixing of local variables and shared variables. In fact, this memory model is a good basis for experimenting cooperative resolution of problems, constructive negation, parallel pruning .... But this implementation does not solve the limited resources problem (how can we parallelize non determinism when the number of agents is bounded) and we know this is the biggest difficulties when implementing or-parallelism. For instance, every agent can be suspended waiting for another agent to release recources even if this is not possible. For the bridge problem, a booking algorithm was an easy solution but the general case is very challenging.

Acknowledgements

I would like to thank François Fages, François Laburthe and my brother Jean Philippe for their help and encouragements.

References

1. K. Ali. Or-parallel execution of prolog on BC-Machine. In *Fifth International Conference of Logic Programming*, pages 1531–1545. MIT Press, 1988.
2. K.A.M. Ali and R. Karlsson. Full prolog and scheduling or-parallelism in muse. In *International Journal of Parallel Programming*, number 19 in 6, page 445:475, 1991.

3. U. baron, J.C. de Kergommeaux, H. Hailperin, M. Ratcliffe, P. Robert, and J.C. Syre nad H. Westphal. The paraller ECRC prolog system PEPSys: an overview and evaluation results. In *International Conference on Fith Generation Computer Systems*, pages 841–849, Tokyo, 1988. ICOT.
4. R. Butler, E.L. Lusk, R. Olson, and R.A. Overbeek. ANLWAM: A parallel implementation of the warren abstract machine. Technical report, MCS division, Argonne National Laboratory, 1986.
5. Yves Caseau and Franois Laburthe. *Claire, reference manual.* Ecole Normale Suprieure.
6. A. Ciepielewski and S. Haridi. Storage models for or-parallel execution of logic programs. Technical report, The Royal Institute of Technology, Stockholm, 1983.
7. A. Ciepielewski, S. Haridi, and B. Hausman. Or-parallel prolog on shared memory multiprocessors. *Journal of Logic Programming*, 7:125:147, 1989.
8. W. Clocksin. Principles of the DelPhi paralle inference machine. *Computer Journal*, 30(5):386–392, 1987.
9. J.S. Conery. Binding environments for parallel logic programs in non-shared memory multiprocessors. In *SLP*, pages 457–467, 1987.
10. D. DeGroot. Restricted AND-parallelism and side effects. In *International Conference on 5th Generation Computer Systems*, San Francisco, August 1987. IEEE Computer Society.
11. M. Hermenegildo and K. Greene. &-prolog and its performance: Exploiting independant and-parallelism. In *1990 International Conference on Logic Programming*, pages 253–268. MIT Press, June 1990.
12. Sverker Janson. *AKL, A Multiparadigm Programming Language.* PhD thesis, SICS, Uppsala University, 1994.
13. Michael Mehl, Ralf Scheidhauer, and Christian Schulte. An Abstract Machine for Oz. Research Report RR-95-08, Deutsches Forschungszentrum für Künstliche Intelligenz, Stuhlsatzenhausweg 3, D66123 Saarbrücken, Germany, June 1995. Also in: *Proceedings of PLILP'95*, Springer-Verlag, LNCS, Utrecht, The Netherlands.
14. Laurent Perron. cc($\mathcal{M}$), a kernel for implementing cc languages. In *Proc. of CCP'95*, 1995.
15. Laurent Perron. A concurrent constraint kernel language based on messages. In *Proc. of ICLP*, 1995. Poster.
16. Laurent Perron. CC($\mathcal{M}$)*, un noyau parallle pour l'implantation des langages concurrents par contraintes.* PhD thesis, Ecole Normale Suprieure, LIENS, 45 rue d'Ulm, 75005, Paris, France, Juin 1997. In French.
17. E. Pontelli, G. Gupta, and M. Hermenegildo. &ACE:a high performance parallel prolog system. In *IIPS 95*, Santa Barbara, CA, 1995. IEEE Computer Society.
18. Enrico Pontelli, Goral Gupta, and Manuel Hermenegildo. &ACE, the and-parallel component of ACE (a progess report on ACE). In Jonas Barlklund, Bharat Jayaraman, and Jiro Tanaka, editors, *Parallel and Data Parallel Execution of Logic Programming*, volume 78, pages 65–78. UPMAIL, June 1994.
19. Vijay Saraswat. Concurrent constraint programming. In *seventeenth ACM Symposium on Principles of Programming Languages*, 1990.
20. Vijay Saraswat. *Concurrent Constraint Programming.* MIT Press, 1993.
21. Christian Schulte and Gert Smolka. Encapsulated search in higher-order concurrent constraint programming. In Maurice Bruynooghe, editor, *Logic Programming: Proceedings of the 1994 International Symposium*, pages 505–520, Ithaca, New York, USA, November 1994. MIT-Press.

22. Christian Schulte, Gert Smolka, and Jörg Würtz. Encapsulated search and constraint programming in Oz. In A.H. Borning, editor, *Second Workshop on Principles and Practice of Constraint Programming*, Lecture Notes in Computer Science, vol. 874, pages 134–150, Orcas Island, Washington, USA, May 1994. Springer-Verlag.
23. E. Shapiro. An or-parallel execution algorithm for prolog and its FCP implementation. In *Fourth International Comference of Logic Programming*, pages 311–317. MIT Press, 1987.
24. K. Shen. *Studies in And/Or Parallelism in Prolog.* PhD thesis, University of Cambridge, 1992.
25. Gert Smolka. A calculus for higher-order concurrent constraint programming with deep guards. Research Report RR-94-03, Deutsches Forschungszentrum für Künstliche Intelligenz, Stuhlsatzenhausweg 3, 'D-66123 Saarbrücken, Germany, February 1994.
26. Gert Smolka. The Oz programming model. In Jan van Leeuwen, editor, *Computer Science Today*, Lecture Notes in Computer Science, vol. 1000, pages 324–343. Springer-Verlag, Berlin, 1995.
27. D.H.D. Warren. An abstract prolog instruction set. Technical Report 209, SRI International, 1983.
28. D.H.D. Warren. Or-parallel execution models of prolog. In *TATSOFT'87*, pages 243,259. Springer Verlag, 1987.
29. D.H.D. Warren. The SRI model for or-parallel execution of Prolog: Abstract design and implementation. In *SLP*, pages 92–102, 1987.

Multi-phase Copying Garbage Collection in LOGFLOW*

Norbert Podhorszki

MTA SZTAKI Computer and Automation Research Institute of the
Hungarian Academy of Sciences
H-1132 Budapest, Victor Hugo u. 18-22. Hungary
E-mail: pnorbert@sztaki.hu
http://www.sztaki.hu/~pnorbert

Abstract. In this paper a new type of copying garbage collectors is presented. The main goal of the modification of the original method was the reduction of the memory area reserved by the collector. The new Multi-phase Copying Garbage Collection (MC-GC) algorithm reserves only a little part of the memory. It works in more than one phases, using all available free memory areas in each phase. Performance measurements show excellent efficiency of the MC-GC implementation in the LOGFLOW parallel Prolog system.
Keywords: garbage collection, parallel Prolog, distributed systems

1 Introduction

LOGFLOW is a parallel Prolog system running on distributed memory multicomputers and workstation clusters [13]. 3DPAM (Data Driven Prolog Abstract Machine) engines execute the Prolog program based on a fine-grain parallel execution scheme. Coarse-grain pieces of work are executed by traditional sequential WAM (Warren Abstract Machines [25]) engines that are coupled with the 3DPAM engines on each processing element.

In the execution of logic programming languages the memory consumption speed is very high because a storage cell of the memory cannot be reused when it is filled once. The memory is exhausted quickly but most of the allocated storage cells are 'garbage', i.e., they are not used by the system. Moreover, there are no deallocating features in declarative languages. Since the birth of the declarative languages much effort has been done on solving this problem. The lost memory areas are called garbage therefore, the common name of the problem is garbage collection.

Since the late 50's many garbage collection algorithms have been proposed. At the beginning they were used by the implementations of LISP and other functional languages. In the 80's Prolog required memory management. In 1981 J. Cohen

* The work presented in this paper was supported partially by the Hungarian-Portuguese joint project 'PAR-PROLOPPE' registered under No. H-9305-02/1095 and by two National Science Research Fund (OTKA) projects under grant number T016091 and T020658.

summarized and classified the work done in the area and these algorithms were altered and developed later, see [6] and [29].

Fig. 1 shows a possible classification of the algorithms including our new *multi-phase copying garbage collection algorithm (MC-GC).*

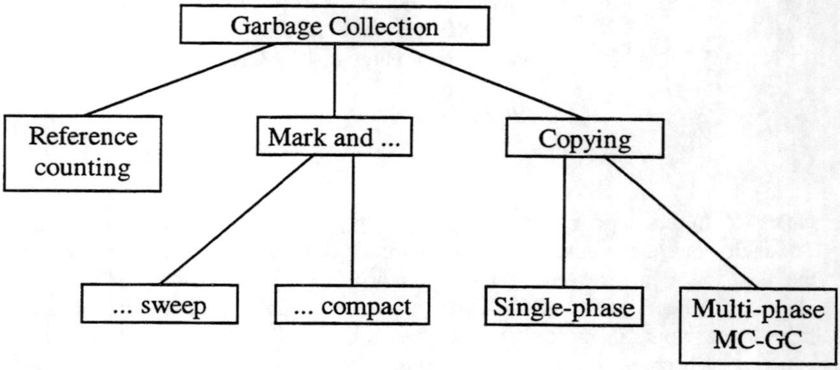

Fig. 1. Classification of garbage collection techniques

- *reference counting*. As it is described in [7] and [28], an extra field, called refcount, is introduced to each object. This field indicates the number of times the object is referenced. This field has to be updated each time when a pointer to the object is created or destroyed. When the counter becomes equal to zero, the object is inactive and can be collected.

  This technique distributes the collection time among the whole execution time providing an appropriate method for real-time and interactive systems. Its locality is a great advantage in systems using virtual memory and caches. However, the method has several disadvantages. First, the extra spaces needed for the counters occupy significant amount of memory. Second, the permanent updating of the counters makes an overhead on the execution time. Third, this method is unable to reclaim cyclic structures.

  A one-bit-size counter method is implemented in [5] (see also [12]). It can reclaim only the garbage of single referenced objects. Deutsch and Bobrow used hash tables for LISP systems to handle the single referenced objects efficiently, see [3],[8],[6]. The "lazy reference counting" method (described in [10]) avoids to allocate additional spaces for single referenced objects, only the multiple referenced ones are handled by indirection cells. The use of weighted references is an efficient method in distributed systems, see [2] and [26].

- *marking and sweeping*. In the marking and sweeping type garbage collectors the collection is executed in two phases. In the first phase, the accessible objects are only marked and the collection is performed in the second phase. The simplest method for reclaiming is that the unmarked cells are incorporated into one or more free lists (*sweeping*). This may be accomplished by keeping a list for each object size commonly used in a program, see [16].

The sweeping algorithm fragments the memory and the handling of structures with different sizes is very cumbersome. The cost of the collection is proportional to the size of the entire memory because all live objects must be marked and all garbage must be collected. Since the structures are not moved - which can be seen as an advantage because of the unnecessity of pointer updating - this method may be unsuitable for a system using virtual memory. Efficient implementation techniques can be found in [29].

- *marking and compacting*. After marking all accessible objects (*living objects*) they are compacted into a continuous area of the memory. Since the structures are moved in the memory, their references must be updated. This is the main disadvantage of these collectors. The compaction may be *arbitrary* (the order of the compacted objects is arbitrary) *linearizing* (objects originally pointing to each other become adjacent after compaction) and *sliding* (the original linear order of the objects is not changed by the compaction). Many algorithms were designed, see [11][24][16][27][17] [23][19] or see summaries in [6] and [29].

- *copying collection*. The copying collectors move all the live objects into a separate storage and the rest of the memory is then reusable because it contains only garbage. The garbage is not touched thus, the "garbage collection" is implicit. While the compacting collectors use a separate marking phase, the copying collectors integrate the traversal of the data and the copying process. Therefore, most objects are traversed only once. The work is proportional to the amount of live data.

  The copying collectors are very efficient if sufficient large memory is available. The cost of one collection is proportional to the amount of the living objects and independent of the size of the memory. The data are transferred fast and only once in the memory. However, the disadvantage of pointer updating remains. For detailed description, see [18][9][4][1].

- *multi-phase copying collection*. To decrease the size of the reserved area used in copying garbage collectors, a multi-phase copying garbage collection (MC-GC) algorithm has been introduced and implemented in LOGFLOW. The main advantage of this algorithm is the efficiency: it provides a sufficiently fast collector, all garbage is thrown away and the continuous heap can be used by the engine without any overhead. The detailed description of the new MC-GC algorithm is given in this paper.

The conventional LP systems can reuse most of the allocated memory cells by freeing them at backtracking. This feature, however, causes more problems in garbage collection, than gives advantages. The objects must be kept in original order of their allocation, otherwise backtracking would be impossible. Because of the need for ordering many efficient garbage collection algorithms cannot be used. For example, the modification of the copying collection algorithms is complex, resulting less efficient methods than the original one.

Fortunately, LOGFLOW does not perform backtracking that would be itself a very complex and inefficient operation in a distributed environment. The 3DPAM exploiting OR-parallelism is an all-solution Prolog engine by its nature. The system searches for all solutions in parallel. There is no backtracking or similar operation in LOGFLOW. Therefore, we need not deal with object ordering in the memory and we can also use copying methods in garbage collection.

A short summary of the memory structure of LOGFLOW is given in Section 2. The detailed description of the MC-GC can be found in Section 3. The implementation issues are examined in Section 4. The performance measurements of the MC-GC are described in Section 5.

2 The memory structure of the 3DPAM

In 3DPAM the following data areas are used: Code, Context tables, Token Queues, Heap, Token tables. The Code area is simply an array for the 3DPAM code. The Heap is used as in the WAM, except its first part holds the ground structures for the sake of optimization. The other data areas are new and specific to 3DPAM and are explained in the following sections. The detailed description of the structure and the handling of these data areas can be found in [20].

2.1 The heap

The heap is a continuous data area in the memory. It consists of cells (with the size of the integer data type). A structure with N arguments occupies N+1 cells in the heap (the descriptor cell [FUNC | Functor ID | Arity] and a reference cell for each argument), see Fig. 2. The heap is consumed continuously by the engine therefore, structures of different Prolog search paths are mixed in the heap.

2.2 Token queues

The execution is governed by tokens. Each token holds at least the following information: identifier, target PE and starting address in the code. Depending on the type, some tokens hold more information. There are three groups of tokens:

1. request token: DO (<environment>, <arguments>)
2. reply token: SUCC (<environment>), FAIL, CFAIL
3. request/reply token: SUB (<environment>)

Identifiers of tokens are placed in one of the token queues: Local, Remote and WAM Token Queue (LTQ, RTQ and WTQ, respectively). Tokens whose identifier is in the LTQ will be processed by the local engine, whereas tokens in the RTQ will be transmitted to another PE. The 3DPAM engine takes the tokens (only identifiers, token data are taken from one of the token tables) only from the LTQ. The resulting tokens (if any) can be placed into the LTQ, RTQ, or the WTQ, or can be processed by the engine. The inherently sequential subtasks are executed by a conventional

WAM engine (see [25]). The tokens representing sequential tasks are placed into the WTQ and are processed by the WAM engine.

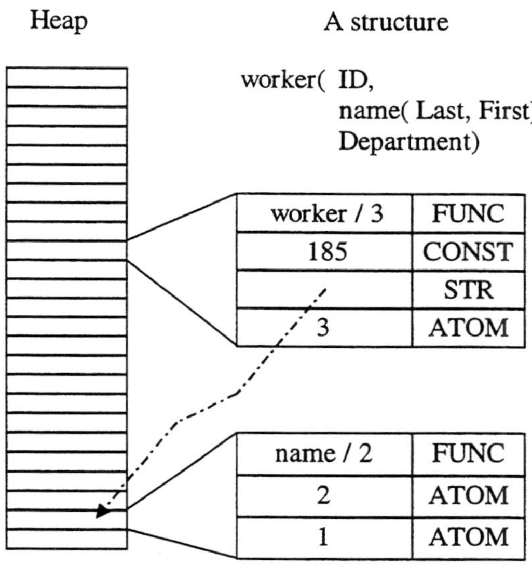

Fig. 2. The heap of the 3DPAM The garbage collector has to concentrate on the heap because other data areas are cleared automatically in LOGFLOW.

2.3 Token tables

The data of the tokens are kept in token tables. There are three kinds of token tables: Do, Fail and Sub/Succ. The token tables are arrays of records that contain a pointer and a token slot. The pointer is used to maintain the list of free token slots (see Section 2.4 where its usage is described). The token slot holds the relevant information of a given token. Its structure is equal to that of a token of the given type.

When a token is processed, its record is freed therefore, the garbage collector does not find any garbage in these tables. *The examination of these tables during the collection is important because the stored tokens contain references to the data structures of the heap.* This fact is true for the context tables, too.

2.4 Context tables

Context tables are used to distinguish different token streams. Their usage is fundamental to realize pipeline AND parallelism. Every operator type (Unify, And,

Or, Cut) has its context table. The theoretical basis is explained in [15] and an example can also be found there.

The Unify and Or context tables. The Unify and Or context tables are similar. The tables are arrays of records that contain a pointer and a context slot. The pointers are used to form a chain of free context slots (similar to token tables) and the context slots hold the relevant information:

When a token arrives to a Unify or Or node, its information content is saved, and a token with new identifier (new colour) will be emitted. When a corresponding token (representing a partial solution) of this colour has arrived at the appropriate point, its original colour will be restored, and the saved information will be updated.

The And context table. The And context table differs from the previous ones since, it must handle multiple overlapped SUB token streams. The And context table is implemented in a different way. The And context table consists of records that contain an array of counters and a state field. The context table is indexed with the colour of the incoming tokens, and the counters are indexed with the identifier of the And node within a Unify/And node.

The Cut context table. The Cut context table consists of a pointer to chain the free items together, and a field for token identifier. It is used to implement the '*cut*' in the distributed environment, where the system looks for all solutions while the 'cut' ignores all solutions except for the first (first in the term of the sequential execution).

The dynamic handling of context and token tables. Token tables and Context tables are handled in such a way that, although, the whole arrays are statically allocated data objects. The elements of these arrays can be allocated and freed dynamically. This feature is obtained by means of pointers, which are in fact array indices. Whenever a new item is to be allocated, the head of the free list will be the next item pointed by the current head. Thus, the current item is removed from the list. Adding an item to the free list means setting the pointer of the given element to the current head of the list, and the given item will be the new head, see Fig. 3. This elaboration combines the flexible and efficient use of pointers with the benefits of arrays, i.e., no run-time memory allocations and error handling are needed.

These data structures are called Dynamically Allocated Static (DAS) data structures [14]. The DAS is much faster[1] than the conventional 'malloc-free' memory management. However, it statically occupies a large amount of memory. Apart from the greater speed this solution can handle the available memory more economically. This technique avoids the loss of memory due to inner fragmentation.

The static tables occupy large memory. The size of a table must be at least as large as the maximal amount of information it should contain in a moment during execution.

[1] The DAS is slightly more than 4 times faster than the conventional method when allocating and reclaiming 50000 data items. On smaller tables the ratio is higher and can reach approximatelly 6. Measurements were done on a T800 transputer and may vary on other systems.

The reduction of the tables would be possible only if the number of tokens and contexts could be limited. This is a question of scheduling strategies.

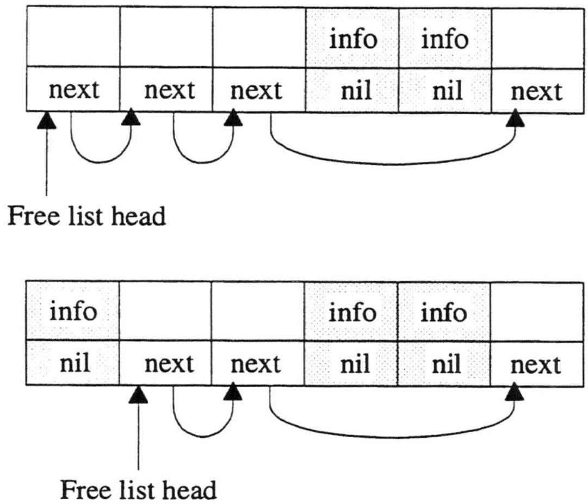

Fig. 3. Dynamically allocated static table

3 The multi-phase copying garbage collection algorithm

The classical copying garbage collection method (see [21][6][29]) provides a very fast one-phase collection algorithm but its main disadvantage is that the half of the memory is reserved for the algorithm. The transputers have only a little amount of memory. LOGFLOW allocates itself most of the available space for the token tables and context tables. The heap size must be kept as large as possible. During the execution of an application, in every moment, the number of all accessible objects on a processing element must be less than the available memory for storing them. Otherwise, the system fails whether garbage collector is implemented or not. If the classical copying collector allocates the half of the heap for own use, most of the applications cannot be executed in LOGFLOW. Of course, it is only a transputer specific problem, in the workstation version of LOGFLOW other difficulties should be solved.

To decrease the size of the reserved area, a multi-phase copying garbage collection (MC-GC) algorithm is introduced and implemented in LOGFLOW. The detailed description of the new MC-GC algorithm is given here.

Let us consider that the last $1/N$ part of the heap is reserved by the collector while the first part is used by the engine, i.e., $(N-1)/N$ part of the heap is usable continuously (see Fig. 4). Notice, that the $(N-1)/N$ limit is not a strict boundary. Processes in the LOGFLOW system can work as far as the available area of the heap is not exhausted. When the available area is consumed, the engine stops and the garbage collector is invoked. The 3DPAM engine examines the heap size regularly and when the available area is exhausted, the collector is invoked. At this time, the first cells of the reserved area may be allocated, too. The unused part of the reserved area can be used as a temporary storage for copying structures.

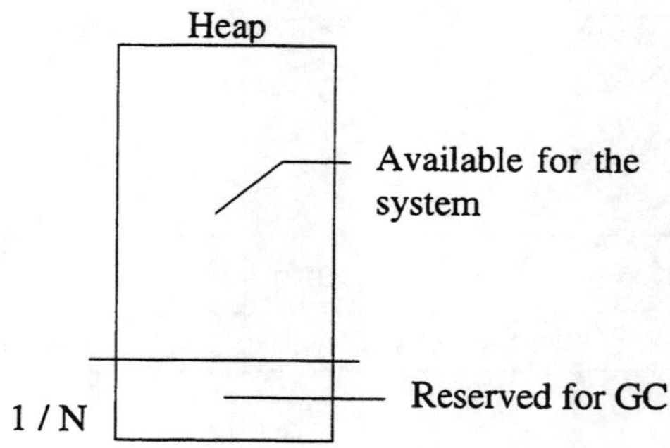

Fig. 4. Logically segmented memory

Before explaining the steps of the collector we give the definition of various areas in the heap as they appear in Fig. 5a-c.

Fixed area — This area contains the structures that are moved to their final position during the garbage collection. It is empty until the end of the first phase of the algorithm. Then it grows continuously from the first cell of the heap.

Free areas — The Free areas are used for temporary storage of the structures accessed in the collection (*living objects*).
One free area is always the reserved area.
Another one will appear after the first phase of collection. It is the 'free hole' between the Fixed area and Copying area. (It is already examined by the collector and all living objects are moved to the Fixed area but it is not occupied by new structures.) This area changes its place and size, from phase to phase.

Copying area — The area in the actual collection phase where the structures are to be moved from when they are found. It is an area changing both in place and size but it is permanent during one phase. Its size should be as large as possible but it must be ensured that all living objects accessed in a phase can be copied into the Free area without loosing data. In the first phase, the copying area consists of the first cells of the heap and its size is equal to the size of the Free area (being in the reserved area in the first phase).

Counting area This area is the one between the Copying area and the end of the consumed heap. The structures found here are only counted. This is used to determine the number of the living objects in this area. By the knowledge of this number, the size of the Copying area can be maximized in the next collection phases.
The Copying and Counting area compose a contiguous area where the structures are examined during the collection.

The steps of the collector are as follows (see Fig. 5a-c):

Phase 1.

Step 1. The Free area consists of the unused cells in the reserved area. The consumed area is splitted into two parts: the Copying and the Counting area. The Copying area starts from the first cell of the heap and its size equals to the size of the Free area. This ensures that all copied structures will fit into the Free area. The remaining part is the Counting area. (The Fixed area starts from the first cell of the heap but it is empty since no structure is collected and moved to its final position yet.)

Step 2. The original copying method is used for the living objects in the Copying area: they are moved into the Free area. The addresses in the references are set as if the objects were moved already into their final position and not into the Free area (this is an optimization, see the third step). The final place of the accessed structure is known: the first cell under the Fixed area. (A pointer is used in the implementation to indicate this position, see Section 4.4 and Fig. 7.) The structures in the Counting area are only counted. To avoid taking into account a structure more than one time, it is marked when it is accessed first.

Step 3. The content of the Free area (the collected living objects) is copied into the beginning of the heap (creating the Fixed area). At this time the structures are placed at their final positions. Since the references have been updated accordingly to the final position of the structures in Step 2, no update is needed in this step.

Phase 2.

Step 4. After the first phase, some part of the Copying area (the last cells that were the part of the Copying area but are not overwritten by the Fixed area) can also be used by the collector as a Free area, i.e., the previous Copying area is divided into the Fixed area and a Free area. The new Copying area starts from the first cell of the previous Counting area. (The Copying area advances forward from the top of the heap towards the last allocated cell, while the Counting area decreases continuously.) Its size depends only the criteria that all accessed structures should fit into the Free areas. The maximum size can be determined by the help of the counting. The method is described in Section 4.5.

Step 5. This step is similar to Step 2 (only the areas have been changed). The accessed structures are copied into the first Free area (between the Fixed and Copying area), i.e., to their final position. When this area is filled, the other Free area is used as in the first phase: the structures are copied here but the references are set accordingly to their final positions. The structures in the Counting area are not modified.

Step 6. This step is the same as Step 3. The Free area in the reserved area is copied behind the living objects (the Fixed and first Free area together). This step ensures that at the end of the garbage collection the living objects will be collected into a continuous area from the beginning of the heap. Thus, no heap management functions or macros are needed for storage allocation during program execution, keeping the efficiency of the Prolog engine. Since no update of the references is needed at this step, this step can be performed by fast block memory copy operations provided by the processor.

Phases 3 - and more

Steps 4-6 are repeated until the whole heap is collected.

The main advantage of this algorithm is the efficiency: it provides a sufficiently fast collector, all garbage is thrown away and the continuous heap can be used by the engine without any overhead. The original access mechanism of the heap in LOGFLOW did not require any special access protocol or heap management algorithm. The garbage collector presented here avoids the need for a heap manager, too. It is not the most efficient collector but its performance is sufficient in most cases. Another advantage is that the MC-GC is asynchronously demand driven on each processor. It means that garbage collection can be initiated on a processor without requiring garbage collection on the other processors.

A disadvantage is that the engine is stopped during the collection (even all processes on the processor in the current implementation of LOGFLOW). This does not seem to be a big problem in our system since it runs on multi-computers therefore, an engine can be stopped meanwhile others still can run. Another disadvantage is the handling of the heap as a whole memory structure. If the system uses virtual memory or cache, the access of the relating structures may be very costly (they can be stored in different areas of the heap). The transputer machines, where the algorithm is implemented, do not have virtual memory or cache therefore, this method can be used there. A garbage collection algorithm designed for workstations, which use virtual memory and cache, is described in [22].

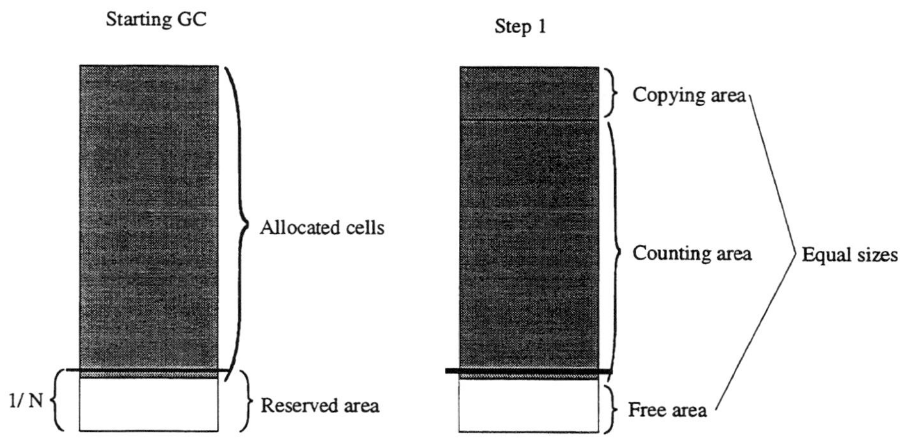

Fig. 5a. The modified copying garbage collection algorithm, starting

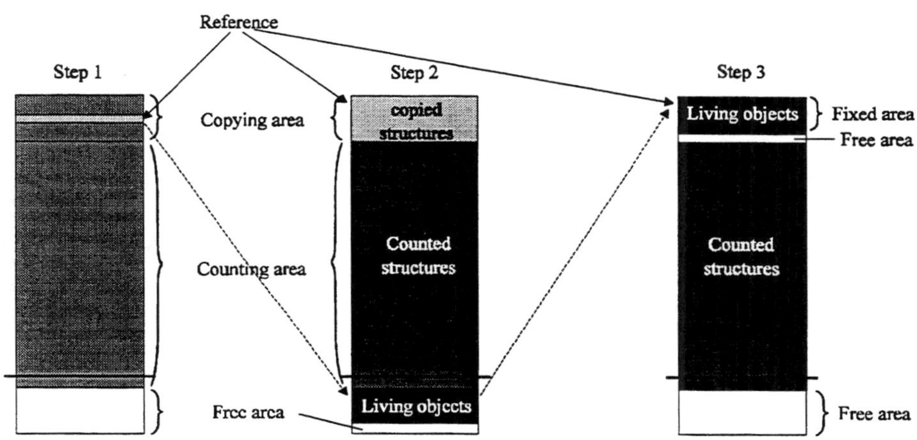

Fig. 5b. The modified copying garbage collection algorithm, phase 1. The *dashed arrows* at *Reference* indicate the real movement of a structure while the *solid arrows* indicate the settings of its references (details in Fig. 7.)

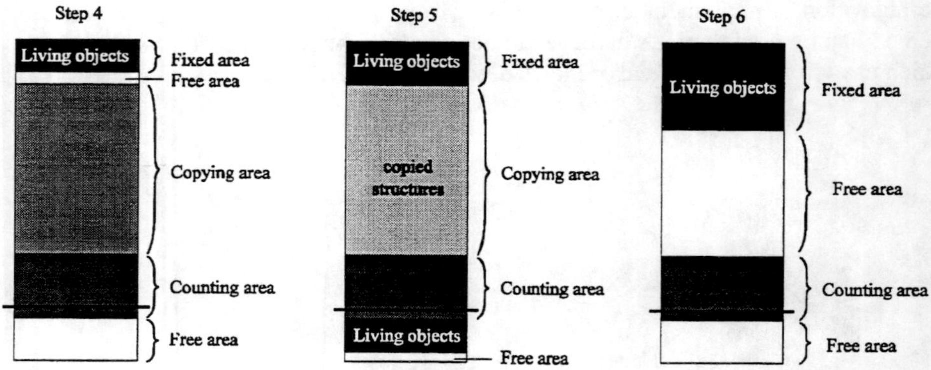

Fig. 5c. The modified copying garbage collection algorithm, phase 2. Further phases work the same way

4 Implementation issues

4.1 Mutual exclusion

A processing element of LOGFLOW consists of several concurrent processes. The parallel 3DPAM and sequential WAM processes perform the subtasks of the application while the Input and Output Managers communicate with other processing elements. All of them can access data stored in the heap. It is the main memory of 3DPAM, the WAM engine places the results of a sequential task into the heap and the managers read and write the heap when sending or receiving tokens representing subtasks or solutions for them.

The heap is a shared object of the system. The exclusive write into it is ensured by semaphore *heap_mutex*. The read has been a secure operation in LOGFLOW before the implementation of the garbage collector because the heap has been consumed increasingly and the cells allocated once have never been changed. During garbage collection neither write nor read is allowed because the cells are moved and changed.

New semaphores are introduced:

gc_input_mutex for disabling write operation of the Input Manager during GC.

gc_output_mutex for disabling read operation of the Output Manager during GC.

gc_wam_mutex for disabling read operation of the WAM engine during GC (the write is disabled by the existing semaphore *heap_mutex*)

The collector is implemented as a function called by the 3DPAM engine. Another solution could be an independent process but it is not needed for this algorithm. The 3DPAM examines the size of the heap before getting a new token from the local token queue. (This operation is performed very frequently since 3DPAM is a fine-grained computation engine.) If the size is over the limit (the reserved area is reached), the collector is called as a function automatically stopping the 3DPAM engine. Therefore, no semaphore for disabling the read and write operations of 3DPAM is needed.

At the start the collector allocates the three new semaphores and the *heap_mutex*. This ensures, that none of the processes can access the heap. The Input and Output Managers are stopped, while the WAM engine can execute the actual sequential task (if it has one) but the write-back of the results and the start of a new sequential task are postponed till the end of the garbage collection.

It is important to note, that this solution may cause problems in task scheduling and load balancing when synchronous message passing is used. In such case, the suspended Input Manager is not able to receive tokens from the neighbours suspending the Output Managers of them when they try to send tokens to this processor.

4.2 References to heap cells

Because of the specialities of the LOGFLOW, only the heap can contain garbage, see Section 2. All references pointing into the heap should be examined and updated during collection. The possible references can be found in the next data structures of the system. Since only structures are stored in the heap, all reference has the same format: [STR | address].

- *Heap structures*
  An argument field of a structure may refer to one of its substructures. When a structure is accessed by the collector, its substructures should also be examined. It is possible in MC-GC that at the time of the first access the substructure is placed in other collection area than the top-level of the structure. For example, the top-level is in the Copying area and it is copied while one of the substructures is in the Counting area and remains in their original position. When the structure (which is at its final position) is accessed in a later phase of the collection, the references must be examined since the substructures may be in one of the collecting areas.

- *Token queues and token tables*
  The references to the heap are physically stored in the token tables but they can be accessed through the token queues. The empty records of the tables need not be examined by the collector. RTQ is used by the 3DPAM engine (putting token) and the Output Manager (getting token). At the invocation of the collector the Output Manager may hold a token (with references to the heap) which is not accessible through the RTQ any more but it is not sent to another processor. This token should be examined, too. The same case is true for WTQ: the WAM engine can

hold a token when the collector disables the read access to the heap. This token should be examined, too.

- *Context tables*
  The pointer field of the Unify context table is used to mark the allocated records. If a record is allocated, the field is set to a specific value (which can not be a valid pointer value). The garbage collector can process the table in a simple cycle and can examine only the marked records (which contains information).

4.3 Heap areas and pointers used by the collector

The following *areas* of the heap can be distinguished during the collection (see Fig. **6**.):

Ground Term Table	The ground terms are stored at the top of the heap. They are never moved. This area must be unchanged.
Fixed area	This area contains the structures that are moved to their final position during the garbage collection. It is empty until the Step 2 of the algorithm.
Copying area	The area in the actual collection phase from where the structures are moved when they are found.
Counting area	The area in the actual collection phase where the structures are only marked when they are found.
Free areas	The reserved area and the area between the Fixed area and Copying area are free areas. They can be used for structure copying.

The following *pointers* are used by the collector:

Heap_begin	The first changeable cell of the heap (except for the Ground Term Table). (It is a fix pointer in the system.)
Copy_start	The first cell of the copying area. (It is fix for one phase of a collection.)
Copy_end	The first cell behind the copying area. (It is fix for one phase of a collection.)
Mark_end	The first cell behind the counting area (same as the first free cell in the heap at the start of the first phase of collection). (It is a fix pointer during one garbage collection.)

Free	The free cell which is the target of the next structure copy. (It moves towards the end of the heap at every structure copying.)
Fix	The cell which will be the final address of the structure to be copied next. (See Step 2 of the algorithm, where the structure is moved to the free area but the reference is updated to another address.) (It moves towards the end of the heap at every structure copying.)
Final_pos	The first cell of the area where the copied structures (the content of the Free area in the reserved area) are moved at the end of a collection phase. (See Step 3 and 6.) (It moves towards the end of the heap when a structure is copied direct to its final position in the Free area between the Fixed and Copying area but it is fix while the accessed structures are copied into the reserved area.)

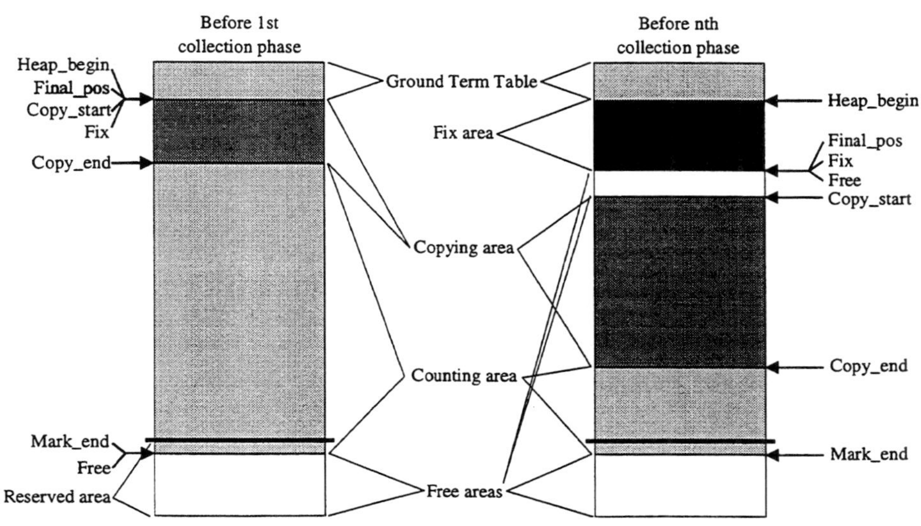

Fig. 6. The heap areas and used pointers during garbage collection

4.4 Examining references

If a reference to the heap is found the accessed structure is collected and the reference is updated. The following cases can occur. The pointed structure is in:

Ground Term Table — The ground terms are never moved. The reference is unchanged.

Fixed area — The structure has been already collected and it is in its final position. The reference is unchanged. However, the references in the cells of the structure can point into other areas of the heap therefore, they should be examined by the collector.

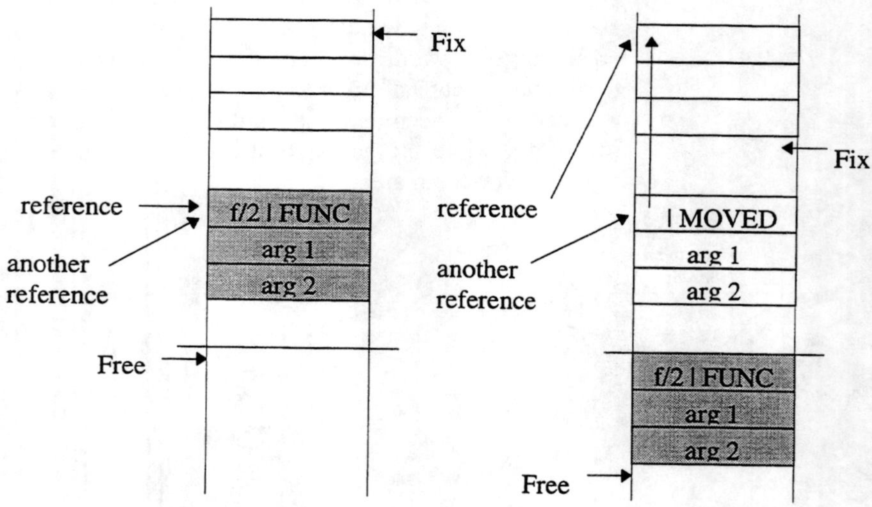

Fig. 7. Copying a structure

Copying area — Two cases can be distinguished. If the structure is not yet moved (this is the first access to it in this garbage collection phase), it is moved into the free area and the original header ([FUNC | functor | arity]) of the structure is replaced with the cell [MOVED | final address] and the reference is updated to the final address, see Fig. 7. (The final address is equal to the Fix pointer.) The substructures must be examined, too.

The second case is the access of an already moved structure. At this time, the header of the

	structure contains the final address of it and only the reference should be updated.
Counting area	Two cases can be distinguished. If the structure is not yet marked (this is the first access to it in this garbage collection phase), the original FUNC header tag of the structure is replaced with the MARKED tag. The number of the marked cells is increased with the size of the structure. The substructures must be examined, too. The second case is the access of an already marked structure when nothing is to be done.

4.5 Counting and determining the copying area

In the second and further collection cycle the copying area should be determined before starting the collection. As many structures as possible should be copied (instead of marking). The size of the copying area depends on the number of the marked structures and the size of the free areas. To give an approximately good size, a counting array is used.

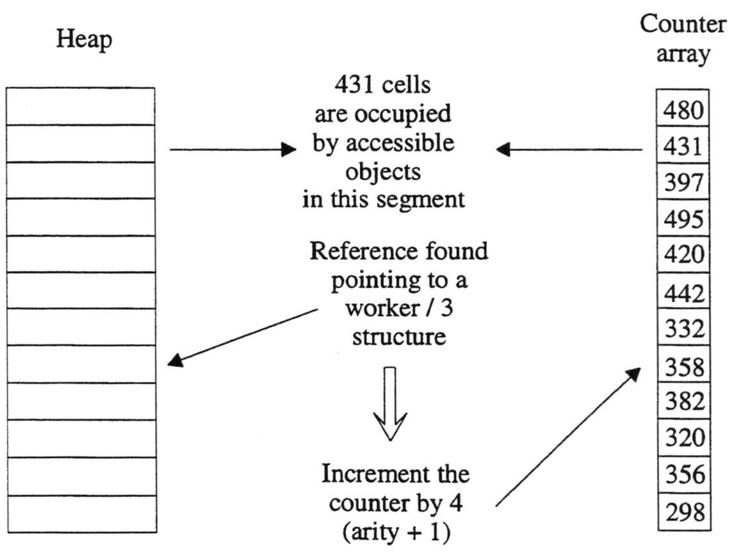

Fig. 8. Counting the accessible structures. '*worker/3*' is defined in Fig. 2.

The heap is considered to be segmented for several segments with the same size. A counter for each segment shows the number of cells allocated by accessible structures in the corresponding heap segment. When a structure in the counting area is accessed and marked the corresponding counter is increased by the number of the cells allocated by the structure, see Fig. **8**. At the end of a collection cycle, the counters contain the number of accessible cells of the corresponding heap area (this is true only for the counters that correspond to an area in the counting area).

The determination of the copying area for the next collection cycle is easy. The new copying area and counting area will be the two part of the previous counting area (since only this area must be collected in the following phases). The new copying area will contain segments from the beginning of the counting area. The number of the included segments depends on the sum of their counters, which must be less then the available free area, see Fig. **9**.

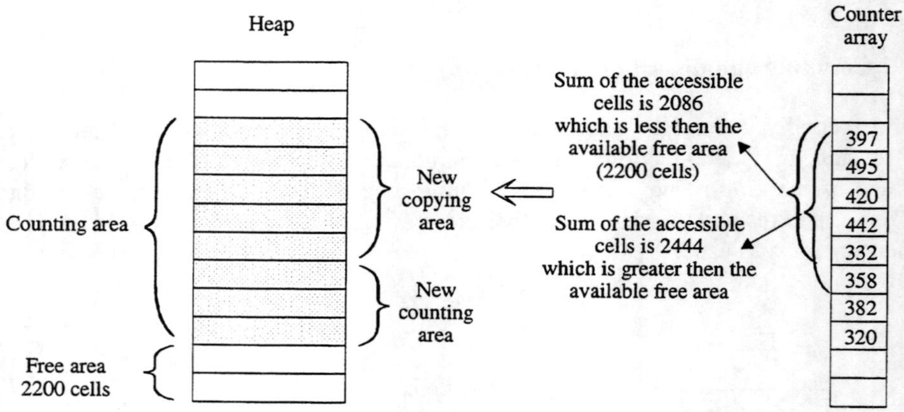

Fig. 9. Determining the new copying area

4.6 Unmarking

The counting area contains several structures at the end of a collection cycle, whose header has been changed to MARKED. The area will be splitted into two new ones in the next cycle. The first part will be the copying area while the remaining cells form the new counting area. The copying area can contain structures with MARKED tags because they do not differ from the original structures in any important information. The new counting area must not contain marked structures because of the counting. The marked structures must be unmarked before starting the next collection cycle.

The unmarking is a very simple action: the MARKED tags should be set back to the FUNC tag. The unmarking consists of examining the cells of the new counting area and unmarking the marked cells.

Fortunately, most cells of the counting area will be in the copying area in the next cycle therefore, only a little part of the area should be examined.

5 Performance measurements on the garbage collector

5.1 Test of LOGFLOW

The test of the system with the new garbage collection gave excellent results. The duration of the collection cycles is much less than the average duration of the execution of a sequential task performed by the WAM engines. As we have predicted, the lock of the 3DPAM engine on a processor does not cause much inference in the execution, since other engines can perform their work during the collection. The corresponding WAM engine works generally with a sequential task longer than the collection is performed therefore, it is not waiting for getting new tasks.
As the test example shows (see Fig. **10**), the overhead of the garbage collection is so small that it cannot be detected; the differences are in the error domain of the measurement. This substantiates our allegation that the new garbage collector is an efficient one.

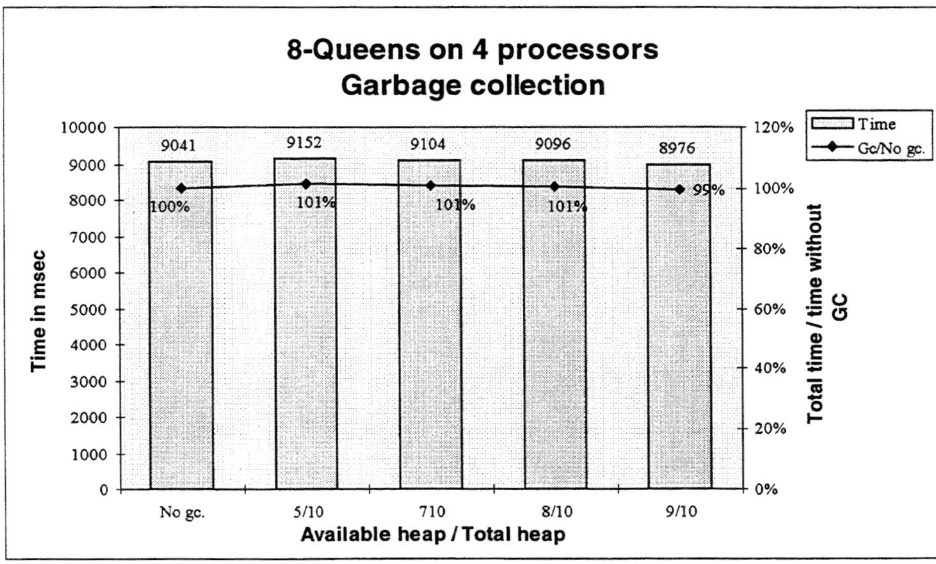

Fig. 10. Execution time of the 8–queens problem on 4 processors with different available heap / total heap ratio. 3DPAM and WAM were working together

On the horizontal scale the ratio of the amount of heap available for the processes and the total amount of heap is represented. The 'no gc.' means the measurement without garbage collection. The 5/10 ratio results in the original copying collection method, where all living objects in the half of the heap are copied into the other half of the heap. 7/10, 8/10 and 9/10 represents our algorithm, where most of the heap is available for the processes and only the 3/10 2/10 and 1/10 of the heap is allocated for garbage collection, respectively. The heap size was 7200 cells in the test. The following table shows the execution time, the number of garbage collections in one run and the number of collection phases in one garbage collection.

Ratio	Execution time	# of collection	# of phases in one collection
5/10	9152	5-7	1
7/10	9104	4-6	2
8/10	9096	2-4	2
9/10	8976	1-3	2

5.2 Tests of LOGFLOW without WAM engines

The previous section showed, that the performance of the LOGFLOW system did not change significantly. We were interested in knowing whether the collector in the pure distributed system (without sequential execution engines) worked also so well. The tests were performed on the 6-queens problem. The pure 3DPAM execution uses enormous memory for token administration therefore, our transputers with 1MB memory cannot execute larger programs than the 6–queens problem. The program was executed with two heap size settings (2400 and 4800 cells, respectively) and performed by 4 processors, see Fig. **11**. and **12**.

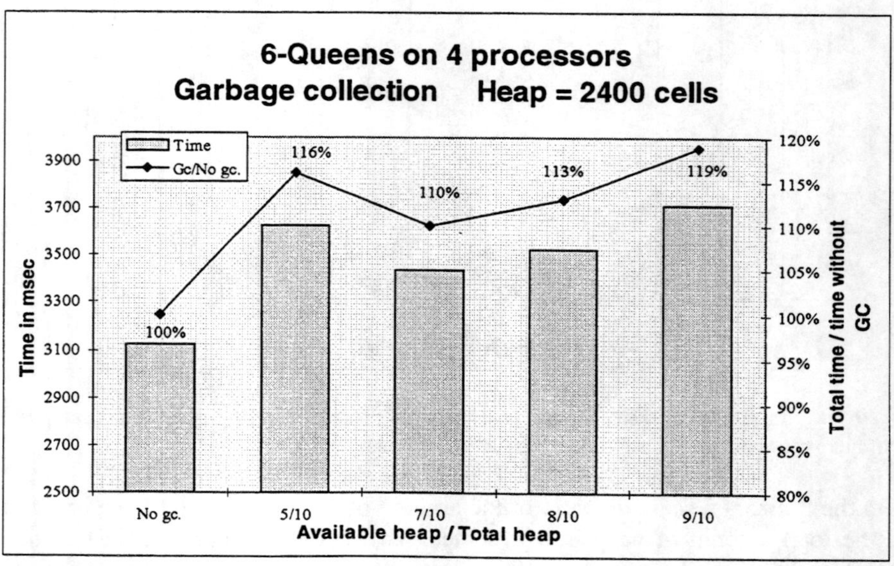

Fig. 11. Execution time of the 6–queens problem on 4 processors with different available heap / total heap ratio. Total heap size is 2400 cells. Only 3DPAM engines were working

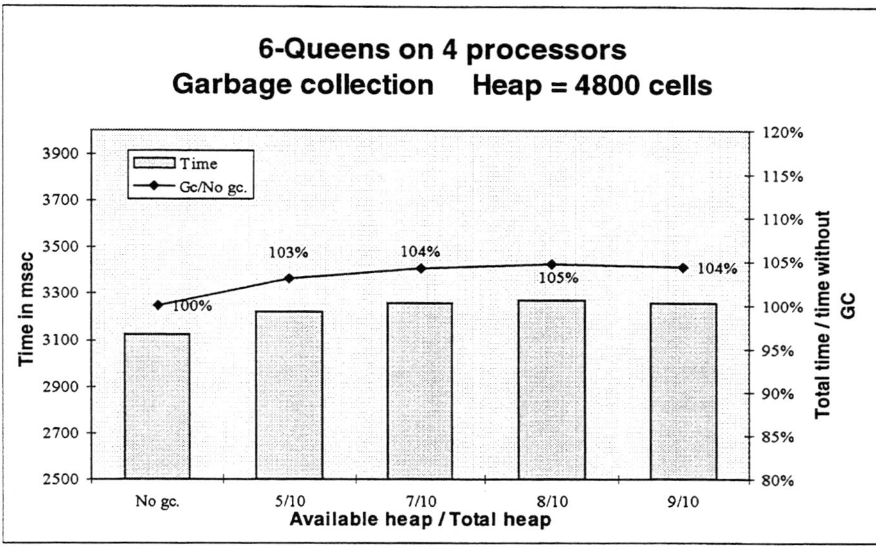

Fig. 12. Execution time of the 6–queens problem on 4 processors with different available heap / total heap ratio. Total heap size is 4800 cells. Only 3DPAM engines were working

When the heap was very small for the program and several collections were performed during the execution, the execution time had 10%-19% overhead. With 5/10 ratio 26 collections was performed while with 9/10 ratio only 11. The number of phases in one collection was 1 in the case of 5/10 ratio while with 9/10 ratio it varied from 2 to 4.

With twice as large heap the performance was much better than with the small heap. The number of collections decreased to 9 and 4, respectively and the number of the phases in one collection was 2 in the case of 9/10 ratio. The execution overhead decreased to 3-5%.

Conclusion

The new Multi-phase Copying Garbage Collector algorithm and its implementation issues have been presented in this paper. The performance tests of the collector showed that it is an efficient garbage collection method for LOGFLOW, which was our primary goal to achieve. By solving the problem of memory deallocation in the heap we have to turn to other problems in the memory management in LOGFLOW. The additional token and context tables, which contain only important data, can be filled up during the execution of a large program. Since they occupy very large amount of memory, their size should be balanced with the size of the heap in a given memory area.

Before implementing MC-GC, the heap was the "weakest" point of the system: programs, representing larger problems than solving the 8–queens problem, could not have been executed because of the insufficient amount of heap. The LOGFLOW system extended with the garbage collector is able to execute larger programs but the size of the token and context tables limits its abilities. Since these tables do not contain garbage, the memory usage can be controlled only by heuristic scheduling strategies, preventing the system from the production of too many tokens in short time interval and filling up the tables. Our new research direction turns to the scheduling and load balancing strategies.

References

[1] H.G. Baker: List-processing in real time on a serial computer. Comm. ACM, 21, 4 (Apr. 1978), 280-294.

[2] D. I. Bevan: Distributed Garbage Collection Using Reference Counting. Conference on PARLE'87.

[3] D.G. Bobrow: A note on hash linking. Comm. ACM, 18, 7 (July 1975), 413-415.

[4] C.J. Cheney: A nonrecursive list compacting algorithm. Comm. ACM, 13, 11 (Nov. 1970), 677-678.

[5] T. Chikayama, Y. Kimura: Multiple Reference Management in Flat GHC. 4th Int. Conference on Logic Programming 1987.

[6] J. Cohen: Garbage Collection of Linked Data Structures *Computing Surveys, Vol. 13, No. 3, September 1981.*

[7] G.E. Collins: A method for overlapping and erasure of lists. Comm. ACM, 3, 12 (Dec. 1960), 655-657.

[8] L.P. Deutsch, D.G. Bobrow: An efficient incremental automatic garbage collector. Comm. ACM, 19, 9 (Sept. 1976), 522-526.

[9] R. Fenichel, J. Yochelson: A LISP garbage-collector for virtual-memory computer systems. Comm. ACM, 12, 11 (Nov. 1969), 611-612.

[10] A. Goto, Y. Kimura, T. Nakagawa, T. Chikayama: Lazy Reference Counting. 5th Int. Conference on Logic Programming 1988.

[11] B.K. Haddon, W.M. Waite: A compaction procedure for variable length storage elements. Comput. J., 10 (Aug. 1967), 162-165.

[12] Y. Inamura, N. Ichiyoshi, K. Rokusawa, K. Nakajima: Optimization Techniques Using the MRB and Their Evaluation on the Multi-PSI/V2. North American Symp. on Logic Programming 1990.

[13] P. Kacsuk: The Distributed Data Driven Prolog Abstract Machine. *Distributed implementations of Prolog. P. Kacsuk, M. Wise editors. Wiley, 1992.*

[14] P. Kacsuk: Memory management in LOGFLOW. *Microprocessing and Microprogramming 39. (1993) pp. 79-82.*

[15] P. Kacsuk: Execution models for a Massively Parallel Prolog Implementation. *Journal of Computers and Artifical Intelligence. Slovak Academy of Sciences, 1997. (accepted for publication).*

[16] D.E. Knuth: The art of computer programming vol I: Fundamental Algorithms Addison-Wesley, Reading, Mass., 1973

[17] B. Lang, B. Wegbreit: Fast compatification. Report. 25-72, Harvard Univ., Cambridge, Mass., Nov. 1972.
[18] M.L. Minsky: A LISP garbage collector algorithm using serial secondary storage. Memo 58 (rev.), Project MAC, M.I.T., Cambridge, Mass., Dec. 1963.
[19] F.L. Morris: A time- and space-efficient garbage compaction algorithm. Comm. ACM, 21, 8, (Aug. 1978), 662-665.
[20] P. Kacsuk: LOGFLOW-2: A Transputer Based Data Driven Parallel Prolog Machine. Transputer Application and Systems '93. R. Grebe et al. (eds), IOS Press, 1993.
[21] N. Podhorszki: Garbage Collection Techniques *PHARE TD&QM report, Jun. 1996. http://www.kfki.hu/~pnorbert*
[22] N. Podhorszki, P. Kacsuk: Garbage Collection in LOGFLOW *PHARE TD&QM report, Dec. 1996. http://www.kfki.hu/~pnorbert*
[23] M. Terashima, E. Goto: Genetic order and compactifying garbage collectors. Inf. Process. Lett. 7, 1, (Jan. 1978), 27-32.
[24] W.M. Waite: Implementing software for non-numeric applications. Prentice Hall, Englewood Cliffs, N.J., 1973.
[25] D.H.D. Warren: An abstract Prolog Instruction Set. *Technical Note 309, SRI International, 1983.*
[26] P. Watson, I. Watson: An Efficient Garbage Collection Scheme for Parallel Computer Architectures. Conference on PARLE'87.
[27] B. Wegbreit: A generalized compactifying garbage collector. Comput. J., 15, 3 (Aug. 1972), 204-208.
[28] J. Weizenbaum: Symmetric list processor. Comm. ACM, 6, 9, (Sept. 1963), 524-544.
[29] P.R. Wilson: Uniprocessor Garbage Collection Techniques. *Proc. of the 1992 Intl. Workshop on Memory Management. Springer Verlag Lecture Notes in Computer Science series.*

Three CLP Implementations of Branch-and-Bound Optimization

Steven Prestwich

Department of Computer Science
University College, Cork
Ireland
s.prestwich@cs.ucc.ie

Abstract. Constraint logic programming systems are becoming increasingly popular for solving real-life constrained optimization problems. An important component of such systems is therefore an optimization function, and typically one or more implementations of the branch-and-bound method are provided. The issue addressed in this paper is that for some problems the choice of implementation is critical, yet there seems to be no available methodology for selection. Instead of attempting to find such a methodology, we decided to examine the robustness of three known implementations under various extreme conditions. We found that the most popular implementation performs badly on certain cost functions, and also exhibits three distinct sources of inefficiency under parallel execution. Another implementation performs badly on different cost functions. The third is not always the fastest but it emerges as more robust than the others. We therefore recommend that only this implementation, or something similar, be provided by CLP systems. This avoids the need for a way of selecting the best implementation, thus relieving the programmer of a difficult but crucial decision.

1 Introduction

Constraint Logic Programming (CLP) has been successfully applied to constrained optimization problems in Operations Research and Artificial Intelligence [3, 20, 21], some implementations approaching the efficiency of specialized, hand-coded algorithms [2]. The main advantage of the CLP approach is its ease of programming and its flexibility. For well-studied problems Operations Research techniques are often the best, but for new problems with complex or non-standard constraints, the flexibility of CLP makes it the tool of choice.

Most CLP systems provide functions for optimization based on the branch-and-bound method. The first two implementations were in CHIP [5]. Various implementations are also provided by commercial versions of CHIP [1] and related constraint solving tools such as ECL^{i}PS^e [6], CHARME [11] and DECISIONPOWER [4]; also by ILOG SOLVER [7], a constraint solver based on C++ instead of Prolog.

Users of such systems, when writing a program to solve a new problem, must test the available implementations to see which is most appropriate. The difference in performance may be more than just a few percent: it may be several orders of magnitude, so the choice is critical. However, there are (so far as we know) no guiding principles for selecting an implementation. A pragmatic approach is to compare the implementations on several sets of data, but there remains the possibility that another implementation would be much better with different data, or in parallel. Moreover, a single problem may exhibit different characteristics on different data or on different machines, and even in different parts of its search tree.

In the absence of a methodology for selecting an appropriate branch-and-bound implementation, we decided to test the behaviour of three known implementations under various extreme conditions (both sequential and parallel). The aim was to see whether one emerges as more robust than the others; if so, we could then conclude that this implementation should be chosen unless there are overriding reasons to the contrary. This paper describes the results of our experiments. In Section 1.1 we provide some background; in Section 2 we describe the three implementations; in Section 3 we test them; and in Section 4 we draw some conclusions.

1.1 Or-parallelism

CLP systems use constraint techniques to prune search spaces, but what remains can still be large. Or-parallel CLP systems attempt to speed up the search by exploring the remaining search space in parallel. This combination of or-parallelism and CLP was first suggested in [17], and first used with finite domain constraints in the Elipsys system [19].

Or-parallelism works as follows. At certain nodes of the search tree each branch is tried in parallel on different processors instead of in sequence by backtracking. These nodes are usually selected by a run-time scheduler from a superset of nodes specified by the programmer in the program source. For example, the programmer may specify that all the branches of any node corresponding to a certain Prolog predicate can be explored in parallel. [1]

A number of researchers have worked on exploiting or-parallelism within branch-and-bound algorithms, both inside and outside the CLP framework [8, 9, 10, 15, 16]. In particular, Szeredi [16] investigated the use of or-parallel Prolog for such problems and had some encouraging preliminary performance figures using Aurora [12].

2 Branch-and-bound implementations

Constrained optimization problems typically have many solutions, and we may assign a cost to each. To solve the optimization problem we must find any one of the optimal solutions, that is one with the lowest possible cost, and also prove

[1] Actually, the branches may not be explored by physically different processors, only by different *workers* (or processes). Several workers can be multitasked on a single machine, but in this paper we shall assume that each physical processor executes exactly one process.

its optimality by failing to find a better solution after exhaustive search. In CLP systems this is often done by the *branch-and-bound* method. We now describe three implementations of this method which we shall call $\mathtt{bb}_1$, $\mathtt{bb}_2$ and $\mathtt{bb}_3$.

2.1 Implementation $\mathtt{bb}_1$

The $\mathtt{bb}_1$ implementation appears to be the most popular, perhaps because it is easily implemented and it usually behaves quite well. It is provided by CHIP, ElipSys, ECL^{i}PS^e, DECISIONPOWER (called `min_max` in each), CHARME (`minim`) and ILOG SOLVER (`IlcMinimize`), and works as follows. It first finds any solution using the underlying constraint solver, under the additional cost constraint $L \leq C \leq H$ where H is the initial upper and L the lower cost bound, and C a domain variable representing the cost function being constructed. Whenever a new solution is found the search is halted and *restarted* under the tighter constraint $L \leq C < C_i$ where C_i is the cost of the new solution ($C_0 = H$). Eventually no further solutions can be found (or $C_i = L$) and the last solution found is therefore guaranteed to be optimal.

2.2 Implementation $\mathtt{bb}_2$

The $\mathtt{bb}_2$ implementation is provided by CHIP, ElipSys, ECL^{i}PS^e and DECISIONPOWER (called `minimize` in each). It does not restart the search when a new cost bound is established. Instead it maintains a global variable which records the lowest cost found so far. On finding a solution with lower cost C_i the global variable is updated. Whenever the domain of C changes during the search this variable is consulted, and a new constraint $C \leq C_i$ added (which is undone on backtracking). The idea behind $\mathtt{bb}_2$ is to avoid the restarting overhead of $\mathtt{bb}_1$.

2.3 Implementation $\mathtt{bb}_3$

This implementation is provided by ILOG SOLVER (`IlcMinim`), CHARME (`minimize`) and was proposed for ECL^{i}PS^e in [14] (where it was called `min`). It works in a similar way to $\mathtt{bb}_2$ except that the variable is consulted at the start of every branch of every node in the search tree, and a new constraint $C \leq C_i$ added as in $\mathtt{bb}_2$. At a node with many branches, if the new constraint fails at some branch then $\mathtt{bb}_3$ need not try the remaining branches.

2.4 Discussion

There are other possibilities than the three implementations described here. For example when a new upper cost bound is found, intelligent backtracking can be used to jump back to an appropriate place in the search tree [18]. However, in this paper we only consider the three implementations $\mathtt{bb}_{1,2,3}$. They each have pros and cons which we discuss here before testing them on examples:

- $\texttt{bb}_1$ may redundantly explore a leftmost [2] portion of the search space, depending upon how well the constraint propagation prunes this part of the space. This is illustrated in Section 3.2. Neither of $\texttt{bb}_{2,3}$ restart the search so they never explore any part of the space more than once.
- $\texttt{bb}_3$ always uses an up-to-date value of C_i because it consults C_i at every labeling; $\texttt{bb}_1$ is also always up-to-date because as soon as C_i is changed the entire search is restarted; in contrast $\texttt{bb}_2$ uses an outdated C_i on backtracking from finding a new solution, and will continue to do so until a new variable binding causes the domain of C to change again. The out-of-date value $C_{i_{old}}$ is higher than the up-to-date value C_i, hence $\texttt{bb}_2$ performs part of its search under unnecessarily weak cost pruning — another form of redundant search. This is illustrated in Section 3.3.
- The extra checking on the part of $\texttt{bb}_3$ is a significant overhead which may make it slower than $\texttt{bb}_{1,2}$. This is illustrated in Section 3.4.

Each of the three implementations perform better than the other two on some programs. Parallelism adds a further dimension: are any of the implementations better suited to parallel execution than the others? The issue of parallelism is explored in Sections 3.5, 3.6 and 3.7.

3 Experiments

In this section we examine the behaviour of the three implementations $\texttt{bb}_{1,2,3}$ by constructing pathological examples. The aim is to test their robustness under extreme conditions. The examples are constructed for clarity so that their behaviour can be understood. They are rather artificial in nature but similar effects may occur in real programs (we have observed at least some of them). The examples may also be useful as benchmarks for new branch-and-bound implementations.

3.1 Preliminaries

For the examples we shall use the standard Prolog syntax whereby predicates and constants are denoted by lower-case and variables by upper-case characters, plus some constraint operators. The `#=/2` operator constrains values of two domain variables to be equal. The `::/2` operator associates a domain with a variable or list of variables. The `../2` operator defines a closed integer interval in a domain. So for example `([X,Y]::0..3, Z#=X)` sets the domains of the variables `X`, `Y` and `Z` to $\{0, 1, 2, 3\}$ and constrains `X` and `Z` to have the same value. To facilitate the description of parameterized families of programs, we also allow sub- and superscripts. A call to a branch-and-bound implementation s with goal `Goal`

[2] We assume the convention that CLP systems search a space from "left" to "right". Leftness and rightness are not properties of the search space alone, but of the search space together with the search strategy used by the CLP system. Hence by "left" we simply mean the parts of the search space reached first by the system.

and cost function `Cost` will be denoted by $\texttt{bb}_s$`(Goal,Cost)`. Finally, we allow `Goal` to be a conjunction (`Goal`$_1$`,Goal`$_2$`,...`).

All timings were obtained on ECL^{i}PS^e version 3.5.2 [6]. Examples which are purely sequential were executed on a Sun SparcStation 5 while parallel examples were executed on a 4-processor ICL DRS6000. Timings are elapsed times (not CPU times) given in seconds, and are the times taken to find the optimal solutions and to prove them optimal.

3.2 Weak cost pruning

Recall that the cost constraint is used to prune the search space, so that the search space is further reduced as each solution is found. How much the space can be pruned depends upon the details of the cost function and the constraint solver, and it turns out that the degree of pruning strongly affects the performance of $\texttt{bb}_1$.

To demonstrate this we construct a family of programs with two parameters s and n, shown in Figure 1. The variable `V` replaces $\texttt{V}_n$ in the cost function, so that $\texttt{V}_n$ plays no part in the cost function; only after labeling are $\texttt{V}_n$ and `V` constrained to have the same value. This means that for lower values of n a variable with higher coefficient plays no part in pruning the domain of `Cost`, thus reducing the possibility of search space pruning. The predicate `label10/1` labels the domain variables, selecting the value `1` before the value `0`. It uses the predicate `member/2` which enumerates the members of the list representing the domain in textual order.

The graph in Figure 1 compares $\texttt{bb}_{1,2,3}$ for different values of n with the query `?-` $\texttt{p}_{s,n}$. It shows that decreasing n has little effect on $\texttt{bb}_{2,3}$ but an exponentially bad effect on $\texttt{bb}_1$. The explanation is that any part space the solver was unable to prune must be re-traversed at each $\texttt{bb}_1$ iteration. All the implementations must traverse this part of the space, but only $\texttt{bb}_1$ traverses it more than once.

3.3 Outdated cost bounds

Here we show that under certain conditions $\texttt{bb}_2$ can be unacceptably inefficient compared to $\texttt{bb}_{1,3}$, because it does not check the cost bound often enough and therefore performs redundant search; that is, by using an outdated cost bound it searches part of the space which cannot possibly contain a cheaper solution than the current best.

First we construct a family of programs with two parameters s and n in Figure 2. The predicate `work/1` is a simple predicate used to increase the amount of work performed, so that timings can be made more accurately. This predicate will also be used below, and is defined by:

```
work(0) :- !.
work(N) :- N1 is N - 1, work(N1).
```

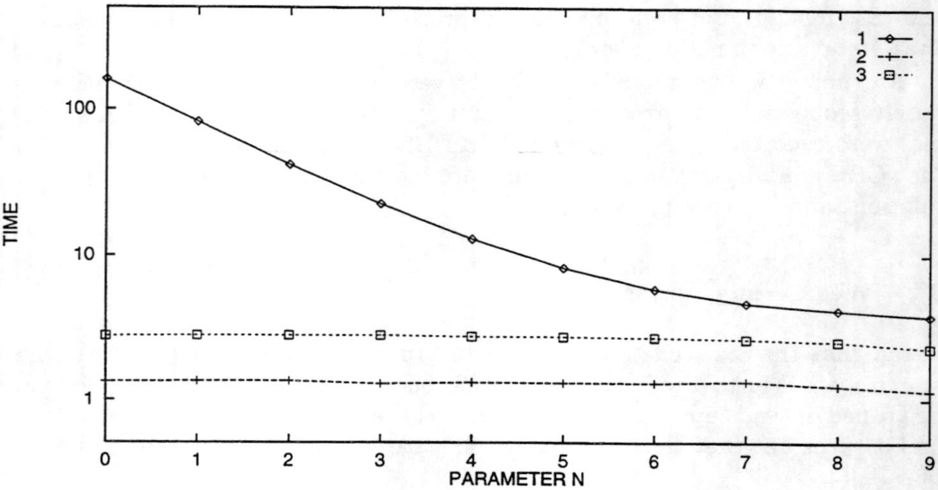


```
p_{s,n} :- L = [V0,V1,V2,V3,V4,V5,V6,V7,V8,V9],
        [V|L] :: 0 .. 1,  Cost :: 0 .. 1023,
        Cost #= 2^9 * V0 + ... + 2^(9-n) * V + ... + 2^0 * V9,
        bb_s( (label10(L), V#=Vn), Cost).

label10([]).
label10([V|L]) :- member(V,[1,0]), label10(L).
```

Fig. 1. Possible effects of weak cost pruning

The graph in figure 2 compares the behaviour of the implementations s with the query ?- $p_{s,n}$ as $n \longrightarrow 0$. Because Cost #= $2^0 * V_0 + \ldots + 2^n * V_n$ the number of possible costs tends to zero as $n \longrightarrow 0$.

The graph shows that both $bb_{1,3}$ speed up exponentially as $n \longrightarrow 0$ but that bb_2 is unaffected. This is because the later labeling events ($n+1$ ... 9) do not affect the cost function, so bb_2 does not check the global cost bound often enough. Hence for large portions of the search, bb_2 is using an out-of-date cost bound, making it extremely inefficient.

This behaviour has been observed in more realistic problems. In [14] it was noted that a set of job-shop scheduling problems behaved well under $bb_{1,3}$ but was orders of magnitude slower under bb_2. Hence (we believe that) bb_2 is used less often than bb_1.

3.4 Cost checking overhead

Here we consider the overhead of cost bound checking in each implementation, with the family of programs in Figure 3. The argument N controls the amount of

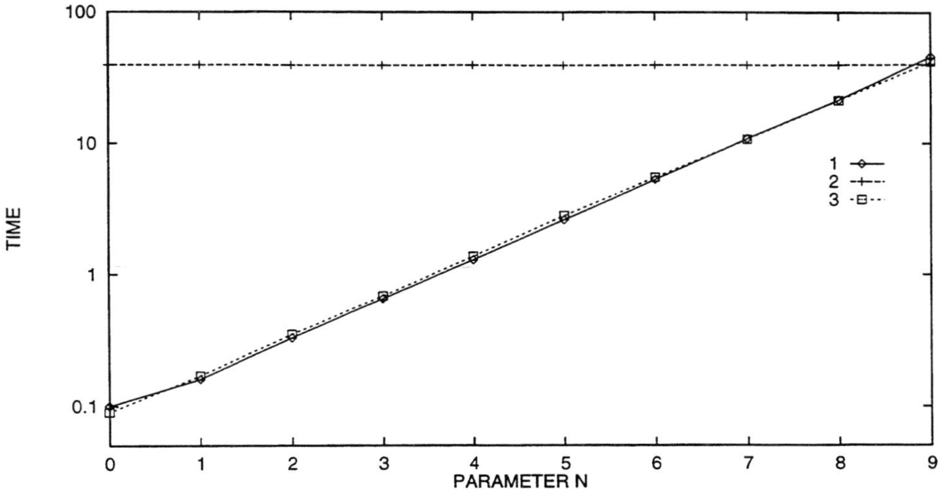

$p_{s,n}$:- L = [V_0,V_1,V_2,V_3,V_4,V_5,V_6,V_7,V_8,V_9],
L :: 0 .. 1, Cost :: 0 .. 1023,
Cost #= $2^0 * V_0 + \ldots + 2^n * V_n$,
bb_s((label10(L), work(10000)), Cost).

Fig. 2. Possible effects of outdated cost bounds

work performed after each labeling, and labeling is performed in reverse order by `reverse_indomain`. The idea of this example is that N simulates constraint propagation. As N $\longrightarrow$ 0 the simulated propagation becomes negligible, and times are increasingly dominated by other overheads such as cost bound checking, resolution and so on. There is only one solution with cost 1 so that the timings are not distorted by the overhead of frequently updating the global cost bound.

Executing this program with the query ?- p_s we obtain the graph shown in Figure 3. As N $\longrightarrow$ 0 bb_3 becomes worse than bb_2, which in turn becomes worse than bb_1. In this example bb_1 is fastest because it has negligible cost bound checking overhead.

Even in the worst case bb_3 is only twice as slow as bb_1. Although this is not conclusive evidence, and moreover applies only to these particular implementations, it does provide evidence that it is hard to make bb_3 much slower than $bb_{1,2}$. Hence the cost bound checking overhead appears to be much less of a potential problem than the forms of overhead described in the previous two sections.

3.5 Wasted speculative parallelism

The effects described above apply to both sequential and parallel optimization. In this and subsequent sections we describe effects associated only with parallel

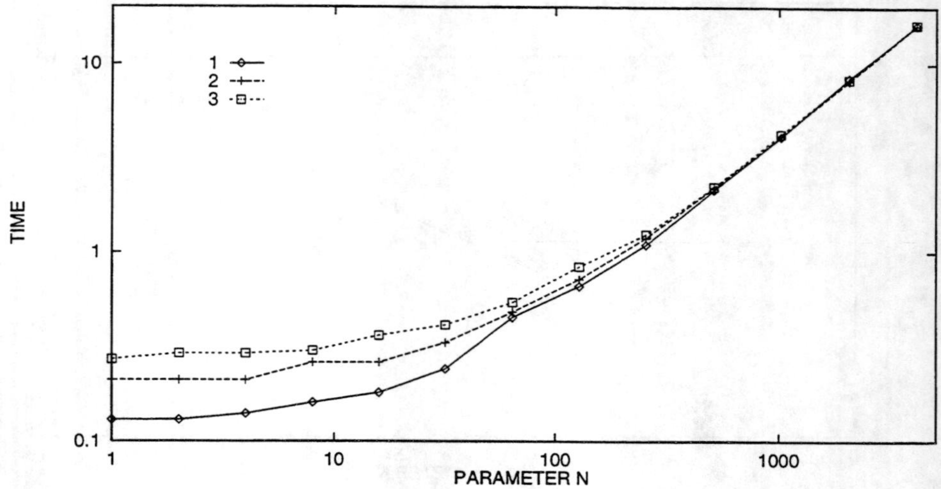


```
ps(N) :- Cost :: 1 .. 1000,
         bbs(g(Cost, N), Cost).

g(Cost, N) :- reverse_indomain(Cost),
              work(N),  Cost #= 1.
```

Fig. 3. Possible effects of cost checking overhead

optimization.

A well-known problem with certain types of parallel program is that of wasted speculative parallelism. *Speculative parallelism* is parallel work which may turn out to have been unnecessary — that is, which would not be performed during a sequential execution of the program. Speculative work which does turn out to have been unnecessary is called *wasted*. Speculative parallelism may lead to superlinear speedups, but if some or all workers perform wasted speculative work then parallel speedup may be poor. All three implementations may perform wasted speculative work, but here we show that $\texttt{bb}_1$ is more prone to this problem than $\texttt{bb}_{2,3}$.

We construct a family of programs with one parameter s, shown in Figure 4. Executing this program with 1–4 workers and the query `?- p`$_s$ we obtain the graph shown in Figure 4. Since $\texttt{bb}_{2,3}$ behave in the same way for this example we merge their results. We see that $\texttt{bb}_1$ has no speedup whereas $\texttt{bb}_{2,3}$ have good speedup (in fact it is superlinear: for example 2.42 for 2 workers). The reason is that, in this example, solutions near the left of the search space are easier to find than those to the right (this is a consequence of the argument of the `work` predicate). Therefore $\texttt{bb}_1$ never finds a solution faster in parallel than sequentially. However, $\texttt{bb}_{2,3}$ continue to search and in a short time find a better

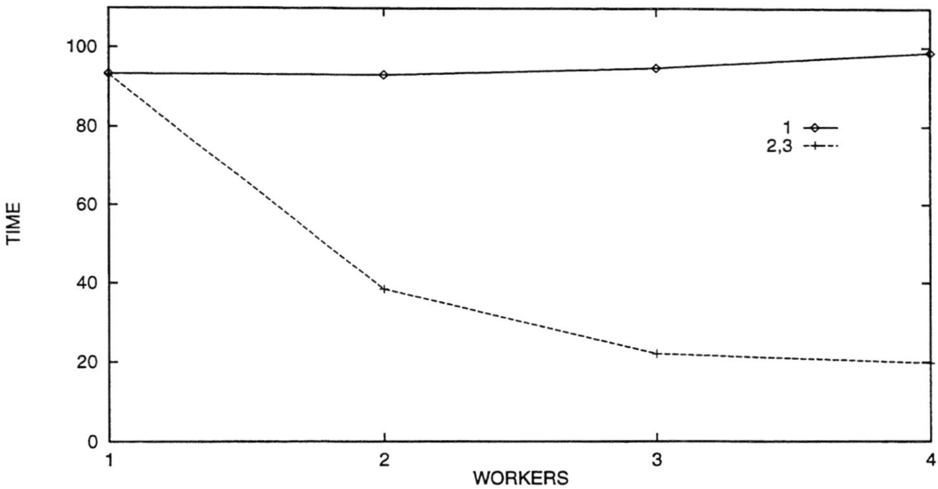


```
ps :- L = [V0,V1,V2,V3,V4],
      L :: 0 .. 1,   Cost :: 0 .. 31,
      Cost #= 16*V0 + 8*V1 + 4*V2 + 2*V3 + V4,
      bbs(g(L, Cost), Cost).

g(L, Cost) :- label10(L),
              N is 2000 * (31 - Cost) + 20000,
              work(N).
```

Fig. 4. Possible effects of wasted speculative parallelism

solution.

This behaviour may be increased by (for example) a value ordering designed to locate solutions faster, which effectively moves solutions to the left of the search space.

3.6 Race conditions

A CLP program may be slower when executed in parallel than sequentially, even if the parallelism overhead is negligible [13]. This is sometimes called *parallel slowdown* (as opposed to the speedup we would like from a parallel implementation). It is a consequence of *race conditions* in the program, where more than one parallel process race each other and the winner decides the future course of the computation. This may occur in or-parallel $\mathtt{bb}_1$.

We construct a family of programs with one parameter s, shown in Figure 5. The predicate `par_member/2` is identical to the `member/2` predicate except that it tries alternatives in parallel where possible (and by backtracking where extra processors are unavailable). In this example, the more expensive the solution the easier it is to find. This is typical of optimization problems: there are often many expensive solutions, and only a few cheap ones.

What is perhaps less typical about this example is that the cheaper the solution, the closer it is to the left of the search space. We have observed somewhat similar behaviour in an application, and it could be increased by a value ordering designed to locate cheaper solutions earlier.

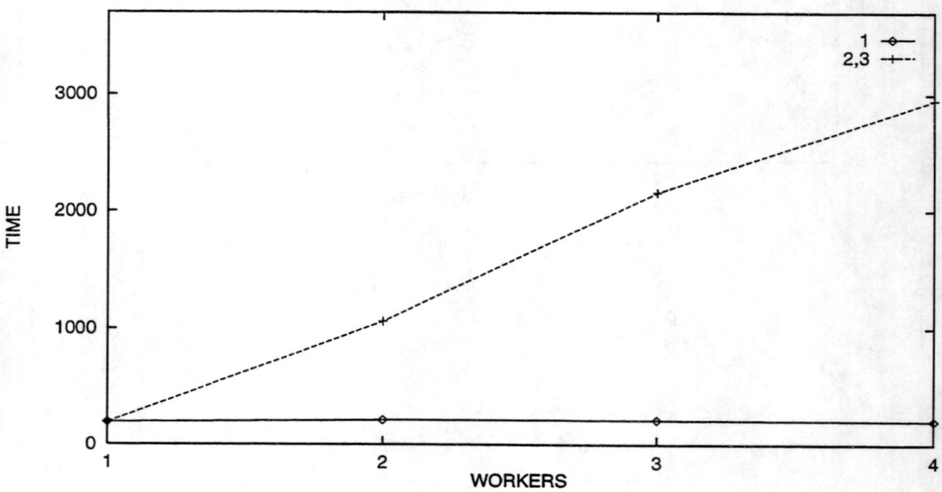


```
pₛ :- L = [V0,V1,V2,V3,V4],
      L :: 0 .. 1,  Cost :: 0 .. 31,
      Cost #= 16 * V0 + 8 * V1 + 4 * V2 + 2 * V3 + V4,
      bbₛ(label01(16,L), Cost).

label01(N,[]).
label01(N,[V|L]) :- W is 50000 * N * (2 - V),
                    N1 is N // 2,
                    par_member(V,[0,1]),
                    work(W),  label01(N1,L).
```

Fig. 5. Possible effects of race conditions

Executing this program with 1–4 workers and the query ?- p_s, we obtain the graph shown in Figure 5. Since $bb_{2,3}$ behave in the same way for this example we merge their results. None of the implementations find the *optimal* solution faster in parallel, though they all benefit from parallelism in the sense that they find *a* solution in a shorter time. The problem with bb_1 is that when a processor searching to the right finds a solution, it restarts the search and interrupts the processors which were about to find better solutions to the left. Parallelism therefore increases the number of iterations and hence the total execution time.

3.7 Parallel overhead

A common problem with parallel execution is the overhead caused by creating parallel tasks and communicating their results. It becomes a serious problem when the time taken to complete each parallel task (their *granularity*) is comparable to the time wasted in parallel overhead. We then say that the parallel tasks are *fine-grained*.

In this section we compare the behaviour of the three implementations as the granularity of the parallel tasks tends to zero. We construct a family of programs with one parameter s in Figure 6. The goal `random_grain(N,Cost)` generates 1000 parallel tasks, each leading to a solution. The costs of these solutions, from left to right, are 1000, 999, ... 2, 1 and the tasks have random grain sizes in the range 0–N.

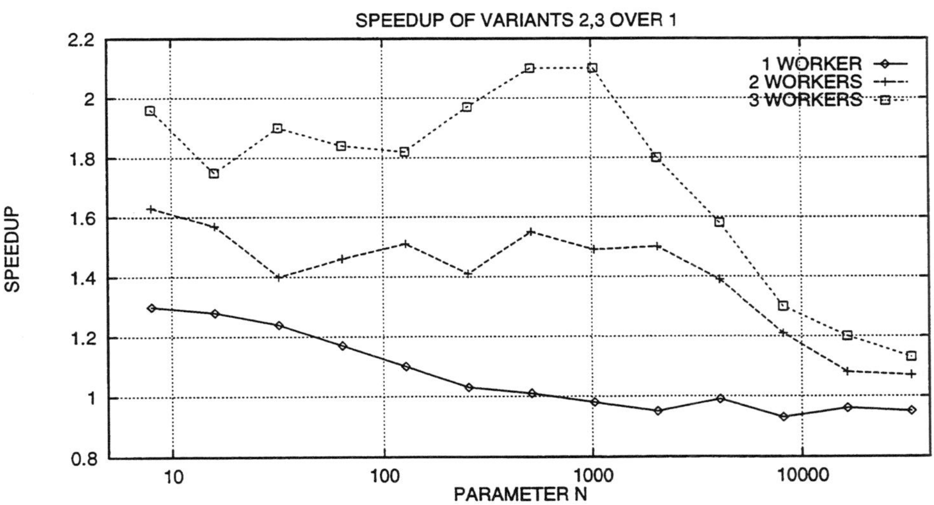


```
ps(N) :- Cost :: 1 .. 1000,
         bbs(random_grain(N,Cost), Cost).
```

Fig. 6. Possible effects of parallel overhead

We are interested in comparing the behaviour of bb_1 with the non-restarting implementations $bb_{2,3}$ for fine-grained parallel tasks. Since `random_grain` is not a "real" predicate we must simulate the effect of cost bound checking in $bb_{2,3}$. We use $bb_{2,3}$ which check the current cost bound after regular intervals equivalent to a grain size of $N = 128$. Figure 6 shows the speedup of $bb_{2,3}$ relative to bb_1 (the execution times of bb_1 divided by those of $bb_{2,3}$) as a function of grain size (controlled by the parameter N) for the query ?- p_s(N), plotted for 1–3 workers. The graph shows that as the grain size shrinks and the number of workers grows, $bb_{2,3}$ performs increasingly better than bb_1.

The precise reasons for this are not easy to prove, because monitoring fine-grained parallel programs distorts the very effects we are trying to observe. However, cautious profiling indicates that for fine-grained tasks bb_1 starts more searches than $bb_{2,3}$. The reason for this seems to be that at each iteration bb_1 starts a task for each worker, but when tasks are fine-grained the leftmost task is usually completed before the others have chance to communicate their results. So bb_1 starts more parallel tasks than necessary and incurs greater parallel overhead. The difference is not great, but because it increases with each extra worker we believe that bb_1 will behave poorly on highly parallel machines.

4 Conclusion

We compared the behaviour of three known branch-and-bound implementations under a variety of extreme conditions, and we conclude that one (bb_3) is superior to the others ($bb_{1,2}$) in several ways.

In the context of sequential execution bb_1 may be very slow if the cost function cannot exploit the labeling of important variables to prune the search space, whereas bb_2 may be very slow if the global cost bound is not checked frequently enough. However, in both cases bb_3 behaves well. In fact, bb_3 is unlikely to be much slower than $bb_{1,2}$ in spite of its increased cost-checking overhead, and it may be a great deal faster. We therefore recommend that, unless these problems can be predicted and avoided, only bb_3 or something like it be used for sequential optimization.

In the context of or-parallel execution bb_1 may exhibit additional undesirable effects: more wasted speculative work than parallel $bb_{2,3}$, more parallel overhead than parallel $bb_{2,3}$, and parallel slowdown caused by race conditions. We therefore conclude that the widely-used bb_1 is particularly unsuitable for parallel optimization.

We should note that bb_3 is also not without problems, and we have not considered how frequently it should consult the current upper cost bound. Here we chose a simple approach: it is checked after each variable labeling (or other nondeterministic step). In problems where propagation is cheap this may be too often, causing high overheads. Conversely, if propagation is expensive it may be too seldom — in a parallel execution workers should check each others' results frequently, to ensure that their cost bounds are not out of date. We provided empirical evidence that the cost checking overhead is not a significant problem, but future work should include a study of this issue.

A possible objection to these conclusions is: if $bb_{1,2}$ and bb_1 are sometimes faster than bb_3 then why not provide them? This seems at first glance to be a reasonable point, but we believe it to be flawed for the following reason. Consider the `label` predicate provided by several languages, which non-deterministically binds a domain variables to each of its domain values in turn. Clearly the order in which this is done may have a very large effect upon execution times. For some applications a variant of `label` which enumerates the values in reverse order would undoubtably be far better than one which enumerates in the usual order; should this variant be provided to programmers? If so, then why not also variants which enumerate first the values in domain positions 1, 3, 5... then those in positions 2, 4, 6...? And so on for many other possible enumeration orders. In current languages these variants are *not* supplied because there is usually no basis upon which to select the best variant, and our view is that the same argument applies to $\texttt{bb}_{1,2,3}$.

References

1. A. Aggoun, N. Beldiceanu. Extending CHIP in order to solve complex scheduling and placement problems. *Proc. of JFPL'92*, 1992.
2. Y. Caseau, F. Laburthe. Improved CLP scheduling with task intervals. *Proc. of 11th Int. Conf. on Logic Programming*. MIT Press, 1994, pp. 369–383.
3. D. Clark, C. Rawlings, J. Shirazi, L.-L. Li, M. Reeve, K. Schuermann, A. Veron. Solving large combinatorial problems in molecular biology using the ElipSys parallel constraint logic programming system. *Computer Journal*, **36**(4), 1993.
4. J.-Y. Cras. A review of industrial constraint solving tools. Survey, AI Perspectives, 1994.
5. M. Dincbas et al. The constraint logic programming language CHIP. *Proc. of Int. Conf. on 5th Generation Computer Systems (FGCS'88)*, ICOT, 1988, pp. 693–702.
6. European Computer-Industry Research Centre, Munich, Germany. *ECLiPSe 3.5.2 User Manual*, December 1995.
7. ILOG SOLVER reference manual version 3.0. Technical report, ILOG 1995.
8. J. M. Jansen, F. W. Sijstermans. Parallel branch-and-bound algorithms. *Future Generation Computer Systems*, 4:271–279, 1988–89.
9. V. Kumar, V. N. Rao. Parallel depth first search — Part I: Implementation. *Int. Journal of Parallel Programming*, **16**(6), 1987.
10. V. Kumar, V. N. Rao. Parallel depth first search — Part II: Analysis. *Int. Journal of Parallel Programming*, 16(6), 1987.
11. M. Leconte. Personal communication, March 1996.
12. E. Lusk, R. Butler, T. Disz, R. Olson, R. Overbeek, R. Stevens, D. H. D. Warren, A. Calderwood, P. Szeredi, S. Haridi, P. Brand, M. Carlsson, A. Ciepielewski, B. Hausman. The Aurora or-parallel Prolog system. *Proc. of the Int. Conf. on 5th Generation Computer Systems (FGCS'88)*. ICOT, 1988.
13. S. D. Prestwich. On parallelization strategies for logic programs. *Proc. of the Int. Conf. on Parallel Processing*, number 854 in LNCS. Springer-Verlag, 1994, pp. 289–300.
14. S. D. Prestwich, S. Mudambi. Improved branch and bound in constraint logic programming. *Proc. of the 1st Int. Conf. on Principles and Practice of Constraint Programming*, 1995, pp. 533–548.
15. T. J. Reynold, P. Kefalas. Or-parallel prolog and search problems in AI applications. *Logic Programming: Proc. of the 7th Int Conf.* MIT Press, 1990, pp. 340–354.

16. P. Szeredi. Exploiting or-parallelism in optimization problems. *Proc. of the JICSLP'92*. MIT Press, 1992, pp. 703–716.
17. P. van Hentenryck. Parallel constraint satisfaction in logic programming: preliminary results of CHIP within PEPSys. *Proc. of the 6th Int. Conf. on Logic Programming*, Lisbon, 1989. MIT Press, pp. 165–180. Giorgio Levi and Maurizio Martelli (editors).
18. P. van Hentenryck. Personal communication, January 1995.
19. A. Veron, K. Schuerman, M. Reeve, L. Li. Why and how in the ElipSys Or-Parallel CLP system. *PARLE'93: Parallel Architectures and Languages Europe*. Springer-Verlag, 1993, pp. 291–302.
20. A. Veron, K. Schuerman, M. Reeve, L.-L. Li. APPLAUSE: Applications using the ElipSys parallel CLP system. *Proc. of the 10th Int. Conf. on Logic Programming*. MIT Press, June 1993.
21. M. Wallace. Constraints in planning, scheduling and placement problems. *Constraint Programming*, Springer-Verlag, 1994.

Ask&Tell Linear Constraints in Constraint Logic Programming

Philippe Refalo*
LIM, URA CNRS 1787
Faculte des sciences de Luminy
13009 Marseille, France
refalo@lim.univ-mrs.fr

Abstract. This article addresses the problem of linear constraint entailment in constraint logic programming. After a brief overview of linear constraint solving, two forms for ask constraints are introduced. Some properties of these forms are provided. The incremental algorithms are also described and have been integrated to a CLP language for handling high-level operators. Practical experiments with operation research problems show that substantial reductions of the search tree and the computation time are obtained.

1 Introduction

Constraint entailment is the basis of new generation constraint logic programming languages (CLP) such as `cc(FD)` [17] or `CLP(BNR)` [2]. It is also the fundamental aspect of concurrent constraint languages [14], which consider (1) a *constraint store* that is monotonically increasing by the addition of *tell* constraints, and (2) a set of *ask* constraints. Goals are associated to ask constraints and are delayed until every solution of the constraint store is a solution of the ask constraint (i.e., the ask constraint is *entailed*).

Ask constraints arise naturally from the use of high level operators such as the *implication operator* $c \longrightarrow B$, where the goal B is delayed until the ask constraint c becomes entailed. Other high level operators have been integrated in CLP languages such as the *cardinality operator* [17], the `if_then_else` operator of `CHIP` [4] and the ability to associate a boolean value to the satisfiability of the constraint in `CLP(BNR)`. These are all operationally equivalent to a conjunction of implication operators. Many applications benefit from these operators; their use simplifies the problem statement and achieves an important pruning of the search tree for some combinatorial problems.

Essentially, constraint entailment has been used over finite domains and interval constraints. In these domains the approximate, but sound, algorithms provide an efficient but incomplete entailment test.

Linear constraints, although integrated in first generation constraint programming languages, such as `Prolog III` [3], CLP($\mathcal{R}$) [7] and `CHIP`, have not

* Now at ILOG, 9 rue de Verdun, 94253 Gentilly, France (`refalo@ilog.fr`)

really been considered for entailment. The existing theoretical works on this subject [8, 9] did not lead to algorithms usable in a CLP language. An application of linear constraint entailment in **CHIP** has been presented in [5], but the algorithms used are incomplete and were not described. The purpose of this article is to address the problem of an efficient algorithm for linear constraint entailment in order to define high-level operators over linear constraints. The associated problem of deciding if no solution of the constraint store is a solution of an ask constraint (*disentailment*) is fully symmetric to the entailment problem in our case and it will not be discussed here.

To handle constraint entailment over intervals and finite domains the entailment test is approximated. The set of solutions is usually approximated by an n-dimensional box or a carthesian product of domains. The entailment test is thus efficient but incomplete. Such an approximation is not applicable to linear constraints over the reals because practical experience shows that the approximation is usually far from the set of solutions. On the other hand, efficient and complete algorithms to solve linear constraints are used in many CLP languages such as **PrologIII**, [3] **CLP($\mathcal{R}$)** [7] and **CHIP** [4], and it is worth using them for linear constraint entailment to provide a complete entailment test. Linear constraint entailment has not really been considered for entailment. The work of Lassez and al. has led to interesting theoretical results like the *subsumption cone* [9] which allows entailment to be decided very efficiently but whose computation is exponential.

The starting point of this work on entailment of linear constraints is the canonical form introduced by Lassez and McAloon [10] and the solved forms for linear constraints used in the languages mentioned above. A *dereferenced form* and a *partial precise form* are introduced for linear constraints, properties of these forms are stated, and we show how to maintain constraints incrementally in these forms. We also describe the entailment algorithm for each type of linear constraint. For shortness, proofs of the properties are not given. They can be found in [12]. These algorithms have been implemented in the CLP language **Athena** [13], and we present practical results showing that our algorithm improves the naive entailment test (i.e., S entails c iff $S \cup \{\neg c\}$ is unsolvable) and that a substantial reduction of the search space and of the computation time is achieved in comparison with standard backtracking.

The rest of this paper is organized as follows: definitions and notations are provided in section 2. In section 3, the normal form for classical linear constraints is described. The dereferenced form is introduced in section 4. It is then applied to the entailment of an equation (section 5) and of an inequation (section 6). The partial precise form for entailment of disequations is defined in section 7. Entailment on a strict inequality is presented in section 8. Some optimizations of the algorithms are described in section 9. The evaluation of our approach on practical problems is given in section 10.

2 Definitions and notations

Let V be an infinite and countable set of variables. A *linear term* is an expression of the form α, x, αx, $t_1 + t_2$, $t_1 - t_2$ where $\alpha \in \mathcal{R}$, $x \in V$ and t_1 and t_2 are linear terms. A *linear constraint* is an expression of the form $t_1 = t_2$, $t_1 \leq t_2$, $t_1 < t_2$ or $t_1 \neq t_2$, where t_1 and t_2 are linear terms. These constraints are called respectively *equation*, *inequation*, *strict inequation* and *disequation*. A *constraint system* is a finite set of constraints. A variable has an *occurrence* in a constraint if it appears with a non-zero coefficient in that constraint. A constraint is *trivial* if it does not contain any occurence of a variable.

An *assignment* is a mapping $\sigma : V \mapsto \mathcal{R}$ which associates a real number with each variable of the set V. A mapping is extended to linear terms in the natural way. An assignment σ is a *solution* of a linear constraint $t_1 \diamond t_2$ if $\sigma(t_1) \diamond \sigma(t_2)$. An assignment is a solution of a constraint system if it is a solution of every constraint of the system. A constraint system having at least one solution is *solvable* otherwise it is *unsolvable*.

An inequation $t_1 \leq t_2$ of a constraint system S is an *implicit equality* if every solution of S is a solution of the equation $t_1 = t_2$. A variable x is *fixed* in a constraint system S if every solution of S assigns the same value to x.

Let S be a solvable system of constraints and c be a constraint. If every solution of S is a solution of c then S *entails* c, which is denoted by $S \models c$. When there exists a solution of S that is not a solution of c, then S does not entail c. This is denoted by $S \not\models c$.

Finally, the expression $\{x \mid S\}$ represents the set of solutions of a system S on a vector of variables x.

3 Normal Form

The normal form is a way of writing a constraint system to guarantee the solvability of the system and to show explicitly every fixed variable. The one briefly presented here is close to the one used in languages such as CLP($\mathcal{R}$) [7] or CHIP [4].

Each inequality is of the form

$$l_i \leq x_i \text{ or } x_i \leq u_i$$

where l_i can be $-\infty$ and u_i can be ∞.

Each equation express a variable (y_j) called a *basic variable* with respect to other variables ($x_1, \ldots, x_n$) :

$$y_j = a_1 x_1 + \cdots + a_n x_n$$

Those equations that contain only bounded variables (i.e. variables x_i for which $\langle l_i,\ u_i \rangle \neq \langle -\infty,\ \infty \rangle$) must be solvable together with inequations. Moreover, this set must not contain implicit equalities (i.e. implicit equalities of the form $l_i \leq x_i$ and $x_i \leq u_i$ are replaced respectively by $x_i = l_i$ and $x_i = u_i$).

Finally, each disequation does not contain variables that appear on the left hand side of equations.

More formally, a system in normal form is a system

$$S = \begin{cases} y = Mz + M^{'}x + f & (S_A) \\ v = Ax + b, \;\; l \leq v \leq u, \;\; l' \leq x \leq u' & (S_K) \\ d \neq Qz + Q'x & (S_D) \end{cases} \qquad (1)$$

where y and z are vectors of unbounded variables and v and x are a vectors of bounded variables and

- S_K is solvable and does not contain implicit equalities;
- S_D does not contain a constraint of the form $0 \neq 0$.

Without going into details, it is important to note that this form can be computed incrementally.

- The form of equations is computed by Gaussian elimination [6, 12].
- The solvability of the subsystem S_K is usually decided with an incremental simplex method [7] or revised simplex method [13].
- For the incremental search of implicit equalities, several methods have been proposed [15, 12]. The one we use is based on the quasi dual formulation of the system S_K [8].

Finally, note that the (revised) simplex method computes a solution of the system S_K. This solution is called the *current solution* of S_K and will be used for simplifying our algorithms for entailment.

4 Linear Constraint Entailment

4.1 Two Approaches

According to the definition of entailment given in section 2.2, proving that $S \models c$ is equivalent to prove the unsolvability of $S \cup \{\neg c\}$.

Let S be a system in normal form. let c be a linear constraint such that $S \not\models c$ and let t be a linear constraint. If $S \cup \{t\}$ can be mapped to a normal form S', then $S' \models c$ if and only if $S' \cup \{\neg c\}$ cannot be mapped to normal form. This is the *naive method.*

The *incremental method* maintains, for each ask linear constraint c_i a system in normal form Q_i equivalent to $S \cup \{\neg c_i\}$. If S' is solvable, then $S' \cup \{t\} \models c$ if and only if the system $Q_i \cup \{t\}$ cannot be mapped to normal form. If it can, the system obtained is reused for constraint added to S' later on. This method is incremental in that the constraint addition to a normal form is incremental.

From the time complexity standpoint, these two methods are equivalent. The major drawback of the naive method is that it decides solvability for the system $S \cup \{t, \neg c_i\}$ while ignoring that the system $S \cup \{\neg c_i\}$ is already solvable.

This information is used by the incremental method but it does not exploit the fact that the Q_i systems are very close (they are different in one constraint only). Consequently, similar operations are repeated. Moreover, the space complexity of this method is high since a system in normal form is maintained for each ask constraint.

The dereferenced form introduced below combines the advantages of the two methods without having their drawbacks. It has the space complexity of the naive method and several properties for entailment.

4.2 Dereferenced Form

After the definition of the dereferenced form, two general properties of this form are given.

Definition 1. *(Dereferenced Form)* A linear constraint $ax \diamond \beta$ with $\diamond \in \{=, \leq, <, \neq\}$ is *dereferenced* for a system S in normal form if it does not contain an occurrence of a basic variable of this system.

Each ask constraint is maintained in dereferenced form. This form has several properties, the more general ones are given here. More specific properties are given in following sections.

The following property establishes a syntactic criterion on the form of some constraints that are not entailed. This enables discarding some constraints from an entailment test.

Property 1 *Let S be a system in normal form and c be an equation, an inequation or a strict inequation in dereferenced form for S. If c contains an occurrence of unbounded variables then S does not entail c.*

When the normal form contains only equations, the following property enables the immediate determination of constraints that are entailed.

Property 2 *Let S be a system of equations in normal form and c be a linear constraint in dereferenced form for S. The system S entails c if and only if c is trivial and solvable.*

These two properties are used for deciding linear constraint entailment. Other properties for each type of linear constraint, are presented in the following. The proofs of those properties are not given here, they can be found in [12].

5 Entailment of an Equation

According to Property 1, an equation in dereferenced form that contains an occurrence of an unbounded variable is not entailed. However, the dereferenced form has a stronger property that simplifies the entailment test of an equation.

Property 3 *Let S be a system in normal form and c be an equation in dereferenced form, S entails c if and only if c is trivial and solvable.*

Deciding entailment of an equation amounts to checking if the equation has the form $\alpha = \alpha$.

6 Entailment of an Inequation

Consider now an inequation in dereferenced form. It is not entailed if it is trivial and unsolvable or if it contains an occurrence of unbounded variable (property 1).

The only inequations that can be entailed are the ones that do not verify these two conditions. Deciding entailment of an inequation is simplified thanks to the constraint propagation theorem given by Lassez and McAloon [10]. The following property is an extension of this result to our normal form.

Property 4 *Let S be a system in normal form 1 and c be an inequation in dereferenced form for S and containing only bounded variables, then $S \models c$ if and only if $S_K \models c$.*

For an efficient entailment test it is essential to note that

$$S_K \models ax \leq \beta$$

is equivalent to verifying that

$$\max\{ax \mid S_K\} \leq \beta \tag{2}$$

More generally, deciding entailment of an inequation is polynomially equivalent to solving a linear program. This linear program can be solved with the simplex method for example. Note that the simplex iterations can be stopped as soon as a solution of the system and of the constraint $\beta < ax$ is reached.

7 Entailment of a Disequation

The dereferenced form is of little relevance for deciding the entailment of a disequation efficiently. Lassez and McAloon have proposed in [10] a precise form for particular disjunctions of linear disequations. This form has interesting properties for entailment. However, for reasons that are explained below, we introduce a partial precise form for deciding entailment of a disequation.

7.1 Precise Form

The precise form of a disequation is a representation of the affine hull of solutions that this disequation excludes.

Definition 2. *(Precise form)* Let S be a system of linear constraints $S = \{y = Mx + m, Ax \leq b\}$. The *precise form* of a disequation $ax \neq \beta$ is the expression $\{Cx = d\}$ where $S \cup \{Cx = d\}$ is solvable and where $\{x \mid Cx = d\}$ is the affine hull of the set of solutions of $\{x \mid Ax \leq b,\ ax = \beta\}$.

The affine hull of a system of linear constraints is the smallest affine space containing the solution of the system. It is characterized by the set of implicit inequalities of this system. Here the affine space defined by $\{x \mid Cx = d\}$ is excluded by the disequation $ax \neq \beta$.

This representation has a nice property for entailment: Let S be a system of equations and inequations, let $D = \{d_1, \ldots, d_n\}$ be a set of disequations in precise form for S and let c be a disequation in precise form for S. Then $S \cup D \models c$ if and only if there exists a disequation d_i from D such that $\{d_i\} \models c$ (see [10]).

However, the precise form has two drawbacks. First, it has the space complexity of the incremental method. It is also difficult to maintain incrementally. Each time a constraint is introduced in the system S we have to recompute the affine hull of each disequation.

This is why we introduce the partial precise form. It is easier to compute and to maintain incrementally, it has the space complexity of a linear constraint and has interesting properties for deciding entailment.

7.2 Partial Precise Form

Like the precise form, the partial precise form of a disequation is a representation of the affine hull of the solutions that are excluded. But this representation is more compact.

The partial precise form only maintains implicit equalities of the system $S_K \cup \{ax = \beta\}$ which are sufficient to characterize the affine hull of excluded solutions.

Definition 3. *(Partial Precise Form)* Let S be a system in normal form 1 and $ax \neq \beta$ be a disequation in dereferenced form for S such $S \cup \{ax = \beta\}$ is solvable. Let $E = \{ux_F \leq v\}$ be the set of implicit equalities of the system $S_K \cup \{ax = \beta\}$. The *partial precise form* of $ax \neq \beta$ for S is the expression

$$\overline{\{ax = \beta\}} \text{ if } E = \emptyset$$
$$\overline{\{x_F = w\}} \text{ if } E \neq \emptyset, \text{ where } w_i = v_i / u_i$$

The space complexity of this form is the one of a linear constraint (i.e. $O(n)$ if n is the number of variables of the normal form).

Note that a disequation that cannot be mapped to partial precise form is entailed by this system. Here is the essential property of this form:

Property 5 *Let S be a system in normal form 1, and let $ux \neq \xi$ be a disequation. Let us consider the partial precise form for S :*

1. *if it is $\overline{\{x_T = w\}}$, then $S \models ux \neq \xi$ if and only if there exists a disequation $ex \neq \gamma$ from S_D such that $S \cup \{x_T = w\} \models ex = \gamma$;*
2. *if it is $\overline{\{ax = \beta\}}$, then $S \models ux \neq \xi$ if and only if there exists a disequation $ex \neq \gamma$ from S_D such that $e.\frac{\beta}{\gamma} = a$.*

This property shows the efficiency of the entailment test for disequations (see [12] for the proof). It amounts to deciding entailment of an equation, which is very simple (see property 3), or to deciding the colinearity of two vectors.

7.3 Computing Partial Precise Form

Let $ax \neq \beta$ be a disequation in dereferenced form for a system S in normal form. The two main steps to map this disequation to partial precise form are

1. decide the solvability of the system $S_K \cup \{ax = \beta\}$;
2. compute the set of implicit equalities $E = \{ux_F \leq v\}$ of $S_K \cup \{ax = \beta\}$.

For the first step, the current solution of S_K is used. If this solution satisfies the expression $\beta < ax$, then finding a solution of $S_K \cup \{ax = \beta\}$ amounts to finding a solution of $S_K \cup \{ax \leq \beta\}$ and thus solving the linear program

$$\gamma = \min\{ax \mid S_K\} \tag{3}$$

for trying to give the term ax the value β (the case where the solution satisfies the expression $ax < \beta$ is symmetric). Note that γ can be equal to $-\infty$. The result of this minimization is then analyzed according to the value of γ :

- $\gamma > \beta$, the disequation is entailed by S_K;
- $\gamma = \beta$, the system $S_K \cup \{ax = \beta\}$ contains implicit equalities that must be computed to obtain the partial precise form;
- $\gamma < \beta$, the partial precise form is $\overline{\{ax = \beta\}}$.

For the second step, note that S_K does not contain implicit equalities. The search for implicit equalities can thus be performed incrementally (cf section 3). In particular, the system $S_K \cup \{ax = \beta\}$ does not contain any implicit equality if the constraint $ax = \beta$ contains an unbounded variable.

The partial precise form for disequations has the advantage that it can be maintained incrementally when a new constraint is introduced in the normal form.

A disequation of the form $\overline{\{ax = \beta\}}$ has no particular structure, and the method described above is applied to it when a new constraint is introduced in the normal form.

For a disequation of the form $\overline{\{x_F = w\}}$, since w_i is equal to one of the bounds of x_i in the system S, searching for a solution of the system $T_S \cup \{x_F = w\}$ is equivalent to searching a solution of the system $S_K \cup \{fx_F \leq fw\}$ with $f_i = 1$ (if $w_i = l_i$) or $f_i = -1$ (if $w_i = u_i$) for $i \in F$, assuming that S is in normal form 1 (cf [12]). The search for a solution is thus equivalent to solving the linear program $\min\{fx_F \mid S_K\}$.

For searching implicit equalities in the system $S_K \cup \{fx_F \leq fw\}$ an incremental method such as the one cited in section 3 can be used since S_K does contains implicit equalities. However to avoid discovering again the implicit equalities that were used for the actual form, they are searched in the system S_K where bounds have been modified such that $l_i = u_i = w_i$, for $i \in F$.

8 Entailment of a Strict Inequation

Entailment of a strict inequation $ax < \beta$ by a system S in normal form is equivalent to the entailment of both the inequation $ax \leq \beta$ in dereferenced form for S and the disequation $ax \neq \beta$ in partial precise form.

However such a decomposition in not efficient and can be improved. If the strict inequality does not contains any unbounded variable, then entailment can be decided by solving the following linear program

$$\gamma = \min\{ax \mid S_K\}$$

This leads to the three following cases:

- $\gamma < \beta$, the constraint $ax < \beta$ is not entailed;
- $\gamma > \beta$, the constraint $ax < \beta$ is entailed;
- $\gamma = \beta$, the entailment of the constraint $ax < \beta$ is equivalent to the entailment of the disequation $ax \neq \beta$.

The last condition is the only one where the entailment of a disequation has to be considered.

9 Implementation

The forms and properties that were introduced previously lead to algorithms that improve the naive method and the incremental method.

However, for every new constraint introduced in the subsytem S_K of the solved form, a linear program must be solved to decide entailment or to maintain the partial precise form.

The ideal method would consider a number of ask constraints which depends on the number of entailed constraints and not on the total number of ask constraints. In practice we try to determine, with an easily verifiable criterion, the greatest possible number of constraints that are clearly *not* entailed.

This criterion is stated like this: if $S \not\models c$, then it is possible to compute a solution σ of the system $S \cup \{\neg c\}$. When a new constraint t is added to the normal forme S, if σ is still a solution of t, then it is clear that $S \cup \{t\} \not\models c$.

Consider an inequality $ax_N \leq \beta$ that is not entailed, it is possible to compute an assignment σ_1 that satisfies $T_S \cup \{ax > \beta\}$. This solution is a non-entailment test for the ask inequality. Suppose that another inequality t over slack variables is added to the normal form. If σ_1 satisfies t then the constraint $ax_N \leq \beta$ is clearly not entailed by the new system (case A. in Figure 1). On the contrary, if σ_1 does not satisfy t the simplex algorithm is applied to find another solution σ_2 of $S_K \cup \{t, ax > \beta\}$ (case B. in Figure 1) or to prove entailment (case C. in Figure 1).

To apply this criterion we associate a solution to every ask constraint over bounded variables. Here are, for a (strict) inequation and for a disequation, descriptions of the solutions to associate and ways to use them.

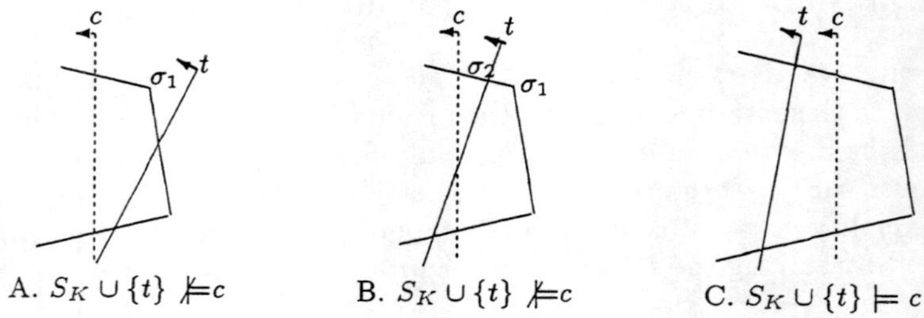

Fig. 1. The three cases for an inequation

9.1 (Strict) Inequation

The solution associated to an inequation $ax \leq \beta$ or a strict inequation $ax < \beta$ is a solution of the system $S_K \cup \{\beta < ax\}$. This solution is available as the current solution of S_K once the linear program 2 is solved. The (strict) inequation must be reconsidered when a constraint introduced in S_K excludes this solution.

In practice, it should be better to choose the solution σ as closest possible to the supporting hyperplane of the inequation since a solution far away from the supporting hyperplane would have more chance to be excluded by a new constraint while the ask constraint is not entailed. Indeed it is difficult to know what a *close solution* is since it depends on the problem considered and it is a good policy to construct σ_1 on the supporting hyperplane of the constraint. This solution is no more a solution of $ax_N + \beta > 0$ but is very close. When an inequation t is added to the normal form, the ask constraint has to be reconsidered either if σ is not a solution of t or if it is on the supporting hyperplane of t.

9.2 Disequation

The solution associated to a disequation in partial precise form, denoted generically by $\overline{\{Cx = d\}}$ is a solution of $S_K \cup \{Cx = d\}$. is available once the linear program 3 is solved. The two following optimizations are then possible:

- the addition of a constraint $ax \diamond \beta$ to the system S_K does nor modify the partial precise form whose associated solution is a solution of $ax \diamond \beta$ without being a solution of $ax = \beta$;
- let $ax \neq \gamma$ a disequation of S_D, if the associated solution is a solution of $ex \neq \gamma$ the $\{ex \neq \gamma\} \not\models \overline{\{Cx = d\}}$.

To prove the first statement, consider the addition of an inequation $ax \leq \beta$. If σ is a solution of $ax \leq \beta$ without being a solution of $ax = \beta$, it is thus a solution of $S_K \cup \{Cx = d, ax < \beta\}$. From the definition of the partial precise form, the system $S_K \cup \{Cx = d\}$ does not contain implicit equalities, and thus the system $S_K \cup \{Cx = d, ax < \beta\}$ does not contain implicit equalities either. So the partial precise form of $\overline{\{Cx = d\}}$ is unchanged.

The second statement is easily proved: observe that the solution σ is a solution of $\{Cx = d,\ ex \neq \gamma\}$. Thus $\{Cx = d\} \not\models ex = \gamma$ and consequently $\{ex \neq \gamma\} \not\models \overline{\{Cx = d\}}$.

Associating a solution to an ask constraint reduces the number of applications of our algorithms. The impact of this association on the efficiency of constraint entailment is evaluated in the following section.

10 Applications

The entailment algorithms described in the previous section have been integrated to the CLP language `Athena` [13] whose linear constraint solver is based on an incremental revised simplex method over rational numbers.

Various problems from operation research and electrical engineering have been solved with this system. The `Bridge` problem is an optimization problem with disjunctive constraints whose first CLP solution appears in [16]. The disjunctive constraints states that two tasks T_1 and T_2, whose starting dates are t_1 and t_2 and whose durations are d_1 and d_2 cannot overlap. This is stated with the following expression:

$$[t_2 + d_2 \leq t_1] + [t_1 + d_1 \leq t_2] = 1$$

The `CNET` problem [11] is a 0-1 mixed integer optimization problem which amounts to selecting the position of the concentrators on a network to minimize the distances between concentrators and plugs and the number of concentrators. The 0-1 constraint over a variable x_i is expressed as follows

$$0 \leq x_i \leq 1,\ [x_i > 0] \rightarrow [x_i = 1],\ [x_i < 1] \rightarrow [x_i = 0]$$

The `Circuit` problem [5] is a simulation of the temporal behavior of a hybrid circuit containing electro-mecanical and digital control devices. The behavior of these devices is easily represented by the high level operators using the implication operator.

Finally, the hoist scheduling problem (`HSP`) is a cyclic scheduling problem with disjunctive constraints [1]. Two instances of this problem from industrial applications have been considered.

In all these problems the presence of high level operators simplifies the statement but does not avoid the use of enumeration for finding a solution or the optimal solution.

Table 1 presents the number of pivoting operations and the time (in seconds) required for the naive method, for using the dereferenced form and for associating a solution to each ask constraint. The dereferenced form always improves the number of pivots and the time requirement. The association of a solution to each

	Naive Method		Dereferenced Form		Solution		
Problems	Pivot	Time (N)	Pivot	Time	Pivot	Time (S)	N / S
Bridge	322512	3706.2	114038	1749.3	13380	221.7	16.7
CNET	14010	385.1	13852	378.2	8751	159.5	2.4
Circuit	520	312.2	236	102.3	47	38.5	8.1
HSP1	18117	401.0	11258	250.2	6541	119.8	3.3
HSP2	25108	682.2	18523	510.3	11736	192.3	3.5
Ar. Mean							6.8

Table 1. Time Requirement for Entailment.

		Standard Backtracking		High level ope.		
Problems	Ask Cons.	Back.	Time (N)	Back.	Time (E)	N / E
Bridge	154	8948	221.7	436	205.0	1.08
CNET	20	173	159.5	45	280.2	0.56
Circuit	46	289	38.5	11	13.4	2.87
HSP1	348	965	119.8	52	14.5	8.26
HSP2	602	1750	192.3	89	21.2	9.07

Table 2. With and without high level operators

ask constraints improves the naive algorithm by a factor of 6 on the average and up to a factor of 16 for the Bridge problem.

The results presented in table 2 show that a significant reduction of the search tree and of the computation time can be obtained when using high level operators over linear constraints. On the other hand, entailment over linear constraints is computationally difficult. As a consequence, complex linear constraints should not be used systematically for solving any combinatorial linear constraint problem. Their use must be studied because not every problem can benefit of them. For instance, for the `CNET` problem the reduction of the search space does not compensate for the cost of reducing it.

11 Conclusion

Solving high level operators over linear constraints is related to deciding linear constraint entailment. Two forms were presented for this purpose: the dereferenced form and the partial precise form. The properties of these forms provides an efficient entailment test for a linear constraint.

The practical results show that a substantial reduction of the search space and of the computation time can be obtained when expressing problems with high level operators over linear constraints. They also show that, although complete, the linear constraint entailment test is computationally expensive.

As a future work, it would be interesting to study the cooperation between the algorithms presented herein and an interval constraint solver. Since interval-based solvers are sound, they can prove easily that some constraints are entailed (in linear time w.r.t. to the number of variables). At the end, the entailment of some constraints would be decided by the interval approximation, the non entailment of some other constraints would be decided by the associated solution, and our algorithms were only applied to the remaining constraints.

References

1. P. Baptiste, B. Legeard, and C. Varnier. Hoist scheduling problem : an approach based on constraint logic programming. In *Proceedings of the 1992 IEEE International Conference on Robotics and Automation*, pages 1139–1144, Nice, France, May 1992.
2. F. Benhamou and A. Touraivane. Prolog IV : langage et algorithmes. Technical report, 1996.
3. A. Colmerauer. An introduction to Prolog III. *Communications of the ACM*, 33(7):69–91, July 1990.
4. M. Dincbas, P. van Hentenryck, and H. Simonis. The constraint logic programming langage CHIP. In *Proceedings of the International Conference on Fifth Generation Computer Systems*, pages 693–702, Tokyo, Japan, 1988.
5. T. Graf, P. Van Hentenryck, C. Pradelles-Lasserre, and L. Zimmer. Simulation of hybrid circuits in constraint logic programming. *Computers Math. Applic.*, 20(9–10):45–56, 1990.
6. J.-L. Imbert and P. van Hentenryck. On the handling of disequations in CLP over linear rational arithmetic. In Frederic Benhamou and Alain Colmerauer, editors, *Constraint Logic Programming: Selected Research*, pages 49–72. MIT Press, 1993.
7. J. Jaffar, S. Michaylov, P. Stuckey, and R.H.C. Yap. The CLP($\mathcal{R}$) language and system. *Transactions on Programming Languages and Systems*, 14(3), July 1992.
8. J-L Lassez. Parametric queries, linear constraints and variable elimination. In *DISCO 90, LNCS 429*, pages 164–173. Springer-Verlag Lecture Notes in Computer Science, 1990.
9. J-L Lassez. Querying constraints. In *Proceedings of the ACM Conference on Principles of Database Systems*, Nashville, 1990.
10. J-L Lassez and K. McAloon. A canonical form for generalised linear constraints. *Journal of Symbolic Computation*, (1):1–24, 1992.
11. G.A. Narboni. Optimization of concentrator positioning in the design of private data networks. In *Conference on the Practical Applications of Prolog*, 1994.
12. P. Refalo. *Resolution et implication de contraintes lineaires en programmation logique par constraintes.* Ph.D Thesis. Laboratoire d'informatique de Marseille, 1997.
13. P. Refalo and P. van Hentenryck. CLP($\mathcal{R}_{lin}$) revised. In *Proceedings of the Joint International Conference and Symposium on Logic Programming*, pages 1–14, Bonn, Germany, 1996.
14. V. A. Saraswat. *Concurent Constraint Programming Langages.* MIT Press, Cambridge, Mass., 1993.
15. P. J. Stuckey. Incremental linear constraint solving and implicit equalities. *ORSA Journal of Computing*, 3(4):269–274, 1991.

16. P. van Hentenryck. *Constraint Satisfaction in Logic Programming.* MIT Press, Cambridge, Mass., 1989.
17. P. van Hentenryck and V. Ramachandran. Backtracking without trailling in CLP($\mathcal{R}_{lin}$). *ACM Transaction on Programming Langages and Systems*, 1(1):0–0, 1995.

This article was processed using the LaTeX macro package with LLNCS style

Realizing Modularity in λProlog*

Gopalan Nadathur and Guanshan Tong
Department of Computer Science
The University of Chicago
Chicago, IL 60637
(773)702-3497, 2575
{*gopalan, guanshan*}*@cs.uchicago.edu*

Abstract. The language λProlog incorporates a module notion that permits the space of names and procedure declarations to be decomposed into smaller units. Interactions between these units can take place through either an accumulation or an importation process. There are both static and dynamic effects to such interactions: the parsing of expressions may require names declared in another module and executable code may utilize procedures defined elsewhere. We describe a method for implementing this feature for modular programming that is based on the *separate* compilation of each module into an appropriate fragment of code. The dynamic semantics of module importation involves enhancing existing program contexts with the procedures defined in other modules. This effect is achieved through a run-time process for including the compiler generated code for such procedures. Our implementation method partitions the code space into distinct chunks corresponding to the module structure, with the management of the sub-parts being realized through a module table. Efficiency of execution requires the use of uniform structures, such as a common symbol table, for the code in all sub-components. To realize this requirement, we describe a suitable communication between the compilation and loading processes. The scheme presented here has been implemented and tested in conjunction with an abstract machine for λProlog.

Keywords: Prolog, λProlog, modularity, separate compilation, implementation.

1 Introduction

Logic programming based solely on the theory of Horn clauses lacks devices for structuring the space of names and procedure definitions. Although the absence of structuring facilities is not problematic in the development of small programs, it can become an issue in programming-in-the-large. This fact has stimulated several proposals of mechanisms that support the modular construction of programs. Bugliesi, Lamma and Mello [2] classify these proposals into two kinds: those that retain Horn clauses as the logical core but endow the framework with metalinguistic mechanisms for composing separately constructed program fragments, an approach exemplified by [1, 7, 14, 15], and those that extract composition and scoping mechanisms from an enrichment of the underlying logic, an approach exemplified

* Work on this paper has been partially supported by NSF Grants CCR-9208465 and CCR-9596119. Comments on this work are welcome and may be sent to either author at the indicated addresses.

by [3, 8, 10]. We consider in this paper the implementation of a modularity notion in the language λProlog [13] that arises from following the latter approach [9].

Programming in a Prolog-like language to a large extent consists of identifying two kinds of collections: the names of constants, functions and predicates that can be used in constructing well-formed expressions, and procedure definitions that might be used in solving goals. The module concept that we consider is relevant to a structuring of programs with respect to both components. Modules in λProlog correspond, in a simplistic sense, to named collections of object identifiers and procedure definitions. The typical use of a module consists of making its content available in some fashion within another module or in the process of answering a query. This operation has both static and dynamic effects. The main impact of making the names of objects declared in a module visible is a static one: these names become relevant to parsing expressions in the new context. The effect with regard to procedure definitions is, on the other hand, largely dynamic. The procedure definitions in the new context might contain invocations to procedures defined in the "imported" module. To make sense of this notion, it is important to determine the exact manner in which procedure references are to be resolved in a situation where the available code is changing dynamically.

In implementing the form of modular programming described above, the main concern is that of handling the dynamic aspects. In particular, it is necessary to describe (a) run-time structures that will realize changing program contexts satisfactorily and (b) compilation and loading methods for extracting and setting up the information that is needed during execution. Such questions have been considered previously in the literature [4, 6, 11]. We expand on prior work in this paper in two significant ways. First, we provide a treatment of information hiding and a notion of module accumulation in addition to a previously considered notion of module importation. Second, in contrast to earlier discussions, we pay attention here to certain "low-level" details that are important to the actual execution model. We present our implementation ideas in the form of enhancements to an underlying Prolog engine such as the Warren Abstract Machine (WAM) [16] serving to realize the dynamic aspects of the module notion.[2] There are several interesting characteristics to the scheme we ultimately suggest, including the following:

1. Assuming some form of interface or signature definitions, it supports the separate compilation of modules.

2. It partitions the active code space into distinct chunks corresponding to the module structure and it manages this space through a global module table.

3. Despite the partitioning of code space, it realizes efficiency in execution by using uniform structures, such as a common symbol table, for all relevant code.

The remainder of this paper is structured as follows. The constructs for modular programming that are of interest to us derive in significant part from scoping devices already

[2] In reality, λProlog has many other new features, each of which requires embellishments to the WAM [5, 11, 12]. We elide this aspect for simplicity in presentation.

present in the core language. An appreciation of this relationship and of the method we have previously proposed for realizing the scoping notions [11] is useful in understanding the present implementation ideas. We provide this background in the next section. In Section 3, we present the important components of the modules language and we sketch the compilation and run-time processes needed to support it. A key ingredient of the scheme we present is a proper communication between the compiler and the loader. We explain some of the details of this aspect in Section 4. Section 5 concludes this paper.

2 Scoping Mechanisms in the Core Language

The higher-order theory of hereditary Harrop formulas underlies the core language of λProlog. From a practical perspective, this logic differs from that of Horn clauses in that it incorporates a typing discipline, supports higher-order programming and provides for scoping mechanisms. The scoping constructs that are of chief interest here result from extending goals in the Horn clause setting with two new logical primitives, those of universal quantification and implication. The first allows an expression of the form $\forall x G$ to be considered as a goal, assuming that G is itself a goal. Operationally, solving such a goal involves introducing a *new* constant c, replacing the variable x everywhere in G with this constant and then solving the resulting goal. Viewed differently, the universal quantifier corresponds to giving a name a scope: in the goal in question, the "name" x has G as its lexical scope and the duration of the attempt to solve G as its dynamic scope. The second new primitive permits an expression of the form $D \supset G$ to be a goal, where D is the conjunction of program clauses, and G is, once again, a goal. The operational interpretation of such a goal is that the program is to be enhanced with the "partial procedure definitions" in D while attempting to solve G. Implication is, thus, a primitive for giving procedure definitions a scope.

The programming character of the new primitives is illustrated by their use in local definitions, a typical application of scoping notions in programming-in-the-small. The following clause defines the *reverse* predicate on lists:

$$
\begin{array}{l}
reverse(L1, L2) \ :\!- \\
\quad (\forall rev\_aux\,((\, rev\_aux([\,], L2) \wedge \\
\qquad\qquad (\forall X\, \forall L1\, \forall L3\, (rev\_aux([X\,|\,L1], L3) \ :\!-\ rev\_aux(L1, [X\,|\,L3]))))) \\
\qquad\qquad\quad \supset rev\_aux(L1, [\,]))).
\end{array}
$$

The body of this clause contains a universal goal whose body is itself an implication goal. Notice that universal quantification over a program clause that is usually left implicit must be made explicit when the clause appears in the antecedent of an implication goal. Suppose now that the goal $reverse([1,2], L)$ is invoked relative to the given procedure definition. This would lead to an attempt to solve the goal

$$
\begin{array}{l}
\forall rev\_aux\,((\, rev\_aux([\,], L) \wedge \\
\qquad (\forall X\, \forall L1\, \forall L3\, (rev\_aux([X\,|\,L1], L3) \ :\!-\ rev\_aux(L1, [X\,|\,L3])))) \\
\qquad\quad \supset rev\_aux([1,2], [\,])).
\end{array}
$$

The semantics of the universal quantifier dictates treating *rev_aux* as a new name, distinct from everything else in the embedding context. Processing the body of the universal goal leads to the invocation of the goal $rev\_aux([1,2],[])$ after the clauses

$rev\_aux([], L)$, and
$(\forall X\, \forall L1\, \forall L3\, (rev\_aux([X\,|\,L1], L3) \;{:}\text{-}\; rev\_aux(L1, [X\,|\,L3])))$

have been added to the program. Universal quantifiers have been retained in the second clause above to distinguish the variables they bind from the variable L in the first clause that is really a "global" bound to a value occurring in the original query. Notice that the computation described up to this point has introduced a definition for the procedure *rev_aux* and that this must be used in solving a new goal. Carrying this process to fruition will eventually result in the query variable L being bound to $[2,1]$.

New devices are needed for implementing the scoping primitives described above. It appears at the outset that rather simple machinery might suffice for universal goals: we merely instantiate universal quantifiers with newly generated constants. However, this scheme is not quite sufficient because universal and existential quantifiers can appear in arbitrary order in goals. For example, suppose that our program consists solely of the clause $\forall x\, p(x,x)$ and that we are interested in solving the goal $\forall y\, p(X,y)$. The variable X has existential strength in the given goal in that it might be instantiated as desired in the course of search. Notice, however, that the interpretation of universal goals prohibits the instantiation for X from depending on any value chosen for the variable y. Now, the suggested treatment would reduce the given goal to $p(X,c)$, assuming that c is a new constant. At this point, the usual notion of unification would result in success by incorrectly instantiating X to c.

The solution to this problem is to modify unification to respect quantifier order. There is a simple way to achieve this that is based on tagging variables and constants with (small) positive integers. We sketch this scheme here, referring the reader to [11] for details. The key step is to think of the collection of all terms as being arranged in an increasing hierarchy of universes. The level 1 universe consists of all the constant symbols that appear in the program clauses and the original goal. These symbols are tagged by the number 1 to indicate their position in the hierarchy. Each time a universal quantifier is processed, a new constant is introduced, giving rise to the next universe in the hierarchy. This requirement is accounted for by increasing a running "universe index" by 1 and generating a new constant tagged with this index. The collection of constants at the new level consists of all those constants tagged with a number less than or equal to that level. When an essential existential quantifier is encountered, it is instantiated by a logic variable. This variable is tagged with the current value of the universe index to indicate that it may be instantiated only by terms in the universe at that level. The actual use of the tags occurs when an attempt is made to bind a variable X with a tag i to a term t. This binding is permitted only if t does not contain any constants with a tag value greater than i.

The main issue in implementing implication goals is to provide an efficient realization of changing program contexts. The essence of the scheme described in [11] is in viewing a program as a composite of compiled code and a layered access function to this code, with each implication goal causing a new layer to be added to an existing access function. Thus, consider a goal of the form $(C_1 \wedge \ldots \wedge C_n)$ => G where, for $1 \leq i \leq n$, C_i is a closed program clause.[3] The C_is are to be added to the front of the program while attempting to solve G. These clauses can be treated as an independent program fragment and compiled as such. Let us suppose that the clauses define the predicates $p_1, \ldots, p_r$. The compilation process then results in a segment of code with r entry points, each indexed with the name of a predicate. In our context, we require compilation to also produce a procedure that we call *find_code* that performs the following function: given a predicate name, it returns the appropriate entry point in the code segment if the name is one of $p_1, \ldots, p_r$ and fails otherwise. The execution of the implication goal results in a new access function that behaves as follows. Given a predicate name, *find_code* is invoked with it. If this function succeeds, then the code location that it produces is the desired result. Otherwise the code location is determined by using the access function in existence earlier.

The process of enhancing a context described above is incomplete in one respect: the new clauses provided for $p_1, \ldots, p_r$ may in fact be adding to earlier existing definitions for these predicates. To deal with this situation, the compilation process produces code for each of these predicates that does not fail eventually, but instead looks for code for the relevant predicate using the access function existing earlier. To realize this function, we associate a vector of size r with the implication goal, the ith entry in this vector corresponding to the predicate p_i. The compilation of the body of the implication goal then creates a procedure called *link_code* that serves to fill in this vector when the implication goal is executed. This procedure essentially uses the name of each of the predicates and the earlier existing access function to compute an entry point to available code or, in case the predicate is previously undefined, to return the address of a failing procedure.

In the framework of a WAM-like implementation, the layers in the access function described above are realized by using a data structure called an *implication point record* that is allocated on the local stack. The components of such a record are the following:

1. the address of the *find_code* procedure corresponding to the antecedent of the implication goal,

2. a positive integer r indicating the number of predicates defined by the program clauses in the antecedent,

[3] In the most general situation, the goal $(C_1 \wedge \ldots \wedge C_n)$ => G may appear within the scope of universal quantifiers and the C_is may contain free global variables; both possibilities are illustrated in the definition of the *reverse* program discussed earlier. Global variables can be handled by treating a program clause as a combination of compiled code and a binding environment in the scheme being described and leaving other details unchanged. Universal quantification over procedure names can lead to two different improvements in this scheme. First, calls to such procedures from within G can be based on using an absolute address and need not be mediated by the procedure *find_code*. Second, the definitions of such procedures within $(C_1 \wedge \ldots \wedge C_n)$ cannot be extended, leading to a determinism that can be exploited in compiling these definitions and obviating entries for such procedures in the next clause vector stored in implication points. Both benefits are significant in practice as the reader might appreciate by considering their effects in the context of the *reverse* program.

3. a pointer to an enclosing implication point record, and thereby to the previous layer in the access function, and

4. a vector of size r that indicates the next clause to try for each of the predicates defined in the antecedent of the implication goal.

The program context existing at a particular stage is indicated by a pointer to a relevant implication point record which is contained in a register called I. Now, a goal such as $(C_1, \ldots, C_n)$ => G is compiled into code of the form

push_impl_point t
  { Compiled code for G }
pop_impl_point

In this code, t is the address of a statically created table for the antecedent of the goal that indicates the address of its *find_code* and *link_code* procedures and the number of predicates defined. The *push_impl_point* instruction causes a new implication point record to be allocated. The first three components of this record are determined immediately from the table parameter and the I register. The last component is determined by running *link_code* relative to the access function provided by the I register. The final action of the instruction is to set the I register to point to the newly created implication point record. The complementary *pop_impl_point* instruction restores the old program context by setting the I register to the address of the enclosing implication point record.

An important operation is the resurrection of an old program context upon backtracking. In the scheme described, the program context at each point is encapsulated in the contents of the I register. Saving the contents of this register in a WAM-like choice point record and retaining implication point records embedded under choice points therefore suffice for achieving the necessary context switching.

3 The Structure of Modules and their Interactions

At the lowest level, the module feature allows a name to be associated with collections of names and program clauses. An example of the use of this construct is provided by the following code that attaches the name *lists* with the predicate names *append* and *member* and the procedures defining them:[4]

module *lists*.
append([], L, L).
append([H|$L1$], $L2$, [H|$L3$]) :- *append*($L1$, $L2$, $L3$).
member(H, [H|L]).
member(X, [H|L]) :- *member*(X, L).

[4] In reality, λProlog is a typed language and so named objects are identified explicitly through type declarations in modules. However, we suppress types in the present discussion.

The module declaration above can be thought of as the declaration of a list "data type". This data type can be made available in relevant contexts by using the name *lists* in specific ways. One possibility is to use the names of modules in a new kind of goal called a module implication. These are expressions of the form M ==> G, where M is a module name. The static effect of such a goal is that the names associated with M become available in interpreting the goal G. Of greater interest from an implementation perspective is the effect with regard to procedure definitions. This aspect is explained by a translation into the core language. We first interpret a module as the conjunction of the program clauses appearing in it. For example, the *lists* module corresponds to the conjunction of the clauses for *append* and *member*. Now, if module M corresponds to the formula D, then the query M ==> G is thought of as the goal $D \supset G$. The run-time treatment of the goal M ==> G thus calls for solving the goal G after adding the predicate definitions in the module M to the existing program.

The modules language incorporates the possibility of hiding data structures. In particular, a declaration of the form

local ⟨*constant-name*⟩, . . . , ⟨*constant-name*⟩.

can be placed within a module to achieve this effect: the names of the constants listed then become unavailable outside the module. The static effect of the local construct is obvious. From a dynamic perspective, another issue arises: the constants defined to be local should not become visible outside through computed answers. This effect can be achieved by interpreting local constants as variables quantified existentially over the conjunction of program clauses in the module. For example, consider the following module:

module   *store*.
local   *emp*, *stk*.
initialize(*emp*).
enter(X, S, *stk*(X, S)).
remove(X, *stk*(X, S), S).

This module implements a *store* data type with initializing, adding and removing operations. At a level of detail, the store is implemented as a stack. However, the intention of the local declarations is to hide the actual representation of the store. Now, from the perspective of dynamic effects, the module can be interpreted as the formula

$$\begin{array}{l}\exists Emp \exists Stk(\\ \quad initialize(Emp) \wedge \\ \quad \forall X \forall S\, enter(X, S, Stk(X, S)) \wedge \\ \quad \forall X \forall S\, remove(X, Stk(X, S), S)).\end{array}$$

If we call this formula *EStore*, then solving a goal of the form (*store* ==> $G(X)$) amounts to solving the goal ($EStore \supset G(X)$). Operationally, the existential quantifiers at the head of *EStore* can be translated into universal quantifiers over the implication to produce a legitimate goal in our core language. Notice, however, that these quantifiers are scoped *within* the (implicit) quantification over X and so the constants supplied for Emp and Stk may not appear in instantiations of X.

A module may interact with others in λProlog by *importing* the definitions appearing in them. A declaration of the following form is utilized for this purpose:

import $M1, \ldots, Mk.$

In such a declaration, $M1, \ldots, Mk$ must be names of other modules, referred to as the *imported* modules. This declaration has, once again, a static and a dynamic effect on the module in which it is placed, *i.e.*, on the *importing* module. The intended dynamic effect is to make the procedure definitions in the imported modules available for solving the goals in the *bodies* of program clauses that appear in the importing module. The exact effect can be clarified by using module implication [8]. Suppose that the clause P :- G appears in a module that imports the modules $M1, \ldots, Mk$. The dynamic semantics involves interpreting this clause as the following one instead:

P :- ($M1$ ==> $\cdots$ (Mk ==> G)).

Using this clause requires solving the goal ($M1$ ==> $\cdots$ (Mk ==> G)) that ultimately causes the program to be enhanced with the clauses in $M1, \ldots, Mk$ before solving G.

The translation of *import* and *local* declarations into the core language indicates a first approach to their implementation. Suppose that a module M imports the modules $M1$ and $M2$. At a conceptual level, the (separate) compilation of $M1$ and $M2$ should associate with these modules the following components:[5]

1. The number of local constants and, if this is nonzero, the names of these constants.
2. The number and names of predicates defined in this module that could be extending previously existing definitions.
3. Analogous to the antecedents of implication goals, the *find_code* and *link_code* routines for the module.

[5] Recalling the discussion of universal quantification over implication goals, it is beneficial to know when definitions of procedures within $M1$ and $M2$ cannot be extended: calls to such procedures can be based on absolute addresses and compilation can profitably utilize (static) determinacy information. Local declarations in modules are not sufficient for this purpose—imported modules may extend definitions for local procedures. Nor are such declarations necessary; in particular, there may be globally visible procedures whose definitions are intended not to be extended. Our modules language actually includes a device for identifying procedures whose definitions, while being exported, cannot be extended, and our notion of signature matching allows the compatibility of interacting modules to be checked in the presence of such declarations without compromising separate compilation. The importance of these aspects to the ultimate practicality of the modules notion should not be underestimated. In particular, most procedures defined in a module are likely to be local or ones whose definitions are 'complete'. However, such information does not call for new run-time devices and its use during compilation is also relatively straightforward. For this reason, we do not discuss this matter any further in this paper, focusing instead on the more 'problematic' aspects that need special treatment during compilation and run-time.

Let the addresses of these "tables" of information for $M1$ and $M2$ be $t1$ and $t2$, respectively. Then the compilation of the body of the clause P :- G in M would produce the following code:

push_import_point $t1$
push_import_point $t2$
  {Compiled code for invoking goal G}
pop_import_point 2

Using its table argument, the *push_import_point* instruction first determines if there are local constants for the module in question. If so, it increments the running universe index and tags the local constants with the new value. It then sets up an *import point record*, a structure similar to an implication point record, to register the addition of the code in the module. The *pop_import_point* instruction complements this operation by removing a number of import point records indicated by its argument and decreasing the universe index as needed.

The scheme described above is naive in the fcllowing respect: if clauses from an importing module are used more than once, it will repeat the addition of code for the importing modules and this is shown to be redundant in [4].[6] To avoid this, we augment import point records with a new cell, called a *backchained* cell, that indicates whether or not a clause from the module has previously been used. Further, we add two new instructions, *add_imports* and *remove_imports* that use the value stored in this cell to condition the pushing and popping of import point records.

module m1.	*module m2.*	*module m3.*
import m2.	*import m3.*	
	local r.	
q :- p.	*p :- w.*	*w :- s.*
s :- r.		*r.*

Fig. 1. Interactions between Local and Import

There is an interaction between local and import declarations that needs to be considered carefully in implementing the scheme described. The particular problem arises from the fact that a module may use a local declaration to hide a (predicate) name defined in a module imported by it. The collection of module definitions shown in Figure 1 serves to illustrate this point. Suppose that the goal q is invoked in a program context in which the code from module $m1$ is available. This goal would ultimately fail. This situation is to be contrasted with one in which the predicate r is *not* defined to be local in module $m2$; in this case, the same goal would, in fact, succeed. Thus, the interpretation of a constant in module

[6] This demonstration is a little subtle because of the presence of local constants.

$m3$ depends on the context into which it is imported, raising the spectre of having to predicate compilation on usage. Fortunately, there is a solution to this problem: we compile each module separately, but in a way that allows the loading process to relativize it to the context of use. In the example being considered, the module $m3$ will be compiled as though the constant r that appears in it is a global. However, loading this module through $m2$ will cause this global to be "renamed" to a local. The actual implementation of this idea is discussed further in the next section.

module m1.	*module m2.*
	accumulate m1.
local a.	
$q(a)$.	$p(b)$:- $q(a)$.
	$r(b)$:- $q(X)$.

Fig. 2. Interactions between Local and Accumulate

There is one additional method for composing modules: several independently defined components can be accumulated into one larger unit. This effect is achieved by using a declaration of the form

accumulate $M1, \ldots, Mk$.

where $M1, \ldots, Mk$ are module names. Such a declaration can, for the most part, be treated by inlining the contents of the accumulated modules prior to the compilation of the module in question. However, there are a few subtle points relating to the scopes of *local* and *import* declarations that must be borne in mind. To understand this matter, we first consider the set of module definitions shown in Figure 2. The semantics of *accumulate* requires us to treat module $m2$ as a composite of the clauses for p and r that appear in it and the code in $m1$. However, the quantificational force of *local* requires us to distinguish between the constants of name a that appear in $m1$ and $m2$. Thus the goal $p(b)$ posed in the context of module $m2$ should *not* succeed. We note, nevertheless, that the scope of the local declaration in $m1$ should be raised to that of all of $m2$ by the composition process. In particular, the goal $r(b)$ should succeed relative to the module $m2$.

A similar point concerning the scope of a *import* is brought out by the modules defined in Figure 3. The accumulation of $m2$ and $m3$ into $m4$ results in the clauses in these modules being added to those already present in $m4$. However, this accumulation is to be done *after* the "de-sugaring" of syntax corresponding to *import* declarations. Thus, different sets of modules are to be imported for the purpose of solving the bodies of clauses arising from $m2$, $m3$ and $m4$. As a specific example, the goal q should succeed relative to the module $m4$ whereas both r and s should fail. The reason for this is that the code in module $m1$ should be added to the program context only when the clause p :- w in module $m4$ that originates from module $m2$ is used, and the (sub)goal w fails without this addition.

module m1.	*module m2.* *import m1.*	*module m3.*	*module m4.* *accumulate m2, m3.*
w.	*p :- w.*	*t :- w.*	*q :- p.* *r :- t.* *s :- w.*

Fig. 3. Interactions between Import and Accumulate

The run-time machinery that we have already presented suffices for handling most of the scoping aspects discussed above and the main requirement is to account for them satisfactorily in the compilation process. We explain how this is done in the next section. However, some modification to the implementation scheme is needed for importing different sets of modules based on the clause being used. Fortunately, a simple generalization of existing devices suffices for this: instead of a single backchained cell, we associate a *vector* of such cells with each import point record. The instructions *add_imports* and *remove_imports* acquire an index into this vector and use the cell determined by it to decide whether or not to execute a sequence of *push_import_point* instructions or a *pop_import_point* instruction, respectively.

4 Compilation and Loading of Modules

In this section, we discuss how modules are compiled and loaded. Before going into details, we give a general description of what should be produced in loading a module and how such information is used subsequently. A user asks for a module to be loaded by typing in a directive of the form:[7]

#load ⟨*module-name*⟩.

The outcome of carrying out this directive is an association between the named module and the following items: (1) the global constants of this module and (2) a table created by the loader for adding the code from this module to the program context when the module is assumed. This association is realized through a global *module table*. Both items get used after the user issues a directive of the form:

#query ⟨*module-name*⟩.

After such a directive, the system will be ready for user queries. The first item associated with the module will be used in parsing these queries and, upon successful parsing, the module relevant code will be used in answering them. Thus, this directive corresponds to relativizing queries through a module implication.

[7] The syntax we use here has been modelled closely on that of Terzo, an interpreter for λProlog that has been implemented in the language SML [17].

4.1 Separate Compilation of Modules

There are interactions between modules that require the sharing of information such as the names (and types) of constants at compile time. These interactions are typically handled by associating interface or signature declarations with modules and our implementation of λProlog incorporates such a notion. Armed with such information, our implementation scheme supports the independent generation of the code needed at run-time for each module.

*module m*1.	*module m*2	
...	...	
*module m*3.	*module m*4.	*module m*5.
*import m*1.	*import m*2.	*accumulate m*3, *m*4.
local r.	*local r*, *w*.	*local q*.
[*clauses in m*3]	[*clauses in m*4]	[*clauses in m*5]

Fig. 4. A module collection illustrating preprocessing

*module m*5.
local q, *r*[1], *w*, *r*[2].

{*import m*2 [*q* → *first local*, *r* → *second local*, *w* → *third local*]
[*clauses from m*4] *with constant references suitably resolved*}

{*import m*1 [*q* → *first local*, *r* → *fourth local*]
[*clauses from m*3] *with constant references suitably resolved*}

[*clauses from m*5] *with constant references suitably resolved*

Fig. 5. Preprocessed form of the definition of module *m*5

The interactions between *local*, *import* and *accumulate* declarations discussed in Section 3 require the preprocessing of the code in modules prior to compilation. Figure 4 contains a schematic presentation of a set of module definitions that serve to illustrate all the significant aspects of the preprocessing phase. Based on these declarations, module $m5$ will be transformed into the form shown in Figure 5. Some explanations are in order with Figure 5. Module $m5$ eventually has four local constants: q, coming from the explicit *local* declaration in $m5$, r and w coming from the declaration in $m4$ and r coming from the declaration in $m3$. This is reflected in the local declaration in the preprocessed form, with $r[1]$ and $r[2]$ indicating the "versions" of r arising from distinct sources. The clauses in the composite form of $m5$ can be partitioned into three sets depending on the import statements that are scoped over them. This structure is made explicit in Figure 5. When the imported modules are loaded into core, some of their global constants will have to be "captured" by the local declarations in $m5$. The loading process will realize this effect, as we explain shortly. However, the compiler must supply the information needed for constructing the renaming function for each such module. The fragments of this function determined by the declarations in $m5$ are indicated within square brackets adjacent to each *import* declaration. A final aspect relates to avoiding inappropriate capture of globals in clauses arising from different sources by the (expanded set of) locals. For example, the clauses in the original presentation of $m5$ may use the names r and w. In this case, some renaming must be done to distinguish these constants from those appearing in the *local* declaration in the composite form. This form of renaming is indicated schematically adjacent to each set of clauses in Figure 5 and would typically be built into the compilation phase.

The compilation of the preprocessed form of a module eventually produces the following components of information:

1. A list of the global constants that are defined and/or used in this module.
2. A list of the local constants that are identified in this module.
3. A count of the segments of clauses that have different importations scoped over them.
4. A list of imported modules paired with partial renaming functions for their global constants. As indicated, these renaming functions are realized as a list of pairs of a name and an offset into the local constant list of the present module.
5. The number and names of predicates (represented as offsets into the list of global constants) in the module that could be extending previously existing definitions.
6. The *find_code* function for the module. (The *link_code* function is completely determined by the previous component.)
7. The byte-code for the clauses in the module. Constant references in this code are provided as offsets into the global and local constant lists.

4.2 Loading Modules

The process of loading a module at the top-level will also involve loading imported modules, possibly triggering further nested loads. There is a difference in final effect between a top-level load and nested loads since nested loads do not produce a module name that is visible at the top-level, i.e., one having an entry in the global module table. As discussed in Section 4.1, constants in a module loaded in a nested fashion may need to be renamed in a way that depends on the context of importation. The loading process realizes this requirement by, in effect, loading specialized copies of modules. The relevant copy that is to be created at any point is determined by an incoming renaming function and the addition to this function that is made by the module from where the one being loaded is imported. The renaming function starts out by being empty for top-level loads.

The idea of loading a specialized copy of an imported module finds a correspondence in other languages. For example, in C++, templates allow generic functions to be defined once for a family of types and the implementation will generate versions of such generic functions for each argument type supplied to the template.

Translation into absolute addresses The structure of the loading process leads to a distinct code space for each module. References to instruction addresses within the code generated for a module are, however, relativized to a start address. The loader translates these into absolute addresses. This translation process affects the (byte)code that is loaded for clauses, the *find_code* function generated for the module and, ultimately, the vector stored in import and implication point records for determining the next clause to try for each predicate whose previously existing definition is being extended.

Resolution of global and local constants A common symbol table is used for all the modules that are loaded during an interactive session. A benefit of doing this is a significant simplification in the run-time manipulation of constants. For example, equality testing of constants is reduced to a comparison of symbol table indices.

An important component of realizing this particular treatment of constants is their translation to symbol table indices. The process for local constants is simple: when a module is loaded either at the top-level or due to importation, each of its local constants is inserted as a new entry into the symbol table. The symbol table index that is determined by this process is used in loading the code for the clauses in the module and also in the renaming function that affects the loading of modules that are imported.

When a top-level module is being loaded, each of its global constants is mapped onto a fresh cell in the symbol table. Before an imported module is loaded, the existing renaming function is extended by utilizing the information generated by the compiler for this purpose. Note that the renaming function can be managed in a stack fashion, with the addition made to it in the course of loading an imported module being popped off after the loading is completed. Note also that the renaming function can be represented as a mapping from constant names to the symbol table indices determined for these (local) constants. Now, when a non top-level module is loaded, for each of its global constants, the incoming renaming function is used to see if it can be resolved with a local constant of one of the "ancestor" modules. If this is the case, the function yields the symbol table index to be used for the constant. If not, the incoming collection of global constants is searched to determine if an index has already been assigned to the constant. If so, we, once again, have the index that is to be used. If neither of these processes yields an index, then we create a new entry in the symbol table for the constant and use the index so generated for the constant.

For efficiency in parsing user queries and in the loading process, the collection of global constants is organized into a binary tree. A pointer to the root of this tree is retained in the global module table entry for each top-level module.

Creation of tables needed for adding module code to the program context When a module is loaded, a table of information of the kind needed by a *push_import_point* instruction for creating an import point record is generated and retained in the corresponding code space. Relativizing earlier discussions to the present context, it suffices to maintain the following items in this table:

1. A count of the local constants and, if this is non-zero, a (pointer to a) vector containing the symbol table indices of these constants, to be used to initialize their universe indices.
2. A count of predicates whose previous definitions might be extended by the code in this module and, if this count is non-zero, a (pointer to a) vector containing the symbol table indices for the relevant predicates. This information is to be used to construct the vector of "next clauses" for these predicates.
3. A count of the segments of clauses in the module that have different importations scoped over them; this determines the size of the vector of backchained cells.
4. A function for finding code for predicates defined in this module and a table of suitable form yielding the address of code. The precise structure of this table would depend on the kind of function used. For instance, if it is a hash function, then a hash table with entries containing symbol table indices for predicates and pointers to code would be constructed.

The way in which the table described above is constructed should be obvious. The loading process eventually returns a pointer to this table. For a top-level module, this pointer is saved in its entry in the global module table, to be utilized in when a *query* directive is encountered. For imported modules, this pointer is used to translate the table argument of *push_import_point* instructions in the importing module into an absolute address.

5 Conclusion

We have presented a module notion in the logic programming language λProlog, and described an approach to its implementation. We have shown that our implementation ideas support the notion of separate compilation even in a situation where the context of use determines the run-time interpretation of modules. We have also discussed some of the details of the compilation and loading processes used in our approach that are intended to facilitate efficiency of execution.

The ideas described in this paper have been implemented in conjunction with an abstract machine for λProlog. This abstract machine utilizes the basic structure of the WAM in the treatment of nondeterminism and unification. However, it also represents a considerable enhancement to the WAM, with mechanisms being added to treat features such as typing [5], scoping over names and procedure definitions [11] and lambda terms as data structures with higher-order unification being used as the corresponding destructuring operation [12]. A satisfactory realization of all these features requires many low-level decisions, such as those pertaining to term representation, to be different from those adopted in typical WAM emulators. We have, for this reason, not been able to use such emulators in our implementation and have constructed an entirely new one for our abstract machine in C. We have tested key features of our implementation, including ones corresponding to the modularity features described here, by hand-compiling and running a carefully chosen set of λProlog programs. We are currently implementing a compiler for this language. We plan to use the system that will result at the completion of this work to obtain an experimental validation of the efficacy of our ideas for implementing a modularity notion that has been found useful in the past in structuring λProlog programs.

References

1. A. Brogi, P. Mancarella, D. Pedreschi, and F. Turini. Composition operators for logic theories. In J.W. Lloyd, editor, *Computational Logic, Symposium Proceedings*, pages 117–134. Springer-Verlag, 1992.
2. Michele Bugliesi, Evelina Lamma, and Paola Mello. Modularity in logic programming. *Journal of Logic Programming*, 19,20:443–502, May/July 1994.
3. L. Giordano, A. Martelli, and G.F. Rossi. Extending Horn clause logic with modules constructs. *Theoretical Computer Science*, 95:43–74, 1992.
4. Keehang Kwon, Gopalan Nadathur, and Debra Sue Wilson. Implementing a notion of modules in the logic programming language λProlog. In Evelina Lamma and Paola Mello, editors, *Extensions of Logic Programming: Proceedings of the Third International Workshop, Bologna, Italy*, volume 660 of *Lecture Notes in Artificial Intelligence*, pages 359–393. Springer-Verlag, 1993.
5. Keehang Kwon, Gopalan Nadathur, and Debra Sue Wilson. Implementing polymorphic typing in a logic programming language. *Computer Languages*, 20(1):25–42, 1994.
6. Evelina Lamma, Paola Mello, and Antonio Natali. An extended Warren abstract machine for the execution of structured logic programs. *Journal of Logic Programming*, 14:187–222, 1992.
7. P. Mancarella and D. Pedreschi. An algebra of logic programs. In Kenneth A. Bowen and Robert A. Kowalski, editors, *Fifth International Logic Programming Conference*, pages 1006–1023, Seattle, Washington, August 1988. MIT Press.
8. Dale Miller. A logical analysis of modules in logic programming. *Journal of Logic Programming*, 6:79–108, 1989.
9. Dale Miller. A proposal for modules in λProlog. In Roy Dyckhoff, editor, *Proceedings of the 1993 Workshop on Extensions to Logic Programming*, pages 206–221. Springer-Verlag, 1994. Volume 798 of Lecture Notes in Computer Science.
10. Luís Monteiro and António Porto. Contextual logic programming. In G. Levi and M. Martelli, editors, *Sixth International Logic Programming Conference*, pages 284–299, Lisbon, Portugal, June 1989. MIT Press.
11. Gopalan Nadathur, Bharat Jayaraman, and Keehang Kwon. Scoping constructs in logic programming: Implementation problems and their solution. *Journal of Logic Programming*, 25(2):119–161, November 1995.
12. Gopalan Nadathur, Bharat Jayaraman, and Debra Sue Wilson. Implementation considerations for higher-order features in logic programming. Technical Report CS-1993-16, Department of Computer Science, Duke University, June 1993.
13. Gopalan Nadathur and Dale Miller. An overview of λProlog. In Kenneth A. Bowen and Robert A. Kowalski, editors, *Fifth International Logic Programming Conference*, pages 810–827, Seattle, Washington, August 1988. MIT Press.
14. Richard O'Keefe. Towards an algebra for constructing logic programs. In J. Cohen and J. Conery, editors, *1985 Symposium on Logic Programming*, pages 152–160, Boston, Massachusetts, 1985. IEEE Computer Society Press.

15. D.T. Sannella and L.A. Wallen. A calculus for the construction of modular Prolog programs. *Journal of Logic Programming*, 12:147–178, January 1992.
16. D.H.D. Warren. An abstract Prolog instruction set. Technical Note 309, SRI International, October 1983.
17. Philip Wickline and Dale Miller. The Terzo 1.1b implementation of λProlog. Distribution in NJ-SML source files. See http://www.cse.psu.edu/ dale/lProlog/., April 1997.

This article was processed using the LaTeX macro package with LLNCS style

The Use of Mercury for the Implementation of a Finite Domain Solver

Henk Vandecasteele, Bart Demoen, Joachim Van Der Auwera
{henk.vandecasteele, bart.demoen}@cs.kuleuven.ac.be

Katholieke Universiteit Leuven, department computerwetenschappen,
Celestijnenlaan 200A, B-3001 Heverlee, Belgium

Keywords: Logic Programming, Constraint Logic Programming.

Abstract. Mercury [SHC94]is a recent phenomenon in the field of logic programming: it is faster than other logic language implementations (e.g. Prolog) and better suited for the development of large applications because of its compile-time error-detection capabilities. The concepts and technology used in the implementation of Mercury are rather new and not yet evaluated thoroughly outside its implementors group. This paper reports on an evaluation of Mercury, by describing the porting from the medium-sized constraint solving tool ROPE written originally in Prolog, to Mercury. At first our aim and hope, was only to arrive at a faster implementation of the constraint solving tool, but in the course of the porting, it became clear that the main feature necessary for efficiency and missing from the current implementation of Mercury, is efficient backtrackable destructive assignment, at least for our application. We report on a naive port of the Prolog implementation of ROPE in Mercury, a redesigned version using more efficient data-structures and finally a version which uses our own hacked together implementation of backtrackable destructive assignment: a future version of Mercury will hopefully support this functionality through user-declarations or analysis.

1 Motivation

In the past years, we have developed a prototype finite domain solver ROPE on top of Prolog [VDS94]. This implementation will further we referred to as ROPE. This prototype lacks efficiency because its implementation doesn't rely on any non-standard support of the Prolog implementation. On the other hand, this helped the development of the ideas of ROPE quite a bit. We believe that the reason for this inefficiency is partly the generality of Prolog (reversible, non-typed predicates) and partly the lack of support for data structures that can be updated at constant cost. When the new logic programming Mercury emerged, it looked very promising to port our prototype to this new system. One of the advantages of Mercury is faster execution: type, mode and determinacy declarations allow to generate more efficient code. On the other hand, exactly because of these declarations the port was non-trivial. For example the mode-declarations do not allow some partially instantiated structures. As a result open-ended data structures are not possible. The prototype of ROPE in Prolog heavily depends on such partially instantiated data structures. Still, we were encouraged to make the experiment as the designers of Mercury claim there exists alternative methods to cure these problems. In the next section we report on the Prolog-implementation of ROPE. This is followed by a description of the initial, pure Mercury implementation of the finite domain solver ROPE. The implementation of the finite domain solver on Mercury will be called mrope in the rest of the paper. This first pure version of mrope did not fulfil our performance expectations and we have experimented with different data-structures. Finally we added backtrackable destructive assignment to the Mercury-system and report on this in section 4. We end with some conclusions.

2 The finite domain solver ROPE

2.1 Finite domain solvers in general

The finite domain solver ROPE [VDS94] is a system within the paradigm of constraint logic programming, an extension of logic programming. In constraint logic programming languages unification is substituted with a more general constraint solving method. This way connections other than sharing can be build between variables where the involved variables do not have to be instantiated. This allows the solver to prune the search space before choices are made. Typical for a finite domain CLP-language is that the possible instantiations of a variable is restricted to a finite set of values.

The working method of such a solver is usually by consistency techniques. Other names for these techniques are a-priori pruning and constraint propagation. This consist in keeping with each variable a set of values which are still candidates for assignment and which are still consistent with the constraints. These sets are usually called the domains. The use of a constraint consists in removing inconsistent values from these domains. A value is inconsistent if there exist a constraint (or in general a set of constraints) such that given the domains of the involved variables, assignment of this value to the corresponding variable violates the constraint (or set of constraints). The removal of inconsistent values from a domain can lead to new inconsistent values for other variables. A fixpoint algorithm like AC3 [Mac77] can be used to accomplish this task.

2.2 Features of ROPE

The finite domain solver ROPE allows the user to express a wide range of different pruning strategies for each constraint. These pruning strategies include forward checking, partial lookahead and full lookahead [Hen89], but also contain many other pruning behaviours in between forward checking and lookahead. The existence of such pruning strategies was suggested in [Nad89]. In [VDS94] these pruning strategies were presented and discussed.

Another feature of the finite domain language is a powerful enumeration primitive [Van94]: consistency techniques (removal of inconsistent values) are not enough to solve a finite domain problem. Most problems also need sophisticated enumeration. This means that a variable is chosen from the list of uninstantiated finite domain variables and that this variable is assigned a value from it's corresponding domain. If such an assignment fails, or if the algorithm searches another solution, this assignment is undone and another assignment is tried. The enumeration strategy (choice of the variable and the value from its domain) is decisive for the efficiency of the search. ROPE contains a primitive which allows to direct the enumeration with three parameters. The first parameter determines a heuristic to select a variable among a list of uninstantiated variables. The second parameter determines which value from the domain is selected for assignment, while the last parameter concerns the backtrack behaviour. This last parameter could express for example that on backtracking a new variable must be chosen for assignment, while in classical methods the same variable is assigned another value.

The language also contains a version of the cardinality constraint [HD91] and the possibility to express an optimization function.

2.3 Implementation of ROPE on top of Prolog

Data representation A domain in ROPE is a finite set of natural numbers which is represented as an union of disjunct intervals. For example the set {1,2,3,8,9,12} is represented as 1..3:8..9:12..12 . The operator ../2 denotes an interval, the operator :/2 denotes the union of the two operands.

A constraint is usually transformed to a set of "in"-constraints, as done in [HSD93]. Each constraint can lead to a different set of "in"-constraints depending on the desired pruning behaviour. For example the constraint X = Y + 1 could result in the set of constraints { X in dom(Y) + 1, Y in dom(X) -1}, {X in int(Y) + 1, Y in int(X) - 1} or { ask(ground(X), Y in X - 1), ask(ground(Y), X in Y + 1) }. The functor dom/1 takes the domain of its argument. The functor int/1 results in approximating the domain of its argument to the smallest interval containing the domain. The construction ask(ground(X), Constraint) leads to the delay of the constraint until the variable X becomes instantiated. As the reader may have noticed the first set of constraints expresses lookahead. The second set of constraints leads to partial lookahead behaviour and the last set of constraints results into forward checking. Cardinality constraints and optimization functions lead to other primitives but we will not discuss these here.

Since our implementation of ROPE does not use any extension to Prolog, the domains and constraints have to be represented as ordinary Prolog data structures. Such data structures must be very easily accessible and also very easy to update. One alternative is to add to every clause an extra input and output parameter. The data-structure in these extra parameters contains information on the domains and the constraints connected to the variables. Every finite domain variable then refers to this global data-structure with a unique number. When information is changed concerning a finite domain variable, a smaller domain for example, then the out parameter reflects these changes where it still contains the old information on the other variables. Such a working method results in efficiency problems as updates to this global store are dependent on the number of finite domain variables in the system. An example of such a data-structure is a flat term where each argument contains information on one finite domain variable (in the sequel, we refer to this representation as "functor"). The unique number connected to each finite domain variable is the position of this argument in the functor. If the information on one variable changes then a new functor must be created where all arguments but one must be copied from the old functor. Time and place complexity of this operation is O(N), where N is the number of finite domain variables in the program. A better alternative is a tree-structure. In this case the complexity of copying in case of changes is logarithmic in the number of existing finite domain variables. Unfortunately, also access without modification becomes logarithmic in the number of finite domain variables.

Therefore we choose to instantiate each finite domain variable to a structure that contains both the domain of the variable and the constraints in which this variable is involved. There exist several references to one finite domain variable, namely each constraint in which the variable occurs. As a result we cannot replace the variable with a new variable when the domain changes. We have to change the domain of the variable by further instantiating it. For this an open-ended data structure is used with logarithmic access depending on the number of updates to this domain. Updating shows the same complexity behaviour. Concerning the constraints, four pieces of information are attached to a constrained variable: a list of constraints to be activated when the variable becomes instantiated, a list of constraints to be activated when the lower-bound of the domain changes, a list of constraints to be activated when the upper-bound of the variables changes and finally a list of constraints to be activated with every change to the domain of the variables. For some types of constraints, for example cardinality, we have to be able to remove constraints from these lists. For this purpose we keep a free variable with each constraint. To remove a constraint from a list, this variable is instantiated.

A final data structure concerns the queue of constraints which were activated, but not used yet. This is an open ended list where new constraints are added at the end of the list. A desirable feature of such a queue is that a constraint can only appear once in the queue. For this purpose an unbalanced binary tree is used in the pure Prolog version. In an impure version, we have used a record database. Every constraint contains a unique number. For every constraint in the queue this number is stored in the tree/database.

Algorithm Given these data structures, the main loop of the solver algorithm performs the following actions: (1) take a constraint from the queue, (2) use the constraint for removal of inconsistent values, (3) if the domain of a constrained variable changed, take the constraint(s) to be checked from the constraint store and add them to the queue, (4) if the queue is not empty restart with (1) otherwise stop. If a domain becomes empty in step (2) then the algorithm fails.

The solver is incremental. Whenever a new constraint is added to the system, the constraint is transformed to internal constraints. These new constraints are added to the constraint store and to the queue of the fixpoint algorithm. Subsequently the fixpoint algorithm described above is activated.

After all constraints are added to the constraint store and the queue is empty enumeration is usually started by the user program.

Enumeration consist of assigning a value to a variable and then activate the propagation mechanism explained above. When the propagation finishes the process is restarted with another variable. On failure the program returns to the most recent choice-point and takes the appropriate actions.

Besides this fixpoint and enumeration code there are some Prolog clauses that compute the intersection, union, addition, multiplication, ... of domains. Also subset properties are computed.

3 A pure implementation of ROPE in Mercury

In this first experiment we restricted the language to "in"-constraints. This implementation allowed to experiment with some small examples. From this we could draw some first conclusions.

3.1 Data-representation

Concerning the representations of the domain only some small changes were needed for the typing system:

```
:- type mrope_srange ---> ..(int, int).
:- type mrope_range ---> simple(mrope_srange)
; :(mrope_srange, mrope_range).
```

The example-set {1,2,3,8,9,12} is then represented as :(..(1,3), :(..(8,9), simple(..(12,12)))) instead of 1..3:8..9:12..12 .

Also for the "in"-constraints similar constructs were used as in ROPE. X in int(Y) + 1 is now represented as in(X, int(Y) + val(1)) . The reason for the val/1 functor, is that Mercury does not support subtypes. The type of such constraints look as follows:

```
:- type mrope_bound ---> val(int)
; lo(mrope_var)
; up(mrope_var)
; mrope_bound * mrope_bound
; mrope_bound / mrope_bound
; mrope_bound // mrope_bound
; mrope_bound + mrope_bound
; mrope_bound - mrope_bound.

:- type mrope_domain ---> :(mrope_domain,mrope_domain)
; ..(mrope_bound,mrope_bound)
```

```
; int(mrope_var)
; dom(mrope_var)
; val(int)
; compl(mrope_domain)
; mrope_domain * mrope_domain
; mrope_domain / mrope_domain
; mrope_domain + mrope_domain
; mrope_domain - mrope_domain.

% Each  constraint contains a unique number as first element.
% The maximum number used so far is stored in the mrope_system.

:- type mrope_constraint ---> in(int,mrope_var,mrope_domain)
; askgroundin(int,mrope_var,mrope_var,mrope_domain).
```

In Prolog to connect a domain to a variable we instantiated the finite domain variable to a structure with an open end. By further instantiating this structure the domain could be changed. Such a data structure is not possible in Mercury. The only possibility left is to use an extra in and out argument in the clauses of the program and most of the clauses of the solver. This arguments then contain a global data-structure with information on all finite domain variables in the user-program at hand. As argued in the previous section, updating such a data structure is usually very time consuming and dependent on the number of finite domain variables in the user-program. In case the update time is logarithmic in the number of finite domain variables, also the access to the domains becomes dependent on the number of finite domain variables. In a first attempt, this global data structure was implemented with the array-library in Mercury. The implementation of this array is based on a balanced tree. Here are the type definition of these extra arguments together with the type-definition of the finite domain variables:

```
:- import_module array.
:- import_module int.
:- import_module queue.

:- type mrope_queues --->
mrope_queues(queue(mrope_constraint),queue(mrope_constraint),
queue(mrope_constraint),queue(mrope_constraint)).

:- type finitevar --->
finitevar(mrope_range,mrope_queues).

:- type variables == array(finitevar).

% mrope_system/3 takes two numbers as input, each being the
```

```
% highest unique number used so far for mrope_constraint objects
% and mrope_var objects.

:- type mrope_system ---> mrope_system(int,int,variables).

:- type mrope_var==int.
```

This subject on representation of constraint-store and changing domains is further elaborated in the subsection on results.

Also the constraints connected to a finite domain variable are represented in this global data structure. As we want the finite domain system to be incremental, also these data structures are subject to change when new constraints are added to the constraint store. One list of constraints connected with a finite domain variable is represented with the queue data type in the Mercury library. Also the queue of constraints still to be consumed in the fixpoint algorithm uses this queue data type from the library.

3.2 Primitives in this first version

Because Mercury is a moded system it is not possible to initialise a finite domain variable implicitly at its first occurrence. As a result every finite domain variable has to be initialised explicitly before use. For these purposes the following primitive can be used:

```
:- pred domain(mrope_var,mrope_domain,mrope_system,mrope_system).
:- mode domain(out,in,in,out) is semidet.
```

Then the "in"-constraints can be formulated with the following primitive:

```
:- pred in(mrope_var,mrope_domain,mrope_system,mrope_system).
:- mode in(in,in,in,out) is semidet.
```

These primitives are used in a small example:

```
% there is a field with both feazants and rabbits
% there are 9 animals and 24 legs
% how many feazants and rabbits are there ?

mrope_main -->
        % initialise the variables.
        domain( F, ..(val(0),val(100)) ),
        domain( R, ..(val(0),val(100)) ),

        % constraint : F+R=9
        in( F, val(9)-int(R) ),
        in( R, val(9)-int(F) ),
```

```
% constraint : 2*F + 4*R = 24
in( F, (val(24)-val(4)*int(R))/val(2) ),
in( R, (val(24)-val(2)*int(F))/val(4) ),

% display result
output([F,R]).
```

In general a problem cannot be solved with constraint propagation only, so a simple enumeration primitive was added to the implementation for experimental purposes. It concerns a predicate that enumerates one variable, with a limited number of heuristics to select a value from the domain of a variable. Also a limited number of backtrack behaviours can be specified

```
:- type selectvalue ---> up ; down ; middle ; split.
:- type backtrackmethod ---> standard ; standard_ex.

:- pred enum(mrope_var, selectvalue, backtrackmethod,
                                        mrope_system, mrope_system).
:- mode enum(in,in,in,in,out) is nondet.
```

3.3 Results

A first observation concerns the order in which solutions are generated. As it happens, the Mercury version of ROPE generates solutions in the opposite order as the Prolog version. Since Mercury is intended as a pure logic language and logic makes abstraction of the order in which solutions are found, Mercury does not care which solutions are generated first. We do, especially in the enumeration phase.

The first results show that this first pure implementation in Mercury is slower than the implementation on top of Prolog using proLog by BIM. Two versions were tried, one with garbage collection and one without. Mercury uses garbage collection at the level of C [BW88]. Timing is given for finding all solutions.

test	mrope	ROPE
queens(10), with gc	95s	39s
queens(10), without gc	47s	

The main difference between the Prolog version and the Mercury version is the different data structure for the domains of the variables and the constraint store. As Mercury is known to be faster than Prolog, for Mercury programs that Prolog can execute, the reason for this slow-down must be because of this different data structure. First we wanted to measure the speedup we got in the parts of the program where the code did not change. A small program was written which computed intersections of random generated domains. Both programs were run on Mercury and ProLog by BIM on a Sparccenter-1000. About 40.000 intersections were computed.

	proLog by BIM	Mercury
40.000 intersections	3.7s	0.36s

This shows that it is reasonable to expect a 10-fold speedup when going from Prolog to Mercury, on the assumption that Mercury offers efficient pure alternatives for the tricks in the Prolog program.

In another experiment we wanted to measure the results of changes to the representation of the data in the extra input and output arguments. The original data-structure was an array from the Mercury library.

```
:- import_module array.
:- type variables == array(finitevar).
:- type mrope_system ---> mrope_system(int,int,variables).
```

Every element of this array corresponds with information on a finite domain variable. This array is implemented as a 234-tree. For testing purposes a simplified special purpose balanced tree was written.

```
:- type mybintree(V) ---> empty
                        ; tree( int, V, mybintree(V), mybintree(V)).

:- type variables == mybintree(finitevar).
:- type mrope_system ---> mrope_system(int,int,variables).
```

The last representation concerns the functor. In the last case every argument of the functor is information on one variable. If the information of a variable changes a new functor is created where all arguments but one, the one that changed, are copied. Then the changed information is put in the corresponding argument.

```
:- type variables --->
    array(finitevar,finitevar,finitevar,finitevar,finitevar,
          finitevar,finitevar,finitevar,finitevar,finitevar,
          finitevar,finitevar,finitevar,finitevar,finitevar,
          finitevar,finitevar,finitevar,finitevar,finitevar).
:- type mrope_system ---> mrope_system(int,int,variables).
```

This test was again on the queens(10) program. The Mercury program was compiled without garbage collection. For the first time we got timings better than the version in Prolog.

	queens(10)
Mercury array	47s
mybintree	25s
functor /20	21s

From this we can see clearly that a different data structure has a large effect on the efficiency of the program.

In another version of the Mercury program checking for duplicates in the constraint-queue was added. This was implemented with the help of the same binary tree used in the previous experiment. Also another example was added to the test-examples. It concerns the bridge problem described in [Hen89].

	mrope	ROPE
queens(10)	65s	39s
bridge1(200)	5s	27s

With the checking for duplicates the queens program is slowed down again, while with the new example we get an interesting speedup. So, it is possible that some examples run 5 times faster in this pure implementation of Mercury. As we will see in the next section better results can be obtained when using backtrackable destructive assignment.

4 Mercury with backtrackable destructive assignment

The previous section reports on the results of a straightforward port from ROPE to Mercury : the results were not so positive for Mercury. The main reason for this seems the absence of appropriate data representations because there is no good alternative to an open-ended data structure in pure Mercury. This section describes the addition of backtrackable destructive assignment to Mercury, and the effect on the efficiency of our constraint solver. In the pure version of the previous section only "in"-constraints were implemented. It was also very difficult to implement for example the cardinality constraint [HD91]. Such a constraint causes the need to remove constraints from the dependency lists connected to a variable. In Prolog this is realized by including a free variable with each constraint. To remove a constraint from a list this variable is instantiated. This is not possible in Mercury. We did not see any good and efficient alternative in Mercury than backtrackable destructive assignment to implement this feature.

4.1 Preview on the gains of backtrackable destructive assignment

Backtrackable destructive assignment is currently not part of the Mercury system. In version v0.5 the modes *unique* and *almost unique* were implemented, but this can only be used at the top-node of a data structure. Allthough the modes are there, destructive assignment is not yet there, so we had to do it ourself. Before jumping into the experiment we wanted to have an idea of the efficiency gain we could get. For this purpose we used SICStus Prolog v2.1 which contains a variant of backtrackable destructive assignment in the from of the builtin predicate setarg/3. The Mercury code for mrope was with some minor changes ported to SICStus v2.1 Prolog. We then again ran the queens(10) problem using different data-representations for the constraint-store and the domains of the variables. Still all variants use two extra arguments, an in and out argument. But in case setarg is used, the in and out arguments are always unified and the update is done locally. We used the same two data structures as before: a functor and a binary tree. Also in both representations a number of artificial variables were introduced. This should indicate how speed scales when larger examples are tackled.

Queens(10) problem in SICStus Prolog	normal	with setarg
functor/20	120s	94s
functor/100	1000s	94s
mybintree	152s	120s
mybintree with more variables	247s	163s

We concluded that it was worthwhile to try to implement a variant of setarg in Mercury. As the aim is to store the information on a finite domain variable in the variable itself we can assume constant access and update. This was the case in the 94s timing.

4.2 Implementation issues

To insert the code in C that implements backtrackable destructive assignment we introduced a dummy module which contains the interface for the code. The C-file generated by Mercury is then replaced with a file which contains the actual code for the backtrackable destructive assignment.

```
% dummy module to generate template for support routines
% to allow backtrackable destructive update in Mercury

:- module mrope_du.
:- interface.
:- import_module std_util.

% announce a backtrack-point
% places a marker on the trail
:- pred du__backtrackpoint_anounce is det.

% untrail all the changes after the last backtrack-point
:- pred du__backtrack is det.

% remove a backtrack-point - will remove marker from trail
% du__backtrack has to be called beforehand to make
% sure that the marker is the last element on the trail
:- pred du__backtrackpoint_remove is det.

% set argument (1), of predicate (2) to given value (3)
% this can be restored by du__backtrack when needed
```

```
:- pred du__setarg(int::in, TP::in, TV::in) is det.

:- implementation.

du__backtrackpoint_anounce.
du__backtrackpoint_remove.
du__backtrack.
du__setarg(_,_,_).
```

4.3 Results

Given backtrackable destructive assignment also the cardinality constraint [HD91] was added to the system. With the additional cardinality constraints a wider range of examples was possible. A new version of the bridge problem was added. In this version all disjunctions are added to the system before any choices are made. The old version of the bridge problem is called "bridge1", the new version "bridge2". A variant of the perfect square [AB92] was added with small dimensions. Also a Japanese puzzle called suudoku.

For comparison the same code was executed in SICStus v2.1 using setarg because the ROPE system on ProLog by BIM and the implementation in Mercury now use totally different data structures.

	mrope(Mercury)	mrope(SICS)	ROPE(BIM)	pure mrope
queens	21s	109s	39s	65s
bridge1	1.9s	10s	27s	5s
bridge2	1.7s	11s	14s	
perfect	23s	125s	126s	
suudoku	1.2s	5.5s	6.8s	

This table shows a bad result for the queens problem. In the version of ROPE in Prolog *the different from* constraint is handled at a higher level, which allows some optimization: a constraint X <> Y can be removed from the constraint store as soon as one variable is instantiated. This is still not done in the Mercury version.

So we should not take into account the queens results; then we can deduce a speed-up ranging from a factor 5 to almost 15 from the table compared to ROPE in Prolog.

5 Conclusions and Future work

This work reports on the use of Mercury for the implementation of a finite domain solver. This implementation is based on an implementation of such a solver in Prolog. Not all features of the original finite domain solver were implemented. For example transformation of high-level constraints to low-level constraints was not included in the new system. This resulted in the absence of some optimisations which are based on the high level constraints. This explains the bad results for queens. For a usable finite domain solving package these missing parts are essential but they will not change much the obtained results and conclusions.

The main result of the experiment concerns data representation: our experiment suggests at least that a straightforward port from Prolog code to Mercury code, will not always lead to a high performance gain. The use of alternative data structures can help, but it seems paramount that because of the lack of open ended data structures, data structures can be locally updated without being completely copied. This seems to be the intention of the Mercury team, with the introduction of support for the modes *unique* and *mostly unique* in release 0.5 (we started this work at the time of release 0.4). However, currently this information is checked, but not yet used and the occurrence of these modes is still restricted to the top-level of data structures. It is not clear whether the intended support is enough for our purposes neither whether in general automatic support is possible within the context of our needs.

References

[AB92] Abderrahmane Aggoun and Nicolas Beldiceanu. Extending CHIP in order to solve complex scheduling and placement problems. *JFPL*, pages 51–66, 1992.

[BW88] H. Boehm and M. Weiser. Garbage collection in an uncooperative environment. *Software Practice and Experience*, 18:807–820, 1988.

[HD91] Pascal Van Hentenryck and Yves Deville. The cardinality operator: A new logical connective for constraint logic programming. In *proceedings of ICLP*, 1991.

[Hen89] Pascal Van Hentenryck. *Constraint Satisfaction in Logic Programming.* The MIT press, 1989.

[HSD93] Pascal Van Hentenryck, Vijay Saraswat, and Yves Deville. Design, implementation and evaluation of the constraint language cc(fd). Technical report, Brown University, 1993.

[Mac77] Alan K. Mackworth. Consistency in networks of relations. *Artificial Intelligence*, 8:99–118, 1977.

[Nad89] Bernard A. Nadel. Constraint satisfaction algorithms. *Computational Intelligence*, 5(4):188–224, November 1989.

[SHC94] Zoltan Somogy, Fergus Henderson, and Thomas Conway. The implemenatation of mercury: an efficient declarative logic programming language. In *Proceedings of the ILPS'p4 Postconference Workshop on Implementation Techniques for Logic Programming Languages*, 1994.

[Van94] Henk Vandecasteele. On backtracking in finite domain problems. In *Proceedings of the Fifth Benelux Workshop on Logic Programming*, September 1994.

[VDS94] Henk Vandecasteele and Danny De Schreye. Implementing a finite-domain CLP-language on top of Polog : a transformational approach. In Frank Pfenning, editor, *Proceedings of Logic Programming and Automated Reasoning*, number 822 in Lecture Notes in Artificial Intelligence, pages 84–98. Springer-Verlag, 1994.

This article was processed using the LaTeX macro package with LLNCS style

The YAIL
An Intermediate Language for the Native Compilation of Prolog Programs

Ricardo Lopes, Vítor Santos Costa
{rslopes,vsc}@ncc.up.pt

LIACC, Universidade do Porto,
Rua do Campo Alegre, 823, 4150 Porto, Portugal

Abstract. A major goal for any Prolog implementor is to achieve the best performance for applications. Advanced compilation is essential for high performance. The last few years have seen improvements in Prolog compilation technology resulting in a return to the idea of native code execution. We present work on designing a novel native code compiler for Prolog. The compiler uses an intermediate language optimised for novel architectures, such as the ALPHA and performs several optimisations to obtain good quality code.

1 Introduction

A major goal for any Prolog implementor is to achieve the best performance for applications. Performance in logic programs can be obtained by using techniques such as advanced compilation techniques, by extensions to Prolog such as co-routining, constraints or tabulation, or by using parallel execution.

Advanced compilation is essential for high performance. Compiler-based systems appeared rather early in the history of logic programming. The first Prolog compiler, the DEC-10 Prolog system, was designed to generate DEC-10 assembly code which that could then be executed by the target machine. The search for portability and simplicity in the implementation in Prolog systems lead to a different approach, where compilers generate code for abstract machines that are then are emulated at run-time. Examples include Quintus Prolog [8], YAP [5], or SICStus Prolog [1], among many others. Most of these systems implement variants of David H. D. Warren's WAM [12] as their abstract machine.

The last few years have seen improvements in Prolog compilation technology resulting in a return to the idea of native code execution [11]. There were two major motivations for skipping emulation in recent systems:

- Overhead Reduction: Native code compilation eliminates the overhead intrinsic to the emulation of abstract machine instructions, which can take a significant percentage of execution time.
- Flexibility: native code computation allows for easier specialisation, whereas the WAM would require new abstract machine instructions for specialised cases. Note that reducing the granularity of WAM instructions is not a good idea, because it would increase overheads.

Native code generation can lead to a significant improvement in performance, at a cost. Portability is harder. The compiler will become much more complex, and usually slower. Whereas a Prolog emulator is a relatively compact piece of code, native code size can grow quite substantially, especially when all possible optimisations are applied. This can lead to large compiled binaries, and ultimately to a reduction in performance due to worse program locality.

In this report we present work on designing a novel native code compiler for Prolog. Our motivation in designing this system is to improve performance of a pre-existing system, YAP, by using native code compilation for user-defined predicates. Our initial goal is to reach the same or better performance than what is achieved by other native code systems, such as Aquarius or native SICStus Prolog. We aim at this work becoming freely available to the logic programming community

As in the case of Prolog by BIM or of SICStus Prolog [7] by we decided to start from a pre-existing system. YAP already provides access to a large library of built-in predicates and a compiler, which we would need to rewrite for a novel system. Moreover, by maintaining both emulated and native code, the user has the attitude to choose what is the best alternative for his or her individual modules. The drawback is that the implementation must support both modes, hence complicating the implementation of native code.

The paper is organised as follows. We first discuss our main design decisions. Next, we describe the YAIL, the intermediate abstract machine we use for the system. We then describe the compilation steps currently used in the system, and conclude with preliminary performance results and with some conclusions and suggestions for future work.

2 Designing the Native Code System

Two major implementation issues must be addressed in native code implementations. First, although most native code systems will use the WAM data representation, it is clear that the WAM instructions are too coarse-grained for a native code system, and that a finer intermediate language must be used. Second, there is a question of what should be the target language and system supported. One alternative is to generate assembly code. This should return the best possible execution, but makes portability harder. A different alternative is to generate code for a high-level language, such as C, and trust the abilities of modern optimising compilers.

2.1 Intermediate Languages

There are several approaches to the problem of intermediate languages for native code systems. In the WAMCC [3], the WAM is used as an intermediate language and compiled code is generated directly from here. This results in a clean implementation, but makes it difficult to obtain the best performance. In

Aquarius [10] or PARMA [9] the WAM is avoided and code is used for an intermediate representation directly. Last, in SICStus Prolog [7] a WAM-like abstract machine is used in the first step, and a lower-level intermediate representation is used for native code generation. The advantages of using this extra step is that the original system already performs several optimisations for generating the WAM-like code. These optimisations can be used directly in the native code system, simplifying its implementation. We decided to use the SICStus approach in YAP. The native code system is an extra step, after WAM-like compilation.

Considering the actual intermediate language, our major goal was to take the best advantage of the underlying hardware. As in most related systems, we followed a RISC-like approach of keeping a set of simple instructions that can be directly translated to assembly code, plus some higher-level instructions that can be implemented either as separated routines or inline. Last, we tried to support novel features in modern architectures that can be emulated in previous architectures, such as `conditional move` operations.

2.2 Compiling the Intermediate Languages

A second question was whether to use C or an assembly language compiler. Notwithstanding the good results obtained with KLIC [2] or Mercury [4], study of Prolog implementations indicates that the best results for native code Prolog systems so far have been obtained with assembly based implementations. Performance of C based implementations is not yet to par with what one can obtain from careful generation of native code. We therefore decided to concentrate on generating assembly code.

An interesting solution would be using an intermediate representation, such as GCC's RTL. This approach allows us to use several steps in the GCC compiler for further optimisation. The main disadvantage is that RTL GCC is a very complex language, subject to major changes at the whim of the GNU CC developers. This means that in practice this solution will be more complex than direct generation of native code. For simplicity we decided to use assembly in the first experiment, and consider RTL for future implementations.

We decided to use the ALPHA RISC architecture as our target architecture. The ALPHA is probably the cleanest architecture currently available, and is an ideal RISC target. A second interesting advantage is that although previous logic systems have been designed for a 32 bit architecture, the ALPHA architecture has 64-bit data registers and a 64 bit address space, which is now being followed by other architectures, such as SPARC and MIPS. For Prolog implementers this has important advantages, such as simplifying the tag scheme. Last, the ALPHA architecture is not yet supported by any other native code system, making the YAIL the first system to do so.

3 YAIL - Yet Another Intermediate Language

The YAIL, "Yet Another Intermediate Language" is an intermediate language between assembly code generation and the WAM instruction set. It aims at fulfilling two goals. Firstly, to isolate the dependencies of the compiler from the target architecture. Secondly, to create a representation that could improve optimisations and transformations difficult (or impossible) in the original WAM. The second factor was the major factor in the current implementation.

The instructions were designed towards independence, so that reordering could be easily achieved. The main characteristics of the ALPHA architecture influenced the design, so that mapping could be implemented easily and efficiently. On the other hand, the design tried to avoid excessive dependency on characteristics from the ALPHA architecture. An important consideration throughout was easy translation to architectural registers. High performance in modern machines depends on avoiding unnecessary memory access overheads. Last, one major goal was minimising the work in compiling from the YAAM (the YAP dialect for the WAM) to YAIL.

3.1 The YAIL Instruction Set

The YAIL instruction set follows Aquarius approach by including simple and complex instructions. We do not have "kernel" instructions, to allow the further steps to decide whether to expand or to call sub-routines. Instructions are mostly represented as groups of simple instructions, with a few complex instructions to support common operations such as trailing and unification. Note that only two simple instructions can access memory in the YAIL: `load` and `store`. All other simple instructions operate on registers.

Instructions have been organised into four categories. They are:

- **Memory Access Instructions** (see table 1). These are just two instructions, one for loading and the other for storing registers.

Instruction	Semantics
`Load(Ra,Rb,disp)`	Ra = *(Rb+disp)
`Store(Ra,Rb,disp)`	*(Rb+disp)=Ra

Table 1. Memory Access Instructions.

- **Register Operation Instructions** (see table 2). These include most general purpose instructions that can be directly translated into Assembly.
  The `test`, `compare`, `comparei`, `move_cond` and `move_condi` require an extra parameter indicating which flag to test. Table 3 describes the test conditions.
- **Complex Instructions** that operate on registers (see table 4). Although all these instructions could be organised as a simpler set of instructions, compacting them simplifies several optimisations. One example is dereferencing variables.
  Note that some of these instructions, such as `deref`, `trail` and friends, `push` and `pop` can access memory. The unification operation is one of the most complex and in some cases may require calling an unification procedure.

Instruction	Semantics
`test(cond,Ra, label)`	if cond(Ra) jump label
`compare(cond,Ra,Rb,Rc)`	Rc=(Ra cond Rb)
`comparei(cond,Ra n,Rc)`	Rc=(Ra cond n)
`move_cond(cond,Ra,Rb,Rc)`	if cond(Ra) Rc=Rb
`move_condi(cond,Ra,n,Rc)`	if cond(Ra) Rc=n
`set(Ra,Rb,n)`	Ra=Rb+n (n with 16 bits)
`add(Ra,Rb,Rc)`	Ra=Rb+Rc
`addv(Ra,Rb,n)`	Ra=Rb+n
`mul(Ra,Rb,Rc)`	Ra=Rb*Rc
`mulv(Ra,Rb,n)`	Ra=Rb*n
`shift(Ra,Rb,n)`	Ra=Rb≫ n

Table 2. Simple Instructions that operate on Registers.

Conditions for `test` and `move_cond`	Conditions for `compare`
`Equal to zero`	`EQual`
`Greater or Equal than zero`	`Less or Equal`
`Greater Than zero`	`Less Than`
`Low Bit Clear`	`Unsigned Less or Equal`
`Low Bit Set`	`Unsigned Less Than`
`Less Than zero`	
`Less or Equal to zero`	
`Not Equal to zero`	

Table 3. Available Flags for Comparison Instructions

- **Tag manipulation instructions** (see table 5). The major goal here is to obtain portability, as different architectures require different tag schemes. Usually these instructions can be implemented as simpler instructions.

Note that the design follows a RISC-like (and WAM-like) architecture in trying to keep often used variables in registers.

3.2 Register Organisation in YAIL

The YAIL supports an infinite number of registers. It is the task of later steps in the compilation process to restrict the number of registers to the ones available in the implementation. This is the current organisation:

- `R0`, zero valued register;
- `R1` - `R9`, general purpose registers for control of execution (see table 6);
- `R10` - `R13`, YAIL temporary registers;
- `R14` - {} , WAM temporary registers `X[i]`;

Instruction	Semantics
deref(Ra,Rb)	Ra=deref(Rb)
failz(Ra)	if (!Ra) goto fail
failnz(Ra)	if (Ra) goto fail
trail(Ra)	trail(Ra)
trailGlobal (Ra)	trailGlobal(Ra)
trailLocal(Ra)	trailLocal(Ra)
unify(Ra,Rb)	unifycells(Ra,Rb)
unifyGround(Ra,Rb)	unifyground(Ra,Rb)
push(Ra)	push(Ra)
pop(Ra)	pop(Ra)

Table 4. Complex Instructions.

Instruction	Semantics
IsVar(Ra,Rb)	Return 0 in Ra if Rb is not a variable
IsAppl(Ra,Rb)	Return 0 in Ra if Rb is not a compund term
IsPair(Ra,Rb)	Return 0 in Ra if Rb is not a pair
RepAppl(Ra,Rb)	untag Rb into Ra
RepPair(Ra,Rb)	untag Rb into Ra
AbsAppl(Ra,Rb)	Ra is Rb tagged as compound term
AbsPair(Ra,Rb)	Ra is Rb tagged as a pair

Table 5. Tag Support Instructions.

Table 6 shows the equivalence between registers in the YAIL and YAAM/WAM registers.

YAIL	YAAM
R1	S
R2	H
R3	Y
R4	ENV
R5	B

YAIL	YAAM
R6	HB
R7	TR
R8	CP
R9	P

Table 6. Equivalence between YAIL and YAAM registers

Temporary registers are used as follows:

- R10 - used when writing structures to control when branch back to read-mode code.
- R11,R12 - used to receive output of dereferencing.
- R13 - used in comparisons.

4 Compilation

Native YAP uses two intermediate languages for Prolog compilation before using the YAIL. First it compiles Prolog to YAAM code, a WAM approximation developed for YAP with some improvements. Second it converts the YAAM code to YAAM 2-streams. This is the YAAM code divided in two area codes, read code and write code. The read code includes the YAAM instructions which execute in read mode. On the write code it includes the YAAM instructions executing in write mode. The YAAM 2-streams has advantages over YAAM because there is a significant reduction on jumps, wich are very expensive on RISC machines. For example, consider the case in which we have one `get_struct` followed by n `unify's`. In the YAAM the `get` instruction set the `Mode` register to write or read depending if the argument is var or nonvar. All the `unify's` instructions that fallow must test that register to decide in which mode they are going to execute. In the YAAM 2-streams the `get` instruction starts by dereferenciating the argument in read code, then it jumps to write code if it concludes to be var, otherwise it continues on read code. The `unify's` that fallow the `get` instruction will execute without the need of any test in boths cases

After converting the Prolog code to YAAM 2-streams, the latter is converted to YAIL. Many unnecessary sequences of register-to-register moves are removed at this stage, but some optimisations are only possible by using a specialised phases that we discuss next.

4.1 Optimising YAIL Code

The techniques that we have used to improve YAIL code are applicable to many languages. A transitive closure is performed on a sequence of eight transformations, i.e., they are applied repeatedly until there are no more changes in code (see figure 1). Each transformation was carefully studied so the resulting code is better, and so the closure operation terminates. By better code we mean code that is either faster, or smaller, or both.

Next, we describe the eight operations used to improve the code. For each operation we present a small example. For simplicity in those examples we use the instruction `jump(label)` that is a short name for the YAIL instruction `test(equal,R0,label)`. Remember that `R0` is always zero.

1. **Label elimination** (figure 2). All `label` instructions that are not used by other instructions can be eliminated. Also, when two `label` instructions appear together the second one can be eliminated after changing all it references to the other `label`.
2. **Dead code elimination**(figure 3). Every non `label` instruction that follows a `jump`, `proceed`, `execute` or `failz R0` can be eliminated. Also, every instruction that do not change the execution state can be removed. Examples of these instructions are: `failnz R0`, `set Rx,Rx,0`, `add Rx,Rx,R0`.
3. **Jump reduction** (figure 4). Replace a `jump` instruction whose destination is another `jump` or a `fail` instruction by a new `jump` identical to the original

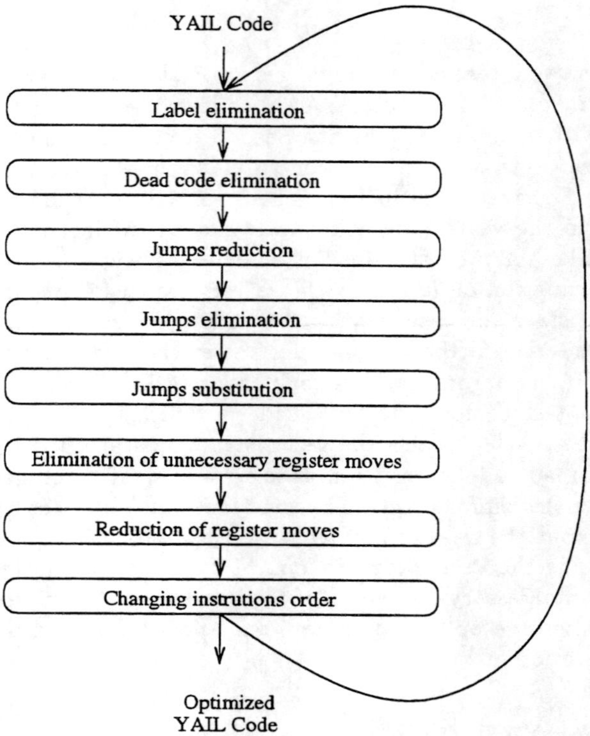

Fig. 1. YAIL transformations

```
<...>                                  <...>
labely:                                labelx:
labelx:              --->              <...>
<...>                                  jump labelx
jump labely
```

Fig. 2. Label elimination

one except that the destination label is replaced by the destination label of the `jump` or by `fail`.

4. **Jump elimination:** (figure 5) a `jump` or `test` instruction followed by the `label` instruction to where it points can be removed.
5. **Jump substitution** (figure 6). Replaces the `jump` instruction by the code it points if that block of code is shorter than a pre-set variable.
6. **Elimination of unnecessary register moves** (figure 7). One instruction that puts a value in register `Rn` can be eliminated if it is followed by a block of instructions that do not use `Rn` plus another instruction that assembles

```
<...>                                               <...>
jump labelx                                         jump labelx
<ins. different of label>                           labely:
labely:                                             <...>
<...>                            --->               <...>
labelw:                                             labelw:
failnz R0                                           <...>
<...>                                               <...>
```

Fig. 3. Dead code elimination.

```
<...>                                               <...>
labely:                                             <...>
jump labelx                                         jump labelx
<...>                            --->               <...>
jump labely                                         jump labelx
<...>                                               <...>
```

Fig. 4. Jump reduction.

another value to Rn.

7. **Reduction of register moves** (figure 8). One instruction that does a register move Rw to Rx can be eliminated if is followed by a block of instructions where Rx can be substituted by Rw, plus another instruction where another value is given to Rx.
8. **Change instructions order** (figure 9).
   Most instructions can be reordered to concentrate the biggest number of `set` instructions so that some of these can be eliminated using the preceding step.

None of those preceding steps work on their own, and in fact they where built to work together. The first five steps are used to reduce size code, eliminating code that is never used, as well as reducing jumps whenever possible. The last three phases are used to eliminate unnecessary moves between registers, using as key idea the fact that some instructions use a register plus a integer in their

```
<...>                                               <...>
jump labelx                      --->               <...>
labelx:                                             labelx:
<...>                                               <...>
```

Fig. 5. Jump elimination.

```
<...>                                      <...>
jump labelx                                proceed
<...>                       --->           <...>
labelx:                                    labelx:
proceed                                    proceed
<...>                                      <...>
```

Fig. 6. Jump substitution.

```
<...>                                      <...>
set Rn,Ra,n                 --->           <...>
<ins. that do not use Rn>                  <no change>
set Rn,Rb,m                                set Rn,Rb,m
<...>                                      <...>
```

Fig. 7. Elimination of unnecessary register moves.

operation.

So that one can understand better the power of the optimisation that can be performed, we present one small extract of code that is very often found when using real programs in Prolog (see figure 10). Note that letters are used in register to make the example more legible, and that `CELLSIZE` is used to represent the size of the word in target machine. On the YAAM/WAM code, presented on the right, no more improvement could be done. In YAIL code, using the fact that the access of memory is done using a register plus a displacement, two instructions can be removed, which is very good considering the whole code has only eight instructions (see figure 11).

4.2 Code generation to Alpha

After optimising the YAIL code, we are almost ready to start the code generation to Alpha. But before that, it is necessary to make register allocation, because in YAIL code it is assumed that an unlimited number of registers are available. We have created a simple scheme to allocate the Alpha registers, and it has

```
<...>                                      <...>
set Rx,Rw,n1                               <...>
set Ry,Rx,m                 --->           set Ry,Rw,m+n1
set Rx,Rx,n2                               set Rx,Rw,n1+n2
<...>                                      <...>
```

Fig. 8. Reduction of register moves.

```
<...>                              <...>
set Rx,Ry,n             --->       store Rw,Ry,n+m
store Rw,Rx,m                      set Rx,Ry,n
<...>                              <...>
```

Fig. 9. Changing instructions order.

```
set   R_S,R_H,0               \  End code of instruction
set   R_H,R_H,2*CELLSIZE      /  unify_last_list_write
addv  R_T,R_Z,value_atom_1    \
store R_T,R_S,0                > unify_atom_write atom_1
set   R_S,R_S,CELLSIZE        /
addv  R_T,R_Z,value_atom_[]   \
store R_T,R_S,0                > unify_atom_write []
set   R_S,R_S,CELLSIZE        /
```

Fig. 10. Non optimised block of code.

proved to be more than adequate for this first version of Native YAP. The YAIL registers `CP`, `B`, `HB` are used as Alpha registers on native code, and as memory positions in YAP emulator. The others YAIL general purpose registers (see table 6) are always used as Alpha registers. The YAIL temporary registers are only used in native code and are always used as Alpha registers. For the WAM temporary registers `X[i]`, we use an region in memory where all that registers are represented. The start of this area is hold on an Alpha register Rn . To access to `X[i]` we use a load operation with Rn as argument plus a displacement of i times the word size (8 in Alpha). The registers `X[i]` could not be used as Alpha registers because the interleaving between the YAP and the native code would spoil the contents of those registers. As more instructions become executed in native code, avoiding the transition between the emulator and the native code, more Alpha registers can be used, and thus archive better performance.

After allocating the Alpha registers, the process of generating Alpha assem-

```
addv  R_T,R_Z,value_atom_1
store R_T,R_H,0
addv  R_T,R_Z,value_atom_[]
store R_T,R_H,CELLSIZE
set   R_S,R_H,2*CELLSIZE
set   R_H,R_H,2*CELLSIZE
```

Fig. 11. Optimised block of code.

bler code from YAIL is very simple. The instructions from tables 1 and 2 can be immediately transformed into one Alpha instruction. The instructions related with TAGS (table 5) implementation are also very simple, and are transformed into one or two Alpha instructions. As with the complex instructions (table 4), its transformation depends upon the instruction. For example, in Native YAP the **fail_X**, **trail_X**, **pop** and **push** are transformed directly into a small block of Alpha instructions. The **unify_X** are transformed in a subroutine call to a YAP function under the same name. The **deref** instruction is treated differently. In the optimisation process the **deref** instruction is forced to stay together to the instructions that use its results. This way when dereferencing a term the jump can be done immediately to the correct place whether the results is a variable or any other kind of term. In figure 12 is presented the deref cycle as implemented on Native Yap. On right is the case where code for X variable comes first. On left is the opposite.

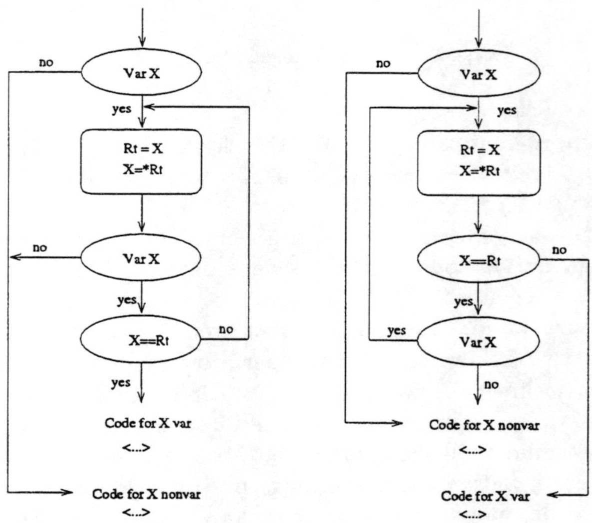

Fig. 12. Deref cyle.

To identify the locations where the code of clauses begin, it are also generated several labels. On the beginning of code for each clause is created a unique label that identifies that clause. It is also created one label for each possible returning point within a clause. The code for each clause would look like the following code :

```
start_clause_code
    ...
    call ()
return_point1:
```

```
        ...
        call ()
    return_point2:
        ...
        proceed
```

Note that the label `start_clause_code` is used to identify the location to where the execution must pass when we pretend to execute the clause in question. The labels `return_point` are used to identify the point to where execution must continue after returning from the call to other clauses.

5 Early Results

This section presents first results of Native YAP performance and compares them to YAP and YAPC (see table 8). YAPC is Native YAP generating `C` as output. We start by comparing YAPC and Native YAP to allow us to access the difference in performance by using C and assembler as our output. Almost all benchmarks presented are well known in the Prolog community (see table 7).

Benchmark	Lines	Description
unification	8	Evaluate unification of a compound term
nreverse	10	Naive reverse of a 30-element list.
tak	15	Recursive integer arithmetic.
qsort	19	Quicksort of a 50-element list.
queens	45	Solve the queens problem
crypt	64	Solve a simple cryptarithmetic puzzle.
query	68	Query a static database (with integer arithmetic).
poly_10	86	Symbolically raise a polynomial to the tenth power.
magic	150	Solve the magic cube puzzle

Table 7. Benchmark descriptions

From table 7 we can see that Native YAP archives the best results, however, one can still ask why the Native YAP could not archive even better performance. In this first version of Native YAP the only code that is transformed to assembler is the clause code. The indexing instructions plus the connection instructions (`try,retry...`), are still executed by the emulator. So, when a program runs, its execution is divided by the emulator and the native code. This results in a major overhead, since the interleaving of native code and the emulator forces the contents of the cache to flushed, resulting in performance loss. More speed can be obtained as more instructions are executed in native code, avoiding at maximum the transition between the emulator and the native code.

The difference between the speedup results can be explained by the fact that some benchmarks spend a lot more time calling certain built-in predicates.

Benchmark	Yap	YapC	NYap
unification	1	1.06	1.69
nreverse	1	1.44	1.74
tak	1	1.00	1.17
qsort	1	1.28	1.69
queens	1	1.30	1.44
crypt	1	1.20	1.20
query	1	1.10	1.10
poly_10	1	1.33	1.62
magic	1	1.02	1.67
Average	1	1.19	1.48

Table 8. Speedup of YAPC and Native YAP over YAP

Since the built-in predicates are the same in Native YAP and YAP, there can not be much of improvement. What other benchmarks, like nreverse, mainly do is to manipulate lists, requiring less calls to YAP, and therefore archive better performance.

The fact that YAPC is slower than Native YAP can be explained by the fact that for some YAIL instructions the compiler generate superfluous assembler instructions. For example, most of the time, when the compiler catches one `if` it tends to generate two jumps even when one would be sufficient. Yet another source for inefficiency is register usage. In C code we can't use so many registers as we can in assembler, because the compiler can also be using the registers without our knowledge.

6 Conclusions

An intermediate machine was developed to support the compilation of Prolog to native code. The YAIL integrates many of the recent ideas on intermediate languages for logic programming execution into a framework designed to support both easy translation from YAAM, and easy compilation into ALPHA assembly code. A first prototype of the YAIL compiler has been developed. Early results are promising, indicating a significant performance improvement over the emulator-based implementation of YAP, even when generating code for clauses only.

We next plan to support full procedure code, and to refine the YAIL instruction set through performance evaluation and perform further optimisations. We also plan to the use YAIL as target for sophisticated Prolog compilers, such as the optimisations being developed within the Proloppe project [6]. This might require changes to the YAIL architecture, such as the introduction of pragmas [11].

Acknowledgments

The authors would like to acknowledge and thank for the contribution and support that Fernando Silva and Luís Damas gave to this work. This work has been partly supported by JNICT under the PROLOPPE project (contract Praxis/-3/3.1/TIT/24/94). Ricardo Lopes thanks PRAXIS (Grant Praxis/2094/94) for supporting his research.

References

1. Mats Carlsson. Internals of Sicstus Prolog version 0.6. Internal Report, Gigalips Project, November 1987.
2. Takashi Chikayama, Tetsuro Fujise, and Hiroshi Yashiro. A portable and reasonably efficient implementation of KL1. In David S. Warren, editor, *Proceedings of the Tenth International Conference on Logic Programming*, page 833, Budapest, Hungary, 1993. The MIT Press.
3. Philippe Codognet and Daniel Diaz. `wamcc`: Compiling Prolog to C. In *12th International Conference on Logic Programming*. The MIT Press, 1995.
4. Thomas Conway, Ferugus Henderson, and Zoltan Somgyi. Code generation for Mercury. In *ILPS95*, pages 245–256, 1995.
5. L. Damas, V. Santos Costa, R Reis, and R. Azevedo. *YAP User's Guide and Reference Manual*, 1989.
6. Michel Ferreira. Um Compilador de Prolog com Expansão de Código. Technical note, LIACC, Universidade do Porto, 1996.
7. R. C. Haygood. Native code compilation in SICStus Prolog. In Pascal Van Hentenryck, editor, *Proceedings of the Eleventh International Conference on Logic Programming*. MIT Press, June 1994.
8. *Quintus Prolog User's Guide and Reference Manual—Version 6*, April 1986.
9. A. Taylor. LIPS on a MIPS: Results from a Prolog Compiler for a RISC. In *Proceedings of the Seventh International Conference on Logic Programming*, pages 174–185. MIT Press, June 1990.
10. P. Van Roy. *Can Logic Programming Execute as Fast as Imperative Programming?* PhD thesis, University of California at Berkeley, November 1990.
11. P. Van Roy. 1983-1993: The Wonder Years of Sequential Prolog Implementation. *The Journal of Logic Programming*, 19/20, May/July 1994.
12. David H. D. Warren. An Abstract Prolog Instruction Set. Technical Note 309, SRI International, 1983.

This article was processed using the LaTeX macro package with LLNCS style

Analysis and Improvement of the Variable Binding Scheme in LOGFLOW*

Zsolt Németh Péter Kacsuk

MTA Computer and Automation Research Institute
H-1518 Budapest, P.O. Box 63. Hungary
{zsnemeth, kacsuk}@sztaki.hu

Abstract
The handling of variables is a crucial issue in designing a parallel Prolog system. There are various binding methods for different architectures or for different types of parallelism. They intend to solve a particular problem in a given implementation and for a certain architecture but there are no general solutions. In this paper the so called closed binding method is analysed and a possible modification is introduced which tries to amalgamate some aspects of several binding schemes. The implementation and performance measurement of the resulted hybrid binding scheme in LOGFLOW is presented.

1 Introduction

Logical programming languages offer a high degree of inherent parallelism. By their nature the kind of exploited parallelism can be categorized as OR-parallelism, when several alternative clauses of a predicate are processed together, and AND-parallelism, when several goals of the resolvent are processed simultaneously.

The most common approach in OR-parallel implementations is assigning branches of the search tree to different processes, to the so called workers. At implementation level the current state of the machine is usually stored in several stacks. Assigning a piece of work to a worker means sharing some parts of the stacks representing a certain stage in computation among several workers. In this case the processes may bind a variable stored in the shared part of stacks to different values according to different alternatives. This is in contradiction to the single assignment property of variables in logical programming.

The central question at implementing an OR-parallel Prolog system is how the multiple bindings can be handled consistently in such a way that the resulting binding scheme accomplishes most of these issues: variable access is in constant time, task switching is in constant time, task creation is in constant time. In [9] it was shown that all the three conditions cannot be satisfied. Additionally, low memory consumption must be taken into consideration at designing a binding scheme.

---

* The work presented in this paper was supported partially by two National Science Research Fund (OTKA) projects under grant number T016091 and T022106. The results were produced while the authors were affiliated at MTA KFKI Research Institute for Measurement and Computing Techniques.

There are a number of techniques for treating multiple bindings [6]. In common, they intended to assure a binding environment so that each worker (process) could handle the shared data as if the worker was traversing the search graph alone.

One of these techniques is the shared stacks concept. It means that the Prolog machine maintains only one, common data structure and each worker has access to it. However, shared variables which may be bound to different values are stored in auxiliary data structures which are private to each worker. In such a way workers try to get the necessary values in the common data areas where they may find a reference to the private data structures when the deferred variable is shared. Some examples of this technique are: hash windows, binding arrays, directory trees and version vectors; they differ mainly in the way they treat the auxiliary data structures.

Another approach, called stack copying scheme, separates completely the data areas of the workers by creating a new copy of the shared part for each worker.

A third approach scraps the idea of sharing or copying: workers build up their own private stacks by recomputing the query up to a given point. Traversing the tree is easy if the computation is deterministic. The idea of the recomputation scheme is making the computation deterministic by predicting the path in the search tree. It is obtained by the so called oracles which encode a certain path. These oracles, representing a given state of the machine and hence a given task, are transferred between workers.

All these techniques have a common feature: references (either physical or logical) are allowed from an environment to any other environments. In a distributed memory system these environments may reside on different processing elements, and deferencing a variable through several processing elements is a tremendously expensive operation. From one point of view the recomputation model aimed at implementing Prolog in a distributed environment. The other method proposed so far for distributed systems is the closed binding environment.

A closed environment in Conery's definition is a set of frames E so that no pointers or links originating from E reference to slots in frames that are not members of E. A closed environment containing just one frame is called a closed frame [4]. In other words the environment holds all the necessary information to continue the computation at a given point. It has two special procedures to close an environment with respect to another one: the (two-phase) unification and the back-unification. The details of closed binding environments are in [4] and [11].

LOGFLOW is a distributed-memory implementation of Prolog [13]. Its abstract execution model is the logicflow model based on dataflow principles [14]. Prolog programs are transformed into the so called Dataflow Search Graph (DSG.) Nodes in this graph represent Prolog procedures, e.g. unification (Unify), handling the alternatives (Or), goals (And), facts (Unit). The execution is governed by token streams. Tokens represent a given state of the machine where the computation is continued. There are different tokens according to the different roles they play: representing a query (Do), representing an answer: solution (Succ) or failure (Fail).

Prolog programs are executed in LOGFLOW by the so called Distributed Data Driven Prolog Abstract Machine (3DPAM.) The machine takes a token from the waiting queue, then executes a portion of code represented by the token and handles the tokens resulted from the previous action. In other words, tokens are moved across the DSG by the engine while it executes the appropriate procedures represented by the traversed nodes. For the sake of granularity control, 3DPAM machines are extended with conventional, sequential WAM machines. Thus, LOGFLOW forms logically a two-layered architecture, where the lower level consists of 3DPAM machines and handles fine grained tasks and communication while the upper level consists of WAM machines and executes coarse-grained tasks sequentially. A given predicate can be annotated parallel or sequential by the programmer and the type of a call is controlled dynamically by the scheduler. (More sophisticated approaches can be found in [8] or [23].)

LOGFLOW is aimed at exploiting OR- and pipeline AND-parallelism. Although the latter resembles AND-parallelism by its name, the source of pipeline AND-parallelism hides in the alternatives, i.e. the pipeline AND-parallelism is a very special way of OR-parallelism.

LOGFLOW is based entirely on the closed binding environment scheme. Thus, tokens holding an environment are allowed to be distributed over the processor space freely, since the piece of work represented by the token can be executed using the information held by the token only.

In the next sections first the widespread binding techniques are introduced then the closed binding environment is studied. In Section 2 the overheads are analyzed then some of the possible solutions are mentioned. In Section 4 the new binding scheme is described and finally, it is evaluated.

1.1 Overview of binding methods

As it was described in the introductory part, all the binding schemes can be divided into basically 4 classes. Let us now take a closer look at the existing implementations and the relationship between the binding schemes and the architectures.

1.2 Stack sharing

The common feature of these models is that they maintain only one, global instance of the shared stacks. The stacks contain variables which may be bound to different values by different workers. In this case the variable is replaced by some kind of reference (pointer, identifier, etc.) and the data itself is held in auxiliary data structures which are private to each worker. Models belonging to this class differ in data structures they apply and how the data structures are handled.

1.2.1 Directory trees

The method called directory trees is intended to implement a binding scheme on a shared memory architecture [7]. The different binding environments are separated by the access mechanism via the directories. A directory is assigned to each OR-process and contexts (activation records) can be found in the directories. If a certain context is not available in the current directory, it can be traced in the parent process' directory and so on. Thus, directories form a tree in the same way as the workers traverse the search tree.

1.2.2 Hash windows

Hash windows can be used in two manners. The first variation, called hashing on contexts is a modification of directory trees, where the 'directory' is a fixed size window and the context access is obtained by hash technique [2][7]. If it cannot be found in the current hash window, the ancestor windows are searched. This method is practically the same as the directory trees but the organization of data structures and thus the cost of process initialization is simpler at the expense of more complex variable access.

The other alternative is hashing on variables [7]. Variables are placed in the hash window directly, there are no contexts stored. Instead, each entry in the hash table is augmented with extra fields to identify the variable. This method eliminates the cost associated with context copying.

1.2.3 Binding array

In this method the values of conditional variables are stored in arrays which are private to each process. Whenever an unbound variable can be found in the shared part, it is represented by an index, and this index serves as an access key for each process to their private arrays [5][6]. Obviously, different workers may see different values for the same variable (physically at the same location in a shared stack). The binding array technique requires only one extra step at dereferencing, thus, the variable access still remains as a fast, constant time operation. The binding array technique is implemented on a shared memory computer (e.g. Aurora [5].)

1.2.4 Time stamping and inheritance binding

It is the only model in this category which is intended to implement a binding scheme in distributed memory environment [11]. Each variable is assigned a time stamp and the validity of conditional variables is detected by the stamp value. The time stamp is increased each time when an OR node is created or an alternative is taken from an OR node. Child processes inherit the parent's time stamp. Time stamps define the so called spans, i.e. a given variable can be bound unconditionally within the span and conditionally outside the span. The auxiliary storage is a double linked chain of variables, therefore the variable access time is proportional to the number of alternative bindings.

1.2.5 Versions-vector

In this model a vector is assigned to each conditional variable [10]. The vector has as many elements, as many processors in the system are (assuming one worker per processor.) A conditional variable contains a pointer to such a vector and each worker can access its own element within the vector. The idea can be used in shared memory system only, and it strongly restricts the number of usable processors.

1.3 Stack copying

In this scheme each worker has its own instances of the stacks and the workers have no access to each others stacks. The share of work is obtained by copying the appropriate portions of stack (and, thus, the computational state at an OR-branch) from one workers' memory location to another.

A common problem in this scheme is that the worker getting a piece of work has to restore its stack to their state corresponding to the time when the actual OR-node was created. One solution is the Kabu-Wake model, where each binding has a logical date, thus, it can be detected whether a binding was made after the creation of the choicepoint and must be undone. The other solution does this un-binding by means of the trail stack.

An important optimization to the basic model is the introduction of incremental copying, where only the differing parts are copied between workers. This scheme was adopted in Muse [18] and in Opera [3].

1.4 Recomputation

The recomputation of stacks is an alternative to copying of stacks. At copying stacks a very fast connection or shared memory was assumed between machines of the same architecture. However, this can not be assumed in every case. For example a cluster of workstation machines (which became wide-spread recently) can contain machines of different type (different data sizes, different endianness, etc.), and they are connected with a relative slow network. In this case, obviously, the copying of stacks is either impossible or not worth due to the slow communication.

Instead copying the state, it can be recomputed as well. It is trivial, when the computation is deterministic, i.e. there is no backtracking. However, the computation to a given node can be made deterministic by 'prompting' to the worker which way to choose at a branch. When a worker explores the tree, it keeps track about the its decisions at the choicepoints. If it shares some of its works with other worker, it simply tells them how to reach the given state where the appropriate piece of work can be grabbed. This can be achieved by the so called *oracles*. This information is relative small to transfer, and can be transferred hardware independently. (An oracle is usually a sequence of integers.) This oracle will guide new worker to build up its stack exactly as they are in the parent worker.

1.5 The closed binding environment

In the conventional 4-stack implementations of Prolog the state of the machine is represented by the content of the stacks. Variables are either in the global stack (heap) or in the local stack (environment stack.) The environment stack is a set of environment frames, i.e. the stack is divided into frames and each frame belongs to a given clause. The binding environment of a worker is a set of stack frames from the root to the current leaf. It means that a worker is processing a clause which has its own environment frame however, variables in the frame may refer to other local variables in another frame or to global variables in the heap.

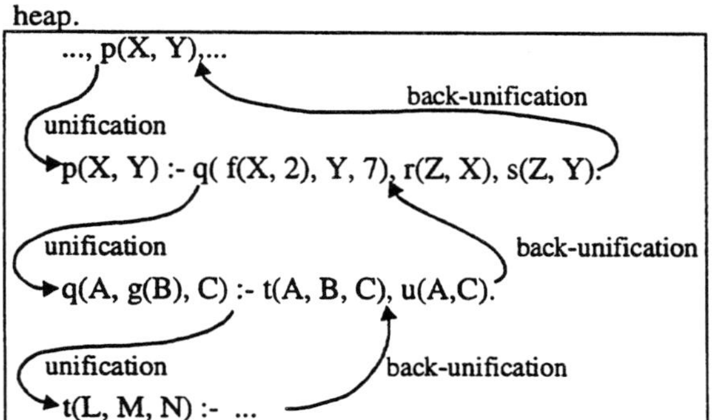

Figure 1. The idea of closed binding environment.

The effect of closed environments is depicted in Figure 1. A clause has its own closed frame. When it calls a goal, a new environment frame is created for the called clause. After unification there may be references between the two frames. Next time the called clause will be processed thus, its frame (working frame) must be closed with respect to the caller frame (reference frame). This closing procedure takes place in the second phase of the unification.

When all the goals in the called clause have been processed, the execution will continue from the next goal in the caller clause. In this case the environment frame of the caller clause must be closed with respect to the frame of the called clause. This operation is called back-unification. Note, that in the closing procedures two frames are always taking part: the one which becomes closed (working frame) and the other, the reference frame.

Additionally, several binding rules of the conventional execution models are broken: the direction of the pointers does not mean younger-older relationship any more, and variables are never placed onto the heap since there are no global variables in a closed environment scheme.

The details of closed binding environments are in [4] [11]. The most important features of the unification and back-unification in the LOGFLOW[1] are described in the following.

[1]There are slight differences between [4] and the closed environment scheme in LOGFLOW.

Basically the environment closing has two steps:

1. reverse the direction of pointers so that no pointer is pointing to the reference frame and,
2. extend the frame with unbound variables for each variable in the reference frame pointed by any term belonging to the frame.

1.5.1 The unification

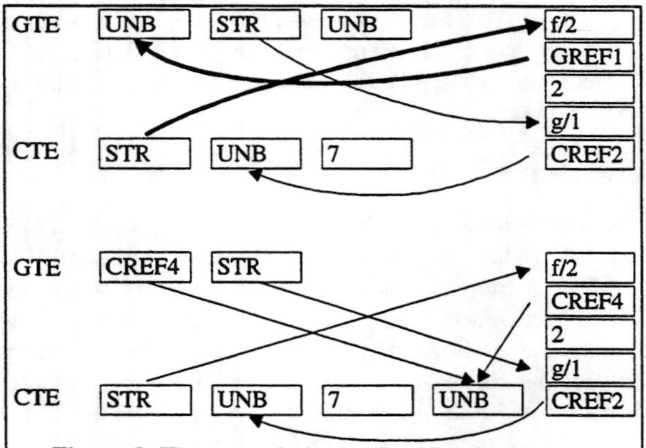

Figure 2. The second phase of unification.

The environment of the caller clause (the incoming environment) is called as Goal Token Environment (GTE). The environment of the called clause, the Clause Token Environment (CTE) is created as a first step of the unification. The first phase of unification is creating the most general unifier in a conventional way. The aim of the second phase of unification is to close the CTE with respect to GTE, i.e. there must not be references from CTE to GTE neither directly nor indirectly via compound terms.

Before unification the GTE is closed and the CTE contains unbound variables only, therefore, it is closed, too. During unification references are set from GTE to CTE thus, there are no direct pointers from CTE to GTE, i.e. the first step of closing can be omitted. However, it is possible that the CTE contains a compound term which has an argument pointing to GTE, i.e. the GTE is referenced indirectly from CTE (Figure 2.) Therefore, for each such unbound variable a new variable is added to CTE and references are set to it for GTE and from the given argument of the compound term. If the deferred variable was bound, the corresponding value is instantiated into the compound term directly.

1.5.2 The back-unification

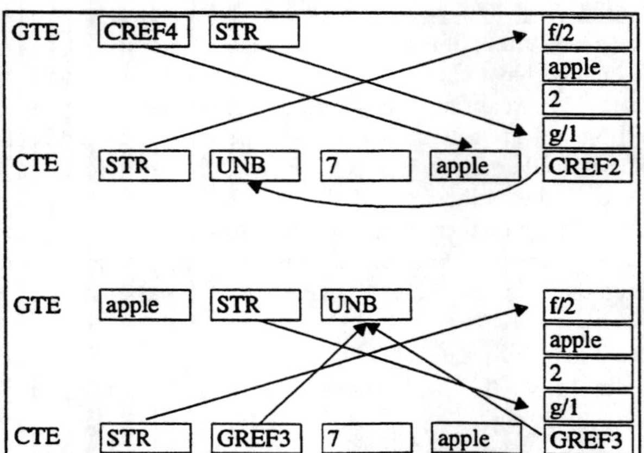

Figure 3. Back-unification.

The back-unification (Figure 3.) is performed after the whole body of a clause has been processed and the token carries the result. In this case the environment of the caller clause (GTE) must be updated with the bindings made after calling the clause (CTE), then the GTE must be closed with respect to CTE. Since originally the CTE was closed with respect to GTE, all the pointers are pointing from GTE to CTE. Therefore, the first step of closing must be performed and the direction of pointers must be reversed. The second step is very similar to that of the unification: the GTE must be extended with new unbound variables for each variable in CTE pointed by any term belonging to GTE.

2 The overhead in closed binding environments

The environment closing is a costly operation both in time and in memory consumption. In [19] the sources of overhead were investigated and divided into three groups as: overhead from environment scanning, overhead from environment extension and overhead from structure copying. Comparing these overheads to each other concludes that the main sources of overhead are: scanning the compound terms and copying the compound terms.

2.1 The scanning overhead in LOGFLOW

Compound terms must be scanned each time when a unification or back-unification takes place. Scanning a compound term means to check each argument of the term whether it is a reference to a variable or not and perform the necessary actions. Since compound terms (structures and lists) are the natural data structures in logic programming languages, they are used extensively. Furthermore, compound terms can have a number of arguments, and can embed other compound terms.

The scanning has three goals: changing the tags from working environment to the reference environment or vice versa, extending the environment whenever the structure refers to a variable that is not in the working environment and finally, instantiating the variables that became bound during the last unification.

2.2 The copying overhead in LOGFLOW

Arguments in structures may be changed by bounding variables or by modifying a reference item during the environment closing. As a consequence, structures must not be shared by different environments. If a token is duplicated (e.g. in Or nodes each incoming token is duplicated; in Unit nodes an incoming token may produce several answer tokens), all the structures in its environment must be copied for each new environment. This results in an enormous memory consumption and slows down the computation.

In LOGFLOW some kinds of optimization have been implemented in order to reduce the structure copying. Structures, which contain atoms and constants only in their arguments (or references to structures of such type) are called Ground terms. These structures are detected at compile time, stored in a special table and handled by dedicated instructions. They never need to be copied or traced, even their unification is much simpler.

Obviously, the reason why structures must be copied is that they contain unbound variables or references. As a second optimization, when all these variables become bound, the structure does not need to be copied again, and may be shared by several environments.

In summary, the copying overhead in LOGFLOW is strongly reduced however, it still remains a critical problem regarding the memory consumption.

3 The proposed solutions

The previously listed overheads may occur because of the very special handling of addresses in the closed binding environment scheme. While in conventional sequential implementations (and in multisequential parallel implementations as well) a variable has an absolute address, in the closed environment scheme a variable can be addressed by a frame address and a relative offset within the frame. Since a process can see at most two environments, the frame address is coded into the type of reference, i.e. the referred item is in the working or reference frame. Variables are never kept on the heap. Whenever a compound term contains a variable, it is placed into the environment and the compound term contains a reference to it.

Each time a unification or back-unification is performed and a compound term is passed between the two environments, the frame address must be changed in each reference within its arguments (since the referred item is moving from reference to working frame.) Additionally, if there has been an extension of the environment, the offset value of the appropriate references must be changed as well.

However, the closing procedure is really necessary only when the computation is migrated to a different processing element. When it remains on the same processor, the complete closure is superfluous.

The proposed solutions so far try to combine the local addressing scheme of the closed environment with the global addressing scheme of non-closed environments. In [17] the molecules are introduced to avoid copying when all the arguments of a structure became ground. In [22] the so called tagged variable scheme is used which is a variation of hash tables for dataflow machines. In [19] the Quasi Closed Environment (QCE) is introduced where variables are divided into two groups whether they can occur in a structure or not. Variables occurring in a structure are stored globally whereas others are stored still locally. In such a way, the most expensive part of the closing procedure, the structure scanning and copying, can be discarded, more precisely, they can be postponed until the task is really migrated between processors.

4 Combining the closed and non-closed binding schemes in LOGFLOW

The new hybrid binding scheme alloys many ideas from different binding methods. The basis is still a variation of Conery's closed environment. The basic idea of avoiding the costly operations with structures is the division of variables into two groups according to their occurrence came from [19]. By default, variables are handled in the usual way according to the closed binding environment principles. Variables are made *global* and thus, are handled differently when they are in the arguments of a structure (hence they are called global variables). The fundamental elements of the new binding scheme are the followings:

1. **The special storage of global variables in such a way that the variable access and the duplication of environment can be done efficiently**. The decision was to implement it as a hash table upon the proposal in [19]. It is a hash technique on variables rather than on environments as Borgwardt's hash windows [2]. There are comparisons in [7] of the two hashing methods.
2. **The way how the global variables are detected, created and named according to a global naming scheme**. The naming scheme is very similar to that of in binding array technique [5].
3. **Binding the global variables to a value**. The scope (time) of binding is implicit by the position of the variable, but the idea is similar to that of the time stamping method [11], where the scope is defined explicitly.
4. **Handling different OR-branches** (the question of conditional global variables.)

5. **The new binding scheme manipulates within a single PE. Some special procedures should be done when the computation migrates between PEs**. The problem shows many common features with the time stamping method [11].

None of the above mentioned binding techniques can solve all the arising problems in LOGFLOW, but their combination could be a promising candidate. In summary, apart from the closed environment method, in more or less extent it inherits ideas from the hash windows, binding array and time stamping techniques. In the rest of Section 4 the above listed issues are described.

4.1 The auxiliary storage: hash tables

In LOGFLOW the Hash Table (HT) is accessed through a Pointer Array (PA) which can be considered as an access path for different OR-branches. Each token is augmented by an extra field that is used to index in the Pointer Array (PA), called Pointer Array Index (PAI) (Figure 4). The records in the Pointer Array have as many fields as many elements the Hash Table (HT) has. The Pointer Array is used to point to the appropriate lines in the Hash Table, so each field contains a pointer to a line in the Hash Table. In such a way, each token (environment) has different Pointer Array Indices. They correspond to different Pointer Array records, i.e. lines in the Pointer Array thus, they reach different areas of the Hash Table. The columns in the Pointer Array correspond to different hash values. In the example in Figure 4 the variable X has a hash value 0. The first token can access X=5 through the nth row of Pointer Array, while the other token can get X=6 through the n+1st row. The clashing items, i.e. variables whose hash values are the same form a chain. The length of the chain can be influenced by the size of the Hash Table. The Pointer Array is used to save some parameters as well, so it has two extra fields. The role of these fields is explained in Section 4.7.1.

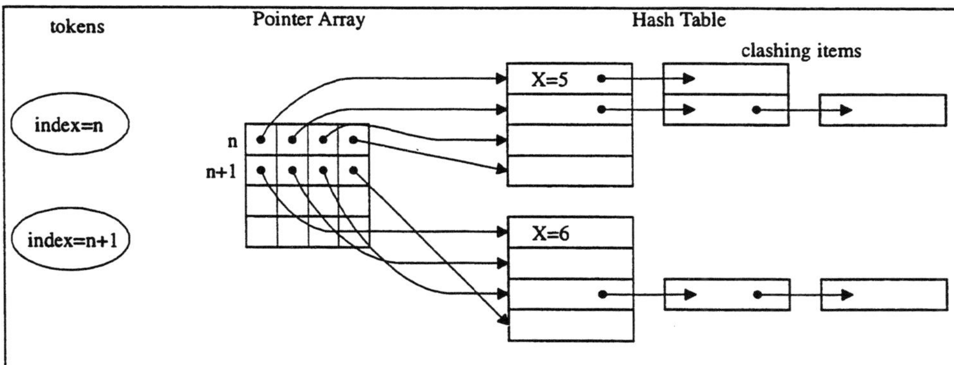

Figure 4. The usage of hash tables. Two tokens representing different binding environments can bind the same variable to different values by using the hash table. The size of the hash table in this example is 4. The key is that they see different areas of the Hash Table through the Pointer Array.

4.2 Detecting global variables

Variables can be put into a structure in two cases: whenever a structure is built up as an argument before a call to a predicate or, the structure is built up during a unification when it is in the head of the called clause. Thus, the scope of instructions to be modified is quite small: they are the write_var[2], write_value and the unify_var, unify_value.

The unify_void and write_void instructions represent a special case. Although these instructions exist analogously to WAM, in closed binding environment there are not *real* void variables due to the nature of the closing procedure, because it incorporates all the unbound variables into the environment. In such a way the unify_void and write_void instructions must be handled the same way as unify_var, write_var regarding the global variables.

As an illustration here follows the pseudo code of unify_var and write_value.

```
unify_var()
{
  if (mode == READ)
      .../* Do the usual way */
  else
    {
      /* Create a global variable */
      new_var = get_global_name();
      add tag to new_var;
      environment_reg[i]=new_var;
      heap[H] = new_var;
    }
}
```

```
write_value()
{
   dereference(environment_reg[i]...)
   /* dereference returns many important
      parameters about the references as
      well. They are used in the next
      lines*/

   if (dereferred variable is unbound)
     {
      if(dereferred variable is global)
         {
         /* It is a global variable
            already. Put it onto the heap*/
          var = the dereferred variable;
          heap[H] = var;
         }
      else
         {
         /* The dereferred variable is not
            GLOBAL. Since it is put into a
            structure, it must be
            transformed to global */
         /* Create a global variable */
          new_var = get_global_name();
          add tag to new_var;

         /* Transform the environment
            variable into a GLOBAL one */
          if(at least one reference)
           environment_reg[last_reference]=
                                  new_var;
          else
            environment_reg[i]=new_var;

          /* Put onto the heap */
          heap[H] = new_var;
         }
     }
   else
     /* environment_reg[i] is a constant
        or referring to a bound variable*/
     heap[H] = environment_reg[i];
}
```

Although, for technical reasons other instructions were necessary to be modified as well, primarily these six instructions are the ones where global variables are created and thus, detected.

---

[2] These 3DPAM abstract instructions correspond to set_variable, set_value, set_void, unify_variable, unify_value, unify_void instructions of WAM respectively.

4.3 Naming global variables

Variables in LOGFLOW are named according to the naming convention of closed binding environments: an environment and an offset in the environment. There may be several variables in the system with the same name, and there is no clashing, since there are two environments visible at a time and the environment names of them are always different.

This is not the case when some variables are global and thus, visible from any environment. These variables must have a unique name for the whole system. The easiest way to generate a new name is assigning a number to each newly generated global variable. The number is coming from a counter, i.e. the successively generated global variables have successive identifiers. It may happen that two variables on two different processing elements have the same identifier, however, as it will be shown in Section 4.7.2, it does not cause any conflict.

4.4 Creating global variables

A newly created global variable is unbound, obviously. The Hash Table contains the bound variables only. Interestingly, creating a new global variable is simply an increment of the counter used for generating identifiers and nothing is put into the Hash Table.

4.5 Binding global variables

Only the bound global variables are in the Hash Table, unbound global variables are never placed into the table. The newly bound global variables are put into the first position of the linked list in the hash table. These important properties of our solution ensure that the problem of multiple bindings of conditional variables can be handled easily.

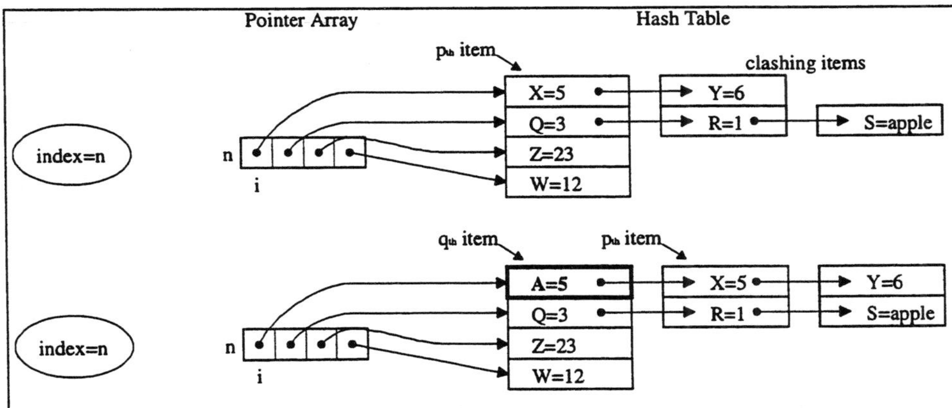

Figure 5. Binding a global variable.

First the engine calculates the hash function of the global variable (*i=f(var)*) and allocates a new free item (q) in the Hash Table (Figure 5.) Then it sets the *i*th pointer field in the Pointer Array to point to q, the newly allocated Hash Table item, puts the variable name and value into the q then sets the pointer of q to the one that was previously the first (p).

4.6 Handling different OR-branches

It is a central and crucial question in a parallel Prolog implementation how the multiple bindings are handled. When several alternatives of a predicate (several branches in the execution tree) are processed in parallel, variables, which were created in the common parent branch may be bound to different values. To solve the contradiction with the single assignment property of logical variables, these conditional variables are handled in a different way.

The usage of the hash tables for such purposes is an old idea. The proposed usage of hash tables in LOGFLOW is different from Borgwardt's implementation [2], where the hashing-on-context method is applied. Our approach is a variation of hashing-on-variables, which is a more efficient alternative according to [7].

The key is in the pointer array that can be considered as an access path to the hash table. In this way different tokens (representing different binding environments) can reach different points in the hash table.

Each time a request token arrives at the incoming arc of the Or node, it is duplicated and put onto the two outgoing arcs. The environment of the incoming token must be inherited by both of the outgoing tokens, however, from this point they represent different environments.

The solution is to allocate a new item in the Pointer Array and copy the content of the item pointed by the incoming token. At this point there are two identical items. Each outgoing token has one of them. It means that they inherited the environment of the incoming token since, they can reach the same variables.

Recall the two very important rules of handling the global variables:

1. Unbound variables are never put into the Hash Table. It means that there are no unbound variables in the inherited part and thus, the problem of multiple bound variables is eliminated. Unbound variables are detected as they can not be found in the table. The price we must pay for this simple solution is that in some cases a relatively long pointer chain must be traversed to check whether a variable is unbound. There are optimizations for this problem in the later sections.

2. The newly bound variables are put into the first position in the chain of clashing elements, i.e. the element in the Pointer Array points directly to the newly bound variable. It means that the newly bound variables are out of the inherited common environment and are visible to that process that has bound them. (See the similarity to the explicit time stamping.)

In Figure 6 and Figure 7 a simple example can be seen how the alternative branches are treated.

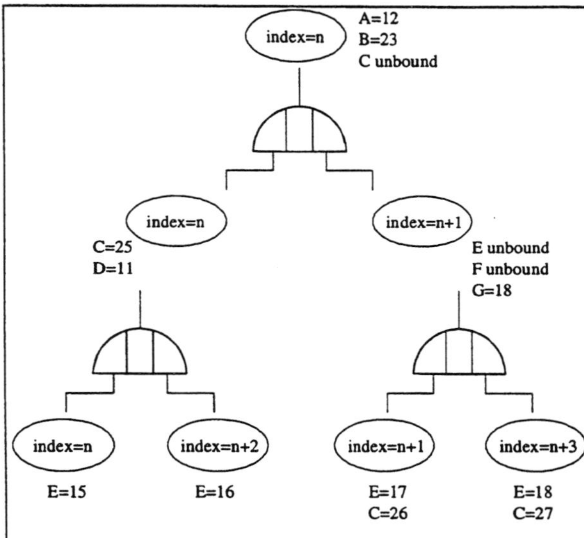

Figure 6. Tokens on different OR-branches.

In Figure 6 the first Or node produces 2 request tokens. The tokens have their own environments where A and B are bound while C is unbound. This is the right end of the Hash Table in Figure 7. There are 2 pairs of arrows pointing to the items representing the two environments.

On the left branch in Figure 6 C and D become bound. This is the upper branch in Figure 7. OR-nodes appear in the hash table as multiple pointers to the same elements. Then the execution is split again. One alternative is E=15 the other is E=16. These are the upper branches in Figure 7. This represents the current situation. Indices n and n+2 point to the pointer array selecting the pointers (the 'head') to the hash table. In such a way the first environment has A=12, B=23, C=25, D=11,E=15 while the second has A=12, B=23, C=25, D=11,E=16. The handling of the right branches in Figure 6 is similar.

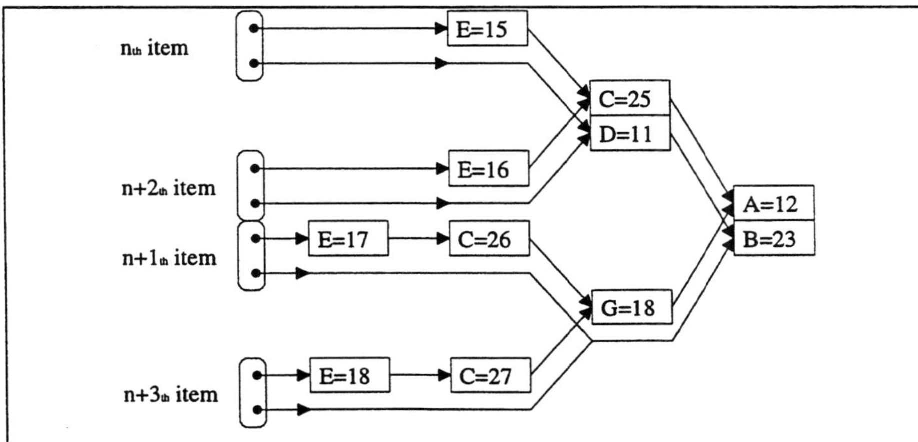

Figure 7. A snapshot from the Hash Table according to the situation in Figure 6. The size of the hash table in this example is 2. The address of a variable is calculated by taking its alphabetical order mod 2, i.e. the clashing items are A, C, E, etc. and B, D, F, etc. respectively.

In this aspect Unit nodes can be regarded as special Or nodes. Unit nodes try to generate all the possible solutions, i.e. the Unit node embodies all the alternatives of a fact. In this way there are (hidden) Or branches and the different solutions must be treated so that they have different binding environments. Therefore, a new Pointer Array item must be allocated for each new solution token.

4.7 Migration between processing elements

So far all the operations were executed on the same processing element. Since LOGFLOW is implemented in a distributed environment, the new binding scheme must tackle with the arising problems when tokens and thus, binding environments are migrating from one processing element to another.

4.7.1 Moving the content of the hash table

When tokens are transferred between two processing elements, the data packet contains all the token context, its environment, arguments and all the structures that are referred from either the environment or the arguments. On the other site structures are extracted and put onto the heap. Thus, when tokens are transferred structures must be scanned and copied no matter what the binding scheme is. This operation is used in our solution to encapsulate the necessary information from the Hash Table into the message packet.

There are processes responsible for the inter-processor communication. In case of request tokens the process, handling the output, takes the token and the relevant structures to put them into a data packet and to send to another processing element. In this phase the process tries to get the value for each global variable and substitute the reference by the value in the environment, arguments and structures. In such a way, all the relevant global information is extracted from the hash table and packed into the existing token structure. This packet will be migrated. The hash table does not need to be moved since, the bound variables are within the packet, *unbound variables are not in the hash table.*

When the request token arrives to the remote site, the process, responsible for handling the input, extracts the data packet. The token has no valid index to the pointer array therefore, the process assigns a new item in the array where each pointer point to an empty slot in the hash table. So, whenever the engine, processing this token, tries to get a variable from the hash table it will find nothing, which corresponds to the situation that the newly received token has unbound global variables only. Of course, variables that become bound during the execution on this site will be placed into the hash table.

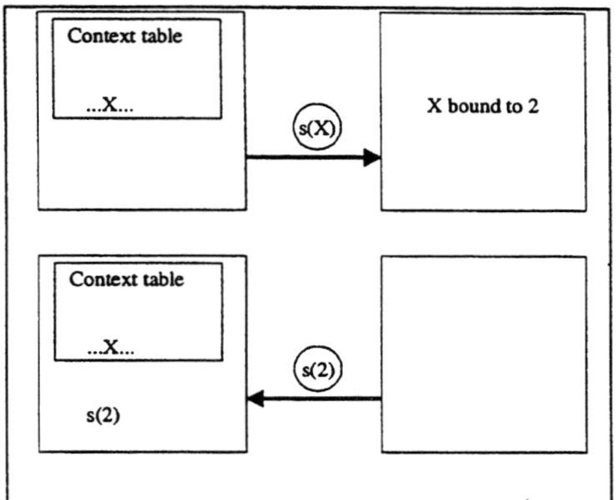

Figure 8. A problem with reply tokens.

This basic mechanism introduced above corresponds to the case of request tokens. However, answer tokens require some additional activities:

It may happen that an unbound global variable is stored in a Unify context table[3]. The outgoing request token from the Unify node is processed on a different PE where, let us suppose, the global variable becomes bound. When the answer token is returned to the Unify node, although the bound value is present, the link between the value and its predecessor unbound variable is lost (Figure 8.) Therefore, answer tokens must contain an extract from the Hash Table to update the unbound variables on the original PE. To reduce the amount of information, the current value of global name counter on the originating PE is recorded, and variables below this limit are traced only. This is a bit similar to that of establishing the scope of a variable by the time spans in the time stamping method. The mechanism is introduced in Figure 9.

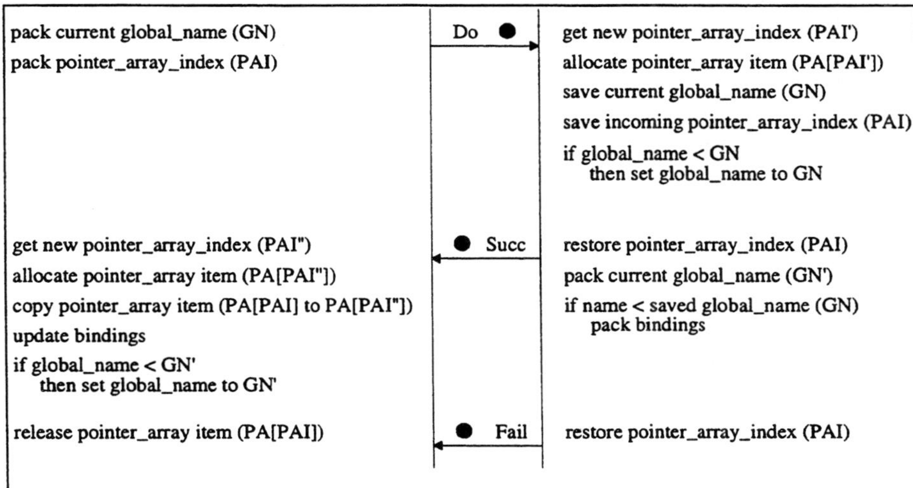

Figure 9. Token transfer between processors.

First the sender PE packs the current value of the global name counter. The Pointer Array Index (PAI) is in the token. On the other PE a new Pointer Array item is allocated to the newly arrived token and the incoming global name value (GN) and PAI is saved to the extra fields introduced earlier. If the global name counter on the given PE is less than the incoming GN, it is set to GN. Otherwise, the engine could create a new global variable that already exists in the newly arrived environment.

[3]Context tables are used to store a state in the computation. Later the computation can be continued from the saved state.

When a solution token is going to be sent back, the original Hash Table will be updated by new bindings. Therefore, the saved PAI is restored from the Pointer Array. It is packed into the message as well as the value of the global name counter (GN'). At this point all the variable-value pairs must be included in the message that were bound on this PE, however the variable was created on the other PE. This condition can be detected by comparing the identifier of the variable to the saved GN. If the identifier is less than GN, and a value to the variable can be found in the Hash Table, this pair is going to be sent with the message packet.

On the other side (this is the original PE where the request token was sent from) a new Pointer Array item is allocated and pointers from PA[PAI] are copied. The bindings are updated in this new environment. The copy is needed because there may be several solutions (answer tokens) to a single request. Then the global name counter is set to GN' if necessary. This step is repeated for each solution token.

Finally, a Fail token terminates the solution stream. At this point the original PA[PAI] item can be deallocated.

4.7.2 Naming the global variables on different PEs

There may be existing records in the hash table when the token arrives. Yet, there is no confusion nor discrepancies when the newly arrived token uses the same Hash Table. The key is that the Hash Table is accessed via the Pointer Array, and it is guaranteed that the pointers point to new hash items that are not in any chain. To put in other way, although the tokens representing different computations use the same hash table, they are logically fully separated.

Theoretically, each global variable must have a unique name (identifier) in the whole system. By the introduced method where the identifier is generated by a counter, the condition above is guaranteed within a single processing element only. However, it was shown above that tokens originating from different processing elements (*different token environments*) use completely disjoint clusters in the hash table so, there may be variables with the same identifier (from different processing elements) but it does not lead to any conflict. The reason why global name counters must be set is to avoid to create two identical identifiers in the *same token environment.*

5 Evaluation of the Hybrid Binding Scheme in LOGFLOW

The performance test of the new hybrid binding scheme aimed at investigating how the new binding method supports different types of programs, different sizes of programs and different sizes of processor networks.

1. First the 3DPAM execution was tested, since the main goal of the new binding scheme is to reduce the cost associated with closing procedures. This cost appears in its most clean form in pure parallel execution (i.e. 3DPAM engines without WAM) on a single processing element.
2. Then the same pure 3DPAM tests were repeated on multiple processing elements where the cost of token transfer (token packing, communication, token unpacking) appears.
3. Since in real applications the 3DPAM engines are supported by WAM engines, the overall performance must be tested in such a case as well. When a WAM is added to 3DPAM, most of the work is done by WAM engines, the 3DPAM engines serve as a coordination layer and hence, the binding method has not much influence to the performance. It can be explained, that the connection of the 3DPAM and the WAM is also a combination of a closed and non-closed binding method, and thus, it eliminates some problems of the closed binding scheme. Implementing the hybrid method in

3DPAM and adding a WAM to it is - from one point of view - somewhat two solutions to the same problem. Test results are not presented in this paper.

5.1 3DPAM Execution speed

5.1.1 Bit-palindromes

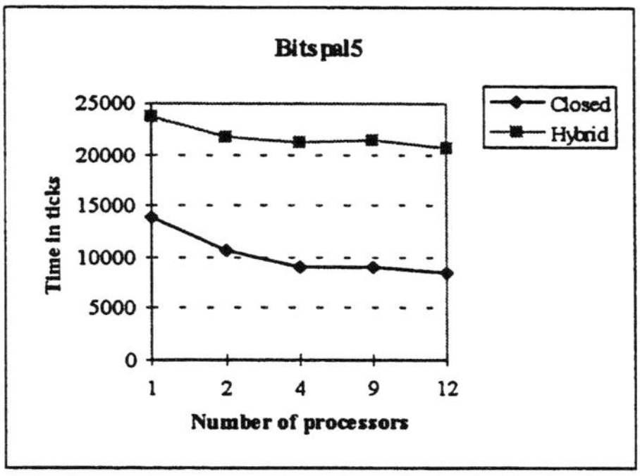

Figure 10. Execution speed of bitspal5

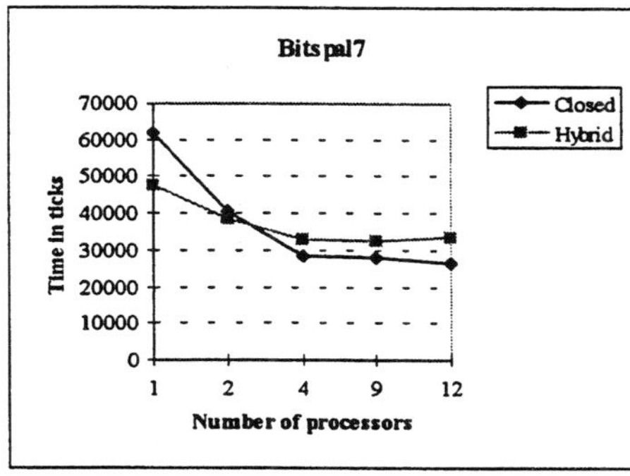

Figure 11. Execution speed of bitspal7

Bitspal is a generate-and-test type of Prolog programs. First it generates all the possible bit lists of length 5 or 7, then it tests whether the reverse list coincides with the original one. It achieved a poor speedup[4] in both versions. The reason in case of bitspal5 is that there are at most 32 possible lists to choose from, i.e. the number of tokens in the body of bitspal/1 is relatively small. Although there are more tokens in rev/3 and bits/1, they represent very fine grained tasks and thus, parallelization does not speed up the execution. In case of bitspal7 the number of possible lists is 128, and the tasks in rev/3 and bits/1 have a bit larger granularity (they are proportional to input list length.) These two factors yielded in a slightly better speedup.

The single node execution of Bitspal5 using the hybrid binding method is slower, while that of Bitspal7 is faster than the old version. It proves the anticipated theorem: the bigger the structures are, the more time can be saved by the new binding method. In case of small structures the overhead caused by variable access (handling the hash table and the auxiliary data items) is bigger than the gain of faster unification and back-unification.

The multiple-node tests show, that the cost of token transfer is higher in the new binding scheme than that of the old scheme.

[4] The speedup usually means the time proportion of the best known sequential and the parallel executions. Since the aspects of binding schemes do not appear in the sequential version, only the 3DPAM (i.e. parallel engine) was tested on increasing number of processors. Hence the speedup means relative speedup.

5.1.2 Queens

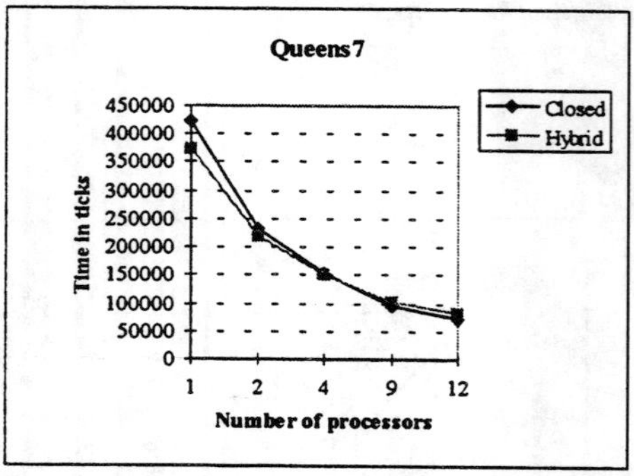

Figure 12. Execution speed of queen7

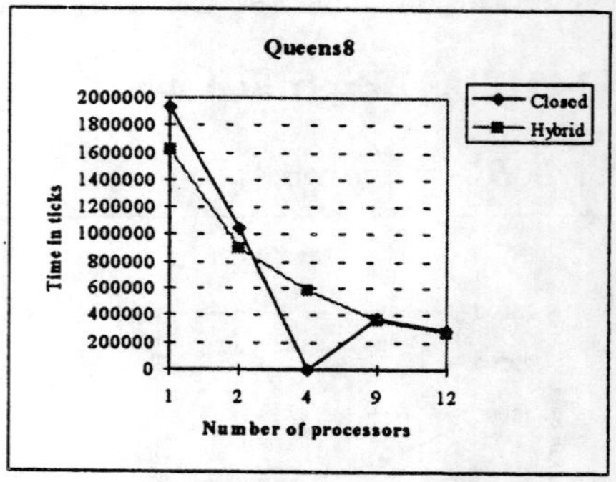

Figure 13. Execution speed of queen8[5]

The specimens of the Queen program are the backtracking versions of the many possible implementations of this problem. The single node version of Queen7 repeats the experience of bit-palindromes: a list containing about 7 items is long enough to gain some speedup by faster unification and back-unification. The multiple node versions of Queen8 add even better results: the same gain in case of about 8-long lists is enough to overcome the slower token transfer, although the ratio of the execution speeds of old and new versions is rising as the number of processors is growing.

5.1.3 Hamiltonian path

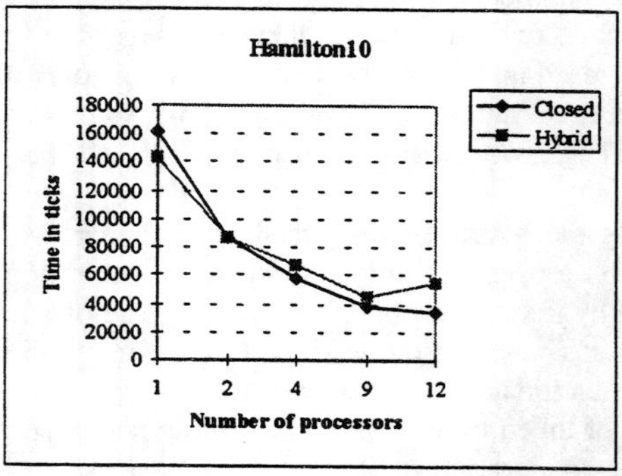

Figure 14. Execution speed of ham10

The Hamilton10 is another program, which achieves quite fair speedup, mainly on 2 and 4 processing elements. However, the difference between the old and new binding environments is not as good as one may expect. Although the average length of lists is enough to expect a better performance, most of the structures are ground terms, which are handled uniquely in both binding schemes, and thus, there is not a big difference between them. Hence the slower token transfer determines the execution speed and jeopardizes the small gain in speedup achieved on a single node.

[5] The measured value for closed environment, 4 processors is invalid.

5.1.4 List permutation

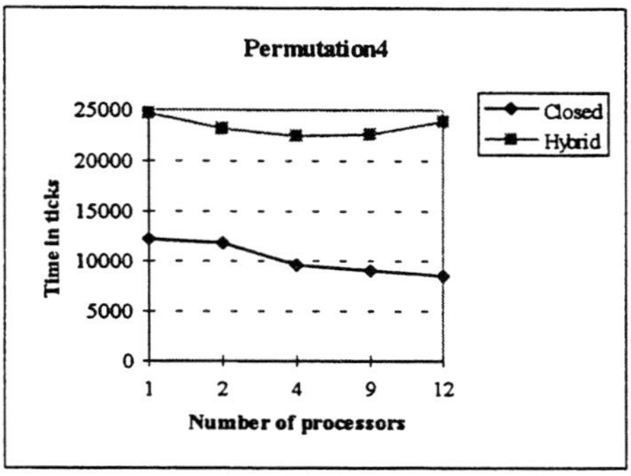

Figure 15. Execution speed of perm4

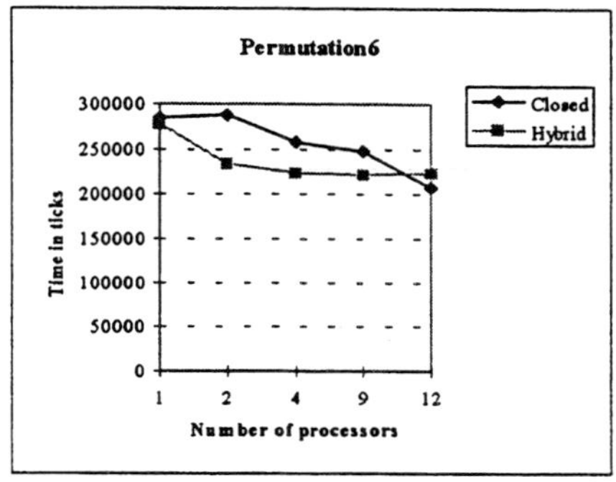

Figure 16. Execution speed of perm6

The behaviour of Perm4 and Perm6 shows many similarities with Bitspal5 and Bitspal7. In case of Perm4 the number of solutions is 24, and so, the number of tokens is very small. The maximum 4 items long lists perform very badly in the new binding environment. However, in case of Perm6 the 1-node execution of the hybrid binding method is better than that of the old one, i.e. there are long enough lists to speed up the unifications and back-unifications. Although Perm6 gives better execution speed with the new binding scheme, this is mainly due to the bad performance of the old scheme (see the slow-down at 2-node execution) and not the good behaviour of the new one. This issue is related entirely to scheduling and load balancing.

5.1.5 Quicksort

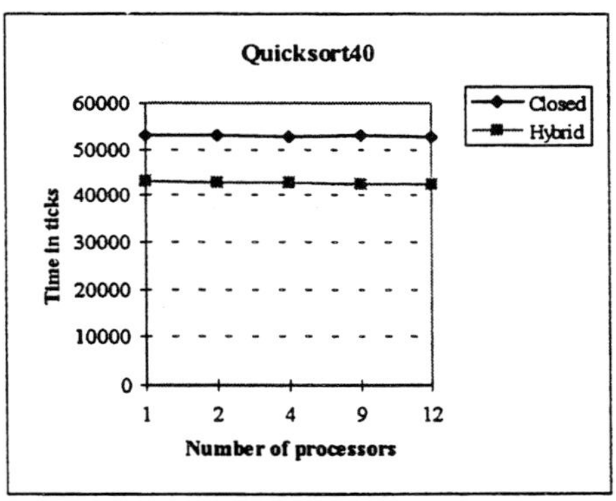

Figure 17 Execution speed of quick40

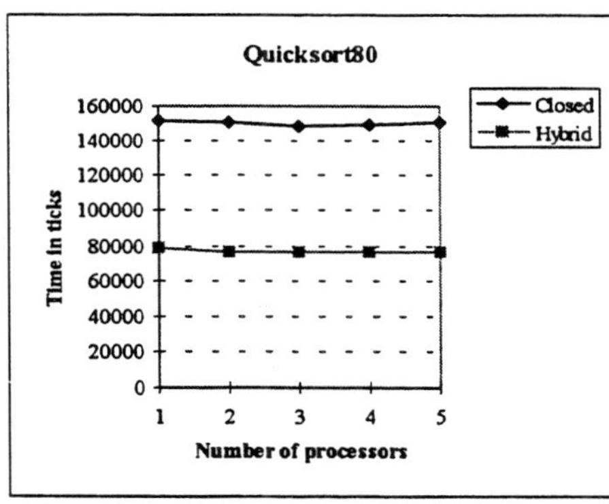

Figure 18 Execution speed of quick80

The quicksort type of programs does not speed up at all no matter how many processing elements there are. One reason may be that clauses of the partition/4 predicate are mutually exclusive and thus, there is always one living branch. The main source of parallelism is the pipeline AND-parallelism in the body of quicksort/2. However, the two quicksort/2 goals are independent, so the second one waits in vain for the result of the first quicksort/2 goal. Since the first quicksort /2 goal will produce only one solution, there is no way to exploit pipelined

AND-parallelism. In summary, this class of problems does not offer parallelism exploitable by 3DPAM[6].

On the other side, there is a big difference between the performance of the old and the new binding schemes. The Quick80 which uses longer lists performs even much more better. However, this version is also unable to speed up, so no doubt, the lack of speedup is not related to binding schemes.

5.2 3DPAM Memory utilization

The other important issue is how the new binding scheme reduces the heap usage. Lists and structures are the natural data representations in declarative languages. They are placed onto the heap. The closed binding scheme requires the copying of these structures quite frequently. The measured values of the heap usage are summarized in the charts below.

5.2.1 1 processor execution

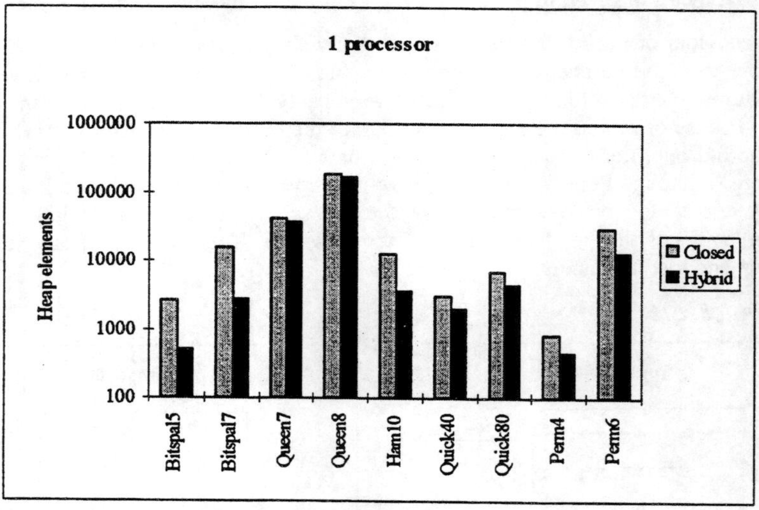

Figure 19. Heap utilization on 1 processor

The heap usage drops spectacularly in the hybrid binding scheme in comparison with the closed one. The newly introduced memory areas in the hybrid scheme are: Pointer Array (PA) and Hash Table (HT). The sum of used heap, PA and HT in the hybrid scheme is usually higher than the heap usage in the closed scheme. However,

- the heap copying is optimized and strongly reduced in LOGFLOW
- there are proposed optimizations for efficient use (detecting and reclaiming unused cells) of PA and HT that have not been implemented yet.

---

[6]This class of programs would be ideal for independent AND-parallel Prolog engines.

5.2.2 2 processor execution

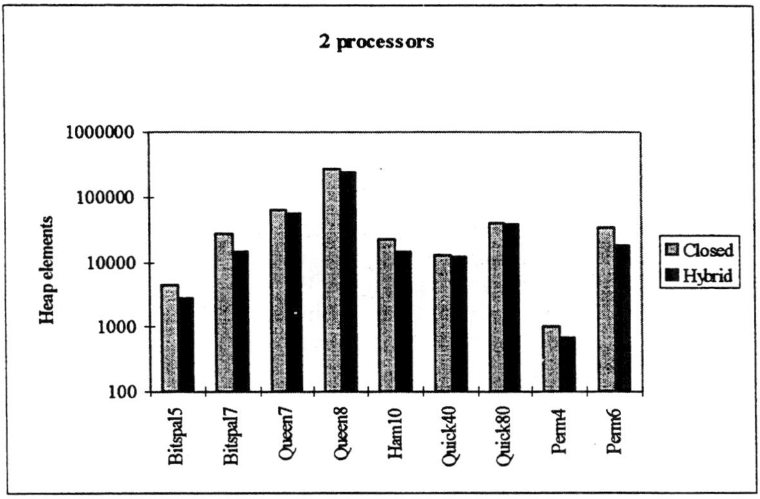

Figure 20. Heap utilization on 2 processors (the sum of used heap cells is shown)

Although the heap utilization is still lower, the proportion of the heap usage shows an increasing trend. It means that a large amount of structure copying is related to token transfer and not to environment closing.

6 Summary

1. The new binding scheme was implemented and tested on a transputer network. The model proved to be functionally correct both in single node and multiple node execution.
2. Performance tests showed that the primary goal, the reduction of closing overhead (both in time and in memory consumption) within a single processing element, was successfully fulfilled.
3. However, the cost of migration between processing elements became higher. It can ruin the performance when structures are either too small or ground ones, i.e. the new binding scheme is not faster than the old one. It was clearly shown that the new binding scheme achieves better performance when the lists and structures are big enough. In practical applications, where usually bigger structures are used than those in standard benchmarks, a better average performance can be expected.
4. The new binding scheme cannot eliminate (at was not aimed at eliminating) the structure copying when tasks are migrated between PEs. This kind of copying remains the main source of high memory consumption.

7 Conclusions

The aim of redesigning the binding scheme in LOGFLOW was to reduce the cost of closing procedure and memory consumption. This problem has been addressed by many researchers and there are several solutions. After analysing the overheads, a new binding scheme was designed and implemented for LOGFLOW. This hybrid binding method tries to combine the benefits of closed binding environments and the efficiency of non-closed environment.

The closed binding environment targeted at distributed memory systems. It was clearly shown that it has a high intra-processor overhead. Other methods, where the context switching overhead is minimized are designed for shared memory systems. Other methods for distributed memory computers (e.g. recomputation, stack copying) assume coarser granularity in contrast with LOGFLOW's fine granularity, where context switch occurs extremely often.

From the summary in Section 6 we can conclude that although the overhead related to environment closing can be significantly reduced within a PE by combining different binding methods. The frequent structure copying between PEs (which is related to the fine granular property of LOGFLOW) can not be eliminated or hidden by binding schemes. It is suggested that some kind of hardware support for accessing remote structures is needed.

The test results pointed out that this kind of hybrid binding scheme is an excellent candidate for binding environment on multithreaded architectures like Datarol-II, where the intra-processor overhead associated with closing procedures is reduced by the binding method, whereas the inter-processor copying overhead is eliminated by the facilities of the architecture. There is an ongoing project in this field and the idea is presented in [15].

Furthermore, several possible optimizations were proposed in [21] which have not been implemented yet (e.g. hash cache, garbage collection in the auxiliary data storage, etc.) Test results suggest that some of them could further improve the performance of the new binding method.

8 Acknowledgments

Authors would gratefully acknowledge the work of Portuguese colleagues, especially J.C. Cunha, J. Lourenco, P. Medeiros, R. Marques and V. Duarte, in the framework of the project. Tests were realized on a 16-node Parsytec machine made available to us courtesy of Universidad Nova de Lisboa.

9 References

[1] Ait-Kaci: Warren's Abstract Machine. MIT Press, 1991.

[2] P. Borgwardt: Parallel Prolog Using Stack Segments on Shared-Memory Multiprocessors. Proceedings of the 1984 Symposium on Logic Programming.

[3] J. Briat, M. Favre, C. Geyer, J. Chassin de Kergommeaux: OPERA: Or-Parallel Prolog System on Supernode. In: P. Kacsuk, M.J.Wise: Implementations of Distributed Prolog. Wiley, 1992

[4] J.S. Conery: Binding Environments for Parallel Logic Programs in Non-Shared Memory Multiprocessors. Proceedings of the 1987 Symp. on Logic Programming, 1987.

[5] M. Carlsson: Design and Implementation of an OR-Parallel Prolog Engine. SICS Dissertation Series 02.

[6] J.Chassin de Kergommeaux, P.Codognet: Parallel Logic Programming Systems. ACM Computing Surveys Vol 26. No 3. Sept 1994

[7] A. Ciepielewski, B. Hausman: Performance Evaluation of a Storage Model for OR-Parallel Execution of Logic Programs. SICS 86003 Research Report.

[8] S.K. Debray, P.L. Garcia, M. Hermenegildo, N-W. Lin: Estimating the computational cost of logic programs. Proc. of the International Static Analysis Symposium, Namur, 1994.
[9] G. Gupta, B. Jayarman: On Criteria for OR-Parallel Execution of Logic Programs. Proc. of the 1990 North American Logic Prog. Conf., 1990, pp. 737-756.
[10] B. Hausman, A. Ciepielewski, S. Haridi: OR-Parallel Prolog Made Efficient on Shared Memory Multiprocessors. SICS R87006 Research Report.
[11] P. Kacsuk: Distributed Data Driven Prolog Abstract Machine. In: P. Kacsuk, M.J.Wise: Implementations of Distributed Prolog. Wiley, 1992.
[12] P. Kacsuk, M.J.Wise: Implementations of Distributed Prolog. Wiley, 1992.
[13] P. Kacsuk: LOGFLOW: Prolog on Massively Parallel Machines. Invited Paper, 6th International Conference on AI and Information-Control Systems of Robots, Smolenice, 1994. pp. 71-80.
[14] P. Kacsuk: Execution Models for a Massively Parallel Prolog Implementation. Journal of Computers and Artificial Intelligence. Slovak Academy of Sciences, 1997. (accepted for publication)
[15] P. Kacsuk, M. Amamiya: A Multithreaded Implementation Concept of Prolog for Datarol-II. Proceedings of ISHPC97.
[16] P. Kacsuk, Zs. Németh, Zs. Puskás: Tools for mapping, load balancing and monitoring in the LOGFLOW parallel Prolog project. Parallel Computing 22(1997) 1853-1881.
[17] Kalé, B. Ramkumar: The Reduce-Or Process Model for Parallel Logic Programming on Non-Shared Memory Machines. In: P. Kacsuk, M.J.Wise: Implementations of Distributed Prolog. Wiley, 1992.
[18] R.Karlsson: A High Performance OR-Parallel Prolog System. SICS Dissertation Series 07, March 1992.
[19] H. Kim, J-L. Gaudiot: A Binding Environment for Processing Logic Programs on Large-Scale Parallel Architectures. Technical Report, University of Southern California 1994.
[20] Zs. Németh, P. Kacsuk: Analysis and Improvement of the Variable Binding Scheme in LOGFLOW. Workshop on Parallelism and Implementation Technologies for (Constraint) Logic Programming Languages, Port Jefferson, 1997.
[21] Zs. Németh, P. Kacsuk: Technical Description of Implementing a Hybrid Binding Scheme in LOGFLOW. Technical report, KFKI-MSZKI 1996.
[22] Sastry, L.M. Patnaik: OR-Parallel Evaluation of Logic Programs on a Multi-Ring Dataflow Machine. New Generation Computing, 10 (1991), pp. 23-53.
[23] K. Shen, V. Santos Costa, A. King: A new metric for controlling granularity for parallel execution. Workshop on Parallelism and Implementation Technologies for (Constraint) Logic Programming Languages, Port Jefferson, 1997

Index

A

B

C

D

E

F

G

H

I

J

K

L

M

N

O

P

Q

R

S